DOROTHY RICHARDSON'S ART OF MEMORY

MANCHESTER
UNIVERSITY PRESS

DOROTHY RICHARDSON'S ART OF MEMORY

Space, identity, text

Elisabeth Bronfen

translated by Victoria Appelbe

Manchester University Press
Manchester and New York

Distributed exclusively in the USA by St. Martin's Press

Copyright © Elisabeth Bronfen 1999

The right of Elisabeth Bronfen to be identified as the editor of this work has been asserted by his in accordance with the Copyright, Designs and Patents Act 1988.

Published by Manchester University Press
Oxford Road, Manchester M13 9NR, UK
and Room 400, 175 Fifth Avenue, New York, NY 10010, USA
www.manchesteruniversitypress.co.uk

Distributed exclusively in the USA by
Palgrave, 175 Fifth Avenue, New York NY 10010, USA

Distributed exclusively in Canada by
UBC Press, University of British Columbia, 2029 West Mall,
Vancouver, BC, Canada V6T 1Z2

British Library Cataloguing-in-Publication Data
A catalogue record for this book is available from the British Library

Library of Congress Cataloging-in-Publication Data
A catalog record for this book is available from the Library of Congress

ISBN: 978 0 7190 8326 6 paperback

First published by Manchester University Press in hardback 1999

First digital edition produced by Lightning Source 2011

CONTENTS

Preface		*page* vii
Note on the text		ix
Introduction		1
	Part I Actual, material spaces	
One	Locations of passage and habitation	10
Two	The spirit of the place	31
Three	Three modes of emplacement	47
Four	In search of lost space	72
	Part II Metaphorical spaces	
Five	World-making as a cognitive process	112
Six	The spatiality of psychic states	173
	Part III Textual space – spatial textuality	
Seven	The space of literature	196
Eight	When the tapestry hangs complete: *March Moonlight*	209
	Appendix: Critical literature on Dorothy Richardson	221
	Bibliography	239
	Index	248

PREFACE

To publish a piece of scholarship based on work done in a rather different form more than a decade ago in another language is always a precarious undertaking. Are the issues still relevant that seemed so compelling then? Is the critical language still adequate in the context of our highly mutable academic discourse? In part because Dorothy Richardson's work continues to be marginalised, despite that fact that in the past decades several monographs and a quantity of articles addressing the issue of gender, genre and modernism have been published, the undertaking seems a justifiable one. At the same time, precisely because *Pilgrimage* has been recuperated from oblivion primarily as a voice of feminine modernism, the philosophical underpinnings to Richardson's work are sometimes overlooked. Furthermore, mapping the early modernist texts against our postmodern interest in real and imagined geographies, in cultural belonging and dislocation, the question of how identity emerges as a result of both corporeal as well as cultural enspacement draws out dimensions in Richardson's work which include but also move beyond the issue of feminine writing. I have chosen not to reformulate my discussion of the importance of corporeal emplacement, psychic topologies and spatial textuality within the terminology that has developed in the past decade because it is my hope that the phenomenological discourse I had initially used may, owing to its unfamiliar ring, invigorate the current debate.

My thanks go to Victoria Appelbe, who has so diligently and creatively translated my German prose into English. I am genuinely grateful to Jean Radford, whose astute critical comments on the first version guided me in my revision. Finally thanks also go to Matthew Frost, my editor at Manchester University Press, who vigorously encouraged the translation and revision process, and to Therese Steffen, without whose generosity and unceasing support this project would never have been realised.

NOTE ON THE TEXT

The final 1967 version of *Pilgrimage* (New York, Knopf) consists of four volumes, each divided into numerous novels which are in turn separated into numbered chapters. All quotations from *Pilgrimage* in the text are detailed with the volume number and page number. The Virago edition (London, 1970) has the same pagination. The sources for all other quotations from Richardson are given, as with all quotations, in the notes, with explanatory information provided where necessary. Italics in the Richardson quotation are added by the present author.

Throughout this study, all translations from French and German are the translator's own, unless an existing translation is cited, and reference is given to the original text.

INTRODUCTION

In an interview for the journal *Little Review*, for which she sent in a photograph of herself as a baby as her 'most recent photograph', Dorothy Richardson expressed the following wishes in response to the first question, 'What should you most like to do, to know, to be? (In case you are not satisfied)':

> Build a cottage on a cliff
> How to be perfectly in two places at once
> Member of a world association for broadcasting the goings-on of metaphors.[1]

While these wishes are of course intended playfully, they articulate one of the novel's seminal concerns: the representation and semantic encoding of actual material (*begehbare*[2]) and metaphorical spaces. For *Pilgrimage* traces the psychological development of its protagonist, Miriam Henderson, by detailing her passage through a plethora of concrete sites and social worlds, a spiritual and aesthetic quest which culminates in her discovery of the scene of writing. At the same time Richardson's portrait of the artist as a young woman also seeks to play through the philosophical and poetic conviction that experiencing and transcribing simultaneous presence is what is at the heart of her aesthetic project, even while psychic reality, ineluctably marked by the presence of a permanent, unchanging essence, may best be represented by describing both the protagonist's phenomenal world and the spatial metaphors she uses to turn her experiences into a meaningful narrative.

The fact that Richardson's first wish should give voice to the longing for a concrete site corresponds to the importance of actual material spaces in *Pilgrimage*. A considerable proportion of the novel is devoted to descriptions of the places which Miriam inhabits, the atmospheres which they possess and the significance which they come to assume for her. At the same time, these spatial descriptions are brought into play as semantically encoded sites and localities which structure the entire text so as to display the enspacement of human existence. In a key passage in *Pilgrimage*, Richardson has her heroine, Miriam, voice the following objection to the traditional novel:

> But in *all* the books . . . the chief thing they all left out, was there. They even described it, sometimes so gloriously that it became *more* than the people; making humanity

look like ants, crowding and perishing on a vast scene. Generally the surroundings were described separately, the background on which presently the characters began to fuss. But they were never sufficiently shown as they were to the people when there was no fussing; what the floods of sunshine and beauty indoors and out meant to these people as single individuals, whether they were aware of it or not. The 'fine' characters in the books . . . were not shown as being made strong partly by endless floods of sunshine and beauty. (III, 243)

By privileging the atmospheric quality in her descriptions of scenes Richardson seeks to expose the existential significance which spaces take on in the psychic life of her protagonist.

In addition, Miriam's quest consists in reaching a privileged site of habitation or dwelling whereby this 'significant space' possesses qualities similar to that of the 'cottage on a cliff' for which Richardson expresses her own desire. For this image evokes a concrete site which, functioning as the nexus between earth and heaven, draws together these two elements and, in marking their intersection, gives them tangible form. By analogy, the subject who dwells in such a liminal site develops a psychic state which makes it possible to experience the boundary between material, corporeal existence and the immaterial, spiritual world, and allows her to conjure up the eternal and immutable elements which lie beyond this intersection. In other words, such a point of liminality can be considered a significant space, because it allows the subject to experience simultaneously a sense of belonging to the earth and an openness towards the universe, the latter conceived as a mode of spiritual liberation from any entrapment in the material world.

This notion of liminality can also fruitfully be related to the Richardson's desire 'to be perfectly in two places at once'; a desire which not only emerges as the thematic leitmotif of *Pilgrimage* but also proves to be one of her seminal narrative strategies: in that she uses a spatial image to express simultaneity, that is, her ideal of being 'perfectly in two places at one' Richardson also highlights her thematic concern with concrete material and metaphorical spaces. This thematic exploration of simultaneous presence as an ideal position not only draws upon numerous philosophical definitions of human existence: her desire to be simultaneously in more than one place is also characteristic of Miriam's attitude towards life, which may be characterised as a refusal to commit herself to any one particular position. This attitude of indefinite oscillation prevails throughout, regardless of whether it concerns her membership of more than one national, cultural, sexual or social group, her affiliation with differing philosophical, religious or artistic schools, or the narrative challenge of including more than one aspect of a question or an event in her own poetic rendition of her life. Indeed for her the ideal psychic, political and spiritual attitude consists in a unifying state of suspension between opposites. In the course of her pilgrimage Miriam discovers that she can come to realise this privileged position by using spiritual and creative activity so as to be present simultaneously in the physical and the imaginative world.

The manner in which Miriam uses memory so as to juxtapose events that were originally experienced as being separate, and in so doing recasts the relationship between events independent of their chronological order, further emphasises the importance she places in achieving a state of simultaneity. The preference for simultaneity is further manifested in her narrative tendency to disregard time, change and the process of 'becoming' so as to privilege instead a state of simultaneous parallelism and unchanging being. Psychic reality is viewed as an unchanging, all-inclusive essence which emerges with a certain reliable sameness, a conviction Richardson displayed so ironically when she decided to submit as her most recent photograph a portrait of herself as a baby. The aspiration towards simultaneity and towards the spatialisation of time thus lies at the heart of her aesthetic project, fully implicating her mode of representing reality but also the prominence of spatial metaphors in *Pilgrimage*. For, as Spencer explains, it is metaphors which have the capacity to synthesise opposites and hold them in suspension, as well as to endow reality with an unchanging essence: 'the most important power of the metaphor is that it holds fused in a condition of stability and synthesis the "truth" that is far too fluid in its natural state to be captured, comprehended, and controlled'.[3]

This brings one to Richardson's third remark, in which she expresses a desire to be a 'member of a world association for broadcasting the goings-on of metaphors'. Here she reveals her suspicion of metaphors in particular, as well as her general ambivalence towards linguistic modes of representing reality per se. While she does acknowledge that metaphors function as one of the most important and effective rhetorical devices in poetic expression, she nevertheless emphasises that they can never give a complete expression of reality. In a letter to her friend Henry Savage, she writes:

> Language is a very partial medium of expression. Poetry indirectly more direct. Music still more so. Yet *all* art, as every artist ... well knows, can never express fully, what he wants to express ... Oh the helplessness surrounding the helpfulness and manifold uses of speech, the dangers within the delights of metaphor.[4]

For Richardson, the ability to be precise in one's linguistic designation is pitted against the constraint imposed upon reality when it is pinned down. She thus concludes that it is the degree of linguistic specificity which determines whether or not a description of an object's essence will be inaccurate and insufficient. The more indirect and ambiguous one makes a description, the more effective it will be as an expressive device. Accordingly, the appeal of metaphor derives from the way in which it captures the essence of a particular thing precisely by skirting around it and refusing to name it directly. The danger is, however, that no act of linguistic naming can ever do justice to the object which it describes. Richardson's fundamental scepticism about language, which leads to a search for the 'right metaphors', thus lies at the heart of *Pilgrimage*'s thematic concern with poetic expression as well as its narrative style.

The following discussion seeks to explore the issue of liminality and simultaneity in *Pilgrimage* by examining Richardson's textual enspacements, whereby, as Max Bense suggests, space should be conceived as the nodal point knotting together a variety of instances – spatial signifiers on the level of plot and theme development but also the significatory processes at work on the level of textuality which allow for the production and transmission of meaning. Describing the inextricable connection between time and being, Bense states:

> Space is not only a physical and mathematical phenomenon, it is also a metaphysical one ... Space is, so to speak, the connection which encompasses the material world ... Something is at once in space and expresses space. Space necessarily constitutes a part of being. The predicative 'is' signifies space or, expressed as a verb: 'to space' ... 'Spacing' corresponds to being. That which *is* 'spaces', by which I mean that being is always already space, regardless whether it involves physical, psychological, mathematical, logical or metaphysical phenomena.[5]

In the following I will, then, explore textual renditions of actual material places in *Pilgrimage* which implicitly refer to a reality outside the text and, at the same time, the use of spatial metaphors which are not related to any actual locations, but rather serve to encode abstract concepts like belongingness, communication or writing within spatial terms. Furthermore, I will examine the diverse ways in which language not only renders tangible concrete places and metaphorical spaces but also itself spaces these representations. Although my discussion is divided into three parts, so as to differentiate between material, metaphorical and textual space, at stake are the similarities between these three different forms of spatiality; indeed enspacement proves to be the point at which these three instances of representation intersect.

Part I focuses on the localities inhabited by the protagonist Miriam, especially the correlation between location and human existence. In this discussion I draw on texts from the area of phenomenology, anthropology, architectural theory and literary criticism which revolve around how an individual is implicated in his or her lived space, notably Graf Karlfried von Dürckheim's and Ludwig Binswanger's studies of the atmosphere or spirit of lived space, Martin Heidegger's essays on the correlation between building, dwelling and thinking and Mircea Eliade's definition of sacred space.[6] My presentation and development of critical terms is also indebted to the work of Walter Götz and Elisabeth Ströker, which offers a systematic overview of the problem of space in philosophy; as well as theoretical writings by the architects Kurt C. Bloomer, Charles L. Moore and Christian Norberg-Schulz, who have worked with a phenomenological approach to the meaning and effect of buildings.[7] In the field of literary criticism, the writings of Gaston Bachelard, Ellen Frank, Jurij Lotman and Mikhail Bakhtin proved to be particularly profitable.[8] The first two critics primarily examine the role of the atmospheres of given concrete material places, the way in which these localities can be invested with different and often plural semantic meanings. This semantic encoding of a given place influences the characters' behaviour in them – their spatial existence or enspacement. The last two authors trace above all the way in which semantically encoded places are used to structure key issues in a text – be they psychological, social, political or aesthetic.[9]

Part II examines the tectonic principle underlying epistemology and cognition and, in this context, addresses the tendency to assign spatial attributes to abstract concepts in order to render them tangible. Writers to whom I refer on these issues include Nelson Goodman, Rudolf Arnheim and Jurij Lotman,[10] given their concern with the use of spatial metaphors and the semantic encoding of spaces which accompanies the processes of perception and understanding. Since any discussion of metaphorical spaces must of course engage with metaphors itself, which is to say with the qualities and effects of this rhetorical device, I have also drawn upon those critics who deal with the relation between metaphors and spatial formation in language. Most fruitful for this purpose were Gérard Genette's essays on language and space, literature and space, John Lyons's work on semantics and Roman Jakobson's and David Lodge's distinctions between metaphor and metonymy.[11]

Part III, the final part, which addresses the analogy between space and text, is indebted on the one hand to the discussion of 'spatial form' which originated with Joseph Frank's essay on the subject and, on the other, the work of Genette, Umberto Eco and Roland Barthes, all of whom offer a structuralist analysis of enspacement in narrative representation.[12]

In contrast to the largest portion of criticism on *Pilgrimage*, I will not be referring to the autobiographical dimension of the text. Speaking of the autobiographical elements which a text may include, Richardson herself asks: 'And is not every novel a conducted tour? First and foremost into the personality of the author who . . . must present the reader with the writer's self-portrait . . . he will reveal whether directly or by implication, his tastes, his prejudices, and his philosophy'.[13] In this respect, the opinions which Miriam voices on various political, religious and artistic movements, on the difference between active and contemplative existence, as well as her discussion of the representability of reality, might permit one to draw conclusions about Richardson's personality, her taste and her *Weltanschauung*. There is indeed ample scope for comparison between Richardson's journalistic essays, her film and book reviews, as well as her letters written in the years when she was working on her novel, and passages in *Pilgrimage* in which Miriam expresses and develops her opinions.[14] Indeed, it is possible to recognise a certain similarity between the positions taken by Richardson and those espoused by her heroine on subjects as diverse as sexuality, writing, metaphysical astonishment, the difference between being and becoming and, finally, the importance of silence and contemplation as opposed to superficial babble and action.[15]

However, although these similarities between the author's views and those of the protagonist of her novel indicate a certain blurring of boundaries, they do not reveal any explicit autobiographical intent. Comparing Miriam with the author, let alone substituting the one for the other, can indeed obscure some of the philosophical and aesthetic concerns of the text. For this reason I will circumvent drawing parallels between the content of Miriam's and Richardson's polemic and instead concentrate on the ways in which the polemical patterns deployed in *Pilgrimage* are structured along tectonic principles. Furthermore, I will be referring to the historical context of *Pilgrimage* only when it has relevance for the question of literary space. The work of Steinberg on the stream of consciousness technique and the work of M. Bell and L. Leshan and H. Margenau[16] does, however, reveal the extent to which Richardson's concerns – simultaneity, the spatialisation of time, lived space, human perception and consciousness, the preservation of the essence of an event and, lastly, her application of innovative formal methods including the stream of consciousness technique – dovetail with the concerns of modernity at large.

NOTES

1 Dorothy Richardson, 'Confessions', *Little Review*, 12 (May 1929), 70.
2 I have coined the term *begehbarer Raum* to designate material spaces, which it is physically possible to enter into, inhabit and pass through. At stake is the distinction between remembered or fancied spaces we might psychically dwell in once they have been conjured up by virtue of the imagination.
3 Sharon Spencer, *Space, Time and Structure in the Modern Novel* (New York, 1971), 94.
4 Dorothy Richardson, Letter to Henry Savage, Good Friday, undated, Beinecke Rare Book Library, Yale University.
5 Max Bense, *Raum und Ich: Eine Philosophie über den Raum* (Munich and Berlin, 1943), 19.
6 Graf Karlfried von Dürckheim, 'Untersuchungen zum gelebten Raum: Erlebniswirklichkeit und ihr Verständnis. Systematische Untersuchungen II', *Neue Psychologische Studien*, 6, ed. Felix Krueger (Munich, 1932); Ludwig Binswanger, 'Das Raumproblem in der Psychopathologie', *Ausgewählte Vorträge und Aufsätze II* (Bern, 1955); Martin Heidegger, 'Bauen Wohnen Denken', *Vorträge und Aufsätze* (Pfullingen, 1954); Mircea Eliade, *The Sacred and the Profane* (New York, 1959).
7 Walter Gölz, *Dasein und Raum: Philosophische Untersuchungen zum Verhältnis von Raumerlebnis, Raumtheorie und gelebtem Dasein* (Tübingen, 1970); Elisabeth Ströker, *Philosophische Untersuchungen zum Raum* (Frankfurt, 1965) See also Max Jammer, *Das Problem des Raumes: Die Entwicklungen der Raumtheorie* (Darmstadt, 1980) and Hedwig Conrad-Martius, *Der Raum* (Munich, 1958). Both texts focus upon the scientific concept of space. Kurt C. Bloomer and Charles W. Moore, *Body, Memory and Architecture* (New Haven, 1977); Christian Norberg-Schulz, *Genius Loci: Toward a Phenomenology of Architecture* (New York, 1980).
8 Gaston Bachelard, *La Poétique de l'espace* (Paris, 1957); Ellen Eve Frank, *Literary Architecture: Essays Toward a Tradition* (Berkeley, 1979); Jurij Lotman, *The Structure of the Artistic Text* (Ann Arbor, 1977); Mikhail Bakhtin, *The Dialogic Imagination: Four Essays*, ed. Michael Holquist (Austin, 1981).
9 The artistic representation of concrete material spaces forms the main subject of enquiry in literary critical analyses of space. Ernst Cassirer's essay, 'Mythischer, ästhetischer und theoretischer Raum', reprinted in *Landschaft und Raum in der Erzählkunst*, ed. Alexander Ritter (Darmstadt, 1975) and Lessing's differentiation between spatial and temporal art in *Laokoon* (1766) are usually taken as the starting point for such discussions. For detailed bibliographical accounts of literary-critical discussions of space, see *Spatial Form in Narrative*, ed. Jeffrey R. Smitten and Ann Daghistany (Ithaca, 1981), Gerhard Hoffmann, *Raum, Situation, erzählte Wirklichkeit: Poetologische und historische Studien zum englischen und amerikanischen Roman* (Stuttgart, 1978) and *Landschaft und Raum in der Erzählkunst*, ed. Alexander Ritter.

INTRODUCTION

10 Nelson Goodman, *Ways of Worldmaking* (Hassocks, 1978); Rudolf Arnheim, *The Dynamics of Architectural Form* (Berkeley, 1977); Lotman, *The Structure of the Artistic Text*.
11 Gérard Genette, *Figures I* (Paris, 1966) and *Figures II* (Paris, 1969); John Lyons, *Semantics*, vols 1 and 2 (Cambridge, 1977); David Lodge, *The Modes of Modern Writing: Metaphor, Metonymy and the Typology of Modern Literature* (London, 1977).
12 See Joseph Frank, 'Spatial Form in Modern Literature', *The Widening Gyre* (New Brunswick, 1963). See also *Critical Inquiry*, 4 (1977), Joseph Kestner, *The Spatiality of the Novel* (Detroit, 1978) and the collection of essays by Smitten and Daghistany. These texts are a continuation of the ideas initiated by Joseph Frank in 1945; Genette, *Figures I* and *Figures II*; Umberto Eco, *The Open Work* (Cambridge MA, 1989); Roland Barthes, *S/Z* (Paris, 1970).
13 Dorothy Richardson, 'Novels', *Life and Letters To-day*, 56 (March 1948), 190f.
14 See *Windows on Modernism: Selected Letters of Dorothy Richardson*. ed. Gloria G. Fromm (Athens and London, 1995).
15 For Richardson's autobiographical comments, see the interviews with V. Brome, 'A Last Meeting with Dorothy Richardson', *London Magazine*, 6 (June 1959), 26–32; Louise Morgan, 'How Writers Work: Dorothy Richardson', *Everyman* (22 October 1931); and Richardson's own texts 'Data for a Spanish Publisher', *London Magazine*, 6 (June 1959) and 'Beginnings: A Brief Sketch', *Ten Contemporaries: Notes Toward their Definitive Bibliography*, ed. John Gawsworth (London, 1933) and the unpublished letters. The conversations which are listed in my bibliography, mostly from the magazines *Focus* and *Vanity Fair*, reveal parallels between Richardson's polemic, her views on philosophy and poetry and the representation of Miriam's opinions in *Pilgrimage*.
16 Erwin Ray Steinberg, ed., *The Stream of Consciousness Technique in the Modern Novel* (New York, 1979); Michael Bell, ed., *The Context of English Literature 1900–1930* (London, 1980); Lawrence Leshan and Henry Margenau, *Einstein's Space and Van Gogh's Sky: Physical Reality and Beyond* (Brighton, 1983).

PART I
ACTUAL, MATERIAL SPACES

CHAPTER ONE

LOCATIONS OF PASSAGE AND HABITATION

While it is difficult to establish the precise chronology of events in *Pilgrimage*, the sequence of the episodes that constitute Miriam's development in the course of the novel may be traced with relative accuracy by examining the places she passes through. Often one does not know exactly when an experience or a remembered episode took place. However, if one records the concrete spaces which Miriam experiences, places she sometimes recalls while located in a different site, a clear trajectory of the stations in her pilgrimage emerges. For Richardson locates each event which is described in the text – even events such as thought processes and conversations which would not appear to be spatially bound – in a specific material space, even though not necessarily in a specific time.

It makes sense, therefore, to outline briefly the novel's plot in terms of its spatial structure. On the one hand, this will allow me to determine the different kinds of actual material spaces Richardson repeatedly represents, and, on the other, to expose a correlation between the specific qualities of these privileged material spaces – open/closed, above/below, interior/exterior, calm/agitated, back/front, near/distant – and the events which take place in them. For, significantly, one of the features of Richardson's topology is that it involves drawing up boundaries between various material spaces that by virtue of their semantic encoding are represented as contrasting each other.

According to the Russian cultural theorist Jurij Lotman, the structure of literary works invites a comparison with space, for the dual nature of the artistic text is such that 'while reflecting a separate event, it simultaneously reflects a whole picture of the world'. He adds that this notion of a work of art as an 'area of space demarcated in some way and reflecting in its finitude an infinite object' lies at the heart of the problem of textual space.[1] Lotman views the frequent attempts to carry out a spatial 'modeling of concepts which themselves are not spatial in nature', and the drawing up of world models which are obviously defined by spatial qualities, as belonging to a visual perception of the world which is peculiar to humanity.[2] Lotman thus sees the 'structure of the space of a text' as becoming a 'model of the structure of the space of the universe', just as the 'internal syntagmatics of the elements within a text' become the 'language of spatial modeling'.[3] Relations exist between the objects described in the text which correspond to conventional spatial relations as a whole. In Lotman's view, this textual structuring of space functions such that 'the spatial order of the world in these texts becomes an organizing principal around which its non-spatial features are also constructed'.[4] Accordingly, he sees the representation of space in the text as a self-reflexive expression of the textual structure as a whole. In the following discussion I will, nevertheless, distinguish between descriptions of material spaces which have an actual presence in the world of the text, and the various metaphorical applications of space within the text. Examples of a metaphorical use of space include the metonymic relation which is set up between material spaces and the people who inhabit them, the immaterial mental spaces and the spatial model which governs the text and organises both material spaces and their immaterial correlates. The function of these metaphorical representations of space will not, however, be addressed until Part II.

By distinguishing between material and figurative spaces in the text, I hope to be able to clarify more effectively the interrelation between these two levels of meaning. For, if one sees the text as the construction of a world, representations of concrete spaces by no means merely have a referential function. Rather, they are in themselves meaningful, indeed self-reflexive. On the level of signification a tension is created, since these actual spaces are already semantically encoded, encodings which in part correspond to conventional perceptions of localities (a room is protective), and in part, however, contradict or transcend them (a room can be infinite). In addition to such semantic encodings of actual spaces, the descriptions of the way in which the protagonist Miriam behaves in a given space, and of the effect this space has upon her, also illustrate that the meaning of a space is determined by the character who inhabits and passes through it. To an extent, this pattern of meaning, which Miriam assigns according to her phenomenological perception of the world, reinforces the spatial structure which governs the text as a whole. *Pilgrimage* thus plays through a correlation between representations of concrete spatial relations, the application of spatial metaphors and the overall structuration of the text as a space. The representations of actual material spaces must, however, also be discussed independently of the metaphorical usage of space and the spatial modelling of the text.

The novel *Pointed Roofs* begins with the same spatial configuration with which the novel *March Moonlight* ends – that of an emptied room: 'Her new Saragota trunk stood solid and gleaming in the firelight. Tomorrow it would be taken away and she would be gone. The room would be altogether Harriett's. It would never have its old look again' (I, 15). Whereas in *Pointed Roofs* the empty room in her parents' house signifies separation from her family and the beginning of a long journey – it is a 'bright bare room' (I, 22) because Miriam has taken from it all her possessions – the last empty room in *March Moonlight* represents a final arrival. The reader perceives the emptiness of this last room owing to the fact that Richardson provides no descriptions whatsoever of the final place of habitation of her protagonist, and by analogy we are given an insight into Miriam's state of mind. For what is implied is that Miriam perceives the room as being empty because she no longer locates reality in her concrete surroundings but rather in the psychic state she will now privilege above all else, namely her creative activity: 'Contemplation is adventure into discovery; reality' (IV, 657). This shift also encapsulates the thematic trajectory of the novel; Miriam's transition from involvement and activity therewith to contemplation and finally to writing about past experiences: 'this sunlit top-back room ... The garden, its washing lines, ash-heap and dust-bins invisible from where I sit alone with the sky, the lime tree and the tops of those poplars ... every distance a clear perspective' (IV, 655). Between these two rooms lie interiors and external places which are sometimes foreign, sometimes familiar. They act at once as hosts of action and meaning and as catalysts for Miriam's experiences during her pilgrimage, a pilgrimage which ends in this final room: the site of her artistic activity.

If we begin to chart Miriam's journey through diverse unfamiliar localities, which are all perceived as transitional spaces, the first significant foreign space[5] in which Miriam stays is Hanover, standing metonymically for Germany. In three respects this place represents something new and unfamiliar for her: it is the first time that she has been separated from her family, it is her first experience of a foreign country and it is her first place of work. In her eyes, Hanover consists of one immobile interior, namely the boarding school in the Waldstrasse where she works as an English teacher. This interior space is, however, divided up into the completely private bedroom upstairs, the schoolrooms down below where Miriam gives lessons to a small group of girls, and the public, communal rooms such as the dining hall and the music hall, in which everything takes place under the constant observation of the headmistress, Frl. Pfaff. These closed, interior spaces are not, however, only places of work for Miriam but also, the music hall in particular, places for transcendental experiences.

In direct contrast to these interior spaces, the exterior spaces – the streets, cafés, church and swimming pool, the nearby woods and the village Hoddenheim – become places of movement and action, destinations for excursions in which Miriam leaves behind the everyday life of the school and, by association, her role as a teacher. The interior space is also closed in the sense that it not only offers protection against the forces of nature (such as storms and heat) but also acts as an utopian space[6] in the sense that it possesses an internally balanced, ordered structure, but one which can be upheld only by blocking out all disturbances and disharmonies (whether they come from outside or emerge from within). Frl. Pfaff tolerates nothing in her boarding school which does not fit into its system and has all those removed who threaten this order, such as the French teacher and later Miriam herself.

This school is the first of many self-contained, enclosed spaces, exhibiting similarities to utopian communities and whose protective yet restrictive closure Miriam finds at once attractive and repellant. Indeed, this first episode establishes a pattern for Miriam's volatile response to interior spaces, which is repeated over and over again in the course of the text. Interior space is felt to be protective as long as it permits a sense of belonging there. In spite of its actual enclosure, it appears porous and open to Miriam when it becomes the site of a transcendental experience: 'dreaming alone in the schoolroom near the closed door of the little room ... she felt herself in vast space. The ceilings and walls seemed to disappear' (I, 108). Miriam experiences the enclosure as restrictive only when she comes up against the boundaries of what is permitted, or the boundaries of what she, as a foreigner, can grasp. This finally leads to her sense of a crushing void when she once again departs from her provisional German home: 'The room was stifling – bare and brown in the gaslight . . . it seemed to be empty. There seemed to be nothing in it but the black screen standing round the bed that was no longer hers' (I, 183f.).

Exterior space, in turn, tends initially to be viewed as open, since it is not subject to an ordering system. Correspondingly, visits to places such as churches or nearby villages allow Miriam to discover traces of a foreign culture: 'This was Luther – Germany – the Reformation – solid and quiet . . . It was the stained-glass windows that made the Schloss Kirche so dark' (I, 76). Ultimately, however, such exterior spaces have a similarly stifling effect once the impression of the foreign becomes more powerful than that of the new and unfamiliar. The boundary between interior and exterior space is thus blurred, since both, when viewed as a whole, become part of the complete, self-enclosed space of Germany, which is an unfamiliar locality rich with potential for discovery not least of all because of its distance from England. By exploring these unfamiliar interior and exterior spaces Miriam is able to experience what she feels to be essential characteristics of Germans: their manners, their outlook on life and their lifestyle. Concrete places are not, however, registered merely in terms of what most typifies them; discovered spaces are also equated with ownership of the life which they contain. Miriam wishes her family were in Hanover: 'if only she could bring them all for a minute into this room, the wonderful Germany that she had achieved . . . She wanted them to come to her and taste Germany' (I, 66). At the same time, the English space which she has left behind acquires immediacy in letters from her family and in her own memories, to the extent that it even suppresses the German space which she experiences in the present: 'The little German garden was disappearing from Miriam's eyes . . . It was all beginning again, after all . . . why had she not stayed . . . how silly and hurried she had been, and there at home in the garden lilac was quietly coming out' (I, 112). Although in the course of such meditations Miriam is physically present only in Germany, she is able to compare and evaluate the two national locations she belongs to by juxtaposing the place she is currently occupying with her memories of the one she has left. Viewed as a whole, then, her stay in Hanover signifies both an experience of an open space, involving mobility and an opportunity to gain insight into an unfamiliar culture, as well as an experience of the hermetically closed boarding school, associated with stasis. Significantly, Miriam's first attempt at appropriating an unfamiliar space so as to achieve a sense of belonging there – foreign in that it meant living away from her family as well as from the familiar English culture – results in a return to England, but not to her parental home, and as such foreshadows the gesture of synthesis which will prove endemic for her entire pilgrimage.

The plot development of the next novel, *Backwater*, juxtaposes two localities with diametrically opposed semantic encodings. At one extreme is Wordsworth

House, a north London high school for girls and a place in which Miriam's life is constrained by poverty and by her role as a teacher, but in which she is able to earn her own income. At the other extreme stands Barnes, the Henderson family's last house in suburban London, a place in which her family keeps up the apppearance of leading an upper-middle-class lifestyle, even though they have lost all their money; organising dances and tennis parties and planning marriages. Upon returning to the school after her first holidays, Miriam describes the conflict between work and marriage which these two different localities embody: 'This is my place. I can keep myself here and cost nothing and not interfere with anybody . . . It'll always be like that now. Short holidays, gone in a minute, and then the long term. Getting out of touch with everything . . . going home like a visitor' (I, 264f.). As in *Pointed Roofs*, Miriam is able to discover sites of recreation that allow her to escape from both her place of work and her estranged home: London's streets, the holiday resort Brighton and the remembered garden of her childhood in Babington.

As in the Waldstrasse, the closed space of the school in North London is divided between Miriam's private bedroom upstairs and the public classrooms and leisure areas below, with the difference that the staircase is now treated as a point of transition, linking the two levels of the house. As in Hanover, Miriam experiences the closed interior space of the school as open when, in moments of transcendence, she becomes conscious of her own essence. However, this school differs from Hanover in that her sense of the porous quality of space and of its protective quality is confined to her private room and the solitude she can experience there:

> reading her two penny books in her silent room . . . she found when the house was still and the trains had ceased jingling up and down outside that she grew steady and cool and that she discovered the self she had known at home, where the refuge of silence and books was always open . . . it was herself, the nearest intimate self she had known. (I, 282)

The rest of the house is, in contrast, perceived as restrictive, 'ugly and shabby'. Miriam describes her life in north London thus: 'She was going to be shut up away from the grown-up things, the sunlit world and the people who were enjoying it' (I, 198), 'North London would always be North London, hard, strong, sneering, money-making, noisy and trammy' (I, 322). These judgments express her rejection both of the social class to which she is a teacher and of her work as a whole. The exterior space surrounding the school, the park and the Brooms' family's house which exemplify the whole of north London is as stifling as the school itself: 'the glazed closed door, with the little strips of window on either side giving onto a crowded conservatory, made the little room seem dark. To Miriam it seemed horribly remote . . . her dreams for the future faded . . . all the space was behind. Things would grow less and less' (I, 289).

Miriam thus never achieves a sense of belonging to north London. In contrast to *Pointed Roofs*, in which the boundary between Miriam and her surroundings became blurred, since the Waldstrasse was perceived as being both foreign and protective, in *Backwater* the interior is clearly separated from all external places. Miriam firmly demarcates her bedroom, as the one place which corresponds to her sense of self, from the rest of north London, including the school. This external locality is experienced as being particularly constrictive or deadening when Miriam perceives it as a screen reflecting her sense of psychic confinement, owing to her dissatisfaction with her work as a high-school teacher.

The other significant site, Barnes, is in turn represented ambivalently, as it is both a place of freedom from the constraints of work and also, owing to her family's tragic circumstances, hostile towards life. The upper and lower interior spaces of her family's home, but especially the exterior space surrounding it, are imaged as free and open when they promise an opportunity for physical movement or spiritual growth. They thus offer a haven away from north London, which Miriam views as a filthy prison. This sense of openness derives primarily from the fact that it is here that Miriam can compare and thus mentally oscillate between the two localities that make up her social reality Thus, during a dance soirée, Barnes signifies an open space in which movement can take place since it offers Miriam the prospect of marriage, although this is never realised. Later on, Barnes acquires the status of an open space since it is a site for holidays and tranquillity. During a boat trip, Miriam meditates upon the discrepancy between the two spaces: 'Six hours ago, shaking hands with a roomful of noisy home-going girls – and now nothing to do but float dreamily in through the gateway of her six weeks' holiday. The dust of the school was still upon her . . . But she was staring up at a clean blue sky fringed with tree-tops' (I, 294). However, Barnes is also the site inhabited by Miriam's sick mother and is therefore extremely threatening: 'Miriam drew up the blind . . . The garden did not seem to be there. The tepid night air was like a wall . . . It was exactly like a grave' (I, 304f.). As the title *Backwater* suggests, ultimately both Barnes and north London are viewed as constrictive and morbid anti-spaces since they signify a stagnation which opposes movement. The only real escape from the confinement both of these places signify is her own room, which can become a 'scene of adventure' (I, 267), a focal point for a plethora of yet undiscovered places: 'All the world would come to her here'.

London's streets and Brighton both act as sites of recreation, but although they make unconstrained movement possible they also deny any sense of inhabiting and thus identifying with these locations. Movement through London's streets provides Miriam with a contrast to the closed space of the school, just as holidays in Brighton offer relief from the closed space of Barnes. It is, however, the remembered garden of Miriam's youth in Babington which represents the most significant supplementary space in *Backwater*. This garden represents an ideal space which, owing to the work of memory, resurfaces again and again, becoming fictive in the process; ever more closely resembling an imagined space. And yet the process by virtue of which Miriam tends to fictionalise spaces which she has experienced is complex. During the initial moment of experience, an actual material space is simply perceived; subsequently it is semantically encoded so as to render that particular experience meaningful. In the course of memory work it becomes ever more fictional, in proportion to the growing distance between the moment of experience and the moment of recollection. At the same time, however, by virtue of this temporal distance and this transformation into an imagined place, the space of the past is felt to be increasingly *real*, precisely because the loss of direct contact with the moment or situation enables its essence to be unveiled. Since the signification of Babington garden will be examined in greater detail in a later section, it is simply worth mentioning here that this remembered site, like Miriam's own room, is posited as an alternative to the inability to communicate with others which she experiences in both of the anti-spaces in *Backwater*. Miriam remarks of her experiences in the garden of her youth: 'Until she could speak to someone about them she must always be alone' (I, 317).

Miriam's recognition that both Barbes and Wordsworth House are uninhabitable places leads her to look for a new position, this time with the Corries; a wealthy family who live outside London. Whereas the Pernes sisters' school was perceived as being exemplary of the entire area of north London, Newlands is, to an even greater extent than the Waldstrasse, portrayed as a utopian space possessing an internally balanced, ordered structure which offers a harmonious society of attractive luxury. However, while the boarding school in the Waldstrasse was perceived as part of the German city of Hanover, Newlands is viewed in complete isolation from the city of London, which again becomes the site for excursions. This difference in part reflects the fact that Germany was ultimately conceived as an utterly foreign location, whereas Newlands embodies an unfamiliar site within the familiar world of England.[7] In other words, the division of England into independent 'islands' (in part protective spaces, in part hostile anti-spaces) is of greater significance, as it represents the foreign within the familiar. However, an experience of a foreign country is in itself an encounter with alternity, such that sub-divisions merely represent nuances of differentiation within something which is ineluctably unfamiliar.

Newlands is depicted as completely separate, its tranquillity, harmony and luxurious beauty making it appear protective and exciting: 'this strange house ... so far away from everything, trams and people and noise – it was in the centre of beautiful exciting life; perfectly still and secure ... No sound came in ... soft moist air and the smell of trees. Nothing but woods all round, everywhere' (I, 360). Nevertheless, Miriam's response to this self-enclosed, utopian site alters, depending upon whether Newlands is described from a distance or from close at hand. Viewed from the perspective of the whole area of London, it represents an idyllic island of luxury, particularly in comparison to the Hendersons' suburban existence: 'there was that other thing ... far from suburban life ... down at Newlands, a brightness' (I, 468). However, once Miriam judges Newlands on its own terms, no longer contrasting it to other places, she falls back on the already familiar pattern of dividing her site of habitation into above/below: once again her room, the only free and porous interior space, is situated at the top of the house. In contrast to the other two houses, the lower rooms in Newlands are rarely used for teaching and instead function as sites for social interaction. In *Honeycomb*, Miriam's discovery of her own room as a place for creative solitude plays through an opposition between a bare, yet permeable, space of creative contemplation and a comfortable, yet therefore hermetically closed, space of social interaction: 'Presently she could, if she held firm, be alone, in a grey space inside this alien room, cold and lonely and with the beginning of something . . . dark painful beginning of something that could not come if people were there . . . Downstairs, warmth and revelry' (I, 432). For the most part, Newlands is depicted as a place of light and beauty: 'beautiful bright rooms, a wilderness of beauty all round her all the time . . . No more ugliness . . . luxuries, beautiful gleaming things' (I, 403). It is not until Miriam recognises that the artificial beauty of Newlands can be maintained only by adherence to strict rules and restrictions upon social behaviour, and that she herself can never belong there, that its closure becomes stifling. Following one such key experience, in which she oversteps the boundaries of permissible feminine behaviour, Miriam feels excluded from this site: 'Miriam found the room dark and chill in the bright midday . . . There was a dark cruel tide in the room, she sought in vain for a foothold' (I, 437). Having realised that Newlands is a beautiful cage in which the women who live there resemble 'coloured birds, fading slowly year to year in the stifling atmosphere' (I, 433), and even appear dead – 'At Newlands people might be dead' (I, 468) – Miriam distances herself from this world, although her final decision to leave Newlands is brought about by her mother's suicide.

The Henderson family's final home stands in sharp contrast to this utopian site of luxury and beauty. Miriam does initially perceive it as open and cheerful because it represents a homecoming as well as the site of her sisters' marriages, but later it is depicted as closed and suffocating in the extreme, particularly with regard to her mother, whose failed marriage casts a shadow over her sisters' prospective happiness. Her sister Harriett's new house, which is also interpreted as the site of her marriage, is described in terms of limitation similar to those used to evoke her mother's room. As receptacles of marital misfortune, both deny the possibility of movement and renewal: in Harriett's house 'the room was too full . . . now she was caught' (I, 448); in her mother's room 'this dreadful little room where despair was shut in' (I, 471). Miriam finds these closed spaces in suburbia even more unbearable than the closed space of Newlands, because they lack its light, beauty and aesthetic lifestyle (I, 468). Furthermore, Miriam associates this physical enclosure with the notion that suburban married life involves sacrificing freedom and thus shutting out reality: 'impossible to be real unless you were quite free' (I, 459).

As in the earlier novels, there are free, open places for excursions in *Honeycomb* as well – Miriam visits London from Newlands and spends a few days with her mother at a spa in Brighton. London's streets appear refreshingly open since they allow for movement; they contain a cheerful lightness since she may encounter the unfamiliar there. As in Hanover, Miriam attempts to appropriate and gain access to foreign localities by traversing them: 'The West End People . . . the mysterious something behind their faces, was hers. She, too, now had a mysterious secret face – a West End life of her own' (I, 419). Interior spaces are described as pleasant whenever they contain, like Newlands, a permanent beauty, as with Mrs Kronen's flat: 'clear light rooms. Nothing is ever grubby. And London there, all round; London . . . was a soft, sea-like sound, a sound shutting in the spring . . . in the pure bright room' (I, 413).

If interior spaces lack this aesthetic quality, however, they appear unpleasant. Miriam describes her admirer's flat thus: 'Bob's bachelor chambers . . . The curious dingy dustiness oppressed her, and there was an emptiness' (I, 477). Again and again it becomes apparent that for Miriam space is indivisible from the life which inhabits it.

In contrast to these London sites of recreation which are, relatively speaking, satisfying and make a pleasurable impact upon Miriam because she approaches them without prejudice, Miriam finds herself unable to respond to the spa she visits with her mother in the face of the tragic circumstances, instead erecting a barrier between herself and her surroundings. The exterior space is described as light and infinitely open: 'Outside was the blaze of the open day, pale and blinding. When they went out into it, it would be a bright, unlimited jewel, getting brighter and brighter' (I, 480). When Miriam is with her mother, however, the exterior space is obliterated: 'When the cook shut the door of the little room the house disappeared . . . the vast open lid of the sky . . . [was] in another world' (I, 482). Nevertheless, she is inclined to believe that it is her own mood which is distorting the appearance of this locality: 'Perhaps in a few days it would be the real jolly seaside and she would be young again' (I, 483).

Following her mother's suicide, Miriam moves to London and takes up a position as a dentist's assistant. The spatial divisions which emerge in the following five novels,[8] spanning a period of ten years, are united by one fundamental pattern. This pattern consists of a tension between London as her privileged space, a kind of centre to which Miriam returns again and again, and the various destinations which make up the locations beyond London. This opposition between London and those places not belonging to the city may be further sub-divided into different sites (which I will term sub-spaces). London consists of three interior spaces: firstly, Miriam's living space, the private space to which she always returns; secondly, the islands, that is, sites which, though initially unfamiliar to Miriam, are semantically encoded; and, thirdly, the neutral spaces which are not semantically encoded and which Miriam experiences as free spaces, though not as her own. The fourth sub-space encompasses the exterior localities of London, the streets and parks which are situated between the significant interior spaces.[9] The space beyond London displays similar spatial divisions, except that it contains no private living space for Miriam. Here too, there are unfamiliar islands Miriam explores, neutral spaces and the exterior space of open nature, whereby all the spaces outside London tend to be viewed as anti-spaces.

Since the length of *Pilgrimage* prevents a description of every single example of a sub-space, and above all since these sub-spaces tend to follow a similar pattern, I will limit my discussion to a description of the general spatial dynamic structuring the entire text. In an autobiographical essay, Richardson sums up the spatial divisions of her years in London in the same way as she came to structure them in *Pilgrimage*:

[18]

what London can mean as a companion, I have tried to set down in *Pilgrimage*. There were of course summer holidays spent with friends at home and abroad, and weekends with relatives and friends ... But from all these excursions I returned to my solitude with the sense of escaping from a charming imprisonment. During these London years I explored the world lying outside the enclosures of social life and found it to be a kind of archipelago. Making contacts with various islands, with writers, with all the religious groups ... with the political groups and ... with the worlds of Science and Philosophy, I found all these islands to be the habitations of fascinating secret societies, to each of which in turn I wished to belong and yet was held back, returning to solitude and to nowhere.[10]

Richardson's description of her oscillation between London and sites outside its peripheries, with her return to the city and her solitary room preferable to all these excursions, in fact accurately reflects the spatial dynamic in these five novels. As in the earlier novels *Pointed Roofs*, *Backwater* and *Honeycomb*, Miriam seeks, on the one hand, to explore foreign and unknown sites in order to gain access to them, while, on the other hand, she never remains in any one of these places, either because she feels excluded or because she declines being part of the world they represent

The first of these private sites of 'solitude and nowhere' Richardson describes is Miriam's room in Mrs Bailey's boarding house in Tansley Street. Initially the significance of this room consists in the fact that it is utterly separated from all the other tenants: 'There was no sound in the house ... its huge thick walls held all the lodgers secure and apart' (II, 77). Situated on the top floor, this site becomes a place of tranquillity and protection from the outside world, and thus also a place of freedom she can always return to. As with her rooms in the unfamiliar homes where she was employed in the earlier novels, this room becomes a seismograph of her changing moods. Miriam views it as light and liberating when she is happy, and as small, dirty and stifling when she is discouraged. At the same time, it is experienced as porous and as stretching into infinity when it becomes the site of the sense of transcendence brought about by reading or writing (III, 273). Most crucially, it assumes the function of a restful counterpart to her actions and discoveries in the outside world: 'There must always be a clear cold room to return to. There was no other way of keeping the inner peace' (II, 321).

To an even greater extent than the rooms of her pre-London life, then, this site of 'solitude and nowhere' becomes not only a place of refuge but also a receptacle for that which she experiences in the outside world. Miriam always brings her diverse experiences of unfamiliar places back into this room with her, whether in the form of physical objects which serve as mementoes, or as thoughts and memories, so that the room becomes a shrine for lived experience. As the following description of a teapot illustrates, the room is not only penetrated but also animated by the outside world: 'the glow of wealthy social life lighting the little wooden window-room, gleaming from the sheeny flecks of light on the well-shaped green teapot' (II, 429).

Richardson thus works with an opposition between Miriam's own room, which remains fundamentally constant, and all the different unfamiliar localities, separate islands which accommodate people and the ideas to which they adhere. These are sites of mobility which facilitate actions, discoveries and changes, although these foreign spaces can, once more, be divided into several sub-spaces. Foreign spaces include, on the one hand, the workplace and the dental practice in Wimpole Street and, on the other, the numerous private houses and friends' rooms, the cafés and restaurants where Miriam meets friends as well as the public buildings in which talks, theatrical performances or political meetings take place. They are in turn expressive of the particular traits of the people who inhabit them. Miriam experiences them as pleasantly invigorating if their 'inhabitants' defend opinions and a lifestyle which is at least partially compatible with her own, or if they represent a life for which she longs. Belonging to this form of space are the flat of the two emancipated women Mag and Jan (II, 87); that of the Bohemian artist Bowdoin – 'the room was full of life and warmth and golden light' (III, 369) – and Café Ruscino, an assembly point for continental London which literally seems to open itself to Miriam: 'the confines of the room were invisible. All about them were worldy wicked people' (II, 394). Miriam feels these places to be oppressive if the life which takes place there conflicts with her own. The YWCA where the impoverished nurse, Eleanor Dear, lives is, for example, described as a 'dreadful little enclosure in the dreadful dark line of women collected together only by poverty' (II, 245).

Regardless of their positive or negative atmosphere, all of these islands are nevertheless ultimately experienced as fascinating foreign places and not as anti-spaces, such as Barnes or Wordsworth House. They retain their appeal until Miriam has fully exhausted their potential for discovery, or until she recognises that she can no longer belong to the world embodied by a particular foreign site. It is thus her refusal to fully belong to any one of these fascinating foreign sites which leads her to withdraw again and again into her own room.

Placed as sites of contrast to the semantically encoded island spaces are those locations which are termed 'neutral territory': the moving trains, taxis and bicycles as well as the motionless cafés but also those rooms which cannot be assigned to any people or ideas. These are empty, free spaces which may have a revitalising influence, since they do not make any demands upon the character who traverses them, yet they are also not experienced as private, protective spaces.[11] The exterior space of London, the streets, boroughs and parks, form a further opposition. Although Miriam experiences individual buildings or entire areas of the city as at times stifling and at times liberating, the exterior space of London is generally and consistently perceived as an open, free, exciting and mysterious space of movement and discoveries. Furthermore, it is also felt to be protective and separated from the rest of the world. In this, it assumes the role of an external approximation to her own room, since both are unique in upholding the tension between porous openness and protection: 'The spirit of London . . . this mighty lover, always receiving her back without words, engulfing and leaving her untouched, liberated and expanding to the whole range of her being' (III, 272).

The area beyond London exhibits a similar tension – between island spaces which are closed and semantically encoded and open, free, nature. One crucial difference, however, is that everything which is outside London is always experienced as a foreign destination for excursions. It does not provide Miriam with a room of her own to which she can continually withdraw, nor does she experience nature as protective. Indeed, it sometimes appears so open that it permits a sensation of spacelessness and thus of transcendence into other lived spaces. The island spaces share certain features with spaces in the earlier novel *Honeycomb*: the north London of the Brooms; her sister Eve's place of work with a rich family (comparable to Newlands); suburbia as the home of both her married sisters and the doctors for whom she works; and her two sisters' second home at the seaside where they have both set up their own boarding houses.

All of the above sites are encoded as harbouring that way of life which would have been open to Miriam had she married, a prospect which she however always resists. In particular, her sisters' second home signifies the settled, bourgeois life which is characterised by home ownership. Ultimately, all of these suburban sites are experienced as stifling and fail to offer the excitement and unfamiliarity of the London island spaces. Since Miriam resists them so strongly, the people and thoughts which they contain inhibit any direct spatial experience. As a result, the spaces assume the role of a façade. Highly stylised as anti-spaces which Miriam rejects outright, their unattractiveness in turn highlights the appeal which London continues to hold. Bonnycliff, the home of the writer Hypo Wilson, is the single, and thus significant, exception to this pattern. Like the London islands, this is a closed space, but also a place for discovering the unfamiliar, in this case writers and scientists. Bonnycliff thus retains the splendour which the other spaces beyond London lack: 'the sun-bathed seaward garden, the joyful brilliant seaside light pouring through the various bright interiors of the perfect little house, the inexpressible *charm*, always renewed and remaining, however deeply she felt at variance with the Wilson reading of life' (III, 263). Although the space is divided between 'upper', 'lower' and 'outer' areas, the boundaries are so permeable that Bonnycliff seems to represent a complete unit. The upstairs bedroom is not experienced as separated from the rest of the house as it was in Newlands, to an extent because the room never becomes Miriam's own space.

The spatial dynamic is only slightly altered by Miriam's move to Flaxman's, to a cheap room which she shares with another woman. As a result, Miriam ceases to have a room of her own, a solitary centre, and the neutral space of her club is the only remaining open and free space: 'this was freedom, in company, enriched. The sense of imprisonment she had felt on coming down the street with Miss Holland ... vanished altogether in the freedom of this neutral territory' (III, 418). The presence of another person inhibits the porosity of the space as well as preventing Miriam from establishing her own centre there: 'Seeking up and down the strip of bedroom for a centre, some running together of effects where her spirit could settle and find its known world about it. There seemed to be none' (III, 418). Accordingly, Flaxman's is depicted as devitalising and restrictive – 'this corner where she had been dying by inches' (III, 508). Her visits to the London island spaces, as well as her walks and journeys through the exterior space of London, continue to take place up until the end of *Trap*, which marks the conclusion of her first years in London.

Following her three failed attempts to find a sense of belonging in houses with closed social structure which thus deny her room for personal discovery, Miriam abandons these suburban sites and moves to London. She no longer tries to settle down in anti-spaces and begins instead to explore foreign spaces in the gesture of oscillation, going out only to return always to her own room, where she is protected from all external contact. Just as Miriam increasingly focuses her life upon London, and with this upon her own room, so she becomes increasingly capable of exposing herself to exterior spaces and to the appeal of these unknown, foreign sites. This is most powerfully demonstrated by the way in which the loss of her own room, as with Flaxman's, is associated with death. These first two novels are thus structured by Miriam's continual oscillation between London and the space beyond London, the latter conceived as an anti-space rather than a fascinating mysterious foreign space. Ultimately, however, the significant boundary is not that between London and the space beyond it but rather between Miriam's own room, which is experienced as both permeable and protective, on the one hand, and the surrounding space of London, the islands and neutral spaces, on the other. Since they are self-enclosed, the island spaces are experienced as both protective and exclusive; the unlimited neutral spaces can in turn give Miriam a sense of freedom, but never one of protection.

With the ninth novel, *Oberland*, this pattern is disrupted. Miriam spends two weeks at a Swiss health resort. This is her second visit abroad, and it differs from her stay in Hanover in that it simply represents a holiday in a completely unbounded locality high up in the mountains, cut off from everything else. Oberland and Hotel Alpenstock do not have any closed, ordered structure and thus have no rules and limits which can be transgressed. Almost all of the figures represented are, like Miriam, tourists in an unfamiliar place and are spending a holiday away from their everyday lives and their familiar native countries. The indigenous population is perceived as natural phenomena and does not exert an influence on the tourists. Whereas Hanover, though a foreign locality, was semantically encoded as the location of her teaching post, so that Miriam made an effort to belong there, Oberland is an utterly neutral space. Because it is completely devoid of any social implications as constraints, it can have a regenerative effect upon Miriam, making no demands upon her but also foreclosing the notion of belonging there from the very start. Here too, the familiar pattern emerges whereby Miriam's own room is situated on the top floor, a place where she can be alone and contemplate the surrounding nature, with social life taking place on the ground floor. Since Miriam feels the entire space to be mysteriously unfamiliar and radiant, interior space is differentiated from exterior space only to the extent that, while inside the hotel nature is experienced as being wholly distanced, once Miriam finds herself outside, the Swiss landscape becomes both an object of contemplation and a site for action.

In comparison to her experience of Hanover, in which descriptions of the school's day-to-day life were predominant, the novel *Oberland* consists primarily of descriptions of nature. The landscape is perceived as a picture: 'Every day through these windows that framed the view in strips, this light would be visible in all its changings . . . Those high, high summits, beetling variously up into the top of the sky, where patches of tawny rock broke through their smooth whiteness against its darkest blue' (IV, 57). This landscape also acts as the scene for ecstatic experiences, for example, sledge rides and ski jumping, sport forms which are associated with a triumph over space and time. One sledge ride is described as follows: 'The joy of flight returned, singing joy of the inaccessible world to which in flight one was translated, bringing forgetfulness of everything but itself' (IV, 119). The stay in Oberland thus represents less an accession to an unfamiliar locality than an experience of an exceptional situation. Although the atmosphere of her surroundings is subject to change, it is evoked throughout in terms such as 'surrounding strangeness' (IV, 35), 'enchantment' (IV, 47), 'brilliant light' (IV, 49), 'radiant stillness' (IV, 47) and 'joyous light'. It is a place which is so open, in the sense of being utterly devoid of social encodings, and which appears to stretch so infinitely far that Miriam can constantly lose and renew herself in it: 'Out in the immense landscape in the downpouring brilliance of pure light, thought was visible . . . to walk and walk on and on amongst them, along their sunlit corridors with thought shut off and being changed, coming back refreshed and changed and indifferent' (IV, 72).

As a location in which Miriam can undertake walks and sports activities which lead to a sense of inner release, it facilitates an experience of infinity: 'Gliding, as if forever; the feeling of breaking through into an eternal way of being' (IV, 87). Furthermore, Oberland is the first place in which Miriam consciously assumes the attitude of a distanced observer; she allows the environment to affect her, while at the same time experiencing it as a phenomenon which is separate from herself. By way of example, one sunrise which Miriam sees from her bed is described as follows: 'Sitting up in bed, she saw hanging in mid-air just outside the window a huge crimson lamp, circular in a blue darkness . . . the gently startling picture, in its sudden huge nearness, of the loveliness of space' (IV, 124). Two modes of perceiving actual material space – firstly, an experience of infinity as a dissolution of time and space, and, secondly, a clarity of spatial experience which is achieved by means of a distanced position – are characteristic for the final volume of *Pilgrimage*.[12] Retaining the mode of perceiving space which she acquired in the unbounded space of Oberland, Miriam returns to London and resumes her work in Wimpole Street, but soon moves back into Mrs Bailey's boarding house. Overall, the spatial model remains as it was prior to her move to Flaxman's. She continues to experience her own room as both free and protective: 'untouched freedom . . . undisturbed space, high above the quiet street, and safely below the old attic with its cruel cold and its sultry stifling heat' (IV, 185). 'In the house, but not too much of it' (IV, 195). Her room's protective openness, made possible by her feeling of freedom there, is most clearly illustrated by a retrospective comparison with Flaxman's:

[23]

'Freedom for thought . . . to expand unhampered by the awful suggestions coming from the Flaxman surroundings (IV, 196).

Her friendship with Amabel, who also takes up a room at Mrs Bailey's in order to be close to Miriam, alters the meaning of the whole house such that Miriam feels it to be 'nothing but a casket for Amabel' (IV, 247). For the first time, she allows another person to enter her room (IV, 243) – until then she had met people only in the diverse London localities she perceives as foreign island spaces or in neutral spaces. Her solitary writing space is indeed affected as a result: 'But after those first evenings before Amabel had settled in the house, the whole of consciousness had flowed, as soon as her work was done, backwards towards Amabel's room down the passage' (IV, 354). None the less, her own room remains a protective centre: 'Once more her room held quietude secure . . . Her being sank perceptibly back and back into a centre wherein it was held poised and sensitive to every sound and scent' (IV, 363). Island spaces, neutral spaces and the exterior space of London are depicted once again, although descriptions of island spaces become noticeably rarer. Just as Miriam's detached attitude towards her environment and her withdrawal into her own room as a solitary place for her writing activity increase, so her visits to unfamiliar or strange localities decrease, or these sites are reduced to a mere backdrop against which events are played out. Bonnycliff alone gains an increasing significance, since it is the scene of her sexual encounter with Hypo. Nevertheless, it remains a self-enclosed site, heavily invested with Hypo's presence, and, though it allows for unfamiliar experiences, not only does her perception of this place depend on her moods but she also ultimately feels excluded from it.

The neutral spaces, not invested with semantic values, assume an ever more influential role as meeting places for Miriam and her friends, especially Hypo and Michael. Since both men compete for her affections, these meetings on neutral territory primarily allow Miriam to assert her independence. In addition, the neutral spaces act as places in which she can again experience the feeling of ecstatic inner release which she had come to know consciously for the first time in Oberland. The significant shift that occurs in Miriam's perception of her phenomenological world at this stage in her life is that she no longer sets up an opposition between island sites and alternative sites; she no longer searches for more suitable locations, but instead revises her whole attitude towards lived space. She uses the power of her imagination, so as to distance herself from sites which she feels to be constrictive, such as the restaurant, in which Hypo has asked to meet her: 'she felt her spirit expand freely in the room and gather to itself' (IV, 224). Similarly she uses her imagination to liberate herself from the restrictions which Hypo's presence seemingly imposes upon nature: 'I wondered, alone for a second with my sea and my sky limitless, as they were before I had heard them scientifically defined' (IV, 255). What is crucial is that at stake is an experience of infinite space in a figurative sense and as such directly connected to the fact that she has begun to assume a detached attitude towards the world. Apolitically put, it expresses Miriam's transition from an unmediated experience of her surroundings to a more indirect, mode of perception, an attitude which articulates a dematerialising symbolisation of spatial experience. Bonnycliff, for example, which was endowed with pejorative values after her sexual encounter with Hypo, undergoes an imaginative transformation: 'the scenes framed by the windows grew beautiful in movement. The framing and the movement created them, gave them a life that was the life of wild nature only . . . watching them she was out in eternity' (IV, 265). As befits her new-found awareness, Miriam separates herself from all constraining relationships – she arranges a marriage between Michael and Amabel, she breaks off her relationship with Hypo and resigns from the position as dental secretary which she has held for ten years, hoping that her savings will allow her to live and write in the country for a year in 'green solitude'.

After brief stays, first with the Brooms in north London, and then with a farmer's wife, she arrives at the Quaker farm Dimple Hill. This community represents the final utopian mode of living which she explores; one which has more similarities with Newlands than with Oberland's Alpenstock. While the appeal of her stay in Switzerland resided in the fact that it foreclosed all desire of inhabiting this site permanently, Miriam once more imagines that she could belong to this community, a desire which is so powerful that she even considers marriage, initially to Richard Roscorla, and later to the newly converted Charles. The attraction of this self-enclosed community, unlike that of Newlands, does not derive from a luxurious lifestyle but rather from the exercise of calm and contemplation typical of Quaker life. As in all the other places described previously, both Miriam's own room and her study are situated up above, while the rooms down below and the exterior spaces are communal areas, though now the interior space is clearly designated as being a feminine site, while exterior space is marked as being masculine.

Miriam explores the Roscorla home, as well as the surroundings of Dimple Hill, and by passing through this new and unfamiliar territory she is able to transform what had hitherto seemed infinite and strange into a protective, because familiar site: 'its quality had changed. No longer stretching out across the world . . . its radius was reduced to visible limits' (IV, 449). Both the Roscorlas' house and the Quaker meeting house are initially viewed as places of tranquillity because they appear to harbour Miriam's ideal mode of being: 'inactive and silent, solitary yet not alone' (IV, 496). Indeed, during Miriam's first stay, Dimple Hill appears to encompass what for her is the perfect location – a site that is both protective and open for creativity and contemplation.

The space of London, which Miriam visits in order to attend Amabel's wedding to Michael and to cancel her membership of the Lycurgan Society, provides a direct contrast to Dimple Hill. Miriam's attempt to eliminate the people and ideas which belong to her London years is in part signalled by the sparse and cursory descriptions of the spaces which she visits. This is expressive of Miriam's conscious, introspective and detached attitude towards her surroundings, which first began in *Oberland*. Actual material spaces are increasingly neglected in favour of remembered and imagined ones. This tendency is made most apparent in the final novel, *March Moonlight*. During a stay with her sister Sally's family, whose house, like all of her family's homes, is described as a self-enclosed island from which she feels herself to be excluded – 'this enclosed circle no effort of mine can open towards the lights that fill my sky' (IV, 586) – Miriam is constantly reminded of Vaud, where she stayed during her second visit to Switzerland. Like Oberland, it is described as an open, free and neutral space, with the advantage that this time she is able to share her experiences of the infinite with her friend Jean.

The increasing juxtaposition of material spaces which are being directly experienced with various remembered or anticipated spaces goes hand in hand with a noticeable increase in Miriam's tendency to compare the different places she has known. In this last novel, the atmospheric qualities of Vaud, Sally's house, Amabel's house and Dimple Hill, acquire their meaning by virtue of being mentally placed next to each other and thus evaluated. As with the visit to her sister Sally, Miriam's stay in Amabel's and Michael's new home exposes the utter self-enclosure of this new house. It is a tastefully furnished house and Miriam sees that Amabel 'has created for her own beauty and for Michael's . . . a perfect setting' (IV, 596). Furthermore, it contains a reproduction of Miriam's room at Flaxman's which Amabel has re-created in an attempt to preserve artificially the life which they used to share. However, Miriam finds this elaborate decoration suffocating when compared to the simple tranquillity of Dimple Hill, not least since it also contains the potential 'loss of unthreatened solitude' (IV, 605) associated with married life.

Upon arriving at Dimple Hill for the second time, Miriam is convinced that she has at last found her significant space: 'Last year this station had meant just the end of the journey towards an unknown refuge. To-day it is the gateway to Paradise' (IV, 606). Nevertheless, she is forced to concede during this second stay that its balanced harmony, as in Newlands, can be sustained only by virtue of an ordered structure to which she as a non-Quaker can never fully belong. In this way, she becomes conscious of the barrier between herself and the Roscorlas, 'aware of herself for the first time . . . as an outsider' (IV, 626). Following her short-lived relationship with Charles which conflicts with Quaker standards, she recognises that she is also excluded from this locality and suddenly feels it to be foreign. 'Life had left her familiar room. Left all that its window looked out upon' (IV, 651). After various intermediate temporary homes, the only one which is described being the YWCA in St John's Wood, Miriam finally arrives at the rented room in Mrs Gray's house to which I referred at the beginning of this discussion. This place is situated in St John's Wood, 'that vague cricket-ground region on the way to Mr. Hancock's place in Hampstead. Far from the sheltering depths of London proper' (IV, 629), that is, in an area of London which is viewed as a frontier between London and the space beyond it, as a part of London and yet not quite London:

> sun-lit top back room . . . Solitude. Secure. Filled each morning with treasure undamaged by compulsory interchange. Every distance a clear perspective . . . the corner of St. John's Wood that inexplicably begins to offer itself as my native heath. Yet every place I have stayed in, at home and abroad, has sooner or later so offered itself, but none with just this indefinable quality. (IV, 655f.)

This room proves to be the most privileged of all her other solitary rooms, like them containing 'this indefinable quality', for the reason that, being completely detached from her outside surroundings, she can here begin to write her novel.

Tracing the trajectory of Miriam's habitation of and passage through various actual material spaces, one notes that she begins in a fully self-enclosed and constrictive interior space (her parental home), moves through various unfamiliar interior and exterior spaces until she finally reaches a second, now privileged interior space which is both porous and protective – the site of her solitary writing. In other words, Miriam's pilgrimage involves a search for a place which is 'significant' for her in the sense that it provides an anchorage in the world,[13] a search which leads her to the realisation that she can belong nowhere but in the solitary room functioning as the materialisation of the scene of writing. Other localities are either foreign in the sense that they are unfamiliar yet rich in potential for discoveries, or foreign in the sense of anti-spaces, because they usually represent familiar spaces which sap Miriam's vitality. At the same time her pilgrimage involves revising the values she was brought up with in relation to locations, but also the way of life they harbour – utterly foreign countries or the city of London prove to be less alienating than the more familiar suburban England.

Miriam's pilgrimage, can, then, be divided into four phases. The first phase consists primarily in an as yet diffuse outwards motion, engendering three attempts on her part to establish herself in an unfamiliar place, though at this point without any sense of her own centre. The second phase involves a movement inwards, an attempt to eliminate everything from her psychic reality except her own room. The realisation that such a radical seclusion from the world leads to a death-like isolation brings about a third phase, in which Miriam comes to conceive her own room as a place which she can leave with impunity because she can always return to it. Miriam's exploration of so-called islands once more increases, and a balance is achieved between interior and exterior space. It is not until the fourth phase, when these diverse localities have become familiar through experience and imaginative refiguration, that Miriam once more gives up her excursions into foreign places in favour of the solitary scene of writing. Once more her writing desk emerges as the centre of her life, and she allows her external surroundings to fade – not, however, before negating them. Rather, they are reintroduced as scenes she remembers and transforms in the act of writing them down. Succinctly put, actual material spaces fade and are exchanged for remembered and imagined ones.[14] With her own room the nexus point of her remembrance of significant places of the past, all other sites come to be perceived as external spaces, even while she still distinguishes between those lying outside her familiar territory and those within 'London's magic-circle' (IV, 196).

A significant aspect of Miriam's pilgrimage consists in drawing boundaries, between herself and others but also between the various localities she passes through. By virtue of demarcating herself in relation to the material spaces she experiences, Miriam is able to shape her sense of self, even while these boundaries are fluid, such that, while Miriam at times feels herself to be included in a particular place, she at other times feels excluded from it. At the same time, drawing boundaries allows her to compare various localities, thus not only endowing them with a more precise meaning but also helping her decide which is most suitable to her. Crucial categories prove to be not only the opposition between interior and exterior but also that between impermeability and porosity, between a self-enclosed, limited site and one that is open, unlimited. While the opposition between limited-interior and unlimited-exterior spaces that Richardson works with to a degree corresponds to conventional semantic encoding of topological sites, it also becomes evident that values attributed to individual sites are usually dependent upon Miriam's perpection. As a result, at stake are not conventional semantic configurations of space but rather the manner in which spaces become meaningful for the experiencing subject.

Thus precisely because spatial perception proves to be a subjective process, given that one of the pivotal themes of *Pilgrimage* involves the mutual implication of spatial perception and the experiencing subject, the distinctions which are set up between various localities remain ambivalent, permeable and subject to change. Indeed the existence of boundaries between different spaces is utterly dependent upon Miriam's perspective, as is exemplified by the different renditions of the Baileys' house Miriam offers us. When she exists exclusively in her own room, the significant boundary is drawn between this room and all the others. Whenever, however, Miriam either moves through the entire house, or when she thinks about the house in Tansley Street as an entity, especially while inhabiting another site, then that very same boundary becomes porous or disappears completely. What was previously separate is now perceived as forming a self-enclosed space.

The boundaries Miriam draws between various localities is further relativised by virtue of the fact that two contrasting spaces may possess identical attributes. For example, both her own room and the island sites are protective hosts of memories; both her familiar native country and the newly discovered foreign countries are considered friendly and happy places, as well as cold and devitalising. At the same time, two contrasting spatial attributes may be ascribed to one space, not least of all in the case of Miriam's own room which is both infinite and protective. Precisely because the semantic encoding of site is so heavily dependent on situation and word, there is no consistent system according to which upper space is always associated with happiness and lower space with unhappiness. Even while one can determine a certain fundamental pattern, owing to which topographical categories such as proximity and distance, interiorcity and exteriorcity, height and depth, infinite openness and limited closure are installed by Richardson's narrative, their actual value depends on the manner in which Miriam uses her descriptions of actual material sites to discuss psychic realities – notably her sense of inclusion in or exclusion from a particular community, but above all her need to remember and recast past places into an autobiographical text.

As a result concrete material spaces in *Pilgrimage* assume two independent functions. They serve to endow non-spatial concepts such as loneliness, creative activity and a sense of belonging with a spatial configuration within the text. At the same time they endow spatial phenomena with additional values such that the meaning of space in this literary text moves beyond its physical and mathematical attributes. As Lotman notes, the scene of action is more than a decorative background: 'The whole spatial continuum of a text in which the world of the object is represented gains its figuration only within a certain *topos*. This *topos* is always invested with a certain "objectification".'[15] Nevertheless he is primarily concerned with the spatial structuring of the text as a whole:

> Behind the description of the things and objects, in whose surroundings the characters of the text act, there arises a system of spatial relations, the structure of the *topos*. While serving as the principle of organization and disposition of the literary characters within the artistic continuum, the structure of the *topos* emerges as the language for expressing other, non-spatial relations in the text.[16]

What the plethora of spatial representations in *Pilgrimage* illustrates, however, is that it is not only possible but also necessary to discuss the meaning of literary space over and beyond both the notion that it serves as the background for plot events and the notion highlighted by Lotman, namely that of the 'modelling function of artistic space in the text'. For, in addition to clarifying both the spatial and non-spatial structure of a given text, descriptions of actual material places point to the fact that it is above all phenomenologically perceived space which allows for a pre-logical or non-logical experience of the world, for an atmospheric, sacred or even metaphysical notion of existence which can be captured only indirectly in language. When we are dealing with questions of literary space, this non-lingual quality, this process of spatial perception, producing meaning and a coherent ordering of perceived reality, is as much at stake as the question of textual structuration. What emerges are three more or less overlapping attributes of space which will be discussed in the following three chapters.

Firstly, the represented actual material space is atmospheric and dependent on the perceiving and experiencing subject. It can be experienced as attractive or repulsive, and can provoke enjoyment or anxiety, since it contains the life, which takes place in it, even while it preserves its atmospheric quality. It can be a mirror for the experiencing character, a seismograph of his or her mood, just as it may, like a catalysis, also summon up particular moods or, like a filter, protect the character from certain influences.[17]

Secondly, because they function more like surroundings than background, actual material spaces should be thought of less as the site in front of which certain events take place and rather as the site in which these events occur, as that in or through which people pass. Actual material spaces are what surround people and objects, indeed that which permits the existence of 'directedness', of an anchorage in the world; that which allows for relationships, tensions or boundaries to exist between people, or between people and objects. Indeed actual material spaces are what make an intermediary position 'between' two entities, as well as a 'meeting' between two entities, possible in the first place.

Thirdly, being more than merely the background or the receptacle for an action, the actual material spaces occasionally transforms into the subject of an action. They are personified, and serve as an addressee for Miriam, in the sense that she conceives of them as her companions. This allows Richardson to articulate more accurately what precise qualities make spaces 'significant' for her heroine.

NOTES

1 J. Lotman, *The Structure of the Artistic Text* (Michigan, 1977), 216.
2 *Ibid.*, 217.
3 *Ibid.*, 218.
4 *Ibid.*, 217.
5 The term 'foreign space' is adopted from from Abraham A. Moles and Elisabeth Rohmer, *Psychologie de l'espace* (Paris, 1972), 58: 'the space of plans, the zone of travel and exploration, the foreign which is more or less familiar, the reservoir of the new'. 'Anti-space', on the other hand, is used to denote space which does not represent a reservoir of the new which permits discoveries, but is rather the old which undermines these discoveries. Occasionally, foreign spaces are felt to be anti-spaces when they are in complete opposition to Miriam's sense of self. The term 'interior space' is used as a topological concept which denotes a space which is separated by walls from exterior space. I am not yet concerned with the metaphorical significance of an interior space in the mind or an interior space in the body, this being a dichotomy which I explore in Part II.
6 See Necdet Teymur, *Environmental Discourse* (London, 1982), 105. He describes utopian space thus: 'space in utopia is both discontinuous and finished . . . since it is closed, that is finished, it is not possible to expect change and development in it'.
7 The name 'Newlands' itself points to the function of the space, as A. Huxley also employs it in his novel *Brave New World*.
8 The novels *Tunnel, Interim, Deadlock, Revolving Lights* and *Trap*.
9 See Moles and Rohmer, *Psychologie de l'espace*, 21. The authors highlight the way in which cultures which are very different, nevertheless all practise a division of space into four types: into 'with myself' (*chez moi*), 'with the others' (*chez les autres*), 'public places' (*lieux publics*) and 'unlimited space' (*espace illimité*). As a whole, these categories also hold true for the pattern which is built up in *Pilgrimage*.
10 D. Richardson, 'Data for a Spanish Publisher', *London Magazine*, 6 (June 1959), 18.
11 See Chapter 4 for a more detailed representation of the 'neutral territories'.
12 This volume includes the novels *Dawn's Left Hand, Clear Horizon, Dimple Hill* and *March Moonlight*.
13 See Chapter 4, where the notion of 'significant' space is defined in greater detail.
14 These four phases are explored more thoroughly in Part II, concerning the psychotopology which is drawn up in *Pilgrimage* of Miriam's development.
15 Lotman, *The Structure of the Artistic Text*, 231.
16 *Ibid.*, 231–2.
17 This is used to an extent as a stylistic device in order to express particular states of mind in the protagonist. Furthermore, this quality of space is itself treated as an independent atmosphere in the text.

CHAPTER TWO

THE SPIRIT OF
THE PLACE

Coming gently into the room, taking her time, as though aware that otherwise something would be destroyed, instinctively aware of the density of invisible life within a room that holds a human being. (IV, 384)

Three critical categories, emerging from a phenomenological discussion of 'lived space', serve as the theoretical point of departure for my own discussion of the actual implication of the perceiving subject and its emplacement within a given space: Husserl's discussion of the 'existential' aspect of space and its anchorage in the lived world; Dürckheim's notion of 'awareness' (*Innesein*) as the experience of an immaterial presence; and Heidegger's notion that space is to not be found in the 'subject', nor that the world is to be found in 'space', but rather that existence is itself spatial.[1] As Binswanger explains: 'The ego's existential fullness or emptiness is here directly related to the fullness or emptiness of his or her world, and vice versa ... Ego and world continually [form] a dialectic unity in which meaning derives from the interplay between the two poles rather than each giving meaning to the other.'[2] As my discussion of the actual material spaces represented in *Pilgrimage* suggests, Richardson's novel can fruitfully be mapped on to the manner in which phenomenology has articulated the question of lived space. For, like Richardson, phenomenological theorists like Binswanger postulate an original, intimate unity between subject and space, so as to insist that space cannot be discussed in isolation from the subject experiencing and perceiving it. Any objective conditions of a given spatial situation are demarcated and are complemented by the effect which it has upon the subject and likewise by the expectations, moods and hopes which the subject projects on to it. Binswanger expands Heidegger's notion of an existence in concrete space by linking it to the notion of spatial atmosphere (*Gestimmtheit des Raumes*). He is thus able to explain the particular expressive quality a given space may have, as well as the possibility that the atmosphere of a space may form the basis for the mood of the one inhabiting it: 'Depending upon my mood ... the expression of the world also alters.'[3] Any change in experience brings with it a change in our experience of the spatiality of the world.[4]

Although, according to Binswanger, this atmosphere is more likely to be found in a space which involves not a goal-oriented space but rather a 'useless but none the less rich and profound existence, one which actually makes the human being human',[5] it nevertheless does not characterise a specific form of space or experience of space. Rather it refers to the quality of every lived space. Binswanger terms a space atmospheric 'in so far as it is the space of our particular mood', yet he makes a distinction between atmospheric and oriented space:

> As I implied earlier, we do of course in some way have a mood in oriented space; for a mood is never entirely absent. In oriented space, however, we deliberately disregard this mood; otherwise the notion of orientation in space would never occur to us . . . We naturally have a mood even in this state of calm observation and intellectual contemplation. However, this mood, in which we dwell calmly upon some thought, does not constitute the quality of the space here.[6]

Although this differentiation, developed further by Ströker,[7] is significant for a discussion of the position occupied by an experiencing subject in space, I would nevertheless like to separate the concept of spatial atmosphere from a discussion of spatial perspective, and treat it in its own right. Even if this atmosphere is not as prevalent in literary descriptions of oriented spaces, one may still recognise the principle of lived space — defined as the existentially significant mutual implication between character and space — regardless of the attitude of the protagonist. A space in which Miriam is standing unaware of her surroundings, a space in which she experiences herself as the centre, a space through which she walks with a goal in mind, a space which she observes contemplatively from a given distance — all these positions presuppose a mutual implication between subject and space. In each case, Miriam's mood affects her lived space, just as the inherent atmosphere of the space in turn affects her own state of mind.

The term 'lived space', coined by Dürckheim, refers to the correlation between spatial and psychological atmospheres or moods (*Gestimmtheiten*), and is an attempt to comprehend the individual's constitutive relation to his or her space. For Dürckheim, this correlation involves the individual imposing his or her own subjective mood on to the objective quality of space, such that lived space is pitted against objective mathematical space. His work stresses the different meaning which any given spatial situation can have for different people, as well as the way in which each individual's experience of space is affected by his or her particular mood. 'Material space differs according to the being whose space it is and according to the life which takes place in it. It changes with the actuality of particular attitudes, inclinations and preferences [*Gerichtetheiten*] which — more or less momentarily — control the entire self.'[8] Lived space is always used to signify a space which is mediated through the body of the experiencing subject. It is therefore differentiated from objective mathematical space in being more than the sum of its parts and is not merely to be viewed as a receptacle of these parts. Space, according to Dürckheim, 'is never merely something which "surrounds" a subject, in the sense that the subject stands in its centre, but nevertheless separated from it, experiencing it precisely by virtue of being demarcated from this spatial situation. Material space is rather imminently and structurally linked to the experiencing subject.'[9] For this reason, space is endowed with an affective quality, a pre-logical or extra-logical atmosphere (*Gestimmtheit*) which can never be reduced to mathematical space, since it can come about only through a subjective experience of space, determined by and related to the perceiving subject. However, lived space is thus also more limited than mathematical space, since its reality is bound to that of the very subject it also phenomenologically constitutes.[10] Significantly, this atmosphere (*Gestimmtheit*) does not concern only something which is transferred on to the space but also its reverse, namely that the experience of a space can itself be the catalyst for a mood. Being at once extended and limited, lived space is the only real space for the psychic and corporeal reality of the subject. Dürckheim describes lived space as 'a medium which allows the self to realise its corporeality' and emphasises that such a mutual implication of the perceiving subject and its spatial situation is both the precondition of human existence in space and the reason why the phenomenological significance of any given space can be determined only individually, varying from one subject to the next:

> However much space may present itself to the person experiencing it as a structure with an independent reality, with its own meaning and immanent significance, as long as it remains lived and experienced space it remains a reality possessing meaning and significance. This reality, that which it is taken to be and the meaning in which it is fulfilled, may be understood only in the context of the particular reality of the subject's life, the way in which the subject keeps it in his mind and lives it.[11]

Gölz, however, warns of the dangers of viewing this relationship as a purely subjective one. The mutual implication at stake signifies that space and the experiencing subject refer to each other, in the sense that the spatial condition correlates with the subject experiencing it.

> Experienced space is neither subjective (*every* human being lives in a space which is structured in this way), nor is it an immanent space which may be differentiated from real outside space. Experienced space is itself the real space which is valid for all human beings, but not as it is in itself, that is, without reference to the person who lives in it, but as it reveals itself to the person who has a standpoint in this space.[12]

For this reason, the atmosphere (*Gestimmtheit*) of a space is neither an arbitrary, belated and supplementary subjective refiguration of a given spatial situation but rather what constitutes our existence in space. According to Gölz, the atmosphere (*Gestimmtheit*) is what makes space present for the subject: 'As a result of this atmosphere, space is a space "for us", that is, a space which is really lived by us . . . atmosphere gives expression precisely to a characteristic quality of the oneness with space which results from anchorage in it.'[13]

One of the theses subtending this critical study of *Pilgrimage* is that Richardson has recourse to precisely such a phenomenological conception of lived space, conceived in distinction to logical, mathematical space, when she has her protagonist Miriam note 'the density of invisible life within a room which holds a human being' (IV, 384).

Indeed, analysing the representations of actual material spaces in *Pilgrimage*, one can distinguish four aspects of spatial atmosphere (*Gestimmtheit*), all of which indicate that Miriam's subjectivity is constituted by the very spaces she inhabits, perceives and ultimately transforms into a narrative.

Firstly, the same space can take on different emotive or affective values depending on a change in the mood of the character experiencing it.

Secondly, as a result of a particular event, the emotive or affective value of space may undergo a transformation, such that spaces which were initially experienced as being pleasant may become unpleasant and vice versa. Occasionally the affective value of a space reverts back to its original atmosphere.

Thirdly, the emotive or affective value of a space may contradict the topological attributes with which it is conventionally associated (a closed, interior space may, for example be experienced as being open) or it may endow this space with additional attributes.

Fourthly, the affective or emotive value of a space – what Miriam calls 'the power of surroundings' (I, 360) – calls forth specific feelings in her which are related to and constructed by this spatial condition. In addition to, and depending on, the manner in which actual material spaces reflect and generate moods in the experiencing person, they are also treated as cryptonymic sites, given that they not only constitute subjective existence but also shelter and preserve past experiences such that the subject can recall them by remembering the site in which this experience took place. In this way, a lived space may also become a catalyst for past emotions and affects, and, equally, the memory of a particular space which was significant in the past may once again call forth the mood which had previously been experienced in it.

To illustrate how Richardson employs the phenomenological conception of lived space as being determined by the emotive or affective value (*Gestimmtheit*) which a given spatial situation assumes for her protagonist, I have isolated two examples: firstly, a description of the walls of Miriam's room, in which each significant shift in Miriam's psychic reality inevitably thematises this boundary between interior and exterior; and, secondly, the representation of her room in Flaxman's Court, in which this principle is most clearly represented because she is now compelled to share her intimate living space with another woman. As objective spaces, neither the walls nor the rooms change. However, since their reality consists in the way they constitute the perceiving subject, even while their significance is inextricably bound to her perception they transform into one of the most vital characters in Miriam's mise-en-scène of her psychic reality.

The passage representing the walls in Miriam's room in Tansley Street, and the 'challenge' they pose to the inhabitant of the space they enclose display five shifts in the affective and emotive value of the space, each corresponding to a shift in Miriam's mood. Let us not forget, however, that walls are conventionally understood as signifying separation. Moles and Rohmer explain: 'the function of the wall (*mur*) which ... presents itself as the very archetype of every enclosure (*paroi*) is to establish a point "here", to enclose a space; to create an interior by opposing it to the exterior.'[14] Richardson describes these walls as follows:

the challenge that lived in the walls of her room. For so long the walls had ceased to be thrilled companions of her freedom, they had seen her endless evening hours of waiting for the next day to entangle her in its odious revolution. They had watched her, in bleak daylight, listening to life going on obliviously all round her, and scornfully sped her desperate excursions into other lives, greeting her empty glad return with the reminder that relief would fade, leaving her alone again with their unanswered challenge. They knew the recurring picture of a form, drifting, grey face upwards, under a featureless grey sky, in shallows, 'unreached by the human tide', and had seen its realization in her vain prayer that life should not pass her by; mocking the echoes of her cry, and waiting indifferent, serene with the years they knew before she came, for those that would follow her meaningless impermanence. When she lost the sense of herself in moments of gladness, or in the long intervals of thought that encircled her intermittent reading, they were all round her, waiting, ready to remind her, undeceived by her daily busy passing in and out, relentlessly noting its secret accumulating shame. During the last three months they had not troubled her. They had become transparent, while the influence of her summer still held them at bay, to the glow shed up from the hours she had spent downstairs with Mrs. Bailey, and before there was time for them to close round her once more, the figure of Michael Shatov, with Europe stretching wide behind him, had forced them into companionship with all the walls in the world. She had been conscious that they waited for his departure; but it was far away out of sight and, when she should be once more alone with them, their attack would find her surrounded; lives lived alone within the vanquished walls of single poor bare rooms in every town in Europe would come visibly to her aid, driving her own walls back into dependence.

But tonight they were radiant. On no walls in the world could there be a brighter light. Streaming from their gaslit spaces, wherever she turned, was the wide briliance that had been on everything in the days standing behind the shadow that had driven her into their enclosure . . . She was going *home*. The walls were traveller's walls . . . They saw her years of travel contract to a few easily afforded moments, lit, thought she had not known it, by light instreaming from the past and flowing now visibly ahead across the farther years. (III, 86f.)

Miriam's initial joyous excitement over her free, independent and unsettled life in London makes the walls of her first room – the fascination of which derives precisely from the fact that they are 'traveller's walls' – become 'thrilled companions of her freedom'. However, as soon as this enthusiasm is replaced by disillusionment – when Miriam recognises her own, inescapable loneliness, becoming aware of how isolated she is from others' lives and of how eventlessly and meaninglessly her life is passing by – the walls become witnesses to her disappointment. The personified descriptions – 'they had watched her', 'scornfully sped her desperate excursions', 'greeting her empty glad return', 'mocking the echoes of her cry', 'waiting indifferent', 'ready to remind her' – make it clear that the four walls to which Miriam must always return act as spatial analogues to her own existence. They represent her conscience, that agency of her consciousness which insists that it is impossible to escape from a radical unencompassable loneliness at the heart of human existence. The 'unanswerable challenge' of the walls consists in their relentless warning that every release from this loneliness, every triumph over and denial of the walls, is only temporary and as such ultimately illusory. Miriam's attempts to escape the enclosure of her room (and with it the existential solitude inhabiting all human existence) – whether it be in her many forays into exterior space, 'her daily busy passing in and out', whether it involves a transcendental experience through reading, or at other times 'when she lost the sense of herself in moments of gladness' – all these departures inevitably lead to a renewed acknowledgment of the walls.

Although the shift in affective values attributed to these walls does not alter this fundamental situation, it does undermine it, precisely because the walls are assigned a porous quality. Once Miriam turns towards the outside world and extends her living space to include the lower part of Mrs Bailey's house, the walls remain, but become 'transparent . . . to the glow shed up from the hours she spent downstairs'. This extension of her living space functions as a spatial correlate to an alleviation of her own loneliness and complete seclusion. Her friendship with Michael Shatov, accompanied as it is by the knowledge that others too share her loneliness, brings further relief. Her new-found 'companionship with all the walls in the world' makes the boundary which she used to view as merciless appear relative. Her final mood, an animation of her surroundings contingent upon her anticipated reunion with her sisters, makes the walls appear 'radiant'. Miriam imagines that she will find a solution to her loneliness by remembering the harmonious life prior to the tragic events which befell her family: she hopes that, with memory bringing the past back into the present, 'the wide brilliance that had been on everything' will reanimate the space she currently inhabits. Her ability to establish a link between her isolated and unsettled social existence, the joy of independence in her own room and her prior feeling of belonging to her family effect a further mitigation of the so harshly felt loneliness.

As Miriam's mood changes, the walls remain 'traveller's walls', spatial signifiers for her continued independent life in London, but in addition they take on a double meaning. Even though they are not part of her past life, they are still touched by the protection her past existence belatedly bestows upon her: 'lit . . . by light instreaming from the past and flowing now visibly ahead across the farther years'. Given, then, that Miriam's mood is what determines the meaning which the walls assume for her, these come to function as a seismograph of the oscillations in psychic reality. In other words at any given moment her psychic condition can be deduced from her reaction to this spatial situation. The walls thus become a spatial embodiment of her phenomenological existence.

If the descriptions of the walls in her Tansley Street room serve to illustrate the constrictions imposed by her loneliness, then the spatial representations of Miriam's room in Flaxman's Court shed light upon another extreme: the constraints imposed upon on when one is forced to share one's living quarters with another person. These shared rooms function as a seismograph of her relationship to Selina Holland and have no reality outside the context of that relationship: 'as long as she stayed in them [the rooms] unaccompanied they would acquire no depth. Their depth was the level of her relationship to Miss Holland' (III, 447).

The initial description of the new room in Flaxman's Court is dominated by hopeful expectations. Flaxman's is seen as a place of refuge from the dirt and noise of London: 'A scrap of old London standing apart . . . The light gleaming from its rainwashed flagstones gave it a provincial air and freshness unknown to the main streets, between whose buildings lay modern roadways dulled by mud or harsh with grimy dust' (III, 399). It is precisely this security which she hopes will offer her an alternative to her room in Tansley Street: 'Soon she would daily be slipping out into this small brightness, daily coming back to it, turning from strident thoroughfares to enter its sudden peace' (III, 400). Although the lower parts of the house appear musty – 'the smell of long-lying London dust' (III, 401) – Miriam soon discovers an illuminated joyful atmosphere in her new rooms on the second floor:

> In this clear upper light, angles and surfaces declared themselves intimately. The thing she loved was there. Light falling upon the shapes of things, reflected back, moving through the day, a steadfast friend, silent and understanding . . . Nothing could be better than . . . this sense of light quietly falling. (III, 403)

In this as yet 'empty' and uninhabited space, Miriam experiences the longed-for feeling of anchorage, a pleasant sense of belonging and fusion with space: 'Long she stood, with life gathered richly about her, in the empty window-lit space where she now asked whether really she had seen up there . . . the thing that lay reflected in her mind, growing dim, changing to a feeling, a part of the warm sense of life all about her' (III, 401f.).

The presence of Selina, however, interrupts this security of belonging. Although they stretch a curtain across the centre of the room in order to secure a certain amount of privacy, the fact that each invests the curtain with different semantic values itself points towards the absence of common ground. Whereas Selina simply regards the curtain as 'an affair of modesty, a physical not a spiritual covering' (III, 406), Miriam views this artificially created and always provisional demarcation of an utterly intimate space only she inhabits as an existential necessity: 'dropping the mask of attention . . . soaring freely within this new life' (III, 406). However, despite the boundary that runs through the room she never succeeds in completely dismissing Selina's presence from her thoughts, and this affects her experiences; 'The thought, too, of reading in the new room, with Miss Holland on the other side of the curtain, changed the proportions of the adventure . . . It was only as private, shared by no one else, that the adventure was glorious' (III, 409). Miriam initially expects her new furnished room with its cleanness and light to provide release from her previous poverty: 'Squalor was banished. No more smell of dust . . . Here in the mornings there would always be beauty, the profile of things growing clear on either side of the pathway of morning light' (III, 410f.). But the joy with which she first greets the beauty of this place is soon dampened by the recognition that her need to share the new room will prevent it from ever becoming intimate and fully her own:

[37]

Seeking up and down the strip of bedroom for a centre, some running together of effects where her spirit could settle and find its known world about it. There seemed to be none . . . Each glance produced the same picture; a picture seen and judged long ago and with which her eyes could do nothing. She took refuge with single objects, finding each satisfactory, but nowhere reaching home. Swimming in transparent shallows, unable to touch bottom, stand steady, and see forth. Her life had somehow ceased. Behind her back unawares, while she had flown from newness to newness, its thread had been snapped. The small frayed end remaining in her hand was drawing her ahead across a level that showed no coverts; no deep places to be invaded by unsummoned dreams and their good end in the recreation of familiar things. (III, 418)

Indeed, as time progresses, the room becomes increasingly restricted, because it is invaded by Selina's presence. Selina insists, for example, upon closing the window at night, which makes Miriam feel uncomfortably constricted: 'It was as if Miss Holland had robbed her of a companion . . . the room seemed now full of Miss Holland, rebuked by her into a dead stillness' (II, 432). Selina's belongings also inhibit Miriam's initial sense of brightness: 'The worst was that nothing shone . . . nothing of Miss Holland's reflected light' (III, 440). Rather than animating, reviving the space – 'Absurdly half believing that the things she saw would change, would somehow become different under her eyes' (III, 440) – Miriam's contemplation actually reaffirms the room's shabbiness. At the same time, she feels a certain fascination with the 'unobtrusive', with 'dowdiness': 'the shock of the furniture had confirmed her sense that something was being offered. Low-toned, apparently gloomy, yet having a strange fascination, a *quality*' (III, 441). The rooms do at least acquire a certain familiarity as hosts for Selina's and Miriam's shared conversations: 'Filled with memories, the rooms had grown dear' (III, 441). When the room becomes a place of communication and shared experience, it temporarily in fact appears animated: 'during their long sitting the room had come to life. Nothing now looked dingy. There was a warm brightness; within the air' (II, 443). However, Miriam always returns to the conviction that, owing to Selina's presence, 'the rooms disowned her'. Precisely because their emotive and affective value is determined by the volatile relationship between these two women, these rooms cannot assume an autonomous reality outside that context: 'the rooms had been changing, growing larger, expanding together with the life lived there, a wealth falling into her hands too swiftly for counting. Apart from that life they were nothing. They stood defined, mean and dismal, crushing her' (III, 447).

Increasingly, Miriam associates Selina's possessions, her presence and the noises which she makes upon returning home at night, with death: 'those other sounds never varied. And spoke of death. That was the worst, that they filled the room with the sense of death and end . . . Centring in the imagined spectacle of the teeth waiting in their saucer for the morning' (III, 500). Once she has acknowledged that the relationship between herself and Selina is deadening and stifling – with the fact that they see the world quite differently spatially materialized in the fact that they are unable to share a room – Miriam recognizes that she must leave 'this corner where they had been dying by inches'. One might say that the two women's incompatibility is expressed precisely by their relationship to space and their sense of the significance of lived space. As Miriam notes, she is unable to bear 'Miss Holland's indifference to surrounding, and her obliviousness of differences in quality of experience' (III, 506). It is precisely Selina's moral response to her environment, in contrast to Miriam's emotional and affective one, which especially reveals their fundamentally different and incompatible response to lived space: 'She would never expand to the atmosphere. Would always sit as she was doing now, upright and insulated . . . But supposing Miss Holland should even for a moment sit back and contemplate her surroundings? She would see only material for pity or disgust. See only morally' (III, 426f.). Selina's presence is above all, however, perceived as being stifling and deadening because she confines and, to an extent, prevents Miriam from fully inhabiting this room, which not only is split in two by virtue of the curtain but also harbours two incompatible ways of inhabiting space. It is thus not simply the fact of sharing this room with someone else which makes Flaxman's an impossible abode for Miriam, but rather that their incompatibility translates into the experience of an utter lack of enspacement.

Following her decision to move back to Tansley Street, Miriam recognises that her experience at Flaxman's will leave no lasting traces:

> No indoor sounds would stay on with her from this house: because after the first few weeks her senses had never been at home, had always been a little on the alert, uneasy, half-consciously watchful for assaults from downstairs and from outside, pressing too closely and difficult to resist. (IV, 194f.)

> Flaxman time would roll up and vanish, for there would be nothing to recall it. She and Selina had left no mark on each other. (IV, 203)

What emerges is that Miriam was never able to achieve a sense of freedom in the Flaxman rooms because they failed to offer any real protection from the outside world, embodying instead a 'perpetual confrontation'; Miriam feels she must constantly resist this alien influence and is thus unable to achieve the anchorage necessary for her existence in space; able to establish a boundary neither between herself and Selina nor between herself and exterior space.

This particular experience of space, the only unremittingly negative one in *Pilgrimage*, thus discloses the one aspect which according to Miriam must not be missing from any given phenomenological condition: an unhampered anchorage in space as precondition for an unfolding and development of the self. In so doing Miriam confirms Dürckheim's principle of lived space:

> The human being and space are thus placed, both immediately and structurally speaking, on top of each other . . . The living subject realises and preserves his innermost self in the plethora of content and meaningful multiplicity of his space, and lived space has a momentary or more permanent psychological reality in the living subject.
> He is to the same extent 'in it' as it is 'in him'.[15]

A second aspect of the mutual implication between subjective existence and lived space unfolds in those spatial representations where the spirit of the place changes owing to a particular event. As the following passage demonstrates, the streets of London come to embody spatially the love Miriam feels for Michael during one of their many shared walks. Indeed, these streets visually objectify the 'thoughts that lay in her heart':

> They wandered silently, apart, along the golden-gleaming street. She listened, amidst the far-off sounds about them, to the gush of the great space in which they walked, where voices, breaking silently in from the talk of the world, spoke for her, bringing out, to grow and expand in the sunlight, the thoughts that lay in her heart . . . But the dust-grains were golden, and her downcast eyes saw everywhere, if she should raise them, the gleam of roses flowering on the air . . . the narrow strip of sky opened to an immensity of smiling spacious blue, and she saw, just ahead, the gleam of flowers and heard, on a breath purer than the air of the open country, the bright sound of distant water. (III, 195)

Similarly, an unattractive room at the Pernes' can suddenly transform into a site of comfort and beauty owing to the happiness reading affords her: 'the ugly gas bracket sticking out above the mirror, her own bed in the corner with its coarse fringed coverlet, the two alien beds behind her in the room and the repellent washstand in the far corner became friendly as the sun shone on the decorated cover of the blue and gold book' (I, 228). Miriam sums up the influence of art upon her experience of space as follows: 'Music and poetry told everything . . . they put you in the mood that made things shine – then heartbreak or darkness did not matter' (I, 374). The reverse of such spatial revitalisation is that the spirit of a place can assume a menacing, alienating note whenever Miriam is unhappy or feels excluded or threatened. After she has broken a rule of etiquette during her stay at the Corries', Miriam finds their living room 'dark and chill in the bright midday. It was as if it were empty. But if it had been empty it would have been beautiful in the still light, and tranquil. There was a cruel tide in the room. She sought in vain for a foothold' (I, 437). At the same time, the spirit of a particular place can be traced back to the life which it harbours. The addition of a hitherto absent component – be it a character's actions, a reference to or discovery of an idea, the entrance or departure of a character – always changes the psychic reality of those inhabiting the particular space, and accordingly their attitude towards it. In this way, when Miriam and Eleanor Dear read *Villette* together, their activity complements the room's atmosphere, 'a looking and a listening so that things came into the room' (II, 261). Reading a philosophical passage which Miriam finds irritating in turn introduces a sense of deadness: 'There was . . . something waiting within the quiet air of the room that would be gone if she read . . . The room was dead about her' (II, 407). Others' comments which threaten or challenge Miriam likewise change her perception of a space's atmosphere. Hypo's advice to Miriam not to work as a journalist, because there are already too many 'editors . . . *beleaguered*, by aspiring relatives' (III, 147), engenders in her the sense that 'a chill spread over the wide stretch of sunlit grass' (III, 147).

In a similar manner, Miriam's visit to her family shortly before Harriett's marriage illustrates how the mood of a place shifts according to how Miriam evaluates the events that take place in it. The sisters' reunion initially results in an intensely happy atmosphere: 'There would not be any talk. But silently the room filled and overflowed' (I, 302). Since Miriam views Harriett's escape from the family tragedy as providing a release for everyone – '[Harriett] with her future life streaming out behind her . . . drawing them all with her out towards its easy security' (I, 302) – the room also appears liberated from this tragic past: 'But these memories were no longer, as they had so often been, the principal thing in the room whenever they were all gathered silently together' (I, 303). However, Sally's remark concerning their mother's illness immediately changes the tone of the room's atmosphere: 'The gas light that had seemed so bright, hardly seemed to light the room at all. Everything looked small . . . The girls were little monkey ghosts babbling together beside Eve's trunk. Did they see that it was exactly like a grave?' (I, 304f.). In other passages Miriam's initial response to a particular place is disturbed by the threatening presence of a stranger. The freedom of the walk after nightfall, at first felt to be positive – 'Outside in the air, daylight grew strong and clear in Miriam's mind. Patches of day came in a bright sheen from the moonlit puddles, distributed over the square . . . From this dark pathway the bright of the wet moonlit road was brighter' (II, 95) – is altered by a man's disruptive greeting: 'the night had become suddenly cold; bitter and penetrating; the square was bleak and endless' (II, 96). Here, too, the disruptive element is to an extent attributed to a discrepancy between the two figures' spatial perceptions. Miriam's altered mood involves rage not only at the man's words but also at his incapacity to experience the space as she does: 'Figures of men . . . the way they saw things, mean and suggestive, always just when things were loveliest. Couldn't the man see the look of the square and the moonlight?' (II, 96). It is not until Miriam has convinced herself that all men are insignificant that the nocturnal surroundings regain their splendour: 'Miriam began singing again when she felt herself in her own street, clear and empty in the moonlight . . . Spring could not be far off. At this moment in the dark twilight behind the thick north wind, the squares were green' (II, 97).

Throughout *Pilgrimage*, Miriam's particular mood – be it joy or sorrow, an openness towards the world or a delimitation of her mode of perception – is transposed on to the lived surroundings, which come to register her emotional state. Pleasurable events, joyful expectations, fruitful meetings with others, or moments when by virtue of contemplation her sense of self is reinforced and she feels reassured in her sense of belonging to a particular place, engender a positive phenomenological experience. Conversely, all events which Miriam feels to be threatening or alienating and which erect a boundary between herself and others, and thus generate a sense of being excluded, of communication failing, or of her solitude being disrupted, produce a pejorative spatial revitalisation. As the following passage reveals, this may also entail the loss of the space's earlier joyful atmosphere. Miriam's recognition that her employer, Dr Hancock, ultimately belongs to 'that side of society' (II, 205) from which, owing to family's poverty, she is excluded, causes the space, which they had until then shared, to lose its particular charm: 'The room was empty ... the room was stripped, a West End surgery, among scores of other West End surgeries, a prison claiming her by the hands of the loathsome duties she had learned' (II, 207). The sudden change in their relation, resulting in a disruption of all romantic ties, renders the shared space arbitrary, because now Miriam no longer has any form of anchorage in this office, not even a negative one.

As a description of Miriam's walk in a north London Park illustrates, a lived space may, however, also lose its phenomenological reality once she is unable to respond to the spirit of the place:

> One day she left the pathways and strayed amongst pools of shadow lying under the great trees. As she approached the giant trunks and the detail of their shape and colour grew clearer her breathing quickened. She felt her prim bearing about her like a cloak. The reality she had found was leaving her again. Looking up uneasily into the forest of leaves above her head she found them strange. She walked quickly back into the sunlight, gazing reproachfully at the trees. There they were as she had always known them; but between them and herself was her governess' veil, close drawn, holding them sternly away from her. The warm comforting communicative air was round her, but she could not recover its secret. (I, 279)

The boundary which she experiences between herself and lived space is interpreted as a loss of the space's atmosphere and thus of her existential being in space.

A third aspect of the way Miriam continually shifts in her spatial perceptions involves situations where the tone of a place may deviate from or contradict its conventional topological attributes, once an additional spatial animation takes place, such as those passages where the elasticity of lived space is discussed, so as to illustrate its capacity to adapt to the body of the experiencing character. After a day's work, the streets and squares of London appear to envelop Miriam like a protective skin: 'The pavement was under her feet and the sparsely lamplit night all round her. She restrained her eager steps to a walk. The dark houses and the blackness between the lamps were elastic about her' (II, 74). In a similar mode, a strong sense of belonging can also allow the lived space to stretch into infinity. When Miriam plays on the Baileys' grand piano in the lower part of the house, 'The room became a background indistinguishable from any other indifferent background. All round her was height and depth, a sense of vastness and grandeur beyond anything to be seen or heard' (II, 335). After she has finished playing, the room regains its contours, the only difference being that it is now imbued with a supportive enriching tone: 'She swung round. The forgotten room was filled with friendly light. Triumphant echoes filled its wide spaces, pressed against the windows, filtered out into the quiet street' (II, 335). Overpowering loneliness may, however, in turn engender a dissolution of lived space. Michael Shatov's request for forgiveness for having had lovers before Miriam creates a gulf between them: 'the dreadful words invested her in yet another loneliness. She seemed to stand tall and alone, isolated for a moment from her solid suroundings, within a spiral of unconsuming radiance' (III, 212).

The central principle revealed in all of the cited descriptions is that it is spatial animation alone – be it a single or a repeated change in the spatial atmosphere: be it a restriction or a complementing of the initial spatial situation – which enables Miriam to feel that she belongs to a given lived space; that by virtue of possessing it she is constituted in her phenomenological being. Space becomes significant to her once an arbitrary spirit of the place is personally inflected. Fundamental about such an animation of lived space, however, is that it relates to sensual perception and the body, and not to an intellectual or imaginative animation of space by means of semantic encoding, which will be discussed in Chapter 4.

A final aspect of Richardson's usage of subjective animation of space involves those passages where a given place animates the subject, since lived space is not only a seismograph of Miriam's emotions, these are, as engendered by her surroundings, not only a mirror and, to an extent, a filter for changes in her psychic reality, but also the catalyst for a vitalising self-empowerment.[16] As she remembers her first night at the Corries', Miriam recalls herself: 'Entrenched in her familiar old dressing-gown, she felt more completely the power of her surroundings. Whatever should happen in this strange house, she had sat for one evening in possession of this room' (I, 360).

If one appropriates a lived space precisely when one becomes conscious of, and responds to, its inherent atmosphere, then an inability to recognise this 'power of surroundings' is emblematic of a disregard for these essential features. Describing a society lady in London, Miriam reflects that 'she and her kind missed the essential both in society and in solitude: the coming to life of the surrounding air, the awareness that within it is a life-breath; in-pouring' (IV, 202). But to Miriam actual material spaces are more than merely places for people: '*Places* to them were nothing but people; there was something they missed out that could not be given up' (I, 358).

Miriam also applies this rebuke to her reading of conventional literature, reproaching novelists for failing to take the existential significance of space into account in their works:

> But in *all* the books . . . the chief thing they all left out, was there . . . Generally the surroundings were described separately, the background on which presently the characters began to fuss. But they were never sufficiently shown as they were to the people when there was no fussing; what the floods of sunshine and beauty indoors and out meant to these people as single individuals. (III, 243)

In so doing Miriam of course, ultimately, refers to Richardson's own narrative technique as well as the compelling significance spatial existence has for her protagonist.

But this call for the 'power of surroundings' to be represented is also grounded in the philosophical conviction of phenomenological theorists that human wonder involves being astonished at one's own spatial existence and at the existence of other objects. Again and again, Miriam speaks of 'the marvel of mere existence' and stresses that 'the fact of there being anything anywhere is more wonderful than any theory about the fact' (III, 165).[17]

Indeed, in a seminal passage in *Pilgrimage* Miriam speaks of 'the astonishingness of there being people *anywhere*' (II, 358), emphasising that 'anywhere' is the spatial location of being. Accordingly, she proposes that Descartes' famous phrase should be rewritten: 'Something exists... It's enough. It answers everything... Descartes should have said, "I am aware that there *is* something, therefore I am"' (III, 171). This interest in spatial being also results in a defence of matter: 'If materialism could be supported empirically, there was something in matter that had not yet been found out. Meantime philosophy proved God. And Hegel had not brushed away the landscape. There was God *and* the landscape' (II, 175). 'Matter' is here, however, used to signify animate vitalised matter, in the context of a phenomenological discussion of 'appearances' or 'things' and not in the sense of the philosophical school of materialism, since it is Miriam's declared intention to prove that matter has qualities which go beyond the purely physical. Visual contemplation of landscapes (as of God) leads to essences of being. A spatial experience is fulfilling when this state of wonderment is in some way encouraged. Thus Miriam refers to the 'power of surroundings' so as to signify an atmosphere which facilitates an empowering anchorage in space, and reinforces precisely that mutual implication between the experiencing, perceiving subject and her enspacement. Miriam asks herself at the end of her pilgrimage:

> Is this conviction of the wonder of mere existence, the amazingness of there being anything anywhere, the secret of my feeling, wherever I go, upon my native heath and wishing to stay there?... Oberland; Dimple Hill... Only from Flaxman's did I fly, from enclosure in squalor I was powerless to mitigate. (IV, 635)

Ultimately the reason why the 'power of surroundings' may effect an empowered sense of enspacement, however, consists in the fact that it enables an individual to overcome the unfamiliarity of foreign spaces and transform them into familiar sites. By being able to construct a continuity between different spaces, Miriam discovers that her identity is contingent upon the attitude towards spatial existence which is inherent to her personality, regardless of the particular place she happens to occupy, even while each particular site resonates with this attitude so fundamental to her. Thus her search for a certain spatial quality and, likewise, her memories of those lived spaces in her past life, which come to fuel this search, are represented as the stable matrix in her psychological development: 'Was this bright space, that drew her, the secret of her nature... the clue she had carried in her hand through the maze?' (III, 244). This psychic matrix also explains the appeal which places such as the Waldstrasse and Newlands have for her, an appeal which is never directly named but rather circumscribed as 'an essence – something you feel in the right surroundings' (I, 413): a secret 'it' (I, 318).

> In Germany she had found it again and again, and at Banbury Park though it could never come out and surround her, it was never far off. It lurked just beyond twilight, amongst the books in the tightly packed bookcase. It was here, too, in and out sunlit days [in Brighton]... it lay along the deserted promenade and roadway as you went

home to lunch, and at night it spoke in the flump flump of the invisible sea against the lower woodwork of the pier pavilion. (I, 318)

This atmosphere, this unifying, constant factor which links otherwise different, joyful spaces, is an unnameable signifier with an endless number of signifieds. It is circumscribed as 'it', 'the thing', 'light' and also as the 'power of surroundings'. It only ever manifests itself indirectly, and Miriam is able to pass through and experience it in an infinite number of variations. At the same time, however, her search for a suitable space involves repeatedly experiencing and retaining this constant, yet unnameable, spatial essence: 'All the dark things of the past flashed with a strange beauty . . . The light had been there all the time; but she had known it only at moments. Now she knew what she wanted . . . beautiful bright rooms' (I, 403).

Since a satisfying, empowering spatial experience obliquely articulates this unifying sameness or essence, it can not only be found in actual material spaces but can refer also to similar *past* and *imagined* spatial experiences. As a result, spaces with this atmosphere do not only bring about a feeling of joy which is directly related to these spaces at the moment of experience, but also call forth, by substitution, memories of other spaces:

> Recalling the song . . . keeping the brightness of her room at its first intensity, Miriam remembered that it had brought her a moment when the flower-filled drawing room had seemed to be lit, from within herself, a sudden light that had kept her very still and made the bowls of roses blaze with deepening colours. In her mind she had seen garden beyond garden of roses, sunlit, brighter and brighter, and had made a rapturous prayer. (I, 405)

In this way, such spaces not only become receptacles of joyful moods but also preserve such empowering atmospheres. A recollection of a stirring moment summons up not only the particular experienced space but also the atmosphere which it then contained. Prior to any semantic and symbolic encoding, this atmospheric quality of space in *Pilgrimage* has a phenomenological significance which lies outside any direct symbolic representation and thus allows Richardson to articulate the 'vital power' of space which cannot be pinned down in language. As Dürckheim writes: 'There is a concrete semantic relationship between the living subject and his space, since the living subject and lived space are related in the extent to which each achieves fulfilment'.[18]

NOTES

1 See G. Hoffmann, *Raum, Situation, erzählte Wirklichkeit* (Stuttgart, 1978), in particular the introductory chapter. Sources for this spatial concept of existence may be found in K. von Dürckheim, 'Untersuchungen zum gelebten Raum', *Neue Psychologische Studien*, 6, ed. Felix Krueger (Munich, 1932); in M. Heidegger, 'Bauen Wohnen Denken', *Vorträge und Aufsätze* (Pfullingen, 1954), 145–162; in Jean Piaget's and Bärbel Inhelder's outline of the stages of spatial awareness in children in *La Répresentation de*

l'espace chez l'enfant (Paris, 1948), and in Maurice Merleau-Ponty's discussion of pre-logical space and the womb in his work *Phénomenologie de la perception* (Paris, 1945).

2   L. Binswanger, 'Das Raumproblem in der Psychopathologie' *Ausgewählte Vorträge und Aufsätze II* (Bern, 1955), 199.
3   *Ibid.*, 199f.
4   See also H. Scheller, 'Das Problem des Raumes in der Psychopathologie', *Studium Generale*, 10 (1957).
5   Binswanger, 'Das Raumproblem in der Psychopathologie', 200.
6   *Ibid.*, 206.
7   E. Ströker, *Philosophische Untersuchungen zum Raum* (Frankfurt, 1965).
8   Dürckheim, 'Untersuchungen zum gelebten Raum', 390.
9   *Ibid.*, 394.
10 If an individual is radiant with joy, then the space of his or her existence will manifest a corresponding joyful abundance; likewise, if despair leads an individual to withdraw into a psychological void, then he or she will feel the space of his or her existence to be empty. See Binswanger, 'Das Raumproblem in der Psychopathologie', 202, and also James Gibson, *The Ecological Approach to Visual Perception* (Boston, 1979), 306. Gibson draws a distinction between lived space and physical space.
11 Dürckheim, 'Untersuchungen zum gelebten Raum', 389f.
12 W. Gölz, *Dasein und Raum* (Tübingen, 1970), 199.
13 *Ibid.*, 203.
14 A. Moles and E. Rohmer, *Psychologie de l'espace* (Paris, 1972), 37.
15 Dürckheim, 'Untersuchungen zum gelebten Raum', 390.
16 K. von Dürckheim terms this the vital quality of lived space, *Ibid.*, 412f.: 'Every experience in exceptional space is coloured by a particular inclination [*Zumutesein*], a peculiar, sensual overall tone which we call the *vital tone* of each spatial experience. Correspondingly, each concrete space has a peculiar, complex vital quality for the experiencing character, in which the sum of the vital fulfilments, opportunities and boundaries which it contains are synthesised to form a emotive objectivity.'
17 See Ludwig Wittgenstein, *Tractatus logico-philosohicus* (Frankfurt, 1976), 114: 'It is not *how* the world is which is the mystical, but *that* it is.'
18 Dürckheim, 'Untersuchungen zum gelebten Raum', 473.

CHAPTER THREE

THREE MODES OF EMPLACEMENT

In the previous chapter my concern was the manner in which Richardson explores the mutual implication of the subject and its enspacement. I will now turn to the question of how lived space is textually engendered. To do so, two aspects will be explored. The first is the position which Miriam assumes in her surroundings, which is to say, the way in which she experiences space as being structured differently according to her attitude towards it. Such variable spatial structuration, changing according to the behaviour of the perceiving subject can be divided into three modes – absorption in the atmosphere of a space, movement through space and detachment from lived space as a result of the protagonist's contemplations. Secondly, this variable spatial structuration is textually produced by virtue of the fact that each mode privileges a different type of linguistic representation of space. In other words, Richardson not only thematises the issue of lived space but, perhaps more crucially, designs a poetic language that stages the difference which a shift in her protagonist's attitude makes towards her phenomenological existence.

Thus in the previous chapter I was concerned with a thematic rendition of the affective and emotive quality of the diverse places Miriam inhabits or passes through. I will now discuss how being enclosed in space and existing in a phenomenological sense prove to be mutually dependent, on a textual level as well. To do so I will use Elizabeth Ströker's[1] tripartite model of phenomenological existence, for she discusses the subject's enspacement according to three experiential modes: the space of human action, the space of human action and the space of human contemplation.

Taking as her starting point the proposition that all being 'in itself' or 'related to itself' already presupposes a self-reflexive position, while a pre-reflexive attitude on the part of the subject consists in an immediate being 'with' objects, in a direct being 'in' the world, Ströker begins by exploring this pre-reflexive position. For her the subject's shift in its relation to space is contingent upon the diverse modes of corporeal existence: 'as an atmospheric body [*Gestimmtheit*], the body is the bearer of expressive content, as an active body it is the starting point for goal-directed activities and as a unity of senses it is the centre of perceptions'. From this she concludes, '*the* single space changes according to the subject's behaviour, and this space is in turn differently structured because it is differently inhabited'.[2] By dividing space into atmospheric space, action space and contemplative space, Ströker attempts to capture the 'subject's inhabitation of space as a physical subject, whereby the nature of this occupation of space differs according to the particular mode of physical existence'. It is crucial to note that Ströker's three spatial attitudes do not, however, relate to different actual material spaces, but rather to different positions in space. According to a given situation, an alteration in the subject's behaviour may cause a space to change from atmospheric to action space, from action space to contemplative space and so on. Furthermore, it is often impossible to pinpoint the place at which one attitude transforms into another; and this indeterminacy engenders hybrid spaces, such as atmospheric action spaces or atmospheric contemplative spaces. Applied to a literary text such as *Pilgrimage*, this tripartite model can be used not only to differentiate between the protagonist's attitudes towards the places she inhabits but also how such shifts in spatial positioning structure the trajectory of her own narrative.

Atmospheric space[3] is an enveloping space which the subject experiences directly and intimately and which is permeated by his or her mood. It expresses the ordinary bond between subject and space prior to the assumption of a reflexive or a functional position. It cannot be grasped with conceptualisations like 'opposition between subject and object' nor with any description of the 'relation' between the subject and its surrounding objects. The subject is immanently in and is absorbed by this enveloping atmosphere. His or her relation to the space is free from any specific intention: 'Experiencing signifies here a peculiar communication between the experiencing ego and a space which is always other and deeply expressive ... atmospheric space is found in a pre-reflexive turning to the world.'[4] Perspective, involving the centredness of subject in space, its orientation in a space perceived as being finite and allowing one to compare different instances of spatial existence with each other, is absent from such atmospheric space. The sense of objects in space being structured sequentially and varying in size is relevant for the atmosphere of a space only if such spatial relations acquire an expressive function, that is, only if they mirror the subject's moods. Atmospheric space must be thought outside categories of measurement: 'Its distances differ from those which may be measured. If one confines the concept of distance functionally to metric measurements, then it stands that there are no distances in atmospheric space.'[5] As Ströker notes, there is no distance between subject and world, no reflexive separation, as if the physical boundaries were porous and it were impossible to determine where the body ends and the surroundings begin.

Since atmospheric space is characterised primarily by its expressive content, it has no system of dimensions which define one place as located in the near distance and another as further away:

> In terms of my emotional state, my experience of a space is unrelated to the position in which I, as a physical being, am at this moment located. My phenomenological location in atmospheric space cannot be determined. As an emotional being, I do not occupy one fixed position in this space ... Atmospheric space has no centre of reference.[6]

By lacking a centred position, the subject also lacks orientation. For the subject, atmospheric space is not directed towards anything, rather it is the expression of an non-intentional, pre-reflexive lingering in space. Without measurable distances, the concept of detachment is also absent. Proximity and distance refer not to measurable, topological conditions but rather to their relation to the perceiving subject: 'Proximity and distance are not attributive classifications of the objects of which one is aware, but my means of becoming aware.'[7] Proximity is simply the condition of being present, and distance is that which is no longer present. As with the subject's mood, so his or her movement adapts to and is determined by the atmosphere of the space. Since the boundary between ego and space cannot be fixed, the inverse is also true:

> Space is not only space *for* my movement – it is, in being so imbued with my mood, also space *by virtue of* my movement. I can negate it with my movement, can document it using my movement so that I become oblivious to its contents – whereby the space does not remain as it was, but becomes momentarily transformed, just as I am not, in the opposite case, merely a receptacle receiving its contents, but bear and am the very first to determine its atmosphere with my movement.[8]

The body is one with objects and space; without intending to be, it is drawn into possessing a mood. Concerning the determination of directions, Ströker concludes: 'Atmospheric space has no marked directions ... [it] is *atropic*'.[9] Thus atmospheric space is dependent upon the experiencing subject and has no separate, individual existence:

> Atmospheric space is not 'outside' me; like objects, it 'surrounds' me, is all around me – this is its mode of actuality. I am not, however, *in* it as objects are in it. Experientially, I have reached the fullest point of my potential to be a mobile, physical being experiencing expression. Atmospheric space is with me as the completion of my atmospheric being, it relates to my being in a condition of mutual determination and fulfilment.[10]

From this issues a strict mutual implication between space and the experience of space. Atmospheric space refers in every respect to the perceiving subject, to his or her body and mood. The subject is situated at the centre of the space, experiences the space as enveloping and as imbued with his or her own mood. For this reason, the subject is not self-reflexively detached from objects, rather, it is absorbed into space. In this pre-reflexive position, the subject does indeed stand at the centre and *as* the centre in space, but it is not centred in himself or herself, and is thus neither oriented in nor directed towards space.

Action space and contemplative space both differ from atmospheric space precisely in terms of the degree to which the subject is oriented and centred in space. For, here, the subject exhibits a definite direction because existence involves clearly defining one's own body as being located 'here' in opposition to everything which is 'there'. For Ströker, such directedness is revealed in two modes of physical existence: 'as an active body it is the starting point for goal-directed activities; as a unity of senses it is the point of reference for sensual contemplation'.[11] In action space, orientation signifies the subject's movement from 'here' to 'there'. In contemplative space, orientation involves the subject reflecting upon the relation between here and there.

Action space is formally defined as providing the 'in which' of potential action. While it is the expressive character of objects which constitutes the affective and emotive quality of atmospheric space, this expressive world disappears in action space and is replaced by the question of spatial suitability or usefulness, which either assists or hinders the subject in achieving a particular goal. In being linked to the activity of the character experiencing it, action space is viewed as a dynamic structure. If atmospheric space involves a unity of meaning and mood, action space may be divided into different areas, since the subject who provides its structure occupies a central site within it. The experiencing subject makes a distinction between his or her own location 'here' and the other location which is 'there' (in the near distance) or 'there' (at a far remove). Thus it is the subject's orientation and certainty of direction which structures the space. 'Here' is the place which the subject never consciously leaves, the vantage point from which the objects are ordered and the space is organised. If he or she moves, it is from 'there' to 'here'. The subject's ever-changing position is always accompanied by reflections upon his or her own centre. As a result, Ströker argues:

> Action space is a topological multiplicity, its structure is determined by areas. Its centre is also an area which is determined by the body's limitations and, at the same time, the body's ability to transcend those restrictions. Ontologically speaking, it is the space which constitutes the outline of a plot, its existence being relative to the situation of the active subject.[12]

In oriented action space, it becomes apparent that the directions do not have equal priority: action space is anisotropic and, in being a centred space, also necessarily non-homogenous. Whereas in atmospheric space the environment surrounds the subject on all sides and, even if the subject does not explicitly perceive the space behind him or her, this site is nevertheless imbued with his or her mood, action space is primarily a frontal space. The active subject faces forwards, even if his or her body is turned sideways. Although the subject includes the rear area in his or her thoughts, he or she is no longer situated in the centre of the objects and the space. In this way, the subject controls the distances, in the sense that his or her movement obliterates and recreates the existing distances. In atmospheric space, proximity and distance were seen to be qualities which relate to the subject's mood and lack measurable distances. Action space, in contrast, is a near space, whereby 'in front of' is nearer than 'beside' and also nearer than 'behind'. Active and judicious, the subject moves in the near region. Not until the subject becomes self-reflexive, theorising his or her enspacement, and in so doing transforming proximity itself into an object, does he or she move from an action space into contemplative space, which is to say into a distanced space containing perspective.

THREE MODES OF EMPLACEMENT

In *Pilgrimage* an action space is depicted whenever the represented spatial condition is related to Miriam's activities, whereby Miriam either sits still, while in a vehicle, and the space moves around her, or moves through an immobile space. In these depictions her surroundings are experienced in terms of availability and functional usefulness, as the trajectory between two places, even while Miriam now self-consciously meditates upon the spatial conditions, which in atmospheric space she had sensed either directly or unconsciously. In action space Miriam differentiates between various possible sites of belonging and habitation by virtue of distinguishing between 'here' and 'there'. Although she is no longer absorbed in space, she still perceives herself to be located in the space, which she divides up by drawing boundaries that change according to her various activities.

In contemplative space, the subject, though centred in lived space, stands as a corporeal contemplative being on the periphery of the surroundings which it perceives only as frontal space, clearly demarcated from it. Contemplative space is perspective space, confined by the limits of the horizon, in which Miriam experiences a loss both of enveloping space and of space behind her. In this spatial attitude, as with action space, the uniqueness of 'here' emerges by virtue of its comparison with every 'there'. Contemplative space is, however, distanced space in a twofold sense:

> Here, distance signifies firstly a spatial relation of separation between the objects and myself . . . The other signification of distance consists in the body being at a peculiar remove in relation to itself . . . In contemplation, the body offers itself in an attitude, whose pre-condition is indeed its own corporeality, but which does not bring the body itself into actuality. Visuality is privileged over all other senses for the reason that it allows the contemplative body to disregard itself and to remain distant from itself. The contemplative body is able to assume visuality effectively only by undertaking a particular spatial separation from the body.[13]

Since, when viewed from the position of an immobile, contemplating subject, contemplative space is centred space, the topology of space acquires its significance only 'through the assumption of a standpoint, it is the description of a place in the context of a physical frame of reference'.[14] Here the phenomenological subject is no longer situated 'in the middle' of objects. Rather, it draws a fundamental boundary between himself or herself and the objects it perceives; however, this boundary is now no longer affected by movement. Instead, the objects are now understood as always standing in opposition to the subject:

> No longer actually *in* space and nevertheless as body still *itself spatial*: in this 'attitude' he or she thus represents that double polarity which is on the one hand within space, between the 'there' of the objects and the 'here' of the subject's position, and on the other hand non-spatial, since it stretches between the spaceless *subject* and the space itself as an *object*.[15]

This absolute opposition between subject and world, of course, ultimately describes both the writer's attitudes toward her lived reality and that of the reader, caught in his or her own act of contemplation.

For each individual act of contemplation, final, irreversible distances are established when objects at close proximity can be fully grasped by the contemplative eye. Distant objects are, however, concealed in part by closer objects, since the subject's standpoint is arrested in its own centredness, which is to say, no longer in the act of moving about in space. If movement is the means by which space is appropriated in action space, then seeing becomes the subject's 'mode of possessing the world'[16] in contemplative space. Ströker not only describes the spatial delimitation of any act of contemplation but in so doing also postulates a connection between phenomenological perception and narrative 'point of view':

> In its being-before-me, space offers itself to me in its depth; it is revealed in the phenomenon of concealment and of becoming concealed. The spatial object alone is hidden, not only because it is *covered* up by others, but because it can never, not even in solitary contemplation, be fully *dis*covered. The object never appears as an entirety personified before me. My looking is an on-looking, it only ever meets the object from particular 'sides'. All solitary contemplation is essentially one-sided, and is thus not sufficiently capable of registering the object in its entirety. Generally speaking, the object becomes accessible only during movement, whether it be one's own movement through space or changes in the object's location. Accordingly, it unfolds its universality only in the successive passage through a sequence of locations.[17]

This passage has two implications for a discussion of textual space: firstly, that the subject's perspective must necessarily be relative and, secondly, on the level of representation, that any description which is linked to a location must necessarily always be subjectively limited as a result of this limited spatial vision.

The horizon in contemplative space is, however, relative only to the extent that what is experienced as a boundary itself implies a further extension of the delimited space. The appearance and disappearance of objects on the horizon is not 'perceived as destruction and re-creation, but as a coming from the "beyond" and a going "there"'.[18] This finitude, inevitably related to the subject, however, does not only point beyond itself. Rather it also allows the subject to transcend his or her own spatial restriction – a precondition for understanding other subjects in space. Communication involves understanding one's own lived space as a space which one shares with others, although each subject is bound to his or her centre. In this, the subject is further estranged from his or her own spatiality: 'In granting the other body the status of selfhood, I at the same time allow him or her to have a place in my space which is not absolutely "there" but also "here". The "here" thus loses its uniqueness; my "here" merely proves to be a "there" for the other.'[19] Owing to self-reflexivity and imagination, a subject can look beyond the uniqueness of his or her 'here' in space and observe himself or herself from the others' corporeal standpoint – as being 'anyone'. 'My contemplative space is indeed mine by virtue of my corporeality, yet it could equally belong to anyone by virtue of my consciousness, and is therefore a space in which it is possible for my experiences to be shared with and coincide with others.'[20] Disregarding one's own spatiality and overcoming an egocentric standpoint in favour of an eccentric one can lead to a transcendence which is characteristic for contemplative space and which permits an understanding between two separate subjects.[21]

Contemplative space may be said to be shaped by a distanced interest in the world which strives for objectivity. Whereas a dissolution of the self was at stake in atmospheric space, at issue here is a dissolution of space *into* the self. Space is experienced neither directly nor functionally, but from the standpoint of the contemplative subject, and, dissociated from the subject, it is perceived as being framed by one particular perspective. The ability to transcend one's own spatiality has various consequences in *Pilgrimage*. Firstly, it allows Miriam to project meaning on to the space which she encounters and to invest it with significant, symbolic value. Thus, it often enables her to construct a boundary between herself and the world as a means of understanding a situation. Secondly, the imaginative capacity to look beyond her own spatial restriction can allow her to communicate with another person. In contemplative space, then, Miriam is able to dissolve actual, lived space and replace it with imagined or remembered space, thereby transforming lived reality into the scene of writing.

Gerhard Hoffmann is right to insist that all textually represented actual spaces are always imagined space for the reader so that atmosphere or plot, contingent upon spatiality, can be understood only obliquely and indirectly. Viewed in its entirety, the text thus always represents contemplative space for the reader. However, since lived space is related to situations, and as such dependent upon any changes in the subject's attitude towards alterations in its spatial situation, literary representation of lived space is likewise related to subjective perception.[22] The centre of orientation is located not so much in the represented world as in the narrator and the experiencing character. Hoffmann thus writes:

> it may either remain constant or change. It makes no fundamental difference whether the space is drawn up from the narrator's or a character's standpoint. It always involves a space related to the subject, that is, a 'lived' space which is formed in the interrelation between object and subject, and therefore does not signify sheer objectivity.[23]

It is, nevertheless, necessary to distinguish between the narrator's and the character's perspective, since the represented lived space, though implicated in the phenomenological attitude of the experiencing character, is not necessarily bound up with the narrative situation, unless narrator and perceiving character are the same. Indeed, one may speak of a space as being atmospheric space or action space for the protagonist, while both the narrator and the reader conceive of the represented spatial situation from a distanced, contemplative point of view, and this distinction occurs regardless of whether the narrator is different from the experiencing character, or whether the experiencing character takes the form of the narrator's remembered self. Contemplative space is always dissolved in favour of the character's lived space, so that the reader can perceive even the act of distanced contemplation in an unmitigated manner. However, when contemplative space becomes a central theme in a narrative – in *Pilgrimage* this is the scene of writing, in which Miriam's real, experienced space is dissolved in favour of an imagined one – the text itself becomes self-reflexive and points beyond itself: towards the scene of its own reception, as a space beyond its boundaries.

By isolating three extremely diverse representations of a particular site – a London tea-shop – it is possible to trace how changes in spatial atmosphere and the protagonist's attitude towards her lived space are linguistically produced. For these three descriptions of Teetgen's teas each express Miriam's momentary mood and her state of mind. At the same time, a comparison between the three episodes also reveals a development in Miriam's psychic reality as this plays itself out in an alteration in her attitude towards lived space. Equally significantly, this psychic *qua* phenomenological change is manifested linguistically not only by a change in adjectives used to describe her mood but more importantly by deploying pronouns, prepositions and verbs in such a manner that they correspond to these changes in Miriam's spatial situation.

The first spatial description depicts an atmospheric space which is dominated by Miriam's despair: her sense of trauma and guilt in relation to her mother's death and, contingent upon this, the feeling that she is trapped in an irrevocable mental stasis. Her fatalistic vulnerability and despair are reflected by her lived space, in the sense that she is driven again and again to revisit this particular London site, signifying an inescapable confinement.

> Why must I always think of her in this place? . . . It is always worst just along here . . . Why do I always forget there's this piece . . . always be hurrying along seeing nothing and then, suddenly, Teetgen's Teas and this row of shops? I can't bear it. I don't know what it is. It's always the same. I always feel the same. It is sending me mad. One day it will be worse. If it gets any worse I shall be mad . . . If not, I should not always be coming along this piece without knowing it, which ever street I take. Other people would know the streets apart. I don't know where this bit is or how I get to it. I come every day because I am meant to go mad here. Something that knows brings me here and is making me go mad because I am myself and nothing changes me. (II, 136)

Convinced that fate has condemned her to imitate her mother's madness and that she must accept this course of events, she feels herself to be both helplessly and unwillingly at the mercy of her lived space. Without intending to, she always finds herself at the one place which reminds her of her mother's death and, since she has not yet found a means of overcoming the traumatic impact of this loss, the building which reminds her of this relentlessly stays 'always the same'. Miriam connects the impossibility of a change in her life – 'because I am myself and nothing changes me' – directly with her experience of this part of London: 'I come every day because I am meant to go mad here.'

Typical features of atmospheric space appear in this passage – space is experienced as immediate, atmospheric and enveloping. The absence of any self-reflexive orientation in space foregrounds the associated absence of direction and of measurable distances, the utter lack of distance between subject and world, as well as Miriam's inability to register discrepancies and differentiations. She cannot distinguish between the streets and is also unaware of them; she does not know how she arrives at the place: 'I don't know ... how to get to it.' The noticeably frequent usage of the words 'here', 'this place', 'this bit' or 'this piece' signify that Miriam is experiencing only *being* in space and not movement towards it or reflection upon it. Lived space is understood exclusively in its relation to an immediate response and derives its significance from this response. It is neither more nor less than a spatial rendition of this mood, i.e. only that section of the entire locality (namely this particular part of London) is depicted which directly corresponds to her mood of despair: 'It is always the same. I always feel the same.' This street is not merely associated with the possibility of insanity on a figurative level, since her continual return to the place is actually equated with the process of going mad. As an actual, material space, it is viewed as the precise site of her future madness: 'I shall be mad. Just here.' This direct and atmospheric space which is related to Miriam's mood and, likewise, her non-distanced attitude towards the space, are furthermore supported stylistically by the use of the first person present, whereby the 'I' is not a self-reflexive, but rather a directly experiencing ego. With regard to the building, one finds almost without exception the verb 'to be' or variations upon it used with the demonstrative pronoun 'here', and surprisingly few adjectives describing physical details.

In his chapter 'Deixis, Space and Time', John Lyons notes the way in which 'the distinction between "this" and "that" and between "here" and "there" depends upon proximity to the zero-point of the deictic context',[24] something which, in this passage, characterises the building as a near space for Miriam. The absence of descriptive details, and the preference for descriptions which emphasise the location of the space, indicate that the focus lies with deictic content. Moreover, in foregrounding Miriam's emotions as opposed to physical details – 'think', 'forget', 'feel' – and evoking her response to the building – 'it's making me go mad', 'it's the same', 'it's worse' – Richardson articulates the fact that this space is, above all, expressive of Miriam's emotions. With regard to the language used, Miriam is right in the middle of the space, located precisely in a 'here' and 'now'; not focused ('directed') but rather passively absorbed in this space.

The extreme restriction of this lived space (deriving from a lack of perspective) which is conveyed in this first description articulates the interconnection between psychological states, topological awareness, the structuring of lived space and textual representation. This inescapable, never-changing place functions as the spatial analogue to Miriam's disorientation concerning her future and her entrapment in her present predicament. Miriam suffers and, since she has not yet developed a self-reflexive distance to her psychic reality, this suffering stands in isolation as an all-powerful emotional condition. She is compelled to experience the space around Teetgen's Teas as relating solely to herself and to this suffering. Topologically, this is demonstrated by virtue of the fact that no spatial perspective is ever developed in this particular representation of Miriam's lived space; there is never any comparison between various near and distant spaces, nor any differentiation between various instances of this space, nor any distance to this lived space. Her psychological stasis mirrors her immobility in space, and her spiritual hopelessness corresponds to the topological absence of perspective. This lack of movement and perspective is anchored linguistically in an absence of transitive verbs. In so far as this passage depicts Miriam's movement, it is shown only as a blind one. She walks along the streets 'seeing nothing' and heading for this point: 'I come every day.'

The second depiction of this place in *Pilgrimage* represents an action space and is clearly distinguished from the first one by movement. This particular description of Teetgen's Teas does not act as an expression of Miriam's mood, but rather as the site of physical and psychological activity. The passage is more complex than the first because two temporal dimensions become enmeshed. Using a third person past-tense narration, Richardson offers us Miriam, located in action space, recalling the beginning of her time in London and, associated with this, her experience of Teetgen's Teas. Significantly, not only temporality is blurred but also modes of behaviour in space. Miriam is both herself remembering and being remembered, and these two manifestations of herself are situated in action space. Thematically the passage emphasises the fact that Miriam, having managed to distance herself from her past suffering, even while she is able to transfer the active manner in which she currently experiences this site on to her recollection of her earlier experience of it, is now able to imagine movement out of the space associated with stasis. In other words, the liberation from her own psychological restriction is mirrored in her lived, action space as well as in the remembered space which has been transformed in her memory into a space of free movement. Strictly speaking, of course, this description is a hybrid, since Miriam, in the act of remembering, moves from action space to contemplative space:

> Two scenes flashed forth from the panorama beyond the darkness, and while she glanced at the vagrants stretched asleep on the grass . . . she saw, narrow and gaslit, the little unlocated street that had haunted her first London years, herself flitting into it, always unknowingly, from a maze of surrounding streets, feeling uneasy, recognizing it, hurrying to pass its awful centre where she must read the name of a shop, and, dropped helplessly into the deepest pit of her memory, struggle on through thronging images threatening, each time more powerfully, to draw her willingly back and back through the intervening spaces of her life to some deserved destruction of mind and body, until presently she emerged faint and quivering, in a wide careless thoroughfare. She had forgotten it; perhaps somehow learned to avoid it. Her imagined figure passed from the haunted scene, and from the vast spread of London the tide flowed through it, leaving it a daylit part of the whole, its spell broken and gone. (III, 106)

In accordance with the primary feature of action space, this description of Teetgen's Teas provides the 'in which' of Miriam's actions. In contrast to the first description, the space is not the site of a continuously recurring, inescapable experience of stasis, but is instead a space through which she propels herself, directed towards a goal. The verbs referring to states of being and feeling from the first passage have been replaced by verbs of movement, adverbs and directed prepositions, thus generating a dynamic structure in the topology which Miriam experiences. What is important now is that Miriam passes *through* space with a goal in mind, and not that she is situated in it: 'she saw ... herself flitting into it ... hurrying to pass its awful centre ... struggle on through ... presently she emerged faint ... in a wide careless thoroughfare'. This 'here–there' relationship ends with Miriam now being able to leave the place: 'her imagined figure passed from the haunted scene'. It thus becomes apparent that it is her actions which have enabled her to gain access to and appropriate the space. Her achievement of a state of centred orientation (so important for action space) is revealed by her perception of the space as being no longer homogenous and exclusively related to her own mood, but rather as anisotropic. The directions which she experiences change according to the relative degree of movement through the space. The first direction, 'flitting into', depicts the space as an 'in front' towards which she is heading directly, but one with which she has as yet little contact. In the second stage, 'hurrying to pass' and 'struggling on through', the space is experienced from the position of 'in the middle of' or bordering 'upon'. The final stage, 'she emerged ... passed' completes the 'here–there' relationship. 'There' has become the 'here' of the experiencing subject, and the 'here' of the past has become the implicit 'behind'.

This centred orientation is further articulated by her self-reflexive disregard for her own present feelings. The direct spatial atmosphere in the first description did not permit any detailed descriptions of the space. The boundary between subject and experienced surroundings in action space does, however, allow for subtle differentiations by means of adjectival naming, as well as by commentaries on the character's actions. The street is 'narrow and gaslit', 'unlocated' with an 'awful centre', and the exit of the 'haunted scene' is a 'wide careless thoroughfare'. Miriam's emotions are not represented verbally as a process, but are instead commented upon. She is 'always unknowingly' entering the street, 'feeling uneasy', and finally 'faint and quivering'. These explanatory and evaluative descriptions are employed in order to underline textually the distance between subject and space.

Similarly, the description of the state of mind which the space calls forth is not static, as it was in the first example. Miriam's psychological experience is imaged as a movement, as a journey through the figurative scene of her emotions: 'deepest pits of her memory ... intervening spaces of her life'; an inner movement which echoes her journey through actual material space. Instead of provoking an inner dialogue with herself, the name of the shop leads to a sequence of descriptions of movement: 'dropped helplessly into', 'images threatening ... to draw her willingly back and back and through'. Here, too, the emphasis on verbs of movement and on pronouns evokes the now metaphorical action space.

Crucial for the opening and expansion of lived space is the perspective from which Miriam is able to perceive it; that is, her ability to see her own lived space in comparison with other spaces and thus to recognise that it forms part of a considerably larger space. The centredness and orientation which her movement creates in turn broaden her field of vision. The boundary of lived space is no longer established as the street in which Teetgen's Teas is located, but changes with Miriam's movement. The 'haunted scene' no longer appears stifling because it is no longer experienced in isolation but as a part of an accessible 'vast spread of London'. This relativisation – it is a 'part of the whole' – allows Miriam's expanded lived space to have a positive atmospheric influence upon this single area: 'from the vast spread of London the tide flowed through it, leaving it a daylit part of the whole, its spell broken and gone'. One should also note the emphasis on movement and on dynamic spatial structure. Since Miriam imagines herself leaving the street for a larger and more open space, light from the area which she has just entered falls on to the old space, filling the place which she once occupied.

This correlation between spatial situation and psychic reality gives voice to the fact that an expansion of the psychological horizon – Miriam has turned towards the world, exchanged her desperate loneliness for a productive oscillation between exploring unfamiliar places and withdrawing into her creative solitude – is mirrored by a corresponding expansion of the spatial horizon. Conversely, in having assumed a new mode of behaviour in space, Miriam can now imagine leaving the haunted place, 'its spell broken and gone', with an ease which would have been unthinkable before. She can now begin to break the bonds of her complete self-absorption. Since London becomes not only a space expressive of her own mood but significantly also a space of movement, she conquers new territory, gains access to unfamiliar sites and thus procures for herself the ability to make choices.

The final example – a contemplative space – renders Miriam in a state of centred orientation. Here, too, her state of mind causes Teetgen's Teas to lose its immediate influence as a place of guilt: 'now their power has gone'. However, in contrast to the second example, movement in space has been replaced by inner meditation and by the projection of meaning on to space. Miriam's memory of the place is concerned not with her previous ability to leave the space but instead with recasting her earlier life in meaningful images:

> and leave her glancing along the shopfronts of this mean little back street. Teetgen's Teas, she noted, in grimed, gilt letterings above a dark and dingy little shop ... Teetgen's Teas. And behind, two turnings back, was a main thoroughfare. And just ahead was another. And the streets of this particular district arranged themselves in her mind, each stating its name, making a neat map. And *this* street, still foul and dust-filled, but full now also of the light flooding down upon and the air flowing through the larger streets with which in her mind it was clearly linked, was the place where in the early years she would suddenly find herself lost and helplessly aware of what was waiting for her eyes the moment before it appeared: the grimed gilt lettering that *forced me to gaze into the darkest moment of my life and to remember that I had forfeited my share in humanity for ever and must go quietly and alone until the end. And now their power has gone. They can bring only the memory of a darkness and horror, to which then, something has happened, begun to happen?* She glanced back over her shoulders at the letters now away behind her and rejoiced in freedom that allowed her to note their peculiarities of size and shape. (IV, 155f., italics in original)

Now the space is experienced neither directly nor functionally, but rather as a distanced space, clearly separated from Miriam's body. By imagining it, she objectifies it and gives it symbolic value. The treatment of space as something situated opposite herself, which is mediated primarily through her contemplative gaze, further highlights Miriam's position at the periphery of her lived space. Perspectival vision is even more pronounced here than it was in action space. As in the first passage, there are no detailed descriptions of the tea-shop's exterior, yet her detached attitude enables her to understand the district's structure and the way in which the individual areas fit together, 'making a neat map'. The single street is seen as relating to the others: 'the larger streets with which ... it was clearly linked'. Even more importantly, Miriam sees the space primarily in her imagination rather than by moving through it. The streets 'arranged themselves in her *mind*',[25] the street is linked with others 'in her *mind*'. Movement is once more absent in this description, underscored (as in the first passage) by verbs of being and deictic descriptions. A second similarity with atmospheric space consists in the shift in narrative perspective from third person past to the first person present. The difference between atmospheric and contemplative space, in turn, consists in the significance which an established and meditated standpoint at the periphery of the space assumes in contemplative space, in contrast to the specified, unmediated standpoint in the middle of space in atmospheric space. In the first description, the use of the first person indicated an utterly porous boundary between subject and space as well as the immediate proximity of the space. In this contemplative space, the 'I' reveals the fundamental opposition and division between subject and world and the subject's distanced, inner meditations.

Whereas this street was depicted in the first passage as initiating a terrible journey through Miriam's psychic reality, here it is simply regarded as meaningful. Neither the experience itself nor the process is of interest, but rather the meaning which the experience has acquired in being remembered from a distance. The sign 'Teetgen's Teas' is encoded semantically as a catalyst 'that *forced me to gaze into the darkest moment of my life and to remember that I had forfeited my share in humanity for ever and must go quietly and alone until the end*'. The 'I' of this description does not relate this lived space unthinkingly to her present state of mind. Rather she disregards her current perception of this place and allows it instead to transform into an explanation for life in the past. The space is experienced as an image, clearly separated from the experiencing subject – an imaginary picture which unites past and present in a meaningful way. The space's immediate, terrible power is lost, because Miriam is able to establish a contemplative boundary between herself and the world and, in so doing, to transcend her spatial confinement. Having become mnemonic in its vividness, the space allows her past life to be spatialised: 'They can bring back only the memory of a darkness and horror.' Miriam experiences this potential for transcendence and the opportunity to disregard herself as liberating: 'she ... rejoiced in freedom that allowed her to note their peculiarities in size and shape'. Since the space takes on neither an affective nor a functional significance, of her present being in the world, it can be aesthetically enjoyed.

Miriam's third rendition of Teetgen's Teas indeed encapsulates her psychic state at this point in the novel. Her detachment from lived space and her objectification of her surroundings at the moment of experience, in the course of which she imbues impressions with meaning, correspond to her increasingly strong sense of her identity as an artist. Lived space – whether it is a space endowed with an emotive or affective quality or whether it is a space she can take possession of – increasingly acts as an illustration. This spatial attitude is the precondition for the scene of writing, in which lived space, along with each memory of lived spaces, is perceived from a contemplative and distanced position and, having been reconceived as an image of past experiences, contributes to the meta-space of art.

What these three renditions of Teetgen's Teas illustrate, then, is the fact that the linguistic representation of lived space is characterised by its connection with the experiencing character, and thus with the character's position in space. Lyons distinguishes between two modes by which 'we can identify an object by means of a referring expression: first, by informing the addressee where it is (i.e. by locating it for him); second, by telling him what it is like, what properties it has or what class of objects it belongs to (i.e. by describing it for him)'.[26] Descriptions of Miriam's spatial existence belong primarily to the first category. Whereas there are surprisingly few descriptions of Miriam herself,[27] there is an abundance of depictions of her position within lived space and her movement through it. In a similar manner, most of the depictions of space are in reference to the experiencing protagonist and to her semantic encoding of her surroundings. There are very few descriptions of spatial situations which are independent of and separated from Miriam's corporeal experience of it. Richardson draws attention to her protagonist's location in space by privileging deictic expressions emphatically associated with *pointing at* and *situating in* space. Lyons elaborates: 'When we identify an object by pointing at it ... we do so by drawing the attention of the addressee to some spatio-temporal region in which the object is located.'[28] Such spatial localisation can be textually performed by having recourse to demonstrative pronouns and adjectives such as 'here–there', 'this–that', which need to be understood 'with respect to the location of the participants in the deictic context',[29] or by means of deictic adverbs – 'now', 'each time', 'someday', 'presently', 'before' – which imply localisation in time.

As Lyons notes, to privilege the location of an object as a perceiving subject in space goes in tandem with a reference to the spatial traits of the represented object, namely: 'their extension in space and their shape'. In other words, both Miriam as the experiencing protagonist and the space she perceives and inhabits are textually localised by means of reference to the spatial relationships which exist between two objects or between Miriam and the objects surrounding her. Such spatial localisation is produced by virtue of the fact that directions are described in relation to one another, that the distances between objects are described or the movement through a given space. It is accompanied by a striking abundance of deictic adverbs and prepositions[30] such as 'beyond', 'back', 'forward', 'from', 'behind', 'ahead', 'through' and 'into' which are typically, but not exclusively, connected with directional verbs, thus evoking a dynamic as opposed to a static space. Lyons elaborates: 'many, if not all of the locative expressions involving dimensionality and orientation can be seen as being implicitly or covertly, directional: i.e. as being dynamic, rather than static'.[31] Such spatial extension becomes significant once it is set in relation to the experiencing protagonist; the locative descriptions equate the 'here' with her position in space, even while they derive their meaning by being different from Miriam's position – implicitly the spatial zero point of the narrative.

Although the development of Miriam's psychic response to Teetgen's Teas – moving from atmospheric, through action to contemplative space – corresponds to the narrative trajectory of *Pilgrimage*, it is necessary to emphasise that the semantic encodings of these three descriptions reflect only Miriam's spatial positioning in relation to this particalar site and can, therefore, not be generalised. Extreme confinement, as it was signified in the first representation of Teetgen's Teas, is not a fundamental characteristic of atmospheric space. On the contrary, atmospheric space is just as likely to represent the pre-reflexive space of an ecstatic sense of liberation. It is always a limited space, yet only in the sense that it is utterly and exclusively related to the subject's state of mind. In other words, while it is impossible to determine the semantic meaning of any one of these three spatial attitudes in any fundamental sense, or the manner in which they correlate with the protagonist's particular psychological situation, what do remain constant are the ways in which Miriam gives structure to her lived space dependent on her attitude towards it.

In atmospheric space the experiencing subject is always situated in the centre of her lived space, incapable of reflecting upon it in any self-conscious manner. In action space, it is the subject's actions which produce a state of centredness and orientation. In contemplative space, it is the subject's detached observation. Although all three forms of space are present in the text from the very beginning, and although Miriam constantly shifts between the three spatial structures, depending on her psychic state, one may nevertheless recognise a developmental trajectory spanning the entire text which traces a heightening progression from atmospheric space via action space towards contemplative space. This overall process corresponds to the passage from the material world to the immaterial or imaginary world of art which Gilles Deleuze[32] outlines in his writings on Proust: 'the material sense is nothing without an ideal essence which it incarnates ... The world of Art is, however, the ultimate world of signs; and these signs, as if *dematerialised*, derive their meaning from an ideal essence.'

In the first part of *Pilgrimage*, Miriam's perception tends to be characterised by a non-centred position in which she is completely enveloped in space and often unreflexively influenced by her own changing moods. As the novel progresses, the emphasis upon the self-reflexive, oriented 'I' gains momentum, bringing with it an increased focus upon an immaterial, contemplative space in which artistic production is possible. Beginning with the London years, orientation in action space is privileged, since it is movement in space which enables Miriam to gain access to the foreign and the new. This gradually ushers in Miriam's recognition that journeying through actual material space ultimately leads her back to her own self. She sums up her Oberland journey to Hypo as follows: 'Of course there is actually no such thing as travel ... There is nothing but a *Voyage autour de ma chambre*, meaning *de tout ce que je suis*, even in a *tour de monde*' (IV, 167).

As she begins to privilege imagined material sites over actual material ones, Miriam concomitantly prefers a contemplative and creative position in the world. During her first translation assignment she perceives her desk as being the 'centre of her life', and, as she reflects upon this experience, she notes that this signifies not only distance between subject and world but, more crucially, her preference of contemplative space over all other attitudes in space:

> Sitting over there, forgetting, she had let go . . . And waking again had seen distant things in their right proportions . . . But the forgetfulness was itself a more real life, if it made life disappear and then show only as manageable space and at last only as an indifferent distance . . . It meant putting life and people second; only entering life to come back again, *always*. This new joy of going into life, the new beauty, on everything, was the certainty of coming back. (III, 135f.)

From the Oberland episode onwards, imagined or remembered spaces assume an increasingly central role, until Miriam finally occupies contemplative space to the exclusion of all others.

In *Pilgrimage* boundary crossings, which according to Jurij Lotman constitute the subject of the text, take place whenever Miriam rejects a concrete material experience of space in favour of an imagined or remembered reality. Such boundary crossings occur continually in the course of the narrative: whenever Miriam, in the act of reading, painting or writing, in dialogue with herself or conversing with others, places herself at the periphery of lived space and experiences her environment either as an image detached from her corporeal existence, or dissolves this material site completely in favour of an imagined space. The absolute precedence of contemplative space is, however, deferred, for until the end of the novel Miriam is represented as being determined by her corporeal existence in lived space, although the withdrawal from the material world into the immaterial world of pure contemplation becomes ever more insistent. Her existence in an utterly immaterial space – the scene of artistic production – is only ever anticipated.

Given that Miriam's trajectory from atmospheric to contemplative space corresponds to the movement from her home through various foreign spaces to the empty room of her artistic production, it is worth looking more closely at other examples for these three positions in space. It is, of course, impossible to draw up a precise system demonstrating the ways in which Ströker's tripartite mode of phenomenological structuration is deployed in *Pilgrimage*; for Richardson's choice of one space rather than another is not programmatically determined. The point, instead, is that one of the three spatial structures is always selected in order to endow contingent phenomenological experiences with meaning.

I begin with a discussion of action space because the semantic encodings of atmospheric and contemplative space are often enmeshed and should, therefore, be treated together. Since travelling, walking, movement between familiar and foreign spaces and between interior and exterior spaces, as well as movement *within* these spaces, are key themes in *Pilgrimage*, there are innumerable different kinds of action space. Nevertheless one can say: action space may either involve a more or less unmotivated movement in space or may act as the site for goal-directed action, with a specific purpose. In both cases, lived space is the 'in which' of a movement, although mutual atmospheric animation between subject and space is often more pronounced in the first case and tends to be absent in the second.

The following description of Miriam's return home after work is a typical example of her many walks through London, which are indeed purposeful, but in which anticipating her goal does not influence her momentary experience of movement. Her euphoria at the prospect of four days' Christmas holiday is of far greater importance.

> She wandered about between Wimpole Street and St Pancras, holding in imagination wordless converse with a stranger whose whole experience had melted and vanished like her own, into the flow of light down the streets; into the unending joy of the way the angles of buildings cut themselves out against the sky, glorious if she paused to survey them; and almost unendurably wonderful, keeping her hurrying on pressing, through insufficient silent outcries, towards something, anything, even instant death, if only they could be expressed when they moved with her movement, a maze of shapes, flowing, tilting into each other, in endless patterns, sharp against the light; sharing her joy in the changing same song of the London traffic; the bliss of post offices and railway stations, cabs going on and on towards unknown space; omnibuses rumbling securely from point to point, always within the magic circle of London. (III, 85f.)

Although goal-oriented action space is also structured dynamically based on Miriam's movement in it, such spatial representations differ from the first example, of unmotivated movement in space, since here lived space is primarily conceived as the condition for leaving one place and arriving somewhere else. In a passage describing how Miriam and her mother leave North London, so as to return home, she notes:

> The high brick walls were drawing away. The end of the long roadway was in sight. Its widening mouth offered no sign of escape from the disquieting strangeness. The open stretch of thoroughfare into which they emerged was fed by innumerable lanes of traffic . . . On the left a tall grey church was coming towards them, spindling up into the sky. It sailed by, showing Miriam a circle of little stone pillars built into its tower. Plumy trees streamed by, standing large and separate on mass-green grass railed from the roadway . . . Wide side-streets opened showing high balconied houses. The side-streets were feathered with trees and ended mistily. (II, 196)

In this passage, Richardson merely describes the space moving past Miriam and not a mutual vivication between the two, since purposeful goal-directedness engenders a separation between the moving figure and lived space. In the most extreme case, such purposeful goal-directedness reduces the action space to a mere background, for once actions become meaningful, independent of the space in which they take place, the subject is able to overlook this space entirely. One might say that space ceases to be *lived* space at precisely those points in the text in which it merely fulfils the role of a setting.

Unlike spatial representations, in which Miriam's focus on her destination structures her perception of space, the decisive factor in representations, in which her exploration and appropriation of her surroundings are at stake, is movement, not destination.[33]

In these examples space functions neither as the space between two places nor as a background; instead, it allows Miriam to possess lived space, as though it were an object. The walk through the Roscorla family's house in Dimple Hill demonstrates particularly clearly how Miriam associates her movement through space with the process of appropriating it and making it accessible.[34]

> Deciding to hoard, she opened the door. There was a bourne close at hand within the realm of this upstairs world: the unexplored sitting-room, seeming so far off on the other side of the wall of the staircase, yet whose door, though set further in, was next to her own. Clearly this was the best sitting-room, the room of state, unfrequented . . . Turning to the near corner whither her eyes were drawn as she stood at the window by something gleaming at her from its deepest shade, she found, within a glass case upon a what-not, the skeleton of a bird, bone-white, unimaginably small and fragile . . . Taking in the chairs in either side of the fire-place whose mantelpiece supported a number of vases, two of them containing dried grasses, and a clock, silent, surmounted by a mild water colour landscape, one a masculine chair, capacious, uncomfortably narrow and minus indulgent support, both protected by crewel-work anti-macassars, the round table between the front windows, a little old writing-table near the end window, velvet-seated drawing-room chairs drawn up there and here against the walls, she left these desolate reminders of a life that no longer flowed through the room and returned to the little bird, so living in his death. (IV, 467f.)

Owing to the use of verbs such as 'deciding to hoard', 'taking in', 'she found', it becomes clear that her visit to the still unfamiliar space is equated with a transgression of and thus a dissolution of the boundary between herself and this unknown world. Furthermore, Miriam's presence in the room is described in terms of spatial possession ('hoarding') and appropriation. Gathering impressions of the space, weighing up the various spatial objects against one another, is thus represented as an attempt on Miriam's part to penetrate the secret of things which are as yet mysterious.

However, in her attempt to fully experience this place, Miriam realises that she must do more than merely occupy it: 'Heavy stillness in the room that seemed now to demand a reason for her visit, confronting her with a past of whose inwards depths she knew nothing . . . Making her way to the door, she felt the room withdraw, satisfied by her acceptance of banishment, into the peace she had disturbed' (IV, 468). Meaningful anchorage in space, though intimately linked to spatial possession, can develop only once one inhabits the lived space. Indeed, the dialectic between moving through a space and retreat from it is a recurrent theme of the novel. Repeatedly, Miriam attempts to make a particular space her own during her walks, only to find herself banished from this foreign site. However, even though she does not achieve the spatial possession she desires, she does acquire images which, gathering them together in imagination, she contrasts with each other in order to discover the essential qualities of her spatial experience. At the same time, these frequent movements through space do not prove to Miriam that spatial appropriation is impossible. Every single movement promises an existentially significant exchange between subject and lived space, even if this interaction can achieve permanence only in the form of remembered images. Accordingly, after an absence from Dimple Hill, Miriam sees her return as representing a new movement through lived space: 'But beneath the high morning sky, the just visible distant marshes, the near green meadows and the piled downlands away to the right . . . seem to promise, if she should face the second journey, a further increase of their inexhaustible response' (IV, 617). Throughout her psychic and corporeal pilgrimage Miriam insists that 'being' signifies 'being oriented', and that possessing and recognising lived space is possible only in the context of a mobile orientation within it.[35]

By contrast, Richardson chooses atmospheric space whenever she seeks to describe the pre-reflexive spatial experiences of her heroine, or when she is concerned with descriptions of extreme egocentricity, when the mutual implication of subject and space is utterly unimpeded. Such depictions involve either the experiences of childhood (depicted in the novel only in the form of memories) or moments of ecstasy and transcendence, when self-consciousness is seemingly bypassed. For this reason it is important to distinguish between the atmospheric space which Miriam experiences in the text and Miriam's memory of atmospheric space, since the latter always takes place in contemplative space. For only in contemplative space can Miriam transcend materially experienced space in favour of her memory of a pre-reflexive spatial experience. In other words, although contemplative space is diametrically opposed to pre-reflexive experiences, because it posits a distance between the perceiving subject and the space she reflects upon, any pre-reflective experience of space can enter Miriam's consciousness only *post facto*; that is, in belated contemplation. Thus Miriam persistently draws attention to the way in which atmospheric space alone permits an unconscious, immediate experience of space: 'the moment of the first vision of spring, the perfect moment before the thought came that spring was going on in the country' (II, 403), 'Mental liveliness *did* obliterate surroundings, stop their expressiveness, already the first expressiveness had gone from the garden' (III, 344) or, 'the immediate truth that shone, independent of speculation, all about her in the English light; . . . something that shook her with gratitude to the roots of her being. But the instant she was called upon there came the startled realization of being in the world, and the sense of nothingness' (III, 238f.). Indeed, self-aware centredness implies the destruction of atmospheric space: 'There is something more than anything that anybody says, that comes first, before they speak . . . life touches your heart like dew' (II, 255).

Though the 'power of surroundings' is felt most poignantly in atmospheric space, only their subsequent conscious reappraisal allows Miriam to transform this ephemeral, immediate essence into something lasting and indirect – a pictorial memory – represented in language. Only then may an experience be shared and preserved, both for the person experiencing it and for others. As the following passage illustrates, pre-reflexive experience beyond linguistic utterance becomes durable only as a mediated image which has been contemplated in memory and which, as a single image, also comes to represent an entire experience:

> Suddenly a mist of green on the trees, as quiet as thought. Small leaves in broad daylight, magic reality . . . Everyone had loved it . . . Wanting, trying and failing to utter its beauty. Everyone had these moments of reality in forgetfulness. Quickly passing, growing afterwards longer than other moments, spreading out over the whole season; representing it in memory. (III, 498)

Miriam repeatedly equates these pre-reflexive spatial impressions with the experience of childhood, describing them as a state of 'childlike wonder':

> the moments of laughter were something like those moments in church; whilst there was nothing but laughter in the room everybody was perfectly happy and good, everybody forgot everything and ran back somewhere; to the beginning, to the time when they were first looking at things, without troubling about anything. (I, 386f.)

While Maurice Merleau-Ponty[36] terms this mode of spatial perception 'pre-logical space', Jean Piaget[37] directly links such phenomenological experiences to the first stage in children's development of an understanding of space, which is conceived as a space of elementary, topological spatial relations, being pre-perspectival, pre-logical and radically egocentric. In Richardson's rendition the formulation 'childlike' in contrast to 'child's wonder', as well as the metaphorical phrase 'everybody ran back', signifies that this is a brief recreation of an original sensation and not a regression into childhood. Accordingly, atmospheric space in *Pilgrimage* is often aligned with childhood space. Not only are all remembered childhood spaces atmospheric ones; Miriam usually associates pre-logical spatial experiences with the gardens of her childhood, particularly with Babington:

> In the instant before her mind had slid back . . . she had been perfectly alive, seeing; perfect things all round her, no beginning or ending . . . But the moment she had just lived was the same, it was exactly the *same* as the first one she could remember, the moment of standing, alone, in bright sunlight on a narrow gravel path in the garden at Babington between two banks of flowers, the flowers level with her face, and large bees swinging slowly to and fro before her face from bank to bank, many sweet smells coming from the flowers and, amongst them, a strange pleasant smell like burnt paper . . . not remembering going into the garden or any end to being in the bright sun between the blazing flowers, the two banks linked by the slowly singing bees, nothing else in the world, no house behind the little path, no garden beyond it. Yet she must somehow have got out of the house and through the shrubbery and along the plain path between the lawns. (II, 212f.)

This correlation serves to articulate those phenomenological essences which remain constant, so as to point to a direct connection between the pre-logical space of childhood and the linguistically self-conscious space of adult reflection and recollection. Piaget[38] defines perception as the recognition of objects through direct contact with them. Imagination, on the other hand, consists for him in seeing absent things in the mind's eye and in making absent objects present by referring to them.

Miriam's notion of 'childlike wonder' thus initially supports her conviction that this pre-logical space can be preserved, indeed returned to, as a remembered space if one learns to disregard oneself during experiences of the 'instant before her mind stepped back'. Furthermore, this notion gives voice to the poignant similarity between atmospheric and imagined space, given that both refer to the state of being 'nowhere', i.e. to an absence of any marked affiliation to space. Their significance differs to the extent that the feeling of 'nowhere' in atmospheric space derives from the absence of self-reflexion and orientation. In contemplative space, on the other hand, the experience of 'nowhere' is facilitated by an extreme, reflexive centredness which is able to transcend the ego. Contemplative space thus involves a conscious transcendence of lived space towards 'nowhere', whereas atmospheric space permits an unconscious, non-oriented dissolution *with* space into 'nowhere'.[39]

This intersection between the materially experienced world and the immaterial, imagined world, experienced in the act of contemplation, is also the point at which the various levels of consciousness and the various remembered, lived spaces converge. The playing of a Chopin nocturne, for example, precipitates an experience of psychic luminosity: 'Closing in upon her from the schoolgirl pieces still echoing in the room, came sudden little abrupt scenes from all the levels of her life, deep-rooted moments still alive within her, challenging and promising' (II, 334). For this reason, Richardson privileges contemplative space in *Pilgrimage* whenever she needs to establish distance between Miriam and her lived space: when Miriam looks outwards and, by virtue of contemplation, transforms lived space into an image; or when her gaze is turned inwards, which enables her to replace lived space with imagined spaces.

As with the discussion of 'childlike wonder', the preference for contemplative space begins with Miriam's dilemma that language deadens reality: 'Speech did something to things; set them in a mould that was apt to come up again; repeated, it would be dead' (III, 129). Unlike the ecstatic transcendence towards a pre-logical proximity to objects, the ecstasy depicted here provokes detachment which, however, leads to the discovery of new words:

> A permanent intoxication in and out amongst life . . . a slight intoxication began it, making it possible to look at things from a distance, in separate wholes and make discoveries about them. It was being somewhere else, and suddenly looking up, out of completion, at distant things, that brought their meanings and the right words. (III, 129)

The realisation that adult consciousness inevitably and irrevocably prohibits any immediate experience of the world leads to a preference for utterly mediated, indirect perception. 'The way to see a sunset', Miriam explains, 'is to be *indoors*. Oblivious. Then . . . just a ruddy glow, reflected from a bright surface . . . The indirect method's the method' (III, 353). As Blanchot astutely notes, seeing presupposes distance, the decision to separate, the ability to not be in contact, indeed to avoid the confusion inherent to one's contact with materiality. Seeing signifies that this separation has, however, become a form of meeting. But can it happen that the manner of seeing becomes a form of touch, once seeing transforms into contact occurring at a distance.[40]

However, Miriam does not only transform her world into an image so as to re-enact it creatively. Rather this contact at a distance allows her to expose the mutability of the material world. Describing her protagonist's experience at her friend Grace's flat,[41] Richardson notes:

> Miriam dropped her eyes and sat back in her chair. The tide of her own life flowed fresh all about her; the room and figure at her side made a sharply separated scene, a play watched from a distance, the end visible in the beginning, to be read in the shapes and tones and folds of the setting, the intentions and statements nothing but impotent irrelevance, only bearable for the opportunities they offered here and there, involuntarily, for sudden escape into the reality that nothing touched or changed. (II, 318)

Indeed, Miriam has recourse to such distanciation whenever she seeks to transform the contingencies of existence into a coherent, comprehensible narrative. For in the distanced position of contemplative space, lived space can be transformed into an image at the moment of perception, and thus be preserved in memory:

> Sitting up in bed, she saw hanging in mid-air just outside the window a huge crimson lamp, circular in a blue darkness . . . she . . . leaped awake to dwell with this strange spectacle, the gently startling picture, in its sudden huge nearness, of the loveliness of space. The little distant moon, enormous rosy in blue mist, seemed to float in the blue as in blue water, seemed to have floated close in sheer unearthly kindliness, to comfort her thought, on this last day, with something new and strange. (IV, 124)

What these different versions of distanced contemplation all have in common is that detachment inevitably transforms the material world in such a way that it facilitates an encounter with immaterial essences. Riding in a tram, Miriam notes:

> Through the sliding door she escaped into . . . an inner world that changed the aspect of everything about her. When the tram moved off, the scenes framed by the windows grew beautiful in movement. The framing and the movement created them, she was out in eternity, gliding along, adding this hour to the strange sum of her central being. (IV, 265)

The novel's abrupt stylistic shift from the third to the first person, occurring increasingly from Oberland onwards, is accompanied by an equally increasing occupation of the contemplative position. Although Richardson does occasionally use the first person in descriptions of atmospheric space, as in the first Teetgen's Teas passage discussed earlier, this shift to first person narrations tends to go in tandem with Miriam's self-reflexions. At these highly self-conscious moments she is usually situated at the outermost periphery of lived space, seeking to go move beyond the boundaries of her corporeal self. The 'I' marks the border between inside and outside, and between material and immaterial space. Drawing upon Plessner, Gölz views this divided position as a significant component of human existence: 'Just as the human being is *also* bound to the here and now, he is at once "*nowhere*", placeless, beyond all ties to space. The human being alone has this mode of eccentric existence. He is at once in himself and beyond himself.'[42] Such human capacity for eccentricity involves the indissoluble tension 'that we always assume a certain position of detachment from ourselves, in particular from our own spatial bodies, but that we can never, on the other hand, fully revoke our indissoluble bondage to ourselves nor, therefore, our entrapment in space'.[43] Richardson's use of the pronoun 'I', to signify an extreme centredness in a 'here' of lived space which contains both self-reflexion and an eccentric movement into nowhere, marks the border between phenomenologically lived space and immaterial, metaphorical space. Since the opportunity to move beyond one's bondage to lived space and thus to experience an eccentric transcendence forms the basis of contemplative space, even while contemplative space is the precondition of every transcendence and thus, too, of all processes which result from such self-disregard (including communicative situations as well as artistic creation and reception), one can ascertain a far more resilient mutual implication between phenomenological and imagined space than is usually assumed. As Lyons states: 'Much of what is commonly thought of as being metaphorical in the use of language can be brought within the scope of the thesis of localism.'[44]

The final novels in *Pilgrimage*, especially *March Moonlight*, evince a progressive intensification of Miriam's self-reflexivity and contemplation, a gradual transition from the experience of the materiality of the world to the recreation of recollected and imagined immaterial sites. Before examining the usage of spatial metaphors in *Pilgrimage*, as well as the notion of the text as space, it is, however, necessary to analyse in greater depth those tangible actual material places, whose significance Miriam must experience corporeally before she can recreate them textually.

NOTES

1 E. Ströker, *Philosophische Untersuchungen zum Raum* (Frankfurt, 1965).
2 *Ibid.*, 20.
3 I have extended the concept of 'atmosphere' in space, since the literary manifestation of space in *Pilgrimage* is almost always atmospheric, in the sense that it is animated by Miriam and her perceptions, regardless of whether she experiences it unconsciously, with a particular aim in mind or whether or not she orients herself within it. Limiting this atmosphere solely to those spaces which fall into Ströker's category of atmospheric space would involve omitting a significant dimension of these spatial descriptions. A space which Miriam experiences as an action or contemplative space may also be subject to a spatial change which is dependent upon her mood (and thus be atmospheric).
4 Ströker, *Philosophische Untersuchungen zum Raum*, 23.
5 *Ibid.*, 31.

6 *Ibid.*, 32.
7 *Ibid.*, 34.
8 *Ibid.*, 37.
9 *Ibid.*, 39.
10 *Ibid.*, 51.
11 *Ibid.*, 54.
12 *Ibid.*, 70.
13 *Ibid.*, 100.
14 *Ibid.*, 102.
15 *Ibid.*, 104.
16 *Ibid.*, 109.
17 *Ibid.*, 117.
18 *Ibid.*, 128.
19 *Ibid.*, 131.
20 *Ibid.*, 131.
21 In *Dasein und Raum* (Tübingen, 1970), 70, W. Gölz writes: 'As a result of the eccentricity of objective spatial imagination, each individual stands where the other stands. – This eccentricity provides the justification for an identification between the space which we experience and that which others experience.' The concept of the 'eccentric standpoint' has been developed most fully by Piaget in his study of children's spatial imagination.
22 See Gölz, *Dasein und Raum*, 185: 'We experience space in experience as the space in which we are ourselves also present. Our own existence in space contributes towards our spatial experience of the parallels which we can only ever experience *from the position of our existence*, because we do not hover above the space like a divine spirit.'
23 G. Hoffmann, *Raum, Situation, erzählte Wirklichkeit* (Stuttgart, 1978), 48.
24 Lyons, *Semantics*, Vol. 2, 646.
25 Emphasis added.
26 Lyons, *Semantics* (Cambridge, 1977) vol. 2, 648.
27 See my research overview in the Appendix, for example R. G. Kelly, 'The Strange Philosophy of Dorothy M. Richardson', *Pacific Spectator*, 8 (Winter 1954), 76–82, or S. J. Kaplan, *Feminine Consciousness in the Modern British Novel* (Urbana, 1925). The latter's criticism of *Pilgrimage* is based upon the almost complete absence of any descriptions of Miriam's physiognomy. Critics judge this either as prudery or as a lack of physical consciousness on the part of Richardson. Kaplan reads Richardson's spatial descriptions as 'her almost compulsive concern with physical objects' and argues that this is 'one of the ways she tries to avoid contact . . . when it comes to relationships . . . it is better perhaps to forgo them in favour of a kind of mystical communion with nature and the things of this world' (40ff.). Both Jean Radford, *Dorothy Richardson* (Bloomington, 1991) and Christin Bluemel, *Experimenting on the Border of Modernism* (Athens: 1997) have convincingly discussed Richardson's writing the body.
28 Lyons, *Semantics*, vol. 2, 654.
29 *Ibid.*, 646.
30 The following examples are taken from the three passages cited above.
31 Lyons, *Semantics*, vol. 2, 699.
32 Gilles Deleuze, *Marcel Proust et les signes* (Paris, 1964), 10f.
33 Ernst Pöppel also speaks of spatial appropriation through movement in his book *Lust und Schmerz: Grundlagen menschlichen Erlebens und Verhaltens* (Berlin, 1982): 'Our visual

34 A further example would be I, 416f. Miriam appropriates the West End by walking through it: 'She, too, now had a mysterious secret face – a West End life of her own.' This example also reveals the corresponding change in description when Miriam no longer moves in space for the sake of space alone, but rather through it with a specific purpose in mind. The spatial descriptions are initially detailed, the space is represented as an object which is enjoyed from all sides and then it is set in motion: 'She sped along looking at nothing.' This movement through a space as a means of familiarising herself with it almost always occurs when Miriam arrives in a new place, whether it is a new station in her pilgrimage – the many rented rooms or the exterior surroundings of these rooms and houses – or her first visit to friends' homes. Her attempt to draw nearer to strangers is most often expressed in terms of spatial exploration.
35 See above all M. Merleau-Ponty, *Phénoménologie de la perception* (Paris, 1945), and Kurt Lewin, *Grundzüge der topologischen Psychologie* (Stuttgart, 1969).
36 Merlau-Ponty, *Phénoménologie de la perception*.
37 J. Piaget and B. Inhelder, *La Représentation de l'espace chez l'enfant* (Paris, 1948).
38 Ibid.
39 See also Chapter 4 and Part II for a discussion of the concept of ecstasy. See also Eveline Killian, *Momente innerweltlicher Transzendenz* (Tübingen, 1997) for a discussion of moments of transcendence in *Pilgrimage*.
40 Maurice Blanchot, *L'Espace Littéraire* (Paris, 1955).
41 This often facilitates the drawing of boundaries which is necessary for her search for an identity. In Miriam's many visits to foreign spaces, for example, one often encounters an action space which is then replaced by a contemplative space, as a result of Miriam's subsequent dissociation and detachment from the new group of people. After a visit to her employer Leyton's family, who belong to London's upper middle class, Miriam explains: 'But all the time she had been half aware that she was only watching a picture, a charmed familiar scene, as significant and as unreal as the set figure of a dance' (III, 269).
42 Gölz, *Dasein und Raum*, 235.
43 Ibid., 254.
44 Lyons, *Semantics*, vol. 2, 728. In his book, *Genius Loci: Toward a Phenomenology of Architecture* (New York, 1980), 16, Christian Norberg-Schulz also draws attention to the differentiation in colloquial language between the naming of particular points in space which, when viewed as objects, are characterised using primary words such as 'wall', 'doors', 'ceiling' and so forth, and the naming of space and spatial atmosphere: 'Space, instead, as a system of relations, is denoted by *prepositions*. In our daily life we hardly talk about "space", but about things that are "over" or "under", "before" or "behind" each other; or we use prepositions such as "at", "in", "within", "on", "upon", "to", "from", "along", "next". All these prepositions denote topological relations . . . Character, finally, is denoted by *adjectives*'.

CHAPTER FOUR

IN SEARCH OF LOST SPACE

> The love of backgrounds, the cause of endless deceptions and the basis of an absurd conviction – that these backgrounds belonged more to herself than to the people who created them. Yet, even here, was mystery and uncertainty. For these backgrounds, thought of without the people to whom they belonged, faded and died. And this would seem to mean that places, after all, were people. (IV, 361)

Until now, my discussion has been concerned with the way Miriam perceives actual material spaces: with the mutual animation which takes place between Miriam and each of the places she inhabits; the ways in which her position in space is responsible for its structuration and with her desire to discover what makes a place 'significant' for her, i.e. what is her fascination with the 'power of surroundings'. At the same time, however, the search for a 'significant space' is what the entire narrative trajectory of *Pilgrimage* ultimately revolves around. The lived spaces are not only animated according to Miriam's mood; they are also subject to a constant process of semantic encoding and are thus assigned a significance in relation to Miriam which, while being based initially on their topological attributes, moves beyond these. Both at a narrative and at a thematic level, semantic encoding of actual material spaces articulates an attempt to establish an order necessary for orientation and understanding. Eliade calls such an attribution of meaning the transformation of chaos into cosmos: 'every territory which is occupied with the aim of using or inhabiting it as a "vital space" has first been transformed from "chaos" into "cosmos"; that is to say that a "form" has been conferred upon it by means of a ritual, which thus makes it become real'.[1] Within *Pilgrimage*, this ritual is enacted by virtue of semantic encoding and naming. The atmospheres of lived space were seen to be flexible, changing according to the particular events in the space or the mood of the perceiving protagonist. Furthermore, although their spatial structure was seen to be determined by the experiencing protagonist's standpoint, the attribution of semantic meaning proves to be relatively constant, because independent of the moment of experience.

Given, then, that it is primarily the process of semantic encoding which creates an orientated, meaningful space out of formless infinity, the concept of 'significant space' must be defined more precisely. Although all of the physical spaces are without exception assigned a semantic value and are thus significant for Miriam, only some of them are understood as significant space in the sense of Eliade's 'sacred space'. For Eliade, this is a place 'where the sacred manifests itself in space, *the real unveils itself*, the world comes into existence . . . the irruption of the sacred . . . project[s] a fixed point into the formless fluidity of profane space, a center into chaos'.[2] Although these features apply to the semantic encoding of most meaningful spaces, the unique quality of 'significant space' is that it engenders a point of intersection between modes of being: 'it also effects a break in plane, that is, it opens communication between the cosmic planes (between earth and heaven) and makes possible ontological passage from one mode of being to another'.

Equally pertinent to my discussion is Heidegger's concept of dwelling, given that he takes as his starting point the principle that existence is synonymous with an existentially meaningful anchorage in space. Human beings may be said to dwell in space if they are capable of orienting themselves within it and thus of experiencing it as meaningful for themselves.[3] For Heidegger, the connection between 'being' and 'dwelling' is to be found in human mortality: 'Being human signifies: being a mortal on earth, means: dwelling . . . Dwelling is the way in which mortals *are* on earth.'[4] Dwelling signifies the original unity, 'preserving the essence of the existential square, which gathers together earth, heaven, the divine and the mortal', that is, 'protecting it in its essence'.[5] A significant space is accordingly a 'marked gathering of the square', a place which permits the square to be formed and which accommodates it: 'The place accommodates the square in twofold fashion. The place permits the presence of the square and the place furnishes the square'.[6] This place, which is seen to become a 'marked gathering' by virtue of any material construction – be it a bridge, a house or another architectural site – preserves the square in such a way that living within this construction enables the individual to stay within the square, thus making it possible to dwell: 'Building namely *calls forth* the square in a thing, the bridge, and *foregrounds* the thing as a place within that which is already present, which has only now been accommodated *by means of* this place . . . The essence of building is permitting to dwell.'[7]

This notion of dwelling points to the meaning which human life can assume in relation to spaces that have been marked as being specific and 'significant' in some mannner or another. In direct reference to Heidegger, Norberg-Schulz applies these philosophical categories to concrete buildings: 'Dwelling therefore implies something more than "shelter". It implies that the spaces where life occurs are *places* . . . which [have] a distinct character.'[8] Given that built or marked spaces must be grounded in a particular semantic encoding in order for their inhabitants to truly dwell in them, Norberg-Schulz argues that architecture should seek to encourage an existential attitude towards dwelling, precisely because built spaces signify more than mere physical sites. As one instance of a marked gathering of Heidegger's existential square, built space implies

> that man *gathers* the experienced meanings to create for himself an *imago mundi* or microcosmos which concretizes his world. Gathering evidently depends on symbol-

ization, and implies a transposition of meanings to another place, which thereby becomes an existential 'centre' ... The existential purpose of building (architecture) is therefore to make a site become a place, that is, to uncover the meanings potentially present in the given environment.[9]

The way in which the act of semantic encoding in *Pilgrimage* transforms spatial sites into significant places can be seen as analogous to Norberg-Schulz's understanding of architecture as a gathering point. He gives a pertinent description of such an analogy when he states that the meaning of an object (the result of a semantic encoding) is synonymous with that which it gathers:

> The 'meaning' of any object consists in its relationship to other objects, that is, it consists in what the object 'gathers'. A thing is a thing by virtue of its gathering ... meaning ... an abstraction from the flux of phenomena ... as a direct recognition of 'constancies', that is, stable relationships which stand out from the more transitory happenings.[10]

For Norberg-Schulz the main characteristics of both natural and artificial 'significant' spaces are 'identification' and 'orientation': 'When the environment is meaningful man feels at home ... When the man-made environment is meaningful man is "at home".'[11] Significant space emerges as the primary form of architectural intensification, as a concretion of the threshold between modes of being, since it signifies identification and existential orientation per se. Norberg-Schulz points to Robert Venturi's definition of architecture: 'the wall – the point of change – becomes an architectural event. Architecture occurs at the meeting of interior and exterior forces of use and space. Architecture ... [is] the wall between the inside and the outside',[12] only to add that 'in the wall ... earth and sky meet, and the way man "is" on earth is concretized by the solution of this meeting'.[13]

The semantic encoding of concrete material spaces as 'significant' is therefore at one level an expression of human desire for being anchored in space. 'Meaning is a psychic function. It depends on identification, and implies a sense of belonging.'[14] At the same time, however, the semantic encoding of actual material spaces acquires a new meaning in the context of marked gathering and building:

> In general, things gather world and thereby reveal truth. To make a thing means the 'setting-into-work' of truth. A place is such a thing, and as such it is a poetical fact ... Through building man gives meanings concrete presence, and he gathers buildings to visualize and symbolize his form of life as a totality ... the meanings which are gathered by a place constitute its genius loci.[15]

Thus what renders a space significant consists in its capacity to gather essences, firstly through being a marked point in space and, secondly, through embodying a meeting point between outside and inside, gathering together essences which, in *Pilgrimage*, are circumscribed as 'same' or 'it'.

The architects Bloomer and Moore employ a similar semantic encoding of significant space. In their architectural writings, they represent the threshold between two modes of being as a place which permits imagination and memory. Drawing upon Bachelard,[16] they view meaningful dwelling as dependent upon whether or not the built space engenders memory, such that for them architecture is successful if it creates a 'memorable place' defined as 'a matter of extending the inner landscape of human beings into the world in ways that are comprehensible, experiential and inhabitable'.[17] These spaces contain 'the potential transactions between body, imagination and environment . . . [they] facilitate the transaction between body, memory and architecture which allows us to dwell'.[18]

In the following discussion of 'significant places' in *Pilgrimage*, what is at stake is the process of signification which allows Miriam to create a meaningful order out of her experience of contingent sites.[19]

The different spatial encodings and their formative role in Miriam's phenomenological existence draw their power from the difference that emerges between spaces which allow her to dwell and neutral spaces which lack precisely this potential for anchorage. Indeed, the semantic encoding of places in *Pilgrimage* can be divided into three categories. The first includes spaces which permit Miriam to dwell because they are perceived as a point of liminality between two modes of being – the childhood garden in Babington, London as Miriam's addressee, and the different versions of her own room, which functions both as a refuge and as a threshold to imagined places. The second category includes mobile and immobile neutral spaces, functioning primarily as intermediate spaces that foster an experience of liminality. The third category pertains to the privileged imagined and remembered spaces which are favoured as substitutes for lived, material space.

Miriam's earliest spatial memories are of her childhood experience of the garden in Babington. It is doubly encoded as a paradisal idyll and place of innocence. Firstly, because Miriam remembers it as a space of sheltered, joyful existence before tragic events cane to mar her family life, it concomitantly signifies an existence not yet marked by guilt. Secondly, it is also associated with an originary connection and unity with space, thus signifying a pre-logical, not yet conscious orientation in space.

Miriam recalls her childhood garden whenever she discovers a similarity between a space she currently inhabits and the place of past bliss and safety. Thus, for example, a liberating experience of disorientation and of endless expansion of space at the moment of waking can trigger her memories of the garden:

> To wake suddenly and fully, nowhere; in paradise . . . In the instant before her mind had slid back . . . she had been perfectly alive, seeing; perfect things all round her, no beginning or ending . . . there had been moments like that, years ago, . . . They were all the same. In each one she had felt exactly the same; outside life, untouched by anything, free . . . But the moment she had just lived was the same, it was exactly the *same* as the first one she could remember, the moment of standing, alone, in bright sunlight on a narrow gravel path in the garden at Babington between two banks of flowers, the flowers level with her face, and large bees swinging slowly to and fro before her face from bank to bank, many sweet smells coming from the flowers and,

amongst them, a strange pleasant smell like burnt paper . . . not remembering going into the garden or any end to being in the bright sun between the blazing flowers . . . All the six years at Babington were that blazing alley of flowers without beginning or end, no winters, no times of day or changes to be seen. There were other memories . . . They did not come first, or without thought. The blazing alley came first without thought or effort of memory. The flowers all shining separate and distinct and all together, indistinct in a blaze. (III, 212)

The garden is viewed as a gathering point of different semiotic layers. At one level, the carefree idyll of childhood is crystallised in this joyful experience of space: 'All the six years at Babington were that blazing alley of flowers.' Even though Miriam also recalls other experiences – 'quarrelling . . . pieces of life indoors . . . all mixed with sadness and pain and bother' (II, 214), these are not her foremost childhood memories. The garden has privileged status because it is expressive of an empathy which existed before thought. At another level, this ecstatic experience of an absorption in space is not only exemplified by the image of the childhood garden perceived as pre-logical space but also emerges in the form of a memory which lies beyond language and thought: 'the blazing alley came first without thought'.[20] In other words pre-logical or non-logical experiences – the moment of waking, 'the instant before her mind had slid back' – become compounded in this image of the garden. Later in the novel, this quality of non-logical memory will be coupled with a gradual recognition of reality:

all about her . . . was the chill darkness that yet might prove to be the reality for which she was bound, she drew back and back and caught a glimpse, through an opening inward eye, of a gap in a low hedge, between two dewy lawns, through which she could see the features of some forgotten scene, the last of a fading twilight upon the gloomy leaves of dark, clustered bushes and, further off, its friendly glimmer upon massive tree-trunks, and wondered, as the scene vanished, why the realization of a garden as a gatherer of growing darkness should be so deeply satisfying . . . And why it was that only garden scenes, and never open country, and never the interiors of buildings, returned of themselves without associative link or deliberate effort of memory. (IV, 299f.)

The image of the garden, as an embodiment of non-logical memory, thus acquires the further connotation as a 'gatherer of growing darkness', a state which is synonymous for Miriam with the 'reality for which she was bound'.

The third and most important meaning of the garden, however, consists in the fact that it gathers to one point the spatial essence which always remains the 'same', regardless of the continual flow of appearances. This sameness of experienced moments involves neither a longing for nor a regression into an unconscious state of being, but rather a synthetic means of recreating pre-logical experience. Miriam offers her own commentary upon her experience of non-oriented freedom when she emphasises that her preferred mode of awareness is a conscious understanding of the world: 'Today, because I am free I am the same person as I was when I was

IN SEARCH OF LOST SPACE

there, but much stronger and happier because I know it' (II, 215). The recognition that she is the 'same' primarily accentuates the permanent aspects of being, the immutable essence within mutable and contingent worldly existence. That which remains permanent can be localised, not only in a lived space but also in the experiencing self. In another passage, Miriam considers how she is still the same person as she was back then in the garden:

> The person who had stood for the first time alone upon the sunlit garden-path between the banks of flowers and watched them, through the pattern made by the bees sailing heavily across from bank to bank at the level of her face, and wondered at them all, flowers and bees and sunlight, at their all being there when nobody was about, and had looked for so long at their bright masses, and now could re-see them with knowledge of their names and ways and of the dark earth underneath, and, still, just as they were in that moment that had neither beginning nor end. (IV, 177)

If the garden is encoded as the space of her earliest experience of permanent essences, so the act of memory establishes a simultaneity between the various stages of Miriam's life. The indication that her memory involves being able to 're-see . . . with knowledge' signals that the criteria according to which something remains the 'same' are independent of the degree of conscious awareness. The 'same' remains constant, regardless of whether the understanding of the world is pre-logical or logical. Thus the remembered garden stands metonymically for the experience of her childhood idyll and allows this atmosphere not only to be continually reproduced but also to be transferred on to her current lived space. The initial sense of joy Miriam feels while staying with the Corries at Newlands is, for example, articulated in an evocation of the garden:

> Coming across the hall, she found a scent in the air . . . the blaze of childhood's garden was round her again, bright magic flowers in the sunlight, magic flowers, still there, nearer to her than ever in this happy house; she could almost hear the humming of the bees, and flung back the bead curtain with unseeing eyes, half expecting some doorway to open on the remembered garden. (I, 392f.)

This wistful equation of remembered space with experienced space, that is, her ability to experience the garden once more in lieu of the actual place she occupies, is unique in the text. It not only sheds light upon Miriam's initial semantic encoding of Newlands as a paradise regained but also anticipates her departure. All other references to Babington garden work by virtue of comparing the present with the remembered space.

Semantically encoded as a paradisal place, the garden is indeed associated with absolute happiness, but also heralds the loss of innocence and the introduction of guilt. The loss of the Babington garden – 'the disappearance of the sun-lit red-walled garden always in full summer sunshine' (I, 32) – is equated with the Fall from grace; i.e. with the entrance into a conscious position in space and with a recognition of worldly guilt. However, as a remembered space the garden also signifies

[77]

Miriam's sense of moral fallibility, for it also comes to represent the promise that guilt may be replaced by forgiveness and mercy:

> Something that was not touched, that sang far away down inside the gloom, that cared nothing for the creditors and could get away . . . from the everlasting accusations of humanity . . . The disgrace sat only in the muscles of her face . . . Deeper down was something cool and fresh – endless garden. In happiness it came up and made everything in the world into a garden. Sorrow blotted it over, but it was always there, waiting and looking on. (I, 425)[21]

In addition to its semantic encoding as an idyllic place of happiness, the garden is thus an image for hopes of atonement and redemption.[22]

Since Babington garden represents a solitary experience of ecstasy, the memory of this place becomes crucial for her thoughts about successful communication. During Miriam's inner conflict over whether she should give marriage to Michael Shatov priority over her independent life, the memory of the garden is employed to represent the preservation of her solitude:

> When she was alone, she moved . . . towards a single memory. Far away in the distance, coming always nearer, was the summer morning of her infancy a permanent standing arrested, level with the brilliance of flowerheads motionless in the sunlit air; no movement but the hovering of bees. Beyond this memory . . . a marvellous scene unfolded . . . But pursuing it, she must always be alone. (III, 197f.)

However, this garden experience which contains such a 'strange independent joy', is not merely Miriam's first and most complete encounter with the attraction held by particular spatial atmospheres to which she finds herself repeatedly drawn. It is also perceived as the seminal experience which, if she were able to communicate it in speech or written narrative, might enable Miriam to break through her own solitude:

> She tried to remember when the strange independent joy had begun, and thought she could trace it back to a morning in the garden at Babington, the first thing she could remember when she had found herself toddling alone along the garden path between beds of flowers almost on a level with her head and blazing in the sunlight . . . She wanted to speak to someone of these things. Until she could speak to someone about them she must always be alone . . . It would be impossible to speak to anyone about them unless one felt perfectly sure that the other person felt about them in the same way and knew that they were more real than anything else in the world, knew that everything else was a fuss about nothing. (I, 316f.)

Successful communication can, however, only be achieved if the listener shares her semantic encoding of the garden as 'more real than anything else in the world'. Conceived in opposition to solitude, communication can, therefore, take place only by virtue of a third space, in this case the sharing of the garden recreated from memory. Yet it can be successful only if the significance of this third space – this image of an experienced space – is shared by the listener. In order to communicate the special quality of her friendship with Amabel to Hypo, 'in which she was more deeply immersed than in any shared living that had fallen to her lot' (IV, 242), Miriam significantly chooses to tell him about a day which they spent together, during which their successful communication triggered a memory of her childhood garden:

> I leaned my head back and for a few seconds was asleep for the first time in broad daylight, and woke so utterly refreshed that I said without thinking: 'This is the birthday of the world', ... I was back in the moment of seeing for the first time those flowerbeds and banks of flowers blazing in the morning sunlight, that smelt of the flowers and was one with them and me and the big bees crossing the path, low, on a level with my face. And I told her of it and that it must have been somewhere near my third birthday, and her falling tears of joy and sympathy promised that never again should there be in my blood an unconquerable fever. (IV, 243)

Not so much the fact that Amabel's presence evokes this memory as the fact that Miriam is able to share it with her is what indicates that this friendship represents the much longed-for answer to Miriam's solitude.[23]

Miriam's own room[24] has already been discussed as a space which is both protective and porous, as the place to which she always returns from her explorations of the outside world, as well as a place for intellectual and creative activity, whether this involves intense contemplation or creation.[25] Concomitantly, the room at Mrs Bailey's is described as a protective place within London: 'the Euston Road, by day and by night, her unsleeping guardian, the rim of the world beyond which lay the northern suburbs, banished' (II, 15), a place whose 'huge high thick walls held all the lodgers secure and apart ... secure from all the world that was not London' (II, 77). At the same time, the room is sufficiently porous so as never to shut out completely the presence of exterior space: 'London just outside all the time, coming in with the light, coming in with the darkness, always present in the depths of the air in the room' (II, 16).

It is a centre which is at once extremely protective and open. Miriam describes her return home through London to her own room as follows:

> she would travel further ... down and down into an oblivion deeper than sleep; and drop off at the centre ... gain her room and lie, till she suddenly slept, tingling to the spread of London all about her, herself one with it, feeling her life flow outwards, north, south, east, and west, to all its margins. (III, 272f.)

This porous security, here viewed topologically, mirrors the psychological encoding of the room. Its protective power consists primarily in its capacity to provide Miriam with a defence against 'solicitude': 'No interruption, no one watching or speculating or treating one in some particular way that had to be met' (II, 17). The weekend which Miriam spends in her room with Amabel is the only time in which this semantic encoding of the room as a solitary place is broken, and even then this is only partial, since Miriam experiences their togetherness as a 'shared solitude':

this being together, alternating between intense awareness of the beloved person and delight in every aspect, every word and movement, and a solitude distinguishable from the deepest, coolest, most renewing moments of lonely solitude only in the enhancement it reaped by being shared. (IV, 242)

Significantly, this is precisely the moment in which Miriam succeeds in sharing her experience of Babington garden.

The threat of 'solicitude' pitted against her search for a safe haven for her solitude is the key reason for Miriam's continual pilgrimage through the various different island spaces. She always leaves living conditions as soon as her own sense of self is too seriously under threat from external disruption, and she always views actual material spaces as 'home' when they preserve this essential core of her self, as is the case with her Tansley Street room: 'the self that was with her in the room was the untouched tireless self of her seventeenth year and all the earlier time. The familiar light moved within the twilight, the old light' (II, 16). Miriam's own room is encoded as a spatial expansion of her own body, as the tangible analogue to her psychic reality. There only can she be left unconditionally in peace and recognise her own essence, though notably not by being outside herself nor by reliving an experience, as in the memory of Babington garden, but rather by giving that which is the 'same' in herself a location in space:

> her own dream world at home in her room, her strange unfailing self, the lovely world of lovely things seen in silence and tranquillity, the coming and going of the light, the myriad indescribable things of which day and night, in solitude, were full, at every moment; the marvellous forgetfulness of sleep, followed by the smiling renewal of inexhaustible *sameness*. (III, 208)

As part of this correlation between tangible space and psychic reality, the continual return to her own room signifies the return to an unchanging self. Regardless of the quality of her experience in the world beyond her room, this final refuge remains the same: 'the adventure would begin and go on and be over. The room would not be in it. Something nice, or horrible, would come back. But the room would not be changed' (II, 154). This tension between inside and outside, or between self and world, is productive only if it is linked with return. Miriam describes a New Year's night in her room: 'The room was full of clear strength. There must always be a clear cold room to return to. There was no other way of keeping the inward peace. Outside one need do nothing but what was expected of one, asking nothing for oneself but freedom to return, to the centre' (II, 321).

The topological porosity of the space articulates yet another aspect of her psychic reality. Miriam feels such freedom in her own room because, in being a place of solitary security, it offers protection against and abstinence from the material world, and therefore also leads to the recognition of her own essential essence:

> it was there; independent, laughing, bubbling up incorrigible, golden and bright with a radiance that spread all round her . . . the last deepest level of her being was joy . . . a hilarity against which *nothing* seemed to be able to prevail . . . always waiting behind

the last door ... Warmly the little shabby enclosure welcomed her ... showing her the time ahead ... extraordinary wealth of going on being alive ... Going back into the room she was once more in that zone of her being where all the past was with her unobstructed; not recalled, but present, so that she could move into any part and be there as before. (III, 321f.)

Miriam's notion that reality can be recognised only in solitary serenity is bound up with her conviction that the diverting movement and continual change in the turbulent outside world distracts people from reality: 'People in themselves want nothing but reality. Why can't reality exist in the world? All the things that happen produce friction because they distract people from the reality they are unconsciously looking for' (III, 188). Yet the only means of safeguarding against stagnation in one's own solitude, against 'isolation in inner space' (Bollnow)[26] is to ensure that the tension is upheld between inside and outside. Ellen Frank addresses the necessity of this movement: 'Our habitations, mental and physical, require empty centers as room for aliveness much as these habitations must look out – for health – upon the open universe.'[27] Miriam does view her room increasingly as a place of refuge, yet it also signifies the site of a devitalising isolation from the outside world, thus implying the necessity of movement in exterior space:

> her room upstairs, alive now and again under some chance spell of the weather, or some book which made her feel that any life in London would be endurable for ever that secured her room with its evening solitude, now and again the sense of strange, fresh, invisibly founded beginnings; often a cell of torturing mocking memories and apprehension, driving her down into the house. (III, 31)

The room, viewed as porous, furthermore upholds this tension between inside and outside since Miriam introduces a piece of experienced world into it each time she returns. In a concrete sense, the room gathers the outside world in the form of objects which have been brought back to it, such as the afore mentioned teapot which acts as a memento of Miriam's experiences in 'wealthy social life'. Figuratively speaking, the room is also a place of contemplative gathering: Miriam brings the outside world into her own room; a broad spectrum of remembered events, from the most recent events as well as from the distant past. Solitude as a form of abstinence from the world is transformed into solitude as a creative production of the imagined, immaterial world:

> Never again, so long as she could sit at work and lose herself to awake with the season forgotten and all the circumstances of her life coming back, as if narrated from the fascinating life of someone else, would they [past solitudes] puzzle or reproach her. (II, 133)

> Rising from the table she found her room strange, the new room she had entered on the day of her arrival ... The years that had passed were a single short interval leading to the restoration of that first moment. Everything they contained centred there; her passage through them, the desperate graspings and droppings, had been a coming

back. Nothing would matter now that the paper-scattered lamplit circle was established as the centre of life. Everything would be an everlastingly various joyful coming back. Held up by this secret place, drawing her energy from it, any sort of life would do that left this room and its little table free and untouched. (III, 133f.)

Since this process of contemplative gathering harbours within itself the tension between inside and outside, even if only in the imagination, the danger of isolation in interior space is dispelled. Indeed, as Blanchot notes, the artist's solitude is not an essential solitude, but rather a form of recollection and gathering.[28]

If one extends the topological porosity of space to include the psychological meanings which are assigned to it in the text, then it becomes clear that Miriam's own room is semantically encoded as an actual material 'significant space'; fully in the spirit of Bachelard, Bloomer and Moore. For the room is the marked space in which she can integrate her thoughts, memories and fantasies; it is a 'memorable place' in that it marks the site of an exchange between lived space and imagined spaces. At one level, the room must be grasped as the focal point of all material interior and exterior spaces. However, since it also acts as the site of all memory and imagination, including solitary artistic activity, it emerges at a second, figurative level as a threshold between the conscious and unconscious, between the products of experience and those of the imagination.

Place of security, existential and creative gathering point and liminality come to be enmeshed in the semantic encoding of the room. A second description of the Tansley Street room highlights this hybrid quality:

> ensconced, high above the quiet street. In the house, but not, too much, of it. Supported and screened by the presence of the many rooms that made the large house; each one occupied by strangers who soon, just because she need establish with them no exacting personal relationship, would be richly and deeply her housemates, sharing the independent life of this particular house, its situation within London's magic circle . . . Freedom for thought, when it made its sudden visits, to expand unhampered. (IV, 195f.)

In her room, Miriam is both within 'London's magic circle' and secure, 'high above the street'; she is at once connected with the other inhabitants of the house and shielded from unwanted encounters: 'not, too much, of it'. Viewed vertically, the room at the top of the house is the threshold, the intersection between security and space (Bachelard), the 'marked gathering' (Heidegger) of heaven and earth. On a horizontal axis, the room represents the gathering point of all of Miriam's movements in material space, in the sense that the ownership of this room is the precondition of and thus the point of departure for every movement beyond it; even while each movement beyond it in turn anticipates the return to this place. At the same time, the room is the gathering point between the material and the immaterial world. It provides the space for 'freedom of thought . . . to expand unhampered', which is to say that unconscious impressions, those 'images before thought', may manifest themselves there as conscious thoughts. Furthermore, the imaginative, psychic activity which takes place within it engenders a connection between experiences in the material, outside world and in the immaterial, inner world.

The semantic encoding of the room – as a marked gathering of all material spaces along with imagined and recollected ones – directly reflects Miriam's creative activity within it: namely, a recollection of the past represented as the gathering together of places inhabited in the past. The prerequisite for this gathering activity is the contemplative space, marking a psychological process of disregarding and transcending lived space. Admittedly, Miriam does experience transcendence in other spaces, but nowhere else is this experience directed towards artistic production. No other material space is semantically encoded as a place of 'gathering transcendence', as a space in which one is 'everywhere and nowhere at once'. She is 'nowhere' in this room because this lived space, viewed as a porous space implies a disregard for spatial restrictions. At the same time, Miriam is 'everywhere' in her room because this creative transcendence permits a simultaneous gathering of events which are temporally and spatially different. Her own room is thus not conceived simply as the place of recollection of lived and imagined spaces. As a space of 'gathering transcendence', it renders tangible the boundary between lived and immaterial space and as such intimates that which recedes from representation – the state of complete psychic dematerialisation.

Signifying a place of liminality, the room engenders the concentration necessary to achieve a psychological balance that runs analogous to the spatial condition of such a marked nodal point between two worlds:

> Once more her room held quietude secure, and the old in-pouring influence that could so rarely and so precariously be shared. Here in the midst of it, everything seemed immeasurably far off and even thought seemed to exist and to express itself in another world, into which she could move, or refrain from moving. Her being sank, perceptibly, back and back into a centre wherein it was held poised and sensitive to every sound and scent, and to the play of light on any and every object in the room. Turning gently in the midst of her recovered wealth, in the companionship that brought, even with movement, a deepening stillness, she saw upon the end wall the subdued reflection of London light, signalling the vast quiet movement of light about the world. (IV, 363)

Centred in her room and thus also within herself, Miriam satisfies the three conditions for appropriate dwelling set up by Otto Friedrich Bollnow.[29] She has created her 'own space of security', while at the same moment withstanding the tension between lived interior and exterior space and between unconscious and conscious lived space. In the room, the outside world seems 'immeasurably far off'; Miriam moves further and further 'into a centre' which is nevertheless rooted in a specific experience of this abode. Furthermore, this form of concentration fulfils Bollnow's third condition: 'to be capable of entrusting oneself to that larger whole of space while at the same time dwelling in the house'.[30] Miriam notices a 'reflection of London light' on the wall, a sign of the 'vast quiet movement of light about the world'.

London, like her own room, is also viewed as a place of porous security and solitary freedom: 'the part of London she had found for herself; the part where she was going to live, in freedom, hidden' (II, 29). Her continual return to London following visits to areas beyond its border, and the associated demarcation of London as a privileged space, may be read as a spatial extension of Miriam's focus on her own room: 'The London life was sacred and secret, away from everything else in the world. It would disappear if one had ties outside' (II, 89). Movement in the streets of London offers freedom because, like her room, it protects her from distractions and thus encourages her to recognise her real self: 'the freedom of London was a life in itself . . . walking in London, she would pass into that strange familiar state, when all clamourings seemed unreal, and on in the end into complete forgetfulness . . . London was her pillar of cloud and fire, undeserved, but unsolicited, life's free gift' (III, 106f.) Like her room, London is a solitary place in which she can withdraw from other people. Its primary appeal is that she can experience it alone, although her being with others may also animate it without denying its fundamental meaning.

> It was time to go, to drop away and face the walk home, alone, through the chilly midnight streets . . . that began to cast, as soon as a space of lamplit stillness lay between her and the scene she had left, their old, unfailing spell. Unsharable. Although, tonight, the mellow, golden light falling upon deserted roadway and silent grey stone building, was deepened by the glow of the hours from which she had come forth. (IV, 173)

In contrast to her room, however, London is not encoded as a marked gathering, as a space for Miriam's recollections and transcendence. Rather, the correlation between the psychic reality and topological semantic encoding consists, on the one hand, in the fact that London is posited as an active subject and assumes the role of an addressee for Miriam's dialogue. Secondly, and this recalls the importance which a communication of the garden experience assumes for Miriam, London also acts as the material space in which successful contact with another person might be possible if she were able to communicate her particular semantic encoding of this place to another.

London does not function in the text only as a backdrop for movements and actions, as a receptacle for various island spaces and, not least, for her own room. Equally, it does not serve merely as a seismograph of Miriam's shifting moods and as the spatial catalyst for particular moments of happiness. Elevated by Miriam to subjecthood, even viewed at times as a privileged conversation partner, London in its status as addressee also gives her the opportunity to develop thoughts, make decisions and to give her insights tangible form. It is her 'companion'[31] who can offer comfort: 'Hidden somewhere here, was relief for the increasing numbness of her brain and the drag of her aching heart. The widening sky understood and would presently . . . offer itself in the old way, for companionship' (III, 207). She notes of her lonely walks through the streets that 'the tappings of her feet on the beloved pavement were blows struck hilariously on the shoulder of a friend' (III, 288). This is not a mere rhetorical flourish. The personification is used neither as a means of comparison between two concepts nor as a linguistic image which renders tangible an abstract idea. It demonstrates the recognition that space claims a subject position in Miriam's life which is equal to that of other people. 'The rosy light shone into far-away scenes with distant friends ... She saw where she had failed ... Her friends drifted forward, coming too near, as if in competition for some central place. Too many forms remained grouped, like an audience, confronted by the evening' (II, 405f.). The personified space provides a response to and a substitute for friendships which Miriam often views as a disruptive 'solicitude'.

Miriam's reasons for choosing London as her preferred partner in dialogue also indicates what for her would be a fully liberating contact with others:

> to-night the spirit of London came to meet her on the verge. Nothing in life could be sweeter than this welcoming – a cup held brimming to her lips, and inexhaustible. What lover did she want? No one in this world would oust this mighty lover, always receiving her back without words, engulfing and leaving her untouched, liberated and expanding to the whole range of her being. (III, 272)

As with her own room, London offers the experience of solitary security, 'engulfing and leaving her untouched', a contact which not only preserves her sense of her own self but also extends it, 'expanding to the whole range of her being'. In contrast to her lived solitude in her own room, which is understood as being completely *with-oneself*, this solitary experience of London is an aloneness *with* London, a representation of the 'shared solitude' she is able to experience with Amabel. London assumes the role of a satisfying and, at times, privileged dialogue partner because Miriam is able to be engulfed by it without losing herself, preserving her autonomy while in contact with another. Miriam's dialogue with London occurs in part in the framework of a wordless communion:

> the light-footed leaping sense of a day new begun ... It seemed to smite her, calling for some spoken acknowledgment of its presence, alive and real in the heart of London darkness ... Roaming along in the twilight she lost consciousness of everything but the passage of dark silent buildings ... the sense of being swept across in an easy curve drawn by the kindly calculable swing of the traffic, the coming of the friendly kerb and the strip of yellow pavement, carrying her on again. (III, 373f.)

To an extent, the dialogue between Miriam and the city is also enacted at a linguistic level. Miriam frequently develops her train of thought in tandem with impressions of the London streets, interrupts her reflections and combines them with descriptions of London as she is currently experiencing it, even while she hopes that the space may provide an answer to her personal difficulties. In the role of interlocutor, London intervenes in her argument with Michael and the ensuing silence:

> But presently all about her, as she sat poised for the length of the journey between the dead stillness within her and the noise of the silence without, a world most wonderful was dawning with strange irrelevance, forcing her attention to life itself from

the abyss of her fatigue. Look at us, the buildings seemed to say, sweeping by massed and various and whole, spangled with light. We are here. We, are the accomplished marvel . . . Wonder rose to her lips, and fell back checked, by the remembered occasion, to which for an instant she returned as a stranger seeing the two figures side by side chained in suspended explanations that would not set them free, and left her gazing again . . . It brought a balm. (III, 210f.)

London allows Miriam to disregard her worldly problems in favour of a state of metaphysical wonder, for her dialogue with the city allows her to shut out all that is threatening as disturbing in the material world. Because she endows the streets of London with the 'power to evoke the continuous moment that was always and everywhere the same' (IV, 176), her contact with the city renders tangible the essence which is ever present in herself: 'The quiet forgotten sky was there again; intelligent, blotting out unanswered questions, silently reaching down into the life that rose faintly in her to meet it, the strange mysterious life, far away below all interferences, and always the same' (III, 16f.).

The enmeshment of solitary and significant space generates a crucial conflict in the text. On the one hand, the failure of interpersonal communication is often explained by an incompatible semantic encoding of lived space. Miriam realises: 'Never the time and the place and the loved one all together' and in response to her question as to 'whether you can see the moonlight like it is when you are alone, when Gerald is there', she receives the following reply from her sister Harriett: 'It isn't the same as when you are alone' (I, 299).[32]

The discrepancies between each individual's perception and semantic encoding of lived space shed light upon the individual's fundamental existential solitude. Lenk describes this in the following manner:

> As a being manifested in space, each person is an individual and is, as such, separated from other individuated beings. The paradox of the doubleness of each human being consists in the fact that each person, precisely because of this oneness . . . must exist for him or herself . . . but that he or she must always, whenever sharing space collectively with others, learn the bitter lesson of being divided from them, shut in.[33]

Concurrently, however, a correlation between different individuals' semantic encodings of lived space provides one of the most important points of interconnection in and through which two people, who will always remain completely separated as subjects in space, may encounter one other. The semantic encoding of lived space thus acts both as a boundary separating people from each other in their modes of perception and as a potential connective bridge between them.

Richardson offers a particularly striking example of this double aspect of human solitude in a passage depicting a nocturnal walk which Miriam and Hypo take together. Miriam views this shared experience of lived space both as a clarification of and as a potential compromise between their very different world-views: i.e. Miriam's faith in mysterious and elusive existential essences, and Hypo's belief in science, progress and evolution.

walking side by side up the street ... Eternity opened, irradiating the street ... So long as he remained silent, she could believe him conscious of all that he denied, aware, as perhaps indeed, with his mind off duty, he really was aware, of the element within the vast stillness pouring in through the ceaseless roar of London, not themselves and yet in communion with them and, itself, the medium of their temporary unity, and to remain when they were within the little backwater in the evolutionary process. (IV, 325f.)

If Hypo were able to recognise the constant essence which she designates as an 'eternity ... [an] element ... not themselves and yet in communion with them' inherent to this lived space, which physically represents 'the medium of their temporary unity', then this shared place would also become, in a figurative sense, the place of a 'temporary unity' by providing a point of contact between their two separate selves.

Miriam realises that Hypo's presence alters her experience of space, for London competes with Hypo, above all since his semantic encoding of the city cannot be reconciled with Miriam's own.

Every step of their way was known to her and was filled with a life that in this midnight hour, transfigured by his presence into a darkened gap between day and day, seemed to stand just out of her reach, pleading in vain for recognition and continuance. Counter to it, kept clear by his nearness, ran the stream of her life with him. (IV, 335)

Oblivious to the atmosphere of the city, Hypo merely regards the night-time streets as 'a darkened gap between day and day'. Their shared walk thus represents an encounter not only between the two characters but also between their respective world-views. Accordingly, Hypo interprets the space as a distance which, as solid actuality, may be measured objectively, while Miriam views it as a limitless expanse which is imbued with a subjective emotional quality:

They were now well within the region of the tall trees lining the stretch of pavement, a hundred yards or so as seen with his eyes, but in reality an illimitable space wherein there always came upon whatever was engrossing her as daily she passed this way to and fro, a subtle influence, modifying it, setting it a little aside and toning down its urgency. (IV, 336)

Although Miriam bows to the dissimilarity of their respective semantic encodings of space, she nevertheless hopes that Hypo may experience the spatial atmosphere as she does, namely as 'powerful magic', an 'influence ... giving her strength':

Even at night ... the powerful magic came forth ... Surely he must be aware of it, must feel it streaming towards him through the stillness ... Under its influence, that was giving her strength to throw, across the interminable distance now separating them, a bridge upon which, as soon as he had recognised it, they might meet and greet one another, he could not fail to respond. (IV, 336)

If Hypo were to respond, the different encoding of this lived space, which up to this point had produced a boundary between them, would become a 'bridge' connecting them. Yet Miriam is unable to impart her understanding of the city, and sees this as proof of the irreconcilability of their two ways of life: 'she braced herself against the truth of their relationship, the essential separation and mutual dislike of their two ways of being' (IV, 336). The last part of the walk restores her tranquillity, since she is again alone and once more free to move through her familiar district with impunity, 'stilled by the familiar presences of its tall grey buildings, and the trees detachedly inhabiting its quiet squares, the inward tumult should subside and leave her to become once more aware of her own path, cool and solid beneath her feet' (IV, 337). This return to her own path is given a double meaning: released from the disruptive presence of another, Miriam's spatial experience of the familiar street is likewise undisturbed. Her perception of the street as 'her own path, cool and solid' is not called into question by any diverging semantic encoding. In psychological terms, this image of her solitary walk signifies her psychic pilgrimage, which she must undertake alone, trusting only in herself.[34]

One can, then, conclude that the 'significance' of a lived space arises from the meanings which it accumulates for the perceiving subject. The significance of the garden for Miriam is that it gathers innocence and redemption from sin; of her own room, that it gathers the material and the immaterial world; of London, that the city gathers two active subjects, either Miriam and London in the role of 'companion' or potentially Miriam and an additional character. All these three spaces allow her to establish a protective anchorage in lived space functioning as a point of orientation both for her actual material and for her psychic pilgrimage, even while they engender an intuitive contact with the essences of being. Furthermore, all semantic encoding of lived space is not only related to the perceiving subject but also, to a greater or lesser degree, unique for each subject. Endowing lived space with meaning does not only allow Miriam to specify what makes a given place significant for her. Rather, it also allows her to recollect the contingent events and experiences of the past into a coherent, meaningful narrative order.[35]

The concept of mobile and immobile neutral spaces, or of a neutral mode of experiencing space, refers to all lived spaces which represent a spatial reality *between* two or more semantically encoded island spaces. The unfamiliar 'islands' conducive to Miriam's presence there, as well as Miriam's familiar 'significant' spaces, contain and represent a particular, quite specifically encoded world, dependent upon who inhabits these places and what events occur there. Neutral spaces, however, are free spaces precisely in the sense that they are masked by an absence of semantic encoding. This is to say that neither one subject nor any specific atmosphere dominates here. Unlike significant spaces, they prevent any anchorage or orientation in space. They are experienced as spaces of 'nowhere' and 'spacelessness', as liminal spaces which, because they do not limit the perceiving subject in any way, come to offer an independent spatial situation which demands compromise at the same time that it also allows the subject to experience the infinity of being.

IN SEARCH OF LOST SPACE

In contrast to all the semantically encoded spaces discussed so far, it is possible for different characters to meet in a neutral space, even if they do not agree on its meaning. Here they need not adapt to each others' perceptions of lived space, since these sites are free of any semantic encoding which demands compromise. Indeed, neutral spaces differ from significant spaces precisely in that they do not allow her the sense of belonging, or even of habitation. Instead they offer an ecstatic feeling of spacelessness and a momentary sensation of unity between self and world.

While Miriam views her own room as a place engendering a feeling of transcendence which heightens and accumulates impressions, i.e. the *transcendence* of recollection, neutral space involves an ecstatic transcendence into nowhere, which disperses and scatters thought and does not strive for any transformative synthesis. Although there are privileged moments of non-logical spatial perception and although various remembered spaces are relived simultaneously in neutral space, their value lies in the experience itself, without seeking to go beyond it. It is only in her room that Miriam can convert transcendental experiences into writing and that she can transform an experience of dematerialisation or of experiencing places simultaneously into artistic representation.[36] Perceived as intermediate space and not as centre, the liminality offered by neutral space is more one of a fleeting sensation rather than a gathering of two modes of being. While significant spaces help Miriam to recognise constant essences, in the form of recurring 'sameness', neutral space reveals constant essences in the sense that here Miriam finds herself on the border between different places and thus temporarily released from all mutability and uncertainty that goes with belonging to any of these so multifariously encoded places. Miriam's position in neutral territory may be described as a combination of action space and contemplative space since in its liminality a neutral site implies the transitional movement from one place to another, even while it allows Miriam to disregard momentarily her corporeal implication in the lived space she inhabits.

When one explores how Richardson depicts such neutral sites in *Pilgrimage*, it is, however, useful to distinguish between mobile spaces, determined by Miriam's movement, and immobile ones. The former include the numerous buses, trains and other vehicles which transport her from one place to another, and thus generate a free site between two semantically encoded places. Miriam calls the Brighton to London train a 'six o'clock preserve of middle-aged City men sufficiently well-to-do to be living in Brighton and evidently enjoying this hour on neutral territory, remote from office and from home' (IV, 647f.). The psychological state called forth by these sites is one of indifference and impartiality. Released from any spatial belonging, Miriam experiences the neutral territory between Bonnycliff and London as a calming and liberating 'nowhere'. This is accompanied by a renewed confirmation of her own sense of self, which she had at times doubted during her stay with Hypo.

> Behind her fixed eyes, something new seemed moving forward with a strange indifference. Suddenly the landscape unrolled. The rim of the horizon was no longer the edge of the world ... Nothing. Everywhere in the world, nothing. She drifted back to herself and clung, bracing herself. She was somebody. (II, 109)

Sitting immobile in such neutral territories can, at times, also bring about a sense of spacelessness which is directed towards an experience of immateriality because it involves a 'suspension of activity' in the material world. Miriam's numerous bus journeys across London, for example, encourage a movement from lived space into the immaterial space of the unconscious:

> In the dimly lit little interior, moving along through the backward flowing mist-screened street lights, she dropped away from the circling worlds of sound, and sat thoughtless, gazing inward along the bright kaleidoscopic vistas that came unfailing and unchanged whenever she was moving, alone and still, against the moving tide of London. (III, 114)

Furthermore, such experiences of nowhere are represented as possible only if Miriam wholly disregards the fact that she belongs to a particular place, in the sense of concrete physical enspacement. A second description of a train journey between Bonnycliff and London illustrates how goal-orientated behaviour in neutral space literally prohibits an experience of precisely such a lack of enspacement:

> There had been a strange exciting sense of travelling, as everyone seemed to travel, preoccupied, missing the adventure of the journey, merely suffering it as an unavoidable time-consuming movement from one place to another. She, like all these others, had a place and a meaning in the outside world . . . it was . . . this basis of preoccupation with secure unshared possessions that . . . checked the expressiveness of surroundings. The gritty interior of the carriage had remained intolerable throughout the journey. The passing landscape had never come to life. (III, 263)

Mobile spaces also function as marked, free spaces between two separate periods of time – whereby temporal experiences are expressed in terms of lived space, with the boundary running between a memory of the past and an anticipation of future experience of space. The following description of a sledge ride between the Swiss railway station and the Alpenstock Hotel captures this aptly: 'And away behind them, standing still and now forever accessible, were the worlds she had passed through since the sleet drove in her face at Newhaven. And ahead unknown Oberland, summoning her up amongst its peaks' (IV, 24). As a result, these neutral sites often allow Miriam to reconstruct past experiences in the form of a simultaneous recollection of different lived spaces. A feeling of spacelessness, of being 'nowhere', is associated neither with a reliance upon her own self-awareness or the unconscious, nor with an animation of space, but instead enables Miriam to disregard lived space in favour of remembered spaces:

> The visit ended in the stillness that fell upon the empty carriage as the train left the last red-roofed houses behind and slid out into the open country. She hung for an instant over the spread of the town . . . her visit still ahead of her. But the interiors of Eve's dark little house and Harriett's bright one slipped in between her and the pictured town, and the four days' succession of incidents overtook her in disorder, playing themselves out backwards and forwards, singly, in clear succession, two or

three together, related to each other by some continuity of mood with herself, pell-mell, swiftly interchanging, each scene in turn claiming the foremost place. (III, 102f.)

Since neutral sites are perceived as the boundary between a spatially localised past and future in neither of which she is currently placed, they help her recognise her own essence. In the car in which she is taken to the Corries', Miriam feels herself to be pleasantly arrested between her parents' poverty and the longed-for respite from poverty at the Corries'.

> Miriam relaxed and sat back, smiling. For a moment she was conscious of nothing but the soft-toned, softly-lit interior, the softness at her back, the warmth under her feet and her happy smile; then she felt a sudden strength; the smile coming straight up so unexpectedly from some deep where it had been waiting, was new and strong and exhilarating . . . it carried her forward, tiding her over the passage into new experience and held her back, at the same time; it lifted her and held her suspended over the new circumstances in rapid contemplation . . . this is me; this is right . . . There was a life ahead that was going to enrich and change her . . . She was changed already. Poverty and discomfort had been shut out of her life when the brougham door closed upon her. (I, 351)

As Miriam finds her thoughts oscillating between the two so differently encoded places, representing two separate periods in her life, she recognises that 'this is me'. For in this neutral site she can become aware of that part of her self which exists beyond any form of belonging to any one place, as it remains untouched by her continual transition from one place to another.

Another set of neutral spaces relates to the subject's movement in space, and thereby to an *inter-spatial* experience. Here, the experience of nowhere and spacelessness does not take place as a result of goal-directed movement between two encoded places, but rather by overcoming the force of gravity. A momentary triumph over gravity, and with it the physical limitations of corporeal existence, occurs in sports activity, when these offer a brief experience of infinity. As she watches others ski jumping Miriam shares their experience of spacelessness: 'Achievement. Thrilling and chastening. Long ago, someone had done this difficult thing for the first time, alone, perhaps driven by necessity. Now it was a sport, a deliberate movement into eternity, shared by all who looked on' (IV, 115). In those passages which pertain to Miriam's own attempts to overcome her corporeal enspacement, the experience of spacelessness is associated with a disregard for a conscious, linguistic understanding of the world. The ecstatic experience of her first toboggan ride is depicted as an instinctive, unconscious movement:

> It slid off at once, took a small hummock askew, righted itself, to a movement made too instinctively to be instructive, and slid onwards gathering pace. But ecstasy passed too swiftly into awareness of the bend in the road now rushing up to meet her ignorance. She . . . stood up tingling with joy in the midst of the joyous landscape, stilled again, that had flown with her and swooped up as she plunged, and was now receiving her exciting news. (IV, 70f.)

Here, her ecstasy comes to an end and the potential to communicate her experience in language begins as soon as she becomes conscious of her own movement, and with it the inevitability of actual material enspacement. Another description of Miriam's toboggan ride illustrates even more clearly the significance that lies in momentarily overcoming corporeal enspacement:

> she let herself go. The joy of flight returned, singing joy of the inaccessible world to which in flight one was translated, bringing forgetfulness of everything but itself. Bend after bend appeared and of itself her body swayed now right now left in unconscious rhythm. The landscape flew by, sideways-upwards, its features indistinguishable. She was movement, increasing, cleaving the backward rushing air. At the last slope she was level with Mrs. Harcourt, safely, triumphantly returned to the known world, passing her, flying down so blissfully that arrival would now be nothing but an end to joy. (IV, 119)

In flight, Miriam feels lived space to be infinite, an 'inaccessible world to which . . . she was translated'. All constraining aspects of material space are disregarded – its 'features indistinguishable' – and only at the close of the ride does it again become the 'known world'. The limitations of her own physical awareness are likewise overlooked – the flight brings 'forgetfulness'; Miriam experiences herself as an 'unconscious rhythm', as pure movement.[37]

Immobile, neutral sites, in turn, either act as a point of connection between two meaningfully marked material spaces or represent a neutral haven which is completely separated from other spaces.[38] The staircase in Miriam's employer's home, for example, transports Miriam from one place to another, while at the same time representing a neutral connection between an upper and a lower level. Like the toboggan ride, movement on the stairs is associated with an opportunity to disregard the material world and her enspacement in it. Moreover, as with the toboggan experience, Miriam views her arrival at the bottom of the stairs as a return to the actual material space from which she was absent during her descent.

> with an emotion independent of that aroused by whatever made the journey necessary, sometimes so strong as temporarily to make her forget her errand . . . making the experience of being on the stairs with the wide eloquent spaces above and below and all about her set in motion by movement, and the beings of the many inmates, and even her own being, momentarily further than usual from her mind and therefore in clearer focus, something distinct from the rest of her life in the house – until she arrived at her destination with a sense of return to a world from which she seemed to have been absent for much longer than the time required for the journey. (IV, 198f.)

Clearly, the experience on the stairs generates a brief sense of being 'nowhere', liberated from all corporeal or psychic bonds to lived space, and thus a sense of temporal expansion: 'she seemed to have been absent for much longer than the time required for the journey'. Moreover, this neutral site also affords a sharpened vision, since it offers detachment from lived space and from her life in it. Observing her life from a neutral distance, Miriam sees it 'in clearer focus'. Such an experience of an intermediary site may also, however, be related to a spatial perception of time. The act of disregarding lived space allows Miriam to experience imagined spaces she anticipates simultaneously with those she inhabited in the past. 'As she passed through the changing lights of the passage, up the little dark staircase ... scenes from the future, moving boundless backgrounds, came streaming unsummoned into her mind, making her surroundings suddenly unfamiliar ... the past would come again' (II, 312). This experience of spacelessness – the space around her is 'suddenly unfamiliar' – is coupled with one of timelessness, and thus engenders a simultaneous awareness of space and time or rather a replacement of diachrony with synchrony.

Movement on the stairs may, therefore, also produce moments of ecstatic transcendence which lead Miriam to a recognition of her own essence:

> The staircase was cold and airy. Cold rooms and landings stretched up away above her into the darkness. She became aware of a curious buoyancy rising within her. It was so strange that she stood still for a moment on the stair. For a second, life seemed to cease in her and the staircase to be swept from under her feet ... 'I'm alive.' ... her impalpable body, sweeping it away, leaving her there shouting silently without it. I'm alive ... I'm alive. Then with a thump her heart went on again and her feet carried her body, warm and happy and elastic, easily on up the solid stairs. She tried once or twice deliberately to bring back the breathless moment standing still on a stair. Each time something of it returned. 'It's me, *me*; this is *me* being alive,' she murmured with a feeling under her like the sudden drop of a lift. But her thoughts distracted her. (I, 245)

On the stairs, Miriam feels herself to be outside space and time: 'life seemed to cease ... the staircase to be swept from under her feet'. This recognition of her own being – 'this is *me* being alive' – is chiefly brought about by overcoming a physical sense of belonging in space as opposed to a semantic one. Here, too, a recognition of her own essence, following an experience of 'nowhere', is incompatible with a logical perception of the world. Her thoughts interrupt her attempt to reconstruct the experience in memory.

The immobile, neutral spaces which do not forge a link between two semantically encoded spaces, the numerous cafés and restaurants, are mainly examples of lived spaces whose neutrality permits an impartial stay within them. As places in which characters meet, they allow for compromise between the various claims which the characters make upon one another. While Miriam usually tries to protect herself from others' 'solicitations' because she holds this to be a crucial requirement for creative activity, in neutral spaces she does not feel the presence of others as an irritating hindrance to her own concentration. In such spaces, Miriam neither seeks to convey to her friends the special meaning a place has for her nor does she fully give herself up to the unfamiliar spirit of the place:

> Fully to recognize, one must be alone. Away in the farthest reaches of one's being. As one can richly be, even with others, provided they have no claims. Provided one is

neither guest nor host. With others on neutral territory, where one can forget one is there, and be everywhere. Hence, for me, the charm of that Euston Miles place . . . I can sit within the differently nourishing variations of the assembled company, reading as receptively as if I were alone, yet feeling one even with that woman who sat at my table last night. (IV, 657)[39]

During her time at Flaxman's Court, when the presence of Selina Holland prevents Miriam's living space from ever becoming a solitary refuge, she discovers the appeal of her club: 'She blessed the club. Its gift, at the moment when solitude had departed from her home-life, of a new solitude; strange lives surrounding her without pressure, and something granting these large quiet moments' (III, 466f.). For this neutral site protects her from the pressurised intimacy with Selina. Since Miriam also transfers their disastrous relationship on to her entire experience of Flaxman's Court, the club offers escape from a sense of imprisonment which is both psychological and spatial:

Away behind was a roomful of independent strangers, also aware of the square set ever before their eyes. This was freedom, in company, enriched. The sense of imprisonment she had felt on coming down the street with Miss Holland, the tangible confirmation when Miss Holland . . . suddenly took her arm, of the note struck too soon, and too high, vanished, altogether in the freedom of this neutral territory. (III, 418f.)

Just as Miriam viewed 'shared solitude' as an enriching consolidation of her own solitude with regard to the communicability of the garden experience, so the disregard for clearly belonging to a given place, which the club affords, is judged as 'freedom, in company, enriched', because Miriam can here share her lived space and its neutrality with others. Although others have an equal stake in this neutral, lived space, they remain 'independent strangers'. The experience of the club is liberating for the reason that it represents an encounter between different subjects in space without the pressure of interpersonal demands.

But the club is also perceived as a 'nowhere' which lies at the outermost edge of material enspacement: 'In this long, empty drawing-room, with morning gone and the afternoon not yet begun, was the end of the world. Life far away, past and done with. The atmosphere of the room, coldly neutral' (IV, 186). It thus provides Miriam with a refuge from the irritating demands which others make upon her even while it serves as an ideal meeting-place for an encounter between her very different friends: it is a 'centre where these old friends and the friends with whom her life was now involved, might meet and understand each other' (III, 452). For here, her friends, who themselves stand for different closed, semantic spaces, can meet with impunity. Michael represents Russia, Densley, the class of the medical profession, and the Taylors, esoteric mysticism: 'Four widely separated worlds met together' (III, 471). Now, if the club permits utterly disparate characters to meet and preserves their position as disparate characters, it also functions as the site where the encounter between her friends allows Miriam to assess her relationships with them. On the one hand, the neutrality of the site weakens what she perceives as restrictive commitments to her friends, because she cannot judge their relationships outside the lived places that usually determine it. On the other hand, she is able to relativise each relationship because in the club it is viewed no longer in isolation but rather in connection with two others: 'watching these two old friends for the first time confronted. It made them strangers to herself, people seen for the first time. Divested of their relationship to her, they were at once diminished and enlarged' (III, 469). Meeting more than one friend in a neutral site allows Miriam to recognise something which she was unable to perceive while confronting each relationship and the lived place it represents, individually, namely that she belongs to none of them: 'her party had, in bringing together three of her worlds, shown her more clearly than she had known it before, that there was no place for her in any one of them' (III, 474).

Finally, immobile, neutral sites can also offer Miriam an experience of ecstatic spacelessness, as her moment of transcendence in a café illustrates. Here, the triumph over the laws of gravity is an imaginary one, since Miriam is physically motionless. Her ecstatic experience of 'being up in the rejoicing sky. For two, three seconds' (IV, 279) instead portrays a psychic transcendence into 'nowhere' in the form of a triumph over the restrictions imposed by language. While observing a waitress, she has the following experience:

> the wordless thought . . . and, before her awakened mind . . . could reach the words . . . she was within that lifting of emotion. With a single up-swinging movement, she was clear of earth and hanging, suspended and motionless, high in the sky, looking, away to the right, into a far-off pearly-blue distance, that held her eyes, seeming to be in motion within itself: an intense crystalline vibration that seemed to be aware of being enchantedly observed, and even to be amused and to be saying, 'Yes, this is my reality'. She was moving, or the sky about her was moving . . . And then the little manageress was setting down the coffee . . . Joy, that up there had seemed everywhere, pulsed now, confined, within her, holding away thoughts, holding away everything but itself. (IV, 279)

As with the other neutral spaces, this transcendence also manifests itself as a limitless suspension in space, in a wordless sensation of sheer movement; and here, too, the experience of spacelessness engenders a recognition of her own essence. Although this is a mental movement into nowhere, it contians a description of a tangible spatial experience, namely of an extreme form of contemplative space in which lived space briefly represents a complete nullification of anchorage in the material world. Above all, however, this passage articulates the way in which experiences of transcendence that move beyond linguistic comprehension nevertheless become communicable only as linguistic utterances. Indeed, this passage enacts precisely this paradox by representing in words an experience which is emphasised as being non-linguistic. Furthermore, Miriam herself even interprets the experience itself in linguistic terms: 'vibrations that seemed to be aware . . . to be saying, "Yes, this is my reality"'. Not until she reflects consciously upon the experience does she become aware of its meaning. In contrast to the experiences of transcendence in her own room, which are increasingly centred on the scene of writing, in the course of which the immaterial is transformed into material and referential signs, Miriam's primary aim in this café experience is to preserve the emotion which it has called forth. Even after re-entry into material space, she is able to prevent the resumption of thought: 'holding away thoughts, holding away everything but itself'.

My final examples for spatial encodings in *Pilgrimage* revolve around Richardson's representation of remembered and imagined spaces. They articulate Miriam's persistent desire to localise past events as well as objects of the imagination; for spatial impressions appear to possess a greater vividness than temporal events – 'the impressions remaining more sharp and deep than the event'.

Imagined spaces are always triggered associatively: either because the spatial situation encourages the visualisation of immaterial spatial experience or because an encounter or atmosphere in a currently experienced space calls to mind a past or imagined lived space, or both. Imagined spaces may be experienced only in contemplative space precisely because here Miriam can disregard her current enspacement so as to allow one or more imagined spaces to become, temporarily, her lived space. In other words, the art of memory and imagination Richardson performs throughout *Pilgrimage* is such that the lived space of her protagonist comes to be enlarged such that it includes simultaneously the corporeally experienced and the imagined space. This spatial juxtaposition is revealed most poignantly when the incorporation of imagined space into currently experienced space consists in Miriam experiencing both at one and the same time. However, such simultaneity also occurs in those passages where Miriam shifts between the spaces, or briefly privileges an imagined space over a currently experienced one, since disregarding a given place is not synonymous with negating it.

Privileging imagined spaces allows Miriam to replace sequential linearity with simultaneous juxtaposition and to reject time in favour of space. In so doing, Miriam reinterprets the concepts 'nearness' and 'distance', in the sense that imaginative visualisation makes temporally distant, lived spaces – because they are at a spatial remove from London – appear nearer to and thus more important for her than the currently experienced space.[40] By virtue of her imagination, that which is absent may be temporally and spatially nearer to her than the place she currently inhabits. At the same time, her imaginative evocation of places allows Miriam to overcome all restrictions imposed by spatial perspective. While remembering or imagining places, Miriam does not assume any specific, anchored position, such that all recollected spaces cannot be inhabited simultaneously but also experienced unhampered by all faces of actual material space.

In many respects, then, imagined spaces represent a precedence of synchrony over diachrony. Imagined space is in itself lived synchronically, allowing for a simultaneity of diverse remembered places along with the space inhabited in the present, such that topological and temporal sequentiality is abandoned in favour of a simultaneous presence. Moreover, the meaning of these imagined spaces is not produced at a syntagmatic level (a temporally determined, linear and irreversible expansion) but rather at an associative level: that is, in a simultaneous connection between two signs.[41] Making immaterial worlds concrete by virtue of the imagination establishes a connection between the present space (together with the mood which it contains) and the mood contained or compounded in imagined space — the mood which it *embodies* as a remembered or imagined space. The production of this juxtaposition may be viewed as a metaphorical process, since the simultaneous presence of one or more imagined spaces together with the currently experienced space either heightens the meaning of both or transfers the meaning of the imagined space back on to the atmosphere of the current one. It is, however, necessary to emphasise that two or more actual material spaces are related metaphorically in relation to their significance as lived spaces for Miriam, even though they do not function purely as spatial metaphors. Textually, this heightening of significance is revealed in the passages in which a lived space calls forth a memory of other lived spaces by means of its similarity to (or fundamental difference from) them. This simultaneous comparison allows Miriam to recognise more clearly the meaning different spaces have for her.

At the same time, imagining lived spaces, deriving either from the past or from fantasy, represents an extended form of spatial vivification. While Miriam creates imagined space, she reanimates remembered space, bringing it back to life. In order to recreate a particular atmosphere, Miriam either remembers places from the past which possessed this atmosphere, or constructs imagined spaces which would contain this atmosphere for her. Thus, imagined space acts as a spatial substitute for a mood or a feeling. Miriam reduces these imagined spaces to the one atmosphere which she views as their primary component, ignoring any fluctuations in the way she perceived this space in the past. Whereas the animation of immediately lived space is subject to change, owing to its dependence upon Miriam's mood, the reanimation of lived space in the form of an imagined space fixes the particular spatial atmosphere which made the greatest impression upon Miriam, becoming, as it were, a substitute for that space. In this way, the process of imagining lived spaces is at once spatial animation and spatial semantic encoding, since the association of a remembered space with one particular mood inevitably results in the assignment of one fixed, constant meaning to this lived space.

The act of imagining spaces may at one level be regarded as an attempt to order the events in one's own life meaningfully and to establish relations between past, present and future. In order to explain it and to gain a better understanding of it, Miriam revisualises past experiences by revisiting places in the past. At the same time, since the imagined spaces are the product of fantasy-work, they act as forerunners of her creative activity; finger exercises, so to speak, for the gathering transcendence which leads to the scene of writing.

One striking feature of the various memories of past events is that Miriam often localises them spatially, as if they had been inscribed in her memory as lived spaces. Three of the four volumes commence with a transitional situation in which Miriam looks back over her life in terms of remembered spaces. In the train which takes her to Hanover, she reviews her life by pinning down different periods of her life with detailed descriptions of the living spaces which accompanied them – Babington garden, Marine Villa on the coast and the upper-class house in Barnes (I, 32f.) Shortly after moving into the room at Mrs Bailey's, Miriam remembers her first months in London by revisualising the various rooms which she has rented there in the past (II, 17). Similarly, her journey to Oberland begins with a recollection of the various 'foreign places' which she has already visited in solitude (IV, 24f.). Personal resolutions about her future and the various opportunities open to her are likewise condensed into imagined lived spaces. This is most obvious in the first books, in which Miriam has not reached a final decision concerning the place in which she would like to live, nor concerning the occupation which she ultimately wishes to take up. A German schoolgirl's invitation to Miriam to move into her home releases the fantasy of a space which might form the environment for this way of life:

> Minna's garden, her secure country house, her rich parents, no worries, nothing particular to do . . . She had been daunted, as Minna murmured, by a picture of Minna and herself in that remote garden – she receiving confidences about the Apotheker – no one else there – the Waldstrasse household blotted out. (I, 216)

Miriam's indecision as to whether she ought to remain in Germany or return to England leads to comparisons between memories of spaces in both countries which she has left behind. In her imagination, the remembered English space replaces Germany for a brief instant: 'the little German garden was disappearing from Miriam's eyes . . . there at home in the garden lilac was quietly coming out . . . and May . . . and everything' (I, 112). In the attempt to reach a decision concerning the ideal living situation, Miriam, in fact, juxtaposes the two cultural locations in her imagination. The vision of a life spent with a second schoolgirl named Emma – 'She imagined a house, everyone kind and blond and smiling . . . There would be a garden and German springs and summers and sunsets' (I, 167) – disappears in favour of a memory of her own home. Rather than simply designating the space as German, the detailed spatial description offers an indication that her home is the place which she favours:

> She imagined Eve sitting . . . in the window space in the bow that was carpeted with linoleum to look like parquet flooring. Beyond them lay the length of the Turkey carpet darkening away under the long table. She could see each object on the shining sideboard. The silver biscuitbox and the large epergne made her feel guilty and shifting. (I, 168)

Her conflict as to whether she should marry, as her sisters have done, or pursue an independent career, is also expressed by means of imagined spaces. Miriam associates employees' own rooms, with which she is familiar from her different workplaces – 'the bedroom at the top' (I, 270) – with the autonomous freedom of an independent life. Marriage, on the other hand, as a liberation from work and poverty, she associates with the ownership of a house, thus revealing that there is a correspondence in her imagination between the assumption of a socially accepted female role and the ownership of her own living space:

> If a victoria came along and in it a delicate, lonely old gentleman who had a large empty house with deep quiet rooms and a large sunny garden with high walls, and wanted someone to be about there, singing and happy till he died, she would go. He would drive away with her and shut her up in the quiet beautiful house, protecting her and keeping people off, and she would sing all day in the garden and the house. (I, 396)

At the same time, however, Miriam localises the potential restrictions in marriage in the example of her suffering mother by describing her lived space:

> [Miriam's] imagined picture of her mother in the first year of her married life, standing in the sunlight at the back door of the Babington house, with the varnished coachhouse door on her right and the cucumber frames in front of her sloping up towards the bean-rows that began the kitchen garden; . . . that neighing laugh had come again and again all through the years until she sat meekly, flushed and suffering under the fierce gaslight, feeling every night of her life winter and summer as if the ceiling were coming down on her head. (I, 234f.)

The first image depicts the space of her original happiness, bathed in sunlight; the second reveals a lived space which expresses her mother's misery and her sense of confinement, 'fierce gaslight . . . as if the ceiling were coming down on her head'.

Experiences which led to an insight into her own existence, and were therefore inscribed particularly clearly in her memory, are also localised spatially. In other words, the spatiality of these experiences is one of their most important features. At night in her dark room at Banbury Park, Miriam pictures two lived spaces, the former linked with the recognition of her own mortality, and the latter coupled with a heightened consciousness of her own self:

> Two forgotten incidents flowed past her in quick succession: one of waking up on her seventh birthday in the seaside villa alone in a small dark room and suddenly saying to herself that one day her father and mother would die and she would still be there and, after a curious moment when the darkness seemed to move against her, feeling very old and crying bitterly; and another of standing in the bow of the dining-room window at Barnes looking at the raindrops falling from the leaves through the sunshine and saying to Eve, who came into the room as she watched, '. . . I feel as if I'd suddenly wakened up out of a dream.' (I, 245)[42]

Here, again, a change in the present space is used to demonstrate that this memory has changed her present life. Having pictured the two lived spaces and the two insights which accompanied them, and thus having remembered her spatial and psychological anchorage, the complete darkness in her room is dispelled: 'The bedroom was no longer dark. She could see the outlines of everything in the light coming from the street lamps through the half-closed Venetian blinds' (I, 245).

Although these passages are instances of simple comparisons, in which present space is disregarded in favour of an imagined space, there are other passages in which numerous imagined spaces are compared with each other as well as with currently experienced space. In this way, Miriam is able to discover one specific, constant pattern for her experience of different material spaces, as well as to trace the distinctive features of her privileged lived space. Such spatial comparing also occurs whenever Miriam, having left one space and the way of living that goes along with it, cannot decide which new place to choose.

During a dinner with Hypo, her feeling of loneliness and her sense that she does not fit to him provoke the question 'What am I doing here' (IV, 166), and thus initiate a comparison between different lived spaces. Miriam localises her motives for her continual pilgrimage in her experience of these different spaces; to be more precise, in the experience that her life there provoked the same questions and doubts as to where she belongs.

> But though it sounded insistently, it held now a promise, as if of an opportunity made towards which, though all her ways seemed blocked, she was invisibly moving. Always had been moving, driven on in the end, whenever she had for a moment thought herself arrived at her destination, by its warning cry. It had sounded everywhere, almost daily, at Banbury Park, at Wimpole Street, at Flaxman's, in the houses of all her friends; everywhere. Except for a while amidst the loveliness of Newlands and, earlier, of Germany, where in the midst of suffering there had been that deep depth of happiness for whose sake she would have gone on enduring for ever. (IV, 167)

Such comparative visualisation of spaces from the past enables Miriam to develop an accurate psychogram for the life which she has lived so far and to discover those constant elements which create a meaningful order out of the disparate events in her past. Having rendered tangible her sense that she must always leave her living situations by spatialising it, it loses its horror and is understood as a 'promise'. Miriam puts this imaginative insight into effect in her present life, not only in order to explain the failed communication with Hypo but also as a means of justifying her return to Tansley Street and her resignation from the dental practice – both being steps which lead to her becoming a writer.

There is an especially significant comparison between different lived spaces which occurs towards the end of the novel *March Moonlight*. Following her first journey to Switzerland, Miriam is, freed from all commitments, at liberty to search for her ideal lived space. For Miriam, the present spaces in the respective homes of her sister Sally and Amabel, like the imagined spaces at Dimple Hill and Vaud, are a tangible representation of the lifestyles and values of the people who inhabit them. Her rejection of certain ways of life in turn expresses her preference for others and comes about by her evaluating the actual material spaces, which are thought to harbour specific ways of life. Thus, Miriam views the dinner at her sisters' home as a chance encounter between different people in space and as lacking any real contact between them: 'the sense of the family gathered together, its natural sympathies and animosities firmly in place, to still the pangs of hunger' (IV, 588). She contrasts this with an image of Dimple Hill and Vaud as lived spaces which she favours since they actively foster communication:

And was translated, while she spoke with her mind truly set upon the image of the small fire slowly struggling towards mastery of the cold, to her place at the Dimple Hill table, to possession of her prentice share of the medium wherein the Roscorlas met and communicated with each other . . . and was aware, the moment her words were sped, of the incompatibility of the two atmospheres . . . Yet in Oberland, where there was neither grace nor Quakerly silence, where communication flowed at once, there was at least an approach to the desirable atmosphere. (IV, 589)[43]

Miriam's recollection of the Dimple Hill kitchen, as she is sitting in Amabel's kitchen, plays a similar role. The opposition which she sets up between Dimple Hill (conceived as a place of relaxed calmness), and Amabel's home (conceived as a place of preoccupied busyness), allows her to recognise clearly where her preference lies:

> Small, compact and brightly burnished, the little kitchener, the heart and meaning of the room, prevailing over its decorative surroundings . . . shows her caught, for life, in a continuously revolving machinery, unable to give, to anything else, more than a permanently preoccupied attention . . . At this moment in the roomy Dimple Hill kitchen, quiet, and dark save where at its far end the practical harsh light of the unshaded oil lamp falls upon the serene figure of Rachel Mary bent over the shabby ancient range, the fire's rosy glow stands out against the blackness of the great flue. (IV, 602)

Ultimately, these imagined spaces affirm Miriam in her decision to return to Dimple Hill since this place, when compared with all others, appears to be the most desirable and suitable lived space. In this way, remembered and imagined actual spaces allow Miriam to give her life a meaningful order, to form a cosmos out of the chaos of different perceptions, feelings and events. Though focused upon change and the future, they also enable her to discover a meaningful orientation in her past as well as her present life.

The imagined spaces which do not serve as catalysts for personal resolutions concerning Miriam's life are characterised not by comparison and evaluation but rather by an objectification of moods and fantasies. They do not help Miriam in deciding upon the path which her life should take, but instead aim at an exploratory examination of her creative acvitity. Following her journey to Oberland and her decision to begin writing, the imagined spaces increasingly act as precursors of her scene of writing, for here she learns to disregard the spaces she currently inhabits in order not only to recollect places she knew in the past but more importantly to recreate them in words. The self-reflexivity of these passages consists in their reference to the text *Pilgrimage* itself, for it also gathers together and reconstructs representations of different material space. At the same time it also implicitly refers to the role of the author, and thus foreshadows the description of Miriam's own attempts at writing.

Genette describes the intimate connection between imagination and the experience of space as follows:

literature . . . also speaks of space, describes places, dwelling-places, landscapes, transports us . . . in our imagination into unknown lands which it for an instant gives us the illusion of traversing and inhabiting . . . since . . . a sort of fascination of place is one of the primary aspects of that which Valéry termed the *poetic state*.[44]

There are numerous instances in *Pilgrimage* in which reading is characterised as a journey into imagined space. Such 'journeys' are not obliquely referred to, but actually experienced as a tangible expansion and extension of lived space. While reading Ibsen's *Brand*, Miriam is transported into the Norway which the text depicts:

> up among the misty mountains, in farms and cottages looking down on fiords with glorious scenery about them all the time, are people, sitting in the winter by fires and worrying about right and wrong . . . Torrents thunder in their ears and they can see mountains all the time . . . You are *in* Norway while you read. That is why people read books by geniuses and look far-away when they talk about them . . . What is genius? Something that can take you into Norway in an ABC. (II, 383f.)

Occasionally, this form of expansion of lived space creates such a lasting impression that the imagined space continues to suppress the currently inhabited space even after Miriam has finished reading.

> In her room, Miriam glanced at the magic pages, hungrily gathering German phrases, and all the way to Aldgate, sitting back, exhausted in her corner she clung to them, resting in a 'Stube' with 'Gebirge' all round it in morning and evening light. When they reached their destination she had forgotten she was in London. (III, 125)[45]

Miriam views her image of the territory of Russia, conjured up by Michael's stories, as an 'irrevocable expansion of her consciousness' (III, 45), as an incorporation of the visualised foreign space, with all its magic, into her familiar London. Both are components of her lived space: 'she gave her flagging attention to the Russia already in her mind; a strip of silent sunlit snow, just below Finland, St. Petersburg in the midst of it . . . she was carried away to villages scattered amongst great tracts of forest . . . She passed down the winding sweep of the Volga' (II, 43). This imaginary journey not only grants her an experience of Russia, it also enables her to appropriate this foreign space. Furthermore, this imagined space signifies a mode of spatial perception which has greater potential than immediate spatial experience since, freed from her restriction to one perspective, Miriam experiences different scenes simultaneously: 'The scenes she watched opened out one behind the other in clear perspective, the earlier ones remaining visible, drawn aside into bright light as further backgrounds opened' (III, 78). Miriam's furious response to Michael's suggestion that she ought to travel to Russia herself highlights a further advantage of imagined space: 'The conviction that she had already been to Russia, that his suggestion was foolish in its recommendation of a vast superfluous undertaking, hung like a veil between her and the experiences she now passed through in imagining herself there' (III, 78). This imaginative process has not just familiarised her with Russia, it has also made any direct experience of that space superfluous.

However, it is not only written and oral descriptions of foreign material space which call forth spatial images in Miriam's mind. She also imagines different ways of life in tangible form, that is, as modes of behaviour in space. Reading Emerson means more to Miriam than simply 'travelling again all over Emerson's world' (IV, 419), it also provokes fantasies about his life in terms of his existence in space:

> A stately house, within the serene immensity of New England, and all his needs supplied, he was for ever free ... to read and meditate and exchange long, leisurely letters ... A slender, but not an austere figure, armchaired ... Detached, in order to be able to focus. Rising, moving across the room to a cliff of books, taking down a volume, reading, with held-in eagerness, a swiftly discovered passage, replacing the book and turning again towards the well-known chair, his place on the invisible battle-field, pausing on the way, window-lit, to gaze nowhere. (IV, 418)

Miriam pictures Emerson's philospher's life as being a life spent in contemplative space, a continual movement in intellectual, immaterial space. This imagined space is, of course, powerfully influenced by her own longing for a solitary writer's life; it is nevertheless interesting that Miriam should locate the desired similarity between herself and Emerson more in a common experience of lived space than in a sharing of ideas.

A remembered space may equally be employed in order to render a particular mood more tangible. On two occasions, Miriam recalls the peaceful summer evenings at the boarding school in Hanover. In both cases, she seeks to clarify and heighten the meaning of her present space through association with the remembered space. Miriam articulates her pleasure in the knowledge that she will be spending the summer in the entire Bailey house and not only, as before, in her room, by imagining a space from the past which had a similar atmosphere: 'Far away within the peace of the room was the evening of a hot summer day at Waldstrasse, the girls sitting about, beautiful featureless forms together forever in the blissful twilight of the cool *Saal* and sitting in its little summer house' (II, 404). In this spatial juxtaposition, the space she currently inhabits is also assigned the atmosphere which is attributed to the remembered space and, as above, expresses a spatial experience of *eternal* 'blissful twilight'.

The second example of this imagined space of the school, prompted by a man's piano-playing at the Alpenstock Hotel, reproduces the boarding school's atmosphere even more closely, and poignantly illustrates how Miriam gives an imagined space priority both over her present space and over the space of the school when she experienced it directly.

> For an instant she was back in it, passing swiftly from scene to scene of the months in Waldstrasse and coming to rest in a summer's evening: warm light upon the little high-walled garden, making space and distance with the different ways it fell on trees and grass and clustering shrubs ... making a little darkness in the summer-house where

Solomon shone in her white dress. And going back to it now it seemed as though some part of her must have lived continuously there, so that she was everywhere at once, in saal and garden and summer-house and out, beyond the enclosing walls, in the light along the spacious forbidden streets. (IV, 35)

Freed from any temporal and spatial restriction to one standpoint (and thus one perspective) in space, Miriam experiences the summer evening in her imagination as a limitless, eternal space which she can grasp in its different spatial extensions simultaneously: 'She was everywhere at once.' For her present existence, this image not only renders her feeling happiness as something tangible – 'piling joy on joy' – but also establishes a connection between the joyful space of the Hanover boarding school and the Switzerland experience which awaits her: 'this ballade was joy. Eternal Sommerabend; and now, to-morrow's Swiss sunlight' (IV, 36).

Whereas the act of imagining an actual material space was in the earlier examples based upon a similarity between the imagined space and Miriam's present activity, Richardson also offers scenes where a particular atmosphere in an imagined space is only arbitrarily related to the place Miriam currently inhabits. In the following, for example, Miriam conjures up an Indian space in her imagination while playing a Chopin nocturne:

> The notes sounded soft and clear and true into her mind, weaving and interweaving the sight of moonlit waters, the sound of summer leaves flickering in the darkness, the trailing of dusk across misty meadows, the stealing of dawn over grass, the faint vision of the Taj Mahal set in dark trees, white Indian moonlight outlining the trees and pouring over the pale façade; over all hovering haunting consoling voice, pure and clear, in a shape, passing, as the pictures faintly came and cleared and melted and changed upon a vast soft darkness, like a silver thread through everything in the world. (II, 333f.)

The atmosphere of the currently experienced space, shaped by music, is transferred on to an imagined space in order to render it tangible. In this way, the immaterial, unnameable mood which the music calls forth in Miriam may be expressed in a spatialised image and thus indirectly be named. This imagined space does not so much provide an intensification of the present atmosphere of the lived space; it rather mediates between unconscious, non-logical feelings and conscious linguistic naming. As an imagined space, it contains both modes of being; it enables the atmosphere to be semantically encoded and is, at the same time, assigned the unnameable aspects of this feeling, since the semantic encoding takes place only by means of transference.

The transference of meaning functions in similar fashion with regard to Miriam's thoughts on the essence of her own existence, her 'unchanging reality'. In her imagination, this continuous essence is intensified in spaces which are brightly lit:

> the sense of the singing of the wind; clear bright light streaming through large houses, quickening on walls and stairways and across wide rooms. Along clear avenues of light radiating from the future, pouring from behind her into the inner channels of her eyes

and ears, came unknown forms moving in a brilliance, casting a brilliance across the visible past, warming its shadows, bathing its bright levels in sparkling gold. (II, 318)

This spatialisation also allows Miriam to render an unnameable atmosphere meaningful. In giving the essence of existence a spatial expression, this imagined space refers back to Miriam's present life, since this continuous presence is what she seeks. The imagined space is a representation of perfect, joyful, lived space in its purest, ideal form. It designates 'brilliance' as one of the most important features of 'significant space', a factor which is so pertinent given that under such conditions boundaries cannot be recognised and are dissolved. In this imagined space, Miriam renders tangible her longing for the deeply satisfying sense of space which she has experienced fleetingly in certain actual spaces.

The contrasting movement of the imaginative faculties which leads directly to the writing process involves a process of summoning up and of gathering imagined and remembered spaces. Here, a space is no longer imagined with the aim of rendering a present atmosphere tangible and thus available for semantic encoding. Instead, the space may be described in its role as an imagined space (as an *image*) and, with it, the whole experience which it representatively embodies. Here, too, imagined and remembered spaces act as a mediating authority between that which is unconscious and immaterial and that which is conscious and material in so far as they are the initial inspiration for a written text.

'Imagination', as Miriam explains, 'means holding an image in your mind. When it comes up of itself, or is summoned by something. Then it is not outside but within you. And if you hold it steadily, for long enough, you could write about it forever' (IV, 613). At this point Miriam has ceased trying to establish a meaningful order for the past and present, and to encode past or present atmospheres and moods semantically. The imagination no longer serves any purpose relating to the material outside world, nor to Miriam's movement and actions, but is instead released from these aims and engaged in the production of the immaterial world of the text. In the writing process itself, Miriam summons up different potential imagined spaces in order to select one she will write about: 'One after another the scenes passed before me, each with its unique claim. Impossible to choose. Impossible without special knowledge to convey . . . the auction in the thirty-acre shot into my mind and got me to my feet' (IV, 610).

Miriam's attempts at oral narration, which become more frequent from *Oberland* onwards, anticipate this development most clearly because they take the form of an exclusively linguistic visualisation. Since, while narrating, Miriam is still anchored in a concrete marked place and not in the solitary contemplative space of a recollecting transcendence, such examples capture a spatial simultaneity between lived and imagined space. At the Brooms' home in north London, Miriam relates her experiences of Switzerland:

she felt the threads of her discourse slipping away and looked across at the row of little villas on the other side of the road, the unchanging outposts of her life in this secluded room, and found them *changed*. And turned back to the table to finish the picture of the ski-contest with the magical strangeness of the villas before her eyes within the background of the scene she was contemplating. Behind the black-clothed figure of the bird-man, poised, with out-flung arms moulded by close-clinging, soft black sleeves from shoulder to glove, for a second against the sky's brilliant blue above the glistening snow-slope, was the vision of these little houses, that once had seemed so sharp in outline, blurred to softness by the English air so that their edges seemed actually to *waver* upon it. (IV, 137f.)

The two spaces merge into one another, each leaving its mark upon the other. The image of the ski jumper in endless 'nowhere', in *eternity*, is transferred on to the present and, in a representation of boundlessness, it blurs the sharp outlines of the place she currently inhabits.

Richardson offers one atypical example for the way a recollection of past events can become attached to an actual material space with the intention of preserving it, but in which this aid to memory takes place in reality rather than in the imagination. During Miriam's visit to the newly married Amabel who has moved into a suburban house with Michael Shatov, she is shown an elaborately reproduced duplicate of her room in Flaxman's Court:

[Amabel's] call either for solicitude or for a speechlessly shared contemplation. A small strip of a room. New. Intimately familiar . . . How to respond? How cross the chasm standing between today . . . and the far past Amabel had here so charmingly recreated . . . 'It's your room,' whispered Amabel . . . 'your Flaxman room. I made it for you' . . . the lingering sound of their voices, hushed as in the past they had been hushed whenever, reaching, by their so widely different routes, awareness of a shared inward life . . . and feel, in that same moment . . . the strength of a united recognition . . . their old world, unrivalled, incorruptible, is all about them and for a moment it seems as though the little room must open and let them through into the past. (IV, 599f.)

As in the other passages the reconstruction of a lived space here, too, acts as a crypt for the events and atmospheres which were once lived in it, so that it emerges as the resilient representation image for the entire past life Amabel and Miriam shared. More than simply conjuring up the past atmosphere, this duplicate of the Flaxman room also enables the past to be continually re-experienced, independent of any particular time: 'for a moment it seems as though the little room must . . . let them through into the past'.

Ellen Frank sees an analogy between architectural buildings and literature, among other things, in the way in which both are used for the preservation and conservation of memory:

Architecture, like literature, may as a device facilitate recall of the past and as an analogue may represent or stand for memory. This leads us, quite naturally, to an idea expressed not by philosophers but by architects: architecture may conquer forgetfulness by embodying the past, by recording the past, or by stimulating recall of the past.[46]

Richardson does imply such an analogy between built sites and narrative sites, given that Amabel's recreation not only duplicates the room Miriam used to entertain her in during her stay at Flaxman's Court. Rather, in that it also duplicates Richardson's prior narrative rendition of this lived space – with special emphasis given to its most dominant spatial features such as 'sideway-falling radiance ... upon the ... green linoleum', 'back-framed mirror' and so forth (IV, 599) – this second room and its narrative depiction functions as a *mise en abyme*. A second aspect of textual self-reference is addressed by virtue of the fact that Amabel's intention – namely to preserve the past by turning it into a material space – repeats Miriam's recollection of remembered places in an effort to retain, but also to communicate, her past experiences in the form of an autobiographical narrative. For the text signals, at least implicitly, that Miriam's poetic activity will consist in creating lived space anew, namely as symbolic, immaterial space.[47]

NOTES

1 Mircea Eliade, *Le Mythe de l'éternel retour* (Paris, 1949), 29.
2 See M. Eliade, *The Sacred and the Profane* (New York, 1959), 63. Sacred space is understood as a break in the homogeneity of space and as the connecting point between different cosmic regions such as earth, heaven and underworld, and is usually viewed as a form of focal point or centre. It tends to be differentiated qualitatively from other places, although they too form a part of the ordered cosmos: 'every sacred space implies a hierophany, an irruption of the sacred that results in detaching a territory from the surrounding cosmic milieu and making it qualitatively different' (26).
3 Martin Heidegger, *Sein und Zeit*, seventh edition (Tübingen, 1953).
4 M. Heidegger, 'Bauen Wohnen Denken', *Vorträge und Aufsätze* (Pfullingen, 1954), 147f.
5 *Ibid.*, 150f.
6 *Ibid.*, 159.
7 *Ibid.*, 160.
8 C. Norberg-Schulz, *Genius Loci* (New York, 1980), 5.
9 *Ibid.*, 18.
10 *Ibid.*, 166.
11 *Ibid.*, 23.
12 *Ibid.*, 88. It should be also noted that Lotman characterises the emergence of a boundary between two spaces, that is, a crossing of the boundary, as a textual *event*.
13 *Ibid.*, 66.
14 *Ibid.*, 166.
15 *Ibid.*, 170.
16 G. Bachelard, *La Poétique de l'espace* (Paris, 1957). In his enquiry into the poetic usage of the metaphor 'house', he attempts to demonstrate 'that the house is one of the most powerful forces of integration for the thoughts, memories and dreams of humanity. The principle guiding this process of integration is the none other than that of reverie' (26).
17 K. C. Bloomer and C. W. Moore, *Body, Memory and Architecture* (New Haven, 1977), 105.
18 *Ibid.*

19 In most cases, Miriam's value system accords with that of the narrator, although there are infrequent, yet important, ironic breaks between the narrator's spatial semantic and the semantic of the experiencing character which shed light upon the significance of a semantic encoding of lived spaces for Miriam.
20 In another passage, Miriam explains her pre-logical understanding of this space to Michael Shatov: 'I never got over the suddenness of the end of the garden and always expected it to branch out into distances, every time I ran down it. I used to run up and down to make it more' (II, 124).
21 In a discussion with Michael, Miriam describes the loss of the garden as a Fall from grace, and represents memory as expressive of the longing for the innocent time which preceded that loss: 'The day we left our first home ... I ran back and kissed the warm yellow stone of the house, sobbing most bitterly and knowing my life was at an end ... I often dream I am there and wake there, and for a few minutes could draw the house ... the way the lawns went off into the mysterious parts of the garden; and I feel then as if going away were still to come, an awful thing that had never happened' (III, 124f.).
22 During one of the last evenings with her mother, Miriam's hope that her mother's health may still improve is expressed by a shift in the semantic encoding of the garden in which they are actually situated. She equates this garden with her memory of the Babington garden: 'the garden was an intensity of deep brilliance, deep bright green, and calceolarias and geraniums and lobelias, shining in a brilliant gloom. It was not a seaside garden ... it was a garden ... all gardens ... The silent motionless brilliance was a guest at their feast ... Miriam felt that a new world might be opening' (I, 482f.).
23 By way of comparison, Miriam's attempt to tell Michael of this garden ends with the realisation that 'he was no longer following with such an intentness of interest. There ought to have been more about those first years' (III, 124). Hypo, in contrast, does not even request an account of the garden experience.
24 Since it would be impossible to discuss all of the forms which Miriam's own rooms take, I will concentrate in the following analysis on her room at Mrs Bailey's house in Tansley Street. The semantic encoding of her other rooms, in Oberland, Vaud, Dimple Hill, at her sister's house, the final most privileged room, as well as its precursor in the homes of Miriam's employers before her London years, does not ever differ markedly from the semantic encoding of her room at Mrs Bailey's.
25 See Bachelard, *La poétique de l'espace*. In his semantic encoding of the house, he locates intellectual activity high up in the roof. Similarly, M. Eliade's concept of the centre in *Le Mythe de l'éternel retour*, 38, possesses similar semantic values: 'The "Centre" is therefore the realm of the sacred *par excellence*, the realm of absolute reality.'
26 Otto Friedrich Bollnow, *Mensch und Raum* (Stuttgart, 1963), 98.
27 E. E. Frank, *Literary Architecture* (Berkeley, 1979), 274.
28 M. Blanchot, *L'Espace littéraire* (Paris, 1955), 9.
29 Bollnow's stipulations are directly related to Heidegger's discussion of space.
30 Bollnow, *Mensch und Raum*, 310.
31 To an extent, the perception of space as an active subject is also transferred onto the landscape outside London, notably in Dimple Hill and in Switzerland. Miriam terms the fields surrounding the Roscorlas' farm 'her companions, left behind long ago' (IV, 433) and refers to the trees as 'the first feature; the first companions to greet her in this renewal of solitude' (IV, 456). Nevertheless, there is no communicative relationship with an intensity which approaches that of her relationship with London.
32 See also the discussion of Miriam's life in Flaxman's Court in Chapter 2, in which I

concluded that one primary reason for Miriam's and Selina's inability to live together was their sharply differing semantic encoding of space.
33 Elisabeth Lenk, *Die unbewusste Gesellschaft: Über die mimetische Grundstruktur in der Literatur und im Traum* (Munich, 1983), 33.
34 An example which runs counter to this failed communication with Hypo is to be found in Miriam's successful contact with Jean, which manifests itself, among other things, in a shared vision of the Swiss landscape: 'And our intermittent silences . . . were fragments of a shared eternity . . . whence our recovered voices boxed by the balcony's sloping roof and enclosing balustrade . . . escaping to challenge . . . the snowbound outer stillness, would simultaneously restore these beloved forgotten surroundings . . . we contemplated whatever had been summoned to stand before us' (IV, 567).
35 Other indications of different ways in which London is semantically encoded chiefly enable Miriam to sort her friends into categories, in order to establish to what extent a shared understanding might be possible. It is indeed mentioned that particular characters view London differently to Miriam, yet, since these different spatial encodings are not explored further in the text and only Miriam's semantic encoding of London is represented, the text cannot be said to stage a confrontation between diverging spatial encodings. The following conclusions – that London is, for the Quakers, 'itself bereft of meaning, regarded merely as a show-room for exhibits' (IV, 440), that London became a holiday destination for Hypo and Alma, or that it represents the space of an alien foreign country for the Irish woman, Julia, and for the Russians, Michael and his friends, the Lintoffs – primarily help Miriam to explain the differences between herself and others. She uses a divergence in spatial encodings in order to define unfamiliar characteristics which she senses in others and value systems which differ strongly from her own. This expresses not least the conviction that the way in which a subject encodes a space sheds light on fundamental features of his or her character. The reader is thus able to deduce some of Miriam's characteristics from the semantic values which she invests in lived space, as for example her preference for solitude, and Miriam in turn assesses her fellow men and women by observing the manner in which they endow their lived space with meaning.
36 Miriam could potentially be creatively active in cafés, trains and so on. However, the only transcendental experiences actually depicted are passive ones, such as reading, remembering and flights of the imagination.
37 Ice-skating is described in similar fashion: 'Gliding . . . the feeling . . . of breaking through into an eternal way of being' (IV, 87). See also the descriptions of cycling or rowing.
38 See *Daidalos: Berlin Architectural Journal*, 'Treppen', 9 (September 1983), a special edition exploring the theme of stairs.
39 The figurative significance of 'neutral territory' is discussed in Part II, although primarily as a means of encapsulating the triangle between art, eroticism and God. Miriam also experiences this feeling of being able to encounter others in neutral space without needing to sacrifice her own autonomy when cycling and during bus and train journeys. In the following description, cycling is portrayed as a form of lived, neutral space, since it is a movement which brings together divided subjects: 'If everyone were on bicycles all the time you could talk to everybody, all the time, about anything' (I, 230).
40 In *Psychologie de l'espace* (Paris, 1972), 29, A. A. Moles and E. Rohmer explain that the individual is not simply situated in extended space but also evaluates it from his or her location in space: 'Space . . . is a field of values, a transposition of the imaginary on to

the real more than the real on to the imaginary. Fundamentally, axiomatically, that which is near is more important than that which is distant, be it an object, a phenomenon or a being.' This principle of the near–far relation in physical, lived space is inverted in the case of imagined spaces. There, too, nearness is more important than distance, but that which Miriam perceives as near may at times be physically, topologically and temporally distant.

41 Roland Barthes, *Elements de sémiologie* (Paris, 1965).
42 Attention is also drawn to other important events by reference to an imagined space; as, for example, the confirmation day which is captured in the memory of a forbidden walk, I, 149.
43 See also IV, 585, for a further comparison between Sally's house and Dimple Hill and IV, 595, for a comparison between Sally's garden and Vaud. Each comparison articulates Miriam's rejection of her family's lived space.
44 G. Genette, *Figures II* (Paris, 1969), 43f.
45 *All* reading experiences become associated with an imagined space. See the description of Miriam reading *Adèle* (I, 228). While reading a poem about a forest, Miriam recalls a forest from her childhood (I, 68f.); while reading Schiller's 'Spaziergang' she visualises this space (I, 100) and even regards it as a heightening of her present space, since she imagines the existence of a harmonious unity between herself, Frl. Pfaff and Minna. See also Michel Butor, *Répertoire II Etudes et Conferences 1959–1963* (Paris, 1964), 43. In his essay on space in the novel, he describes a similar phenomenon: 'When I read the description of a room in a novel, the furniture which is before my eyes, but which I am not looking at, grows more and more distant in the face of that which is emerging and transpiring from the signs inscribed on the page. This "volume", as it is called, which I hold in my hand, liberates, beneath my gaze, evocations which impose themselves, which haunt the place which I inhabit, and disorientate me.'
46 Frank, *Literary Architecture*, 246.
47 The reader does not know exactly what Miriam is going to write. One further anticipatory reference is provided by Amabel's duplication in the material world of the Flaxman room which she shared with Miriam, which acts as a contrast to Miriam's new creation which will only be achieved in the form of a poetic reinvention in immaterial space. Miriam assigns her response to the newly created room the same meaning as she does her response to Amabel's baby. She thus sets up an implicit analogy between Amabel's spatial duplicate and material procreation and her own symbolic procreation, namely that of her poeticised imagined and remembered spaces which are the precursors of her writing. Miriam views all three – Amabel's spatial duplicate, her baby and her own linguistic reproduction of her shared life with Amabel, which usually occurs by means of descriptions of spaces which they experienced together such as the Sunday morning in her room – as expressions of the 'inexpressible quality of our friendship' (IV, 658). Grace Broom and her house acquire a similar function. During Miriam's final stay there on the way to Dimple Hill, she praises Grace for the 'treasure-house of Grace's faithful memory', and describes her house as a place 'in the stateliest of whose upper rooms the whole of one's life as known to oneself, was stored up' (IV, 406).

PART II
METAPHORICAL SPACES

CHAPTER FIVE

WORLD-MAKING AS A COGNITIVE PROCESS

Concerning the possibility of understanding another individual and of communicating this in language, Miriam says of her friend Eleonor Dear:

> It is tempting to tell the story. A perfect recognizable story of a scheming unscrupulous woman; making one feel virtuous and superior; but only if one simply outlined the facts, leaving out all the inside things . . . Speech is technical. Every word. In telling things, technical terms must be used; which never quite apply. To call Eleonor an adventuress does not describe her. You can only describe her by the original contents of her mind. Her own images; what she sees and thinks. (III, 285)

This passage may be read as a legitimation of Richardson's own mode of representation. For her, also, stories cannot and ought not to simply outline the facts, the linearly narrated sequences in Miriam's life, because this would fail to capture what is unique about her. Rather, her protagonist can be described only by her spatial perceptions, and by the way she reflects upon past events, shaping phenomenological experiences into images which possess a personal significance – 'her own images'.

In Part I, I explored Miriam's phenomenological perception of space. I would now like to apply her notion of successful story-telling to the way in which in *Pilgrimage* her identity comes to be represented by her 'own images', as these result from vision and creative thought. Nelson Goodman argues that perception and understanding can be viewed as a meaningful process of producing (creating) meta-worlds:

> if worlds are as much made as found, so also knowing is as much remaking as reporting. All the processes of world-making I have discussed enter into knowing. Perceiving motion . . . often consists in producing it . . . Recognizing patterns is very much a matter of inventing and imposing them. Comprehension and creation go on together.[1]

Applying this to *Pilgrimage*, one could say that Richardson creates a narrative meta-world, which is devoted to examining how her protagonist uses world-making in order to form her own identity and to understand the world around her and her position within it. For in the manner suggested by Goodman, Richardson focuses upon the creative aspects of this learning process, 'the creative power of understanding'. Furthermore, Miriam is described in her 'own images', in terms of her observations and reflections upon the world which she inhabits; she learns who she is through these images. And if in Chapter 4, I sought to trace Miriam's personality by looking at how she endows her lived space with meaning, at stake now is the way in which she, like any reader, uses her method of world-making in order to learn about her personality. Miriam herself explains: 'How not to be struck by the inside pattern of life? It is so obvious that everything is arranged. Whether by God or some deep wisdom in oneself does not matter. There is something that does not alter . . . The *way* you contemplate is your temperament' (III, 282). Miriam's recognition of her own identity as a means of creating it thus involves two aspects: firstly, she reinvents the lived world and creates out of it her own personal world and, secondly, she recognises the underlying principle which governs her world-making. This principle, *the way she contemplates*, is linked also to the discovery of an 'inside pattern of life', in the sense that her recognition (or understanding) serves to validate a pattern of expectation, the 'deep wisdom within'. Put another way, the correlation which Miriam identifies between her way of seeing and her temperament, both of which inform her cognition and understanding of the outside world, also suggests that perception is determined by certain pre-existent ideas.

Jane Miller discusses Miriam's polemical thoughts on men and women, active and contemplative life, time and false fiction by examining how these claims separate all experiences, characters and ideas into a sequence of dichotomies. In so far as Miriam continually qualifies and revises her judgments, such that her polemic is often self-contradictory, suggested tentatively or withdrawn with a gesture of self-dismissal, Miriam's claims represent

> one of a number of strategies for locating herself during a tortuous journey towards the stability which might enable her to write the kind of novel [Richardson] wrote herself . . . her extreme points of view . . . suggest the movement of her mental life and the interplay of reflection with mood and sensation.[2]

To describe Miriam's cognitive strategy it is useful to draw upon Goodman's definition of world-making, of which he explains: 'It always starts from worlds already on hand; the making is a remaking . . . the process involved in building a world out of others.'[3] For his concept of world-making, a spatialisation of the concept of cognition, also helps to clarify the central questions around which *Pilgrimage* revolves – namely in what sense can one speak of the existence of multiple worlds and how is world-making linked with understanding and knowledge? According to him, this strategy involves a process of moulding disparate experiences into various ordered units of meaning or 'worlds'. Three of the criteria he develops in his discussion of world-making are particularly applicable to *Pilgrimage*:

Firstly, his criterion of 'composition and decomposition' refers to the way an entity as a complete system for a narrative text – this refers to the entire, experienced outside world – is divided into different parts even while individual parts are separated from one other and then reassembled into a new configuration. Miriam takes all of her experiences and impressions of her surroundings and reorganises them by assigning them to particular 'worlds' according to the differences and similarities which she has established between them. Furthermore, these worlds tend to have nothing, or little, in common with one another nor with Miriam herself. Miriam's identification, often only partial, with a particular 'world' thus occurs in relation to the contents which she has assigned to it.

Secondly, the criterion of 'weighting' refers to the manner in which certain features may be important in one 'world', yet irrelevant in another. One example of this weighting in *Pilgrimage* is that Miriam usually links characters and ideas to one 'world' but, when exposed to a second 'world', these figures lose their significance and their presence appears irrelevant or disruptive. Such weighting may also be witnessed during the phase of Miriam's world-making in which she moderates her judgments and discovers attributes of one world in its supposed opposite. Thus, for example, she qualifies her claim that men lack any consciousness, realising instead that they are simply unaware of it: '[Mr Orly] was unconscious of his consciousness' (IV, 132).

Thirdly, the criterion of 'deletion and supplementation' refers to the way in which those elements of the entire world which do not fit into the system are rejected whenever a new world is created, a strategy which applies also to Miriam's tendency to augment supplementary attributes. In the course of world-making, characters and ideas are reduced to particular primary features; intellectual positions and arguments, along with the traits of the characters' representing these ideas, are simplified, such that they can be appropriated for the world-making process, by being sorted into single worlds and made to stand in for these. Goodman states that 'even within what we do perceive and remember we dismiss as illusory or negligible what cannot be filled into the architecture of the world we are building'.[4]

World-making thus involves a process of separating and combining, in which given values are emphasised, deleted, supplemented, extended or distorted. Goodman elaborates: '[it] begins with one version and ends with another'.[5] This selection process is not, however, random but is governed by specific ideas and patterns of expectation. One of the reasons I suggest applying Goodman's categories to Richardson's as well as to her heroine's world-making, is my own claim that *Pilgrimage* does indeed possess an organising system so that one does the text an injustice if one reads it as a random succession of Miriam's impressions and feelings. The text is not a mere accumulation of Miriam's immediate impressions; rather it depicts 'her own images' and expresses her mode of arranging experience and of understanding it by organising it. From the outset, her perceptions are characterised by a pattern of expectation; there are specific criteria according to which Miriam judges whether to admit a particular view into her own world or reject it. This pattern changes as the novel develops, becoming more subtle and thus more precise.

Miriam's construction of various opposing worlds which are either subsumed into a third world that contains both, or are simultaneously retained as different worlds, correlates with Goodman's recognition that there are multiple worlds which must be preserved:

> There are as many different worlds as there are such mutually exclusive truths ... to demand full and sole reducibility to physics or any other version is to forgo nearly all other versions ... unity is to be sought not in an ambivalent or neutral *something* beneath these versions, but in an overall organization embracing them.[6]

Indeed, one of the seminal claims Miriam makes in *Pilgrimage* is that different worlds ought not to be reduced to values which must be made compatible, but should rather be grasped side by side in their incompatibility. Ultimately Miriam's world-making is an attempt to realise such a vision of simultaneity.[7] At the same time, however, Goodman emphasises that world-making is possible only as the outcome of a decision and a prioritisation: 'a willingness to welcome all worlds builds none'.[8] This claim also holds true for Miriam's cognitive strategy: firstly, because despite her argument for impartiality, she expresses her complete aversion to certain worlds right from the beginning (as, for example, the world of housewives in the upper-middle-class suburbs) and, secondly, because although her movement in the immaterial space of her own artistic production permits a simultaneous preservation of different worlds, it also involves a firm commitment to one particular world, namely that of writing.

The following excerpt from Richardson's autobiographical essay implicitly casts the formation of identity in terms of a world-making process:

> During these London years I explored the world lying outside the enclosures of social life, and found it to be a kind of archipelago. Making contact with the various islands, with writers, with all the religious groups ... with the political groups ... with the worlds of Science and Philosophy, I found all these islands to be the habitations of fascinating secret societies, to each of which in turn I wished to belong and yet was held back, returning to solitude and to nowhere, where alone I could be everywhere at once, hearing all the voices in chorus.[9]

In Chapter 1, I was concerned only with the spatial division of London. At stake in this chapter is the way Miriam's pilgrimage through diverse places involves, in the first stage, a process of dismantling and reordering the entire lived, outside world, whereby it is the 'world of social life' which plays a key role in the fundamental establishment of polarities. This outside world is sub-divided into different worlds ('political groups', 'religious groups', 'Science' and 'Philosophy'), whereby Miriam's engagement with their contents (people and thoughts) enables her to clarify the contents of her own world.[10] This first stage may also be interpreted as a psychological and metaphorical action space, in which the outside world functions as the scene, which allows her to compare worlds so as to establish differences and similarities between them.

The second stage, in turn, involves withdrawal into her own solitude, her own world, in which she has the unique opportunity to be simultaneously nowhere (not belonging entirely to any single world) and everywhere, 'hearing all the voices in chorus'. This psycho-metaphorical contemplative space enables her to retain a multiplicity of worlds – worlds which are incompatible in the material world.

Furthermore, it is in this privileged solitary world that she can create an overall organising structure of the kind which Goodman demands, namely that of the immaterial world of art.

A crucial aspect of Miriam's search for identity is precisely the manner in which she perceives herself, as well as all other characters, as a wholly unique world. When Miss Haddie calls her an 'independent young woman', she chooses to rephrase the comment and states: 'I'm something new – a kind of different world' (I, 260). As this statement suggests, the primary opposition within Miriam's formation of her identity is between Miriam, who is characterised as 'her own world', and the 'outside world'. Miriam is, however, herself further divided between a conscious, reflective subject and a subject of the unconscious, the 'world within'. Furthermore, the concept 'world' is at times used to refer in a very general way to the outside world as that which is other, as the accepted norm from which she deviates. This general concept of the world is even used idiomatically, with 'world' being posited as an abstract point of reference for an utterance or as an abstract observer, for example, 'for all the world', 'announcement to the whole world'.[11] As part of her search for a psychological orientation, Miriam's world-making involves a general attempt to determine to what extent and under which conditions she is part of the outside world and is thus 'in' it. The opposite extreme of this inclusion in the outside world is her withdrawal 'back into her own world' as well as her ecstatic, liminal experiences 'outside' or 'beyond the world'.

Furthermore, the outside world is divided into sub-groups which are also viewed as worlds, namely as 'new worlds'. In contrast to the notion of the entire 'world outside', they represent quite specific values and traits, encompassing one individual or group or representing particular ideas which Miriam is actively exploring. Here, Miriam seeks also to determine with which worlds she can or cannot identify and what conditions and circumstances might enable her to belong to a particular world. However, since she invariably breaks off contact with a world once she has experienced the sense of belonging there, the important question is rather that of recognising those psychological, ethic or aesthetic elements represented by the different worlds, which she wishes to incorporate into her own. For Miriam compiles her own world by finding aspects in one of the worlds, which she is in the process of exploring, which correspond to her own experiences. The knowledge that this value exists in a 'world' beyond her self then enables her to notice it and name it. As the novel progresses, she views herself increasingly as a meeting-point for different worlds. If her relation to the general outside world may be said to consist in a continual process of distancing and separating herself from it, then what she seeks in the particular worlds is the potential for reciprocation, for a correlation between her own world and the foreign worlds:

> 'It's finding the *same* world in another person that moves you to your roots. The same world in two people . . . It makes you feel that you exist and can *go on*. Your sense of the world and of the astonishingness of there being anything anywhere, let alone what there seems to be turning out to be, is confirmed when you find the same world and

the same accepted astonishment in someone else . . .' 'Wherever two or three are gathered together' . . . there is something that is themselves and more than themselves. (IV, 333)

The discovery of mutual worlds confirms and encourages Miriam's recognition of the make-up of her own world. At the same time, this discovery forms the only possible basis for interpersonal communication. Miriam realises:

> most people brought their worlds with them, their opinions and the set of things they believed in; forcing in the end direct questions and disagreements. And most people were ready to answer questions, showing by their angry defence of their opinions that they were aware, and afraid, of other ways of looking at things. (III, 241)[12]

Since every instance of interaction is viewed as a relationship between two worlds, interaction must mean that two separate subjects either share one world or one way of seeing, that they agree that there may be multiple worlds, or indeed that they share the conviction that there are no mutual worlds, which is termed a 'world apart'. Communication is perceived as taking place if one recognises oneself in the other and if the other in turn also accepts such an encounter with alterity.

Miriam's psycho-topological *pilgrimage* begins with the loss of the only world which she has so far known – her home: 'a world which would go on without her, taking no heed. There would still be blissful days. But she would not be in them' (I, 16). This marks the beginning of her search to find the 'real' and the 'same' in another world and yet, initially, this search emerges as a negative discovery of the absence of precisely these features. At first, then, it is possible to ascertain only what the 'real' implicitly means to Miriam, in its conspicuous absence from the worlds available to her given that she associates her presence there with 'role' and 'pretence', concepts which are placed in opposition to the 'real'.

In Volume One (*Pointed Roofs*, *Backwater* and *Honeycomb*), the spaces with the greatest semantic significance in the outside world are the middle-class world and the world of foreign countries. The world of financially independent women, as opposed to married women, is polarised within these two worlds. The first is represented by Miriam's family, which stands for the entire middle-class population of the London suburbs and comes to stand for bourgeois marriage. Although suburban married life involves being free from the drudgery of work, it is the world which Miriam least favours, since it signifies an intellectual as well as an aesthetic void: 'In the suburbs people were everything and there was nothing in them. They did not understand anything; but going on. They were helpless and without thoughts . . . They did not even have busts of Beethoven' (I, 468).

Contrasting worlds include north London: 'shut up from grown-up things' (I, 195), 'hard, strong, sneering, money-making' (I, 322). Miriam associates it with independent money-making but also with stagnation, since she would not be free to structure her future according to her needs: 'North London meant twenty pounds a year and the need for resignation and determination every day' (I, 322). The Newlands world of the Corrie family, who live in the countryside, presents itself at the other extreme. Admittedly, this world is likewise perceived as a place of stagnation ('prison') and as an intellectual void, because its inhabitants are also distracted from their own selves by trivialities.[13] Nevertheless, it has an undeniable appeal: 'she ... envied the ease and despised the ignorance' (I, 382). Beyond the attraction of luxury, she also associates Newlands with an unqualified aesthetic enjoyment of everyday life: 'At Newlands people might be dead; the women in bright hard deaths of cold, cruel deceitfulness, the men tiny insects of selfishness, but there were things that made up for everything, full and satisfying' (I, 468). Having weighed up the potential areas of identification with each world against those aspects which conflict irreconcilably with her own sense of self, Miriam resolves not to adopt any of these middle-class worlds as her own. This decision marks the end of Volume One.

The world of foreign countries, embodied by the girls' boarding school in Hanover as well as by foreign friends, serves primarily to reveal to Miriam the components which make up Englishness, helping her establish to what extent she is part of this and to what degree she rejects conventional English values. Miriam's stay in Germany is thus marked by her fascination with the culturally unfamiliar which she at times even favours. This preference is reflected in Miriam's reasons for being drawn initially towards the German schoolgirls and for rejecting the English schoolgirls. It is highlighted most dramatically when Miriam describes the difference between the German girls' manner of performing music and that of the English girls. In stark contrast to 'English self-consciousness ... they did not think only about the music, they thought about themselves too' (I, 45), the German style of performance appears to offer an opportunity to overcome this awkwardness and to be absorbed momentarily into the music. Miriam attempts to imitate this: 'She had almost forgotten her wretched self, almost heard the music ... Grave and happy she sat with unseeing eyes, listening for the first tune' (I, 56). By pitting England against Germany, Miriam is able to negotiate one of the seminal dichotomies subtending *Pilgrimage*, namely that between self-consciousness (as the inability to move beyond the material world) and self-forgetfulness (as transcendence – whether music-inspired, contemplative or creative – leading to the immaterial world).

At the same time, however, her stay in Germany increasingly reinforces her Englishness, whether this is exemplified by her response to the school system, which is indifferent to the girls' intellectual development, to the role of the German housewife or with regard to German religious sentimentality. Ultimately she finds herself unable to identify with this cultural space so that, when she is invited to stay in Germany for good, Miriam responds in the following way: 'She could not pretend long enough. Everything would be at an end long before there was any chance of her turning in a happy German woman' (I, 167). The idea of staying in Germany remains a fantasy, yet Miriam does retain individual attributes which are peculiar to German space, such as freedom from inhibition, and incorporates them into her world. In the course of the novel, Miriam looks back upon these with affection. Ultimately, it is by comparing the two national spaces that Miriam becomes aware of her capacity to identify with that which is English, however limited that identification may be. 'All the English girls were there . . . They shone. They were beautiful. She wanted to cry aloud. She was English and free. She had nothing to do with this German school' (I, 180).

Miriam's foreign friends in England also highlight certain English features due to their cultural difference; however more than anything they expose the narrow boundaries which are prescribed by the English norm. During a dance party at her family home, the presence of Max, a German Jew, compels Miriam to regard the familiar world in a new and sobering light: 'How battered and ordinary everyone had looked, frail and sick, stamped with a pallor of sickness' (I, 221). Their dancing together is viewed as a transgression against the norm and it is this which opens Miriam's eyes to the unbearable small-mindedness and emptiness of her family's bourgeois world, as well as revealing the impossibility of marriage to her friend Ted, something which she associates with it. The character Julia, an Irish woman, plays a similar role, in that she causes Miriam to recognise the narrowness of middle-class norms. Julia stands metonymically for Dublin (I, 275) and is also endowed with spatial attributes: 'Julia was a deep, deep nook, full of thorns' (I, 340). Her response to Miriam's news of her sister's engagement exposes the lie which is concealed in Miriam's joyful anticipation: 'Julia's eyes . . . seeming to say that nothing was really touched or changed' (I, 342). Again, on the day of the farewell party when Miriam feels an uncertain, sentimental sense of belonging to the north London world, Julia embodies that which lies beyond the north London world and thus exposes its ugliness and superficiality: 'far away, Julia was alone with life and death. She made two worlds plain, the scornful world of the girls and her own shadow-filled life' (I, 345).

A second dichotomy structuring *Pilgrimage* involves the oppositions between independent work and marriage, and it serves primarily to negotiate the difference between the masculine and feminine world as well as the difference between her own world (solitude) and life in the outside world. Negotiating this difference varies according to Miriam's living circumstances, but it is upheld in all worlds and not confined to one single world. It is particularly significant that Miriam not only feels estranged from the middle-class world as well as from the world of foreign countries, but also feels alienated by the modes of behaviour which these two worlds permit. In these worlds, she associates the work she is able to perform there to the notions of femininity prevalent there and the social behaviour expected there with 'pretence', so that they come to form the antithesis to solitude and worldly abstinence.

Travelling to Germany where she is to work as a teacher, Miriam considers that what awaits her is 'a false position ahead and, after a short space, disaster' (I, 31). Later, she views her social role as a teacher as an absolute sham: 'practising deception' (I, 72), 'she begins to perceive . . . a complete failure of her role of English teacher . . . cheating pure and simple' (I, 91). Since Miriam views her failure primarily as a deception of her employer, her relief at being offered the opportunity to escape this role (I, 127) may also be read as self-deception, even if her second decision to leave the boarding school divests her of her social role: 'She was nothing again' (I, 183). This pattern repeats itself in Miriam's perception of her position as governess in Newlands, as well as in her dissatisfaction with that role. There, she sees her work as a mistake (I, 352), as a lie (I, 359) and as tantamount to deceiving the Corries (I, 382).

Equally, Miriam views the world of marriage, with its conventional expectations of femininity, as a deception and as an insufficient role. From the beginning, she distances herself from the world of women, viewing herself as belonging there only when she engages in pretence: 'those hateful women's smiles ... she loathed women ... Pater knew how hateful all the world of women were and despised them. He never included her with them; or only sometimes when she pretended' (I, 21). Her primary objection to this world and her reason for rejecting it is that women conceal their true selves deceitfully: ' "I hate women ...," she retorted ... feeling all the contrivances of toilet and coiffure fall in meaningless horrible detail ... "Ragbags, bundles of pretence" ' (I, 436). At the same time, she regards feminine behaviour as a response to men's wishes: 'But men like actresses. They liked being fooled' (I, 400). Miriam's own defiance of conventional feminine behaviour, in gestures such as smoking in public at an evening gathering, gives her a degree of freedom to shape her own identity, although this behaviour is also felt to be a form of role-play: ' "I suppose I'm a new woman – I've said I am now, anyhow" ... [she wondered] how she would reconcile the role with her work as a children's governess. "I'm not in their crowd, anyhow" ' (I, 436). She rejects flirting and indeed all attention-seeking forms of conversation as fraudulent strategies. Miriam has similar doubts about the merits of marriage, namely that it demands continual pretence and self-concealment and that it conflicts directly with a developing identity and with inner reflection, although she is aware that it would free her from solitude and work:

> Miriam caught at a vision of the well-appointed man ... no more need to make money: a stylish, contented, devoted sort of man, who knew nothing about one. It would be a fraud, unfair to him ... so easy to pretend to admire him ... well, there it was ... an offer of freedom... that was admirable ... But there was something wrong somewhere. (I, 451)

Miriam attempts to make a decision by directly opposing marriage to solitude. During a visit at home, which is occasioned by the weddings of two of her sisters, she pursues the following train of thought. Firstly, she considers that independent life is 'free' and 'real' yet 'troubled': 'Impossible to be real unless you were quite free ... But money ...' (I, 459). Secondly, she encodes marriage as a site of security: '*somewhere* then always to be ... a presence, understanding' (I, 460), but also – as in her parents' marriage – rooted in profound ignorance of the other: 'Don't mother ... he can't understand ... Silence, darkness and silence' (I, 460). Miriam presents nature, which may only be experienced in solitude, as a possible alternative: 'It was enough ... and things happened as well' (I, 459). In this comparison, both opposing choices are shown to possess appealing as well as unacceptable attributes. Nevertheless, it becomes apparent that Miriam's decision is informed by the contrast between certain fundamental values, that is, the reality of freedom versus the pretence of marriage. Since both the world of marriage and that of work as a teacher are chiefly characterised by continual role-play and would therefore alienate her from the 'real' rather than bringing her any closer to it, Miriam ultimately decides to reject them both.

In the course of reaching a decision, Miriam oscillates between extremes and weighs them up against one another. Like the world of Germany, which, though it possessed an appeal, Miriam felt it necessary to resist, the world of women does have a certain charm and she also experiences a brief sense of belonging in the 'worldly world Newlands' (I, 435) and in the harsh, professional world of north London (I, 235). This mixture of attraction and aversion highlights another feature of Miriam's world-making, since it gives voice to her sense of her own identity as being situated *between* different worlds. Significantly, in the course of her pilgrimage, this intermediate position shifts in emphasis – away from a general rejection of all worlds towards the recognition of her own self as a meeting-point of different worlds; most notably in her oscillation between the masculine and the feminine world, and between solitude (abstinence from the material world) and bondage to the material world.

Expressing her awkward position between the masculine and the feminine world, as well as her reluctance to belong in either, Miriam states at the beginning of *Pointed Roofs*: 'I don't like men and I loathe women' (I, 31). She distances herself most emphatically from the role of housewife, both in Germany and England, and from women's 'pretence', which they use to attract the attention of their potential or present husbands. Furthermore, she attempts to adopt the values of the world of men, even while she is forced to acknowledge that this behaviour excludes her from both worlds: 'Now I've offended the men and the women too' (I, 380). As she begins to compare the two worlds, so too she begins to revise her judgments. In Mrs Kronen, a representative of the world of women, she recognises not only the attribute of pretence but also a secret, inner resolve: 'It was a world she lived in that made her able to carry off these things without being disturbed by them, a rosy secret world in which she lived secure. A richness at the heart of things . . . She possessed it. At any rate she wanted to suggest that she did' (I, 402).

Similarly, although women's empty-headedness – 'women have no thoughts' (I, 439) – is one of her main reasons for rejecting their world, Miriam also views this flaw as providing a connection with the divine: 'Mrs Corrie . . . Dead in ignorance and living bravely on . . . Nearly all women like that, living in a gloom where there were no thoughts . . . no room for ideas . . . She was a good woman; a God woman . . . Women were of God in some way' (I, 404). Dividing the world into a masculine and a feminine realm, in fact serves two different purposes. Miriam uses this difference in order to discuss what she considers to be an adequate linguistic representation of existential truths, even while her distinction between the two sexes allows her to convince herself that she occupies a position between these two worlds, her identity transcending both.

According to Miriam, men have an advantage over women with regard to their abstract, self-reflexive knowledge: 'Men knew there were gardens everywhere, not always visible. Women did not seem to know' (I, 405). The concomitant disadvantage of possessing a conscious language is, in her view, men's insistence upon one single standpoint, their inability to see things from many angles and to concede that truth is relative: 'Men always thinking something, only one thing at a time and unless that is agreed to they murder' (I, 438). Miriam invests the traditional masculine objection that women are intellectually inconsistent – 'woman says one thing one minute and another the next' (I, 423) – with new meaning, presenting it as a desirable mode of expression: 'two sides to every question ... a million sides ... no questions, only sides ... always changing' (I, 438). The strategy which men use in discussions is, she argues, too concerned with details: 'you can't look at anything from the point of view of life as whole ... small clever things ... immediate near causes that appear to explain, and explained nothing!'. Miriam seeks instead to explain things in their entirety: 'You think – in propositions ... Of course you can go back, and round and up and everywhere. Things as a whole' (I, 443). In other words, her privileged mode of expression is a combination of masculine knowledge and feminine inconsistency.

The difference between masculine and feminine speech Miriam proposes of course relies also on an opposition between sequential, primarily temporal narration and associative, primarily spatial narration in which, as Miriam says, *you can go back and round and up*. Miriam's oscillation between the masculine and feminine worlds causes her to view her own androgyny at first in negative terms – 'I'm a sort of horrid man' (I, 404) – but later to see it as a positive balance between independent persuasive powers and intuitive understanding: 'that strange hard feeling that was always twining between her and the things people wanted her to do and to be. Manhood with something behind it that understood' (I, 471).

In her radical vacillation between solitude and sociability, Miriam investigates the extent to which she is able to reconcile her own sense of self with society's demand for role-play. In an imaginary conversation with her sister Eve, she replies to her demand that she 'be like other people' with the remark: 'But you can't keep it up' (I, 165). Initially, then, her identity consists of a simple desire to be other, to be different: 'Miriam always likes to be different ... I *am* unsociable' (I, 31). Her world-making at this stage involves the following division: active involvement in the world, in addition to its appealing promise of security, comes to be associated with superficial, distracting talk and with continual, deadening motion: 'all the fuss and noise people made all day was a pretence' (I, 254), 'everything every one did ... a distraction from astonishment' (I, 458), 'to *be* a fair mask ... knowing that everything was kept out ... Taking each fair mask was a fine grown-up game ... They were not real' (I, 391). Solitude, on the other hand, is regarded as a 'strange independent joy' (I, 317), 'something real, something cool and true and unchanging' (I, 394), as a process of focusing upon and becoming aware of her own aliveness ('being alive', I, 458).[14]

This distinction between an involvement in the world and solitude allows Miriam to negotiate the value that an eternal, continual essence – the permanence of being which connects us with the real and is present above all in silence and solitude – takes on for her in contrast to constant movement, transformative becoming, which is encapsulated by talk (the 'noise of the world') and action. Here, too, traces can be found of the opposition between a primarily temporal process of becoming – focused upon movement and transformation – and a primarily spatial, continual essence which is always itself and always returning to itself; the same polarity played through in the opposition between masculinity and femininity. Thus, Miriam sees herself as faced with the following dilemma in the creation of her world: 'What was life? Either playing a part all the time in order to be amongst people in the people, or standing alone with the strange true real feeling – alone with a sort of edge of reality on everything' (I, 320). Accordingly, she rejects marriage – 'a glad world where there was no need to be alone in order to be happy' (I, 319) – and affiliation to a worldly space for the same reasons, namely that they are a distraction from the real. For a while, she does indeed toy with the idea of religious asceticism, but only to reject both the religious and the worldly life: 'There was something too sad about worldliness and too difficult about goodness' (I, 387). It is not until her withdrawal into solitude becomes the site for the first signs of creative activity that it is associated with the real. Miriam's first attempts at painting thus offer her 'an experience ... far in away from any "glad mask", a thing belonging to that strange inner life and independent of everybody' (I, 431).

Nevertheless, this opposition between solitude and society remains unresolved at the end of Volume One. At times, Miriam decides in favour of worldly attractions and at times she tends towards solitude, although she does associate the worldly with the absence of a conscious existence in space:

> That was feminine worldliness, pretending to be interested so that pleasant things might go on. Masculine worldliness was refusing to be interested so that it might go on doing things. Feminine worldliness then meant perpetual ... pretence at the door of a hidden garden ... Masculine worldliness meant never being really there; always talking about things that had happened or making plans for things that might happen ... Nobody was ever quite there, realizing. (I, 388)

By the end of Volume One, Miriam's world-making – her technique of dividing up, differentiating and reorganising the outside world – has helped her recognise a mode of existence which unites intuition (feminine) with reflection (masculine).

In Volume Two the central opposition between solitude and social allegiance is preserved, although Miriam's move to London introduces a plethora of new worlds, which in itself shifts the emphasis towards Miriam's relationship with her surroundings. The world of the 'suburbian middle class' remains the site of marriage, embodied by her married sisters and by Grace Broom who lives in north London. Likewise, the world of independent work is still represented, in the form of Miriam's position as a dental assistant, whereby her employers also stand for the middle classes, some of the patients act as representatives of the upper classes and, most importantly, her relationship with Hancock ensures that marriage continues to remain a possibility. Finally, the world of the foreign is also retained, embodied by her foreign acquaintances. There are new worlds – different groups of people which she has never encountered before and regards as 'secret societies' (II, 117): the world of intellectual socialists, scientists and artists, metonymically represented by her school friend Alma and her husband, the writer Hypo Wilson; the world of independent women, embodied by the working women Mag and Jan and the adventuress Eleonor Dear, as well as numerous, less differentiated worlds which give London special priority over all other places and which can, broadly, be said to converge in Mrs Bailey's boarding house: 'London life was sacred and secret, away from everything else in the world' (II, 89).

In contrast to her perception of her home and work in the first volume, Miriam does not associate London, her room at Mrs Bailey's nor her work as the Wimpole Street practice with role-play and pretence. As a result, she regards the basis of her relationship to the outside world differently. Solitude is still encoded semantically as the site of new insights which facilitates contact with the 'secret', the 'sacred' and the 'real'. Similarly, it continues to be understood in opposition to an outside world which is a site of distraction from one's own self and of self-deception, and is associated with feelings of loneliness when others are present and with a lack of understanding and mutual exchange. At the same time, however, Miriam abandons the static 'either–or' stance which she assumed in the earlier volume and recognises that the insights which are possible only in solitude cannot be gained before a dynamic interplay has taken place between the subject and the outside world. There are two new influences in Miriam's life which make her aware that this is the case. Firstly, her London life makes her feel released from the need to conceal herself in role-play, enabling her to recognise further aspects of her own self and, furthermore, she now accepts the entire London world as valuable for the development of her own world, although she does continue to discover certain discrepancies between the two. She states: 'I am back now where I was before I began trying to do things like other people ... none of these things can touch me here' (II, 13). In the context of the comprehensive metaphor of 'identity as world', Miriam thus voices a sense that she has formed a part of the space of her identity, a space which she is convinced corresponds to her own self and which she can depend upon.

The knowledge that she can always return to this space where her identity is located enables her to stop viewing the outside world in terms of totalising belonging. She no longer rejects it completely as a place of pretence as soon as she notices certain unacceptable features. Since she is no longer searching for perfect symmetry with her own world, the different worlds may now be partially accepted and partially rejected. An interplay develops between the various worlds, according to which they are examined side by side and then separated once again, and in which they form areas of convergence with, or divergence from, Miriam's sense of self. Miriam does not consider renouncing the material world utterly; instead she is concerned with the joys and dangers of social affiliation and the way in which commitment to a group does not necessarily involve sacrificing her solitude, but can co-exist with her own world. She no longer regards the constant change and movement in the outside world as a threat to her unchanging essence, but as something without which she could not appreciate that essence and as a vital factor in the development of her identity. Just as the opposition set up between the concepts of essence (sameness) and becoming (transformation) is not confined to one world, so the opposition between masculine and feminine continues to play itself out in different semantic worlds.

In the second volume (*Tunnel, Interim*), allowing characters to represent world metonymically is employed with greater frequency. As she realises that 'people were arranged in groups' (II, 316) Miriam also recognises that contact with one character signifies contact with an entire world, so that judging one allows one to judge the other as well. In this respect, Miriam's unique relationship with each single character is not spatial only in the sense that both individuals are regarded as worlds or territories but also in the sense that each relationship brings Miriam into contact with the space which that particular character represents.

Although Miriam resolves to keep 'free of all groups' (II, 20) at the beginning of Volume Two, her life in London in fact consists wholly in forming, and communicating with, various groups (worlds), to the extent that her friend Mag states quite the opposite at the end of the volume: 'You have so many sets of people' (II, 424). Miriam's contact with others is in no way a simple process of recognising the same in the other, but much more a process of recognising aspects of herself through differentiation from the other. This is exemplified most clearly by Miriam's involvement with her employer Hancock. Since he represents two, in her view, separate worlds – the world of the Wimpole Street dental practice and of independent work and the world of the 'professional Englishman' (II, 200) which is also her family's world that she has left behind – her relationship with him initiates a comparison between the two worlds.

The quality of her relationship with her employer Hancock which Miriam treasures most is a kind of sympathetic honesty – 'the wonder of the Wimpole Street life . . . instead of an employer there had been a sensitive isolated man . . . He had not hesitated to seek sympathy' (II, 205) – and Hancock looks upon their relationship as being 'real and changeless and independent' (II, 207). Nevertheless, she continues to associate his other side, the social world of the professional class, with 'pretence' (II, 191). For her, it represents a closed world from which she is excluded: 'They sat inside a little fortress, letting in only certain people' (II, 196). She was an upstart and an alien' (II, 192). Despite having once been a member of this world (II, 196), she has not simply gained a new perspective on this familiar space but now actively distances herself from it, since she perceives it as a safe world which shuts out the real and is thus empty:

> their lives were empty of everything but principles and a certain fixed way of looking at things . . . never could she belong to that world. It was a perfect little world: enclosed . . . the experience of it as an outsider was pure pain and misery; admiration, irritation and resentment running abreast in a fever. (II, 201)

Furthermore, although Miriam enjoys a frank understanding with Hancock as her employer, she experiences his behaviour and his expectations of her behaviour, influenced as they are by this social circle, as a self-deception which prohibits true communication. As with the Corries' worldliness, she associates the worldly Hancock with superficial activity and talk from which the real is absent. Since he voices his thoughts solely in the form of 'statements', Miriam must pretend to assume his mode of expression in order to converse with him and, as a result, sacrifice her own reality:

> It was only by pretending to be interested in these statements and taking sides about them that she could have conversation with him. He liked women who thought in these statements. They always succeeded with men. They had a reputation for wit . . . was it a trick, like 'clothes' and 'manners' . . . Perhaps there was something in it . . . But it would mean hiding so much letting so much go; all the real things. (II, 107)

The precise significance of role-play, which is necessary in order to participate successfully in Hancock's social world, now becomes clearer, since it is seen in direct relation to a specific understanding of reality which Miriam can accept. This leads to a shift in Miriam's justification for her rejection of this world and of the marriage which it might offer. While in the earlier novels she had come to recognise that marriage in this world would be deadening because accompanied by a suffocating security and a fixed and inflexible way of seeing, she now also takes into account the self-deception which life in this world would demand, namely that she would have to conceal or deny her own vision of reality.

This realisation is based upon Miriam's increasing sense of the fundamental separation between the masculine and feminine worlds, a separation which she already intimated in the Corries' world. Feeling that allegedly masculine values are privileged in the 'social world', Miriam concludes that feminine participation must necessarily involve transferring the self into a foreign realm. She expresses this more clearly in a discussion concerning the difference between masculine and feminine speech:

> In speech with a man a woman is at a disadvantage – because they speak different languages. She may understand his. Hers he will never speak nor understand. In pity, or from other motives, she must therefore, stammeringly, speak his. He listens and is flattered and thinks he has her mental measure when he has not touched even the fringe of her consciousness . . . Men and women never meet. Inside the life relationship you can see them being strangers and hostile; one or the other or both, completely alone. That was the world . . . In social life no one was alive not the lonely women keeping up half-admiring half-pitying endless conversations with men, with one little ironic part of themselves . . . But outside the world – one could be alive always. (II, 210)[15]

For Miriam, presence in the masculine social world involves a double pretence for women: both in the sense that women shift from their own space into an alien one and in the sense that they deceive each individual representative of this foreign, masculine space by feigning an understanding which merely distracts attention from the insurmountable barrier between men and women. This leads either to the complete loss of women's own world or to a conscious game of hide and seek which is upheld by a continual shifting between foreign, masculine speech and women's own ontological mode of speech. To counter this necessity for self-concealment, Miriam offers complete withdrawal from this world: 'outside . . . one could be alive always'. Accordingly, she characterises a friend's marriage as involving the unconditional sacrifice of her own world: 'Grace was ready to take all she possessed into a world where it would have no meaning: ready to disappear and be changed' (II, 317).

At the same time, since it is women who are repeatedly asked to act in a world foreign to them, Miriam ascribes to them what men lack, namely the capacity to speak two languages. She views women's simultaneous mastery of their own true speech and the adopted 'masculine' speech as an opportunity which allows them to benefit from and not be hampered by their lack of affiliation to one exclusive space.

Miriam's ultimate decision to reject the Hancock world also corresponds to her unshakable sense of her own independence, her 'self-sufficiency', which is determined by an increasing awareness of her own essence:

> I have nothing but my pained self again . . . But I stand for something . . . I make people hate me by . . . dashing my head against the wall of their behaviour . . . I shan't leave until I have proved that no one can put me in a false position. There is something that is untouched by positions. (II, 209)

Miriam's growing awareness of her independence is particularly encouraged by her contact with the 'world of independent women'. She regards the self-assured freedom of her working friends, Mag and Jan, as a favourable alternative to the security offered by a marriage in the 'social world'. In this, she sets up her own solitude and the company of her two girlfriends as a counter to her failed communication with Hancock: 'Never again would she go out in the evening unless alone or with the girls' (II, 108).

Nevertheless, she remains ambivalent towards this world as well. Although there are certain points of agreement between Miriam's world and that of her friends Mag and Jan, especially as regards their unanimous rejection of the world of marriage, Miriam distances herself from their obliviousness to nature (II, 152), from their incessant talk (II, 211) as well as from their pronounced activity in the outside world, all of these being attributes which she regards as distractions from the real: 'Mag . . . goes in amongst people and the complaints and fuss, and takes sides. But they both come out again; to be by themselves and talk about it all' (II, 211). At the same time, she recognises that their independence gives them the opportunity to move freely and that this is in turn accompanied by a very particular awareness of the world: 'They were doing things . . . that made independently elderly women . . . who were free to go about, have that look of intense appreciation' (II, 211).

With regard to her own independence, Miriam again sees her identity as situated between two worlds, since she is not prepared to break off all ties to the middle class which Wimpole Street represents: 'The girls had broken with the past and were fighting in the world. She was somehow between two worlds, neither quite sheltered nor quite free' (II, 163). Nevertheless, Miriam incorporates the independent, unimpeded movement which is inherent in Mag's and Jan's free world into her own, since it allows her to shift between the different worlds and enables her to embrace her own world as a 'various world' (II, 310). In addition, she associates her sense of independence with an attitude of ambivalent judgment. Unlike Mag and Jan, whose independence ultimately involves their making a resolute stand ('fighting the world'), Miriam views her intermediary position as a crucial component of her own world. Similarly, although she adopts aspects of the uncompromising stance taken by Mag and Jan, who entirely reject the Wimpole Street world, she is also able to see the charms of this world. However, Miriam is only in a position to articulate her sense of these attractions if her addressee is equally prepared to acknowledge the multiplicity of every situation: 'She drove these thoughts away; they were only one side of the matter; there were other things; things she could not make clear to . . . any one who could not see and feel the whole thing from inside, as she saw and felt it' (II, 163). The attribute 'independence' thus signifies not only Miriam's withdrawal from the social world, the world of marriage, but also her rejection of all one-sided meanings and all unequivocal stances and attitudes. Independence, as one of the seminal attributes of her world, is thus conceived as synonymous with a willingness to view a thing empathically from many sides: 'see and *feel* the *whole* thing from inside'. This notion of independence, which Mag and Jan cannot share, is ultimately why she withdraws from them.

Her attitude towards the 'world of science and art', represented by Alma and Hypo Wilson, is characterised by a similar ambivalence and inconstancy. During a scientific lecture which she attends with Hancock, she recognises that this world is also a distraction from the real, although she feels it to be less disruptive than the worldly world:

> They would never stop 'looking'. Culture and refinement; with . . . a raw school harshness about them that was quite unlike the deadness of the worldly people, not nearly so dreadful . . . always with the advancement of science on their minds; never really aware of anything behind or around them because of the wonders of science. (II, 102)

In this, Miriam reaches her most important conclusions about the world of science prior to her encounter with Hypo, although her attitude is developed more clearly in the context of her conflict with him. In opposition to the sequential, forward-looking (and thus emphatically temporal) thinking of the scientific world, she posits a thinking which insists upon simultaneity, encompasses past and future, seeks to engage seriously with 'life as a whole', lives in a state of continual self-referentiality and is thus not 'unconscious of itself'.

Since Hypo and Alma also represent a fascinating new world in which she sees herself to an extent reflected, Miriam is constantly torn between a desire to belong and a need to distance herself actively from it. From the beginning, she separates Alma from her London life – 'she was outside . . . and extra . . . a curious bright distant resource, nothing whatever to do with the wonderful present . . . the

London life' (II, 88). She associates Alma's lifestyle with a shallow mode of existence: 'Alma ... trying to be real; in a bright outside way' (II, 110), 'playing some part she had taken up ... Some wrong hurried rush' (II, 112). Furthermore, she refers to Alma and Hypo as a 'difficult, different world' (II, 112), also associating them with a one-sided, superficial mode of expression which seeks to make an impression upon others and leaves out that which she sees as real: 'saying nothing, or only the clever superficially true things' (II, 112), 'making statements' (II, 113), 'men's talk, argument and showing off ... taking sides, both right and both wrong' (II, 116), 'approval of a certain chosen set of things ... which excluded everything else with derision' (II, 118). As a result, she believes that affiliation to this group would, as with other worlds encountered previously, involve pretence: 'It would be necessary to be brilliant and amusing ... to tell lies. To get on here, one would have to say clever things in a high bright voice' (II, 113).

At the same time, however, she acknowledges that this world is a part of her own world and recognises herself in it: 'These were her people. There was something here ... It corresponded to something in herself, shapeless and inexpressible; but there' (II, 117). Above all, the fact that its members do not question her difference leads her to conceive of this world as a potential home: 'They know one was 'different'; and liked it and thought it a good thing: a sort of distinction ... It made them a home and a refuge. The only refuge there was, except being by oneself' (II, 131). While she criticises thinking which is based upon one supposedly indisputable standpoint as 'all wrong' (II, 119), she begins to sense for the first time the fascination which this intellectual activity holds for her: 'Speech and action had launched her, for good or ill, into the strange tide running in this house ... she was no longer quite herself ... she had accepted something she neither liked, nor approved, nor understood; refusal would have left its secret unplumbed' (II, 120).

Although she terms Hypo's progressive science 'scandal-mongering; gossip about the universe' (II, 417) and his pragmatic artistic doctrine a 'clever trick', 'mannish cleverness' (II, 131) and, moreover, despite the fact that this world loses its significance in London – 'Here in London it seemed wrong' (II, 132) – her confrontation with this world plays a crucial role in the development of her identity. Her discovery of an outside world which corresponds to something in herself consolidates her sense of self. Correspondingly, her return to London, back to her own world, is accompanied by the affirmation: 'She was somebody' (II, 109).

It is, however, not only the Wilsons' world which loses its significance in London; the world of science in general is also assessed in a less positive light there. In London, Miriam recognises that the world of science contains misogynist elements. After having read T. H. Huxley's statements regarding feminine underdevelopment, she concludes of science as a whole: 'Books were poisoned. Art. All the achievements of men were poisoned at the root ... Religion ... insults for women ... life is poisoned, for women, at the very source. Science ... will grow more and more horrible. Space is full of dead worlds. The world is cool and dying' (II, 222). Having experienced many different worlds, Miriam is able to stage an interaction between the various possibilities, to compare the worlds with one other and, if she rejects a particular aspect of one, to replace it with a new aspect from another world. Just as she opposes the world of independent women to the Hancock world of professional suburbia and the Wimpole Street dental practice, so she in turn plays the Wilson world against those three worlds. This process becomes even more pronounced when Mrs Bailey's guest house is converted into a boarding house in which the inhabitants meet at meal times, since this brings Miriam into contact with representatives of yet more worlds: the London medical world (II, 364), Bohemia (II, 367) and continental London (II, 394). These are all compared and differentiated from one another in order to establish their respective significance for Miriam. Indeed, it is precisely the multiplicity of available worlds which enables her to perceive differences, each helping her clarify by the limitations of others, rendering each single world relative, even while momentarily privileging one allows others to diminish in importance. This multiplicity is what makes both the boarding house and London at large such a resilient world: 'living in London was going about happy ... outside ... houses, looking at nothing and feeling everything, like people wandering happily from room to room in a well-known house at some time when everybody's attention was turned away' (II, 156).

Whereas solitude was perceived in Volume One as being opposed to and incompatible with affiliation to a world outside, in Volume Two the recognition of one's own essence is portrayed as necessitating a dynamic interplay between the two worlds: 'perhaps only those who had moved from one experience to another could get that curious feeling of a real self that stayed the same through thing after thing' (II, 101). On the one hand, freedom from all worldly ties is still viewed as the precondition of the most intense happiness: 'I'm up here alone, frantically happy' (II, 211), 'happy and free without anything' (II, 98). Frequently, it is only in solitude that Miriam is able to experience her own aliveness as well as her own reality: 'I'm alive and alone' (II, 237), 'one's own real realization ... Things that no one could share, coming ... to remind you that the innermost reality comes to you when you are alone' (II, 351). Equally, solitude is the environment which facilitates an experience of the boundary between the conscious self and the unconscious inner world; it sensitises Miriam to an experience of continual essence: 'If you keep quiet ... not being anything, not holding on to anything in your life, nor thinking about anything in your life, there is something there ... behind you' (II, 355). In consequence, Miriam regards those who do belong to groups as engaged in a desperate attempt to conceal their own solitude: 'Loneliness? It was always the people arranged in groups and seeming so lost and isolated and lonely who said that' (II, 350). She regards participation in the outside world as deadening the senses (II, 87): 'a fussy excited thoughtless way people seemed to do things', 'a talkative nothingness sliding on about nothing' (II, 350), 'distraction and sham'. Furthermore, she interprets the compulsion to continual activity in the outside world, as well as the incessant search for something which is superficially new, as a distraction from the real, recognisable only when movement ceases:

> never have a moment to realize anything at all; rushing along saying things, that covered everything and never stopping to realize. Talking *about* people and things and never being or knowing anything, and perpetually coming to the blank emptiness . . . unconscious of everything. (II, 372)

Nevertheless, Miriam is also forced to accept that complete withdrawal from the outside world leads to a deadening sterility. The turning point in Miriam's development takes places on one New Year's Eve, which brings with it the resolution to abstain from the world as much as possible and to give her solitude, 'the calm steady innermost part of her', priority over her 'other selves': she desires to be 'alive without personality or speech' (II, 321). The ecstasy possible in this state of lonely abstinence is evoked as follows:

> There was no thought in the silence, no past or future, nothing but the strange thing for which there were no words, something that was always there as if by appointment, waiting for one to get through to it away from everything in life. It was the thing that was nothing. Yet it seemed the only thing that came near and meant anything at all. It was happiness and realization. (II, 322)

This identity is one formed out of nothingness, with no correlation whatsoever to the outside world. It is characterised by a negation of the mutual determination between self and world. However, Miriam is forced to accept that it is unbearable to live entirely without recognition from outside; that complete withdrawal would lead to entropy, would mean being 'left out of life forever' and that there would be 'no one in the world who would care if she never appeared anywhere again' (II, 326).[16] Admittedly, she regards her return towards the outside world with ambivalence – as a 'restoration to shame' (II, 327) – but at the same time she accepts that it is necessary. She thus recognises that it is not by rejecting the world completely, but rather by upholding a dynamic interplay between subject and world, that she will preserve her own reality (being 'alive'), as well as those moments of ecstasy, 'happiness and realization' which may only be experienced in solitude: 'Always and always in the end there was nothing but to be alone. And yet it needed people in the world to make the reality when one was alone' (II, 379).

Miriam rejects the eternal sameness of the 'social world' (II, 199) since it involves stagnation on the surface of things and insistence upon one viewpoint – 'certainty about everything' (II, 314), 'agreement, ignorant of reality' (II, 373) – and thus inhibits recognition of that real essence which she regards as situated beneath the surface and as encompassing all viewpoints. She therefore distances herself from the constant movement necessary in the outside world, since it is associated with distraction and indifference to the real. However, it now becomes apparent that she also rejects the eternal sameness of complete withdrawal from the world, since this too involves stagnation and insistence upon one viewpoint and begins to accept the necessity for movement and change. This effectively creates a synthesis between the concept of motionlessness and that of movement. Indeed, the sameness which is necessary in order to perceive the real is possible only by shifting between stillness and motion and by renewed contact with the foreign and the exterior.

The potential dangers for Miriam of returning to the world are that she may lose her secure sense of self and, with it, her sense of hermetic self-sufficiency. The pleasures which she anticipates are, in turn, the opportunity for self-renewal: 'I grow more and more unknown and more and more like what people think of me. But *I* know; and things go on coming; scraps of other people's things' (II, 336). The multi-faceted quality of her own world thus consists not only in the various aspects of the outside world which Miriam has deemed worthy of inclusion into her own inner world but also in two opposing and yet also mutually dependent manifestations of her self: one constant, inner self and one inconstant, shifting and changeable outer self: 'some source of light within her ... the freedom of following certainties. Outside it was this other self untouched and always new, her old free companion attending to no one' (II, 392).

Concomitantly, the affirmation that time spent in one world prevents a recognition of the real is gradually replaced by a recognition that an overly intense participation in one world excludes the others. Miriam explains this to Mag in response to her remark that she has so many 'sets of people' (II, 424): 'You can't like everybody at once. You have to choose. That's the trouble. If you are liking one set of people very much you get out of touch with the others' (II, 424). Here, Miriam implies her own ideal condition, a psychological position in which she would be able to inhabit multiple worlds simultaneously without having to declare allegiance to one standpoint or one world. This ideal is revealed also in Miriam's continued negotiation of gender difference as well in as her search for an adequate mode of representing reality.

Miriam's recognition that she is capable of entering the masculine world only by practising a certain degree of deception is not confined to Hancock's 'social world'. Even in Bohemian circles she witnesses this fundamental division between men and women (II, 371). In the Wilsons' world she also feels she must assume a masculine mode of expression, the 'clever statements', in order to participate successfully. As a result Miriam becomes even more adamant in her need to distinguish the attributes relating to women's presence in the masculine world from those which she views as being genuinely feminine.

The first category involves the feminine charm which is designed to attract men's attention – 'a brilliant death', 'deliberate "charming" feminine effect', 'a trick', 'the whole advertising manner' (II, 105). This quality is also cited in the context of a polemic against women's attempts to appropriate masculine language, which Miriam views as another manifestation of feminine charm: 'All "clever" women seemed to have that, *never* speaking what they thought or felt, but always things that sounded like quotations from men; so that they always seemed to flatter or criticize men they were with ... *What* was she like when she was alone and dropped that bright *manner*' (II, 251).

At the same time, she admits that although the allegedly masculine world of intellectuals and scientists may represent a world alien to women, in which each member employs exclusive categories in order to describe reality, it is not only engaging but in fact much closer to her than the conventional world of women.

During a discussion of *The Merchant of Venice*, she tries to encapsulate her ambivalent position regarding the masculine and the feminine worlds, as well as her sense that her own identity is located between the two:

> How much more real was the relation between Portia and Nerissa . . . Did a man *ever* speak in a natural voice – neither blustering, nor displaying his cleverness . . . speaking in put-on voices to hide their shame, pompous and philosophizing . . . The knowledge of woman is larger, bigger, deeper, less wordy and clever than that of men . . . [Men] have not real knowledge, but of things; a sort of superiority they get by being free to be out in the world amongst things; they do not understand people.
> (II, 187)

Within this negotiation of gender difference, masculinity is assigned an eloquence which is at once intelligent and showy, as well as a broad abstract knowledge about the world of things. However, this mode of expression apparently fails to recognise what Miriam views as real. She sees women, in turn, as possessing less abstract, verbal talents but instead a deep, intuitive and 'natural' wisdom about people; a direct connection with the sacred, as opposed to the 'masculine' relation to God which Miriam represents as being mediated through the language of philosophy and religion. Of women, she says: 'when they were alone together, the beauty they knew and felt and saw, holy beauty everywhere' (II, 187).

Feminine space is thus implicitly assigned a quality of restful, constant, pre-linguistic or non-linguistic knowledge and behaviour, whereas masculine space is characterised by free, continual movement and reflective speech. Miriam expresses the opposition between feminine and masculine space in terms of the notion of constant, permanent knowledge. In women's lives she discerns a 'deep certainty. There is no deep certainty in the lives of men' (II, 407).

At the same time, Miriam views her position as somewhere between the two spaces: 'I am like a man in that, overbearing, bullying, blustering. I am something between a man and a woman; looking both ways. But to pretend one did not see through a man's voice, would be treachery. Nearly all men will hate me – because I can't play up for long' (II, 187). Conscious of the doubleness of her own position, Miriam is attracted in one respect by the expressive capacity of masculine speech, as well as by the unsettled freedom of movement which is attributed to masculine space, and this is why she often favours the company of men and attempts to adopt masculine modes of behaviour: 'I am going to lead a man's life, always getting away' (II, 230). She desires not to be confined exclusively to feminine space and, significantly, when she is about to leave the company of Eleanor Dear, a representative of what Miriam considers to be typically feminine, she encodes this departure as the achievement of an androgynous position: 'She would be again, soon . . . not a woman . . . a Londoner' (II, 266).

Nevertheless, Miriam also recognises that she can adopt masculine speech only temporarily since she must ultimately reject it: for 'not to see through a man's voice would be treachery'. This leads her to take on the hitherto unacceptable feminine attitude to the world, without needing to relinquish the advantages of masculine speech. She endows her opinion of women, intended previously as a criticism of feminine 'pretence', with a new, positive meaning: 'The secret life of women. They smiled at God. But they all flattered men' (II, 267). What emerges is that the 'feminine' position in the world is also inconstant – not in the sense of continual movement in the outside world but rather in the sense that it functions as a threshold between a direct relation to God, an articulation of the constancy and permanence of the 'deep certainties', on the one hand, and, on the other, that of masculine speech and constant motion lacking 'deep certainty'.

In *Pilgrimage*, Miriam is the only one who can occupy an intermediary position between the masculine and the feminine world; in command of both modes of self-expression. All the other characters are either situated firmly in feminine space, as, for example, the women in the Corrie world and Eleanor Dear, or they occupy masculine space through deceit, such as Alma, Mag and Jan, whom Miriam accuses of adopting fixed opinions and of speaking in 'clever statements'. Just as she was able to reconcile the opposition between self and world by recognising two forms of the self – a constant self which is associated with the notion of 'following certainties' and an inconstant, mobile self which is conceptualised as being 'untouched and always new' – so Miriam synthesises the polarity between the sexes by assuming a third position, in between. This allows her to achieve a simultaneous presence in numerous different worlds, a pattern which emerges also in her discussion of what an adequate representation of reality would be. Miriam's point of departure lies in her belief in the plurality of each thing, event or person: 'Things are not simply right and wrong. There are a million sides to every question; as many sides as there are people to see and feel them, and in all big national struggles two clear sides, both right and wrong' (II, 189). From this she concludes that each attempt to report and pin down the multiplicity of reality is doomed to fail; firstly, since it can represent only one position and, secondly, since any intense absorption in one aspect of reality involves being blinded to all others (II, 140). If mutually contradictory descriptions are valid, then it follows that no utterance is totally or exclusively true. Instead, she favours

> a tangle of statements . . . All contradictory, up and down, backwards and forwards, all true. The things they would grasp, here and there, would misrepresent herself and the whole picture. Why would people insist on talking about things – when nothing can ever be communicated . . . Yes would be a lie. No would be a lie. Any statement would be a lie. All statements are lies. (II, 306)

Since it is never possible to capture an object in all its multiplicity and ambiguity, every linguistic representation is a mere collection of biased expressions and is more likely to place a barrier between the object of speech and the addressee than to draw them closer together: 'It was impossible to show everything, the more opinions you expressed the more you misled people and the further you got away from them' (II, 297).

Furthermore, Miriam is critical of the use of language when at issue is an extralingual sensation or truth. The word 'fascinated', which the other inhabitants of the Bailey boarding house use to describe her extremely ambivalent and complex relationship with Mendizabel, is wholly inadequate in Miriam's eyes. Not only does it fail to capture the true nature of their relationship, it also attempts to put something which cannot be said into words: '*Fascinated.* How did they find the word? It was true; and false. This was the way people talked. These were the true-false phrases used to sum up things for which there were no words' (II, 434). Here, Miriam touches upon one of the central themes of her own poetics: the search for the right linguistic representation for the essence of an event which can never fully be communicated in symbolic language; in part, because the real is infinitely various and, in part, because its essence inevitably eludes language.

At the same time, however, Miriam is forced to acknowledge that language is the only means of expressing one's inner reflections, however clumsy and unreliable it may be. Language places her in a position between utter certainty and complete confusion as to her own capacity to express herself to others. Ironically, however, it is precisely linguistic ambivalence which also opens up endless possibilities, since every utterance implicitly contains overtones of countless other supplementary and contradictory meanings:

> *All* that has been said and known in the world is in *language*, in words . . . the meaning of words changes with people's thoughts. Then no one *knows* anything for certain. Everything depends upon the way a thing is put . . . language is the only way of expressing anything and it dims everything . . . then there is nothing to be afraid of and nothing to be quite sure of rejoicing about. (II, 99)

Equally empowering is the recognition of a delay and deferral between an object and its utterance. For when something is represented, the object at stake already belongs to the past. Such belatedness, however, endows the represented object with a certain independence: 'If you can speak of a thing, it is past . . . Speaking makes it glow with a life that is not its own' (II, 317). In other words, even while representation is inevitably one-sided, the resulting imprecision implies the presence of a multiplicity of sides; even while language cannot name the real accurately, its strength lies precisely in the vagueness, which permits an infinite circumscription of that which eludes any direct articulation. As Miriam relinquishes her attempt to devise a language which would confirm an object's solidity and reliability, the opportunity to describe an object obliquely, 'seeing all round a thing' (II, 94), and to represent it as an endless expansion of oneself acquires increasing relevance. Ultimately, speech is perceived as an act of creation since it is always linked with the object's acquiring a life of its own; creativity is contrasted with falsification. In the following passage, Miriam outlines this positive vision of language and thought as being multi-faceted, endless, associative; a spatial process of encountering and traversing the real:

> a single world holding all the possible variations of everything at once . . . anything that the mind can conceive is realized, somehow, all possibilities must come about . . .

> you go on and on and on, filling space . . . You ought not to think in words. I mean
> – you can think in your brain, by imagining yourself going on and on through it,
> endless space . . . You don't GRASP it. You go through it. (II, 93)

What emerges in Miriam's search for the multiplicity of her own world and of the outside world is that the notion that the 'real' can be located proves to be a paradox in itself, since the real can emerge only when opposites are held in a state of simultaneous suspension. What Miriam has come to recognise is that *being* is preserved in the process of *becoming*, that essence and permanence are upheld in movement and change; that femininity is sustained by masculinity.

In Volume Three (*Deadlock, Revolving Lights, Trap*), Miriam continues to perceive her own identity as located in an intermediate position in which she can share in a multiplicity of worlds without needing to commit herself to one and reject the others. Miriam rejects her employer's social world and the 'suburban middle class world' of her married sisters for the same reasons she had come to articulate earlier, even while she still feels an ambivalent attraction towards the Tansley Street boarding house as a meeting place for new, unusual people which contrasts with the various political, scientific and religious worlds within London and with the Wilson world of writers, characterised by 'clever wit'. Although aspects of these worlds also deviate sharply from her own sense of self, she considers belonging to each of them. She sums up her shifting attraction to each world as follows:

> Away behind, in the flatly echoing hall, was the busy planning world of socialism, intent on the poor. Far away in tomorrow, stood the established, unchanging world of Wimpole Street, linked helpfully to the lives of the prosperous classes. Just ahead, at the end of the walk home, the small isolated Tansley Street world, full of secretive people drifting about on the edge of catastrophe . . . In the space between these surrounding worlds was the everlasting solitude; . . . and here, at the end of the stairs, was the showcase of cold Unitarian literature. Yet another world. (II, 233)

As before, these worlds are weighed up against each other and render each another relative, even while they help Miriam clarify what she values most in each, what she wants to retain and what she wants to relinquish.

To the same degree that she intensifies her movements and actions in the outside world, so her need to withdraw into her own world as the site of 'self-realization' likewise becomes more acute. In this way, she resists that world's 'becoming' by focusing upon the permanence of being. In contrast to the previous volume, however, her decision to withdraw represents a deliberate renunciation of the different outside worlds, a renunciation which is a direct consequence of her involvement with these worlds and ought not to be seen as resulting from a lack of available outside worlds. For the first time, Miriam explicitly refers to a sub-division within her own world, by addressing the immaterial 'regions within inner zones' (III, 53). She describes

> this incomparable sense of being plumb at the centre of rejoicing . . . It compensated the failure of her efforts at conformity . . . It was forgetfulness, suddenly overtaking

her in the midst of her busiest efforts . . . memory . . . a perpetual sudden blank . . . and upon it broke forth this inexhaustible joy. (III, 288)

Movement in the outside world is opposed to a convergence upon her own world, which is itself now conceived as a centre controlling all actions. This concentration marks the beginning of her decision to privilege one world over all the others, namely the immaterial world of creative solitude.

Volume Three is primarily structured around Miriam's confrontation with two foreign worlds; namely that of Russian-Jewish intellectuals and revolutionaries (III, 24), represented by Michael Shatov, and that of art and science, as well as socialism, represented by Hypo Wilson. Both worlds help Miriam clarify her increasing sense of the importance of the individual, her sense of her own unchanging personality as opposed to commitment to one cultural or social group. Moreover, these two worlds lead Miriam to prefer tranquil contemplation to worldly activity and, with regard to Michael, to cherish familiar English qualities above foreign ones. Miriam's encounter with these two particular worlds again allows her to negotiate the three oppositions so seminal to her own self-fashioning: the difference between worldliness and solitude, between masculinity and femininity as well as the incommensurability between representation and what she perceives as being existentially real.

On many occasions, Miriam's contact with Michael helps her to define the contents of her own world. At one level, his appeal consists in his role as an ambassador of all foreign countries. Contact with him promises to provide a continuation of the fascination exerted by her many experiences of the culturally foreign even while his person and his stories appear to offer a means of appropriating these foreign worlds for herself. This attitude is reinforced also by her conviction that Russia possesses a particularly powerful kind of spirituality, an indifference to worldly values, calling it 'the strongest kinetic force in Europe' (III, 45). At another level, her encounter with this wholly alien world enervates and intensifies all others, since her experience of Michael's Russian world briefly enables her to observe the other worlds from a distance. As with all of Miriam's previous foreign friends, Michael's presence and his comments – 'completely foreign, a mind from an unknown world' (III, 113) – act as expressions of alterity, which enables Miriam to recognise the characteristics that may be resolutely English. Her encounter with him leads her to wonder: 'What *is* England? What do the qualities mean?' (III, 113) and this foreign perspective leads her to view the familiar aspects of her surroundings in a new light: 'passing forward to some fresh sense of things that would change the English world for her . . . But even seeing England from his point of view, was being changed; a little' (III, 151). Michael thus gives her a more pronounced sense of belonging to a national space. She says of Michael: 'he seemed to see people only as members of nations, grouped together with all their circumstances . . . All her meaning for him was her English heredity . . . he gave her her nationality and surroundings, the fact of being England to him made everything easy' (III, 151). Miriam is especially drawn to Michael since he functions as an actual adressee for her cognitive discoveries, able to renew and supplement her experience of the outside world. One may thus view Miriam's relationship with him as a fulfilment of the knowledge which she gained in *Interim*, namely, that solitude, the site of self-realisation, is dependent upon an experience of the other, person as a representative alterity:

> He forced her to think. She reflected that solitude was too easy. It was necessary, for certainties. Nothing could be known except in solitude. But the struggle to communicate certainties gave them new life; even if the explanations were only a small piece of truth . . . The extraordinary new thing was that she *could* think, untroubled, in his company.

However, to the same degree that his foreignness broadens her horizons, so it also embodies the qualities which she finds unacceptable. By negating and rejecting certain features of Michael's world, Miriam is able to discover and affirm the most important attributes of her own world. His foreignness acts not only as an invigorating influence but also as a boundary inhibiting closer contact: 'Not again could she suffer nearness, until the foreigner in him, dipped everyday more deeply into the well of English feeling, should be changed' (III, 197).

As well as highlighting her own English characteristics, Miriam's perception of Michael primarily in terms of his national identity, rather than as an individual, also brings her face to face with the greatest and most insurmountable discrepancy between their two worlds. In his Zionist world, ethnic allegiance is valued more highly than personal development as an individual. In Miriam's world, however, it is precisely the individual who has absolute priority. She refers to Michael as a 'poor little man . . . in a world without individuals' (III, 166) and also regards his own Zionist movement as subordinate to the individual:

> There's something behind all those outside things that goes on independently of them, something much more wonderful . . . he must be an individual to be affected at all, and no two people are affected in the same way.
> . . . you must begin with the individual. (III, 169–71)

Her refusal to enter the world of Judaism, a step which marriage to Michael would require, is based upon similar objections: 'I can't bear Jewesses . . . because they reflect the limitations of the Jewish masculine. They talk and think the Jewish man's idea of them. It has nothing to do with them as individuals' (III, 221). Privileging groups over individuals, an integral feature of Michael's Zionist world, also involves commitment to a one-sided and exclusive vision of reality. This attitude stands in direct conflict with Miriam's own inability to commit herself to one position and her belief in multiple worlds:

> All these people had one mind . . . and were gay in unity . . . statements about different ways of looking at things were irrelevancies . . . Personal life to them was nothing . . . They lived for an idea . . . She offered them a comprehensive glimpse of the many pools of thought in which she had plunged, rising from each in turn, to recover the bank and repudiate; unless a channel could be driven, that would make all their waters meet. (III, 239)

Since Michael's world is characterised by the pursuit of an idea which makes no concessions to the individual, his world also embodies an indifference to the spatial phenomenon of the 'real' which is so important to Miriam. Her vision of the 'real' is to be found only in the self and in the depth of each single moment, not, however, in a superficial view of time, which privileged the past and future over a continual present:

> But they themselves were absent, set far away, amongst their generalizations. Of the actual life of the passing moment they felt no more than Michael. Itself, its uniqueness, the deep loop it made, did not exist for them. They looked only towards the future. He only at a uniform pattern of humanity. (III, 314)

This world is not attuned to the permanent essence, not alive to the uniqueness of the present moment and, as her conflict with Michael makes clear, it is this essence, experienced 'away from speech and behaviour' (III, 295), which makes up the significant part of her world. Hence Miriam's main criticism of Michael is that 'there was no permanent marvel for him in the present' (III, 316).

Their differing assessment of the individual's position in relation to his or her community, as well as Michael's obliviousness to the existence of multiple worlds and to what Miriam calls the *depth* of each single moment, leads Miriam to conclude: 'we are living in two utterly different worlds' (III, 219). It is clear that Michael's world contains nothing which corresponds to her understanding of reality; her 'sense of endlessness' and 'incommunicable blissfulness' and her celebration of the 'marvel of existence'. Equally, Miriam is not prepared to trade in her vision for his world, focused as it is upon an impersonal idea. Therefore, she is forced to accept that their differences cannot be resolved: 'there was less reality between them now than there had been when they first met . . . Since she could not hold him to these shifting visions, nor drop them and accept his world, they had no longer anything to exchange' (III, 304).

This realisation marks the beginning of her withdrawal into her own solitude as the place which offers an experience of the real. Even if her contact and exchange with Michael's world — with him as an incarnation of the other and of the unknown addressee per se — did sensitise Miriam to the drawbacks of an exclusive presence in solitude and redressed this imbalance, her discovery that her own world does not correspond sufficiently with Michael's in turn leads her back to solitude:

> solitude had failed and from its failure she had been saved by the companionship of a man; of whom until to-day she had been proud in a world lit by the glory and pride of achieved companionships. But it was an illusion, fading and failing more swiftly than the real things of solitude. (III, 208)

In the context of her struggle to discover her own identity and the features integral to her own world, Miriam has thus not only established the crucial importance of the individual and recognised that she must continue to insist upon the existence of multiple worlds and upon a willingness to experience the depth of each moment which leads to permanent essence, but has concluded, furthermore, that solitude and permanence, the 'real things', must take precedence over companionship with another person.

A similar polarity develops in her continuing contact with Hypo. The writers' world which he and his friends represent remains the embodiment of a 'wit-wrecked world' (III, 349), being associated with the attributes 'cold' and 'clever' (III, 342) and also with 'fuss ... dead empty loss' (III, 349) because it does not acknowledge her vision of reality, her joy in the depth of each moment and her marvel at existence: 'They didn't know how to be joyful; only how to be clever' (III, 356). Hypo's world is thus at once unacceptable and compelling (III, 337), a world which she still admires and from which she is nevertheless excluded, since she cannot share its perception of reality nor of its mode of representing it. In the Wilsons' 'writing-world', she discovers 'a social atmosphere that was, in spite of its scepticism, and its scorn of everyday life, easier to breathe than any other' (III, 148). At the same time, she is unable to conform and again withdraws from contact with this world: 'a hesitating sense of guilt, unable to be beguiled by gross sentimentality ... meant belonging outside the world of clever writers' (III, 148).

In additionally representing socialism, in the guise of the Lycurgan Society, the Wilsons' world is, like that of Michael Shatov, oriented towards one all-inclusive, exclusive idea (as opposed to a multitude of personal interests), in which people are assessed as members of a group and not as individuals. Furthermore, the members of this world seek to effect change for the future and place more emphasis upon action in the world than upon a contemplative frame of mind which is sensitive to the reality of every personal moment. As in her conflict with Michael, Miriam cannot accept the denial of a unique, personal perception of the real and always places the uniqueness of each individual above any affiliation to a group. In Miriam's eyes, it is impossible to develop any ideas unless one has achieved a measure of fulfilment as an individual:

> The world of clear ideas summoning mankind to follow like an army, seemed again ... to contain a trick, to be too clear, too hard, too logical to embrace the rich fabric of life ... they were idealists, blind with the illusion that humanity moves with one accord. Each one moves singly. To join the movements of others is harmful until you have moved yourself. Movement is with the whole of you. Ideas come afterwards.
> (III, 475)

Miriam refuses to accept the individual's subordination to one single scientific idea, since an idea cannot encompass anything more than the most superficial aspects of a person and subsequently excludes and denies those characteristics which may have contradictory or unsavoury aspects. Of the Lycurgans, Miriam states that they 'reduced them [the things of life] to the terms of what could be said about them' (III, 475).

In response to Hypo's accusation that Miriam's problem is her individualism (III, 253), she argues that socialism is crucially flawed by its one-sided position and by its failure to acknowledge that the individual is the wellspring of all ideas and of revolutionary energy: 'socialists . . . seem ignorant of *humanity* . . . It's *individuals* who must change, one by one' (III, 374). Hypo describes the fundamental reason for their incompatibility accurately: 'The difference between you and me is that you think to live and I live to think' (III, 377). In direct opposition to the Wilson world, Miriam highlights the individual and not the group, placing key emphasis upon the self with its own experiences and perceptions rather than upon ideas. She views this concentration upon life, as opposed to abstract thought, as a decisive component of her existence and thus too as a core feature of her own world.

Since it is Hypo's role as a writer, rather than as a socialist, which dominates Miriam's perception of him, her engagement with his world continues to involve discussions of the discrepancies between their conceptions of reality and their modes of depicting it. Hypo's position is perceived as paradigmatically masculine, while she increasingly assumes a feminine standpoint. Hypo offers his own opinion of Miriam's unstable position, her insistence upon a multiplicity of valid explanations for reality, 'seeing everything simultaneously' (III, 393), and of her attempt to retain an impartial, intermediate position, 'reading keeps one simply always balanced between different sets of truth' (III, 377), 'taking sides annihilates me' (III, 394). He analyses her position as follows: 'You're feathery . . . You have . . . a surprising lack of expression . . . You're too omnivorous . . . scattered' (III, 375). Miriam, however, views the ambiguity and formlessness of her language as an expression of a specifically feminine rhetoric, in the sense that women look to their own lives and experiences rather than to abstract ideas and things: 'Women see in terms of life. Men in terms of things' (III, 393).

In opposition to Hypo's sequential narration of facts, his clarity and his unambiguous yet also one-sided and superficial descriptive mode, Miriam defends the ambiguous and variable rhetorical mode which is most suited to her preferred mode of capturing reality, her 'shapeless outpourings' and 'wide generalities' (III, 255). However, she does not view this mode of expression as a negation of his descriptive modes, but as a means of drawing attention to, supplementing and preserving what he has disregarded, what she calls 'the reality that fell, all the time, in the surrounding silence, outside his shapes and classifications' (III, 360).

Indeed, her rejection of Hypo's language resides largely in her disdain for descriptive structures which rely upon the temporal dimension and upon sequentiality:

> Sacrificed to its sharp expressiveness were the real moments of these people's lives; and the moments of the present, counting themselves off, ignored and irrecoverable, offering, as their extension, time that was unendurably narrow and confined, a narrow featureless darkness, its walls grinning with the transfixed features of consciousness that had always been and must, if the pictures were accepted as true, for ever be, a motionless absurdity. (III, 255)

In the context of a more general treatment of the tension between self and world, Miriam's encounter with the worlds of Michael and Hypo leads to a renewed withdrawal into solitude. This withdrawal into solitude is, however, also marked by Miriam's resolution to begin writing. Miriam is increasingly resolute and uncompromising when she encounters attributes of the outside world which conflict with or nullify her own sense of self. Nevertheless, her rejection of the outside world continues to further her awareness of the features of her own world. She continues to locate her identity in an intermediary position and, similarly, a considerable part of her identity still consists in a sense of being different: 'Was there any one, anywhere, who suffered quite in this way, felt always and everywhere so utterly different?' (III, 315).

As before, Miriam's justification for her 'social incompatibility' is that she associates exclusive membership of one group with confinement to one point of view, 'having opinions' and 'taking sides', as well as the exclusion of all differences. Uncomplaining participation in a group is thus seen to reduce life to one shallow aspect — 'narrowed life down to a restive discomfort' — and to involve deceit and role-play, making one 'insincere and fickle' (III, 19). Finally, then, Miriam can fulfil her desire to preserve multiple worlds only by resisting commitment to any group: 'It is only by the pain of remaining free that one can have the whole world round one all the time' (III, 20).

This is further accentuated by Miriam's increased defence of her impartial and distanced individualism. She does indeed accept the accusations which are levelled against her, admitting that her preference for her own company, or her 'social incompatibility', gives her a 'feeling of meanness' (III, 20) and 'cruelty' (III, 75) and makes her feel like a 'murderess' (III, 75). At the same time, she encodes her refusal to conform as a 'curious boundless promise' (III, 323), since it represents the only chance for 'personal realization'. As well as perceiving solitude as a place which allows her to remain different and accommodates her desire for multiplicity, she now also views it as a place in which she can protect and fulfil her individuality. She terms solitude a 'safeguard of individuality . . . Always to be solid and resistant . . . having no opinions and only one enthusiasm — to be unmoved' (III, 241).

Solitude is thus affirmed as the only possible site of transcendence and personal realisation, yet Miriam is unwilling to occupy this position fully and to exclude all others, since the outside world, with all its subtle discrepancies and contradictions, retains a certain appeal. She comments: 'the kingdom of heaven is within . . . Yet the kingdom within is a little grey and lonely' (III, 482). As a result, she does not deny herself all involvement with the material outside world, what she refers to as a 'triple tangle of art, sex and religion' (III, 482), deferring the resolution of this confrontation to the end of the last volume, in which she finally commits herself exclusively to the immaterial space of her writing.

Miriam's second reason for preferring solitude to affiliation to groups consists in her increasing conviction that the real is not to be found in the outside world, and that life there represents a spiritual death. It is not only her belief that the movement required in the outside world is a distraction from reality which inspires this conviction, but also her sense that the emphasis upon time in the outside world actually eliminates life:

> Life *ceased* when time moved on. Out in the world life was ceasing all the time . . . Why can't reality exist in the world? All the things that happen produce friction because they distract people from the reality they are unconsciously looking for. That is why there are everywhere torrents of speech. (III, 188)

For Miriam, the necessary conditions for the emergence of the real are silence and motionless calmness. The real may be experienced only by assuming a distanced position and by observing the world without a specific purpose in mind. Here, the concept of contemplative space is transferred on to the topology of the mind and is no longer confined to descriptions of Miriam's position in actual material spaces. As a result, she associates the recognition of reality with the qualities attributed to solitude. Furthermore, this recognition of reality is linked directly with temporary immateriality and with the suspension of time. She describes one such revelatory moment as follows:

> Now that the stillness had returned, life was going on, dancing, flowing, looping out in all directions . . . so long as time stayed still . . . people alone in themselves when time is not moving . . . Silence is reality . . . Life does show, seen from far off, pouring down into stillness . . . the contemplation of it as part of a picture, which no one who is in the picture can see . . . a stillness of reality, a mind picture that does not care, out of the rush of life . . . The outsider sees most of the game. (III, 188)

The immaterial reality experienced in solitude appears to provide the perfect environment for her self, conceived as a dependable, secure centre: 'her own dream world at home in her room, her strange unfailing self, the lovely world of lovely things seen in silence and tranquillity . . . solitude' (III, 208). All other phenomena merely supplement this private world. Miriam affirms that her own independent, spiritual and immaterial world is not simply her chosen environment but in fact the *only* valid world, and sees the outside world as drained of all meaning and reality: 'There is no need to go out into the world. Everything is there without anything; the world is added. And always, whatever happens, there is everything to return to' (III, 67). The intimacy with the real which solitude offers, including an experience of heightened awareness, aliveness and ultimately joy – 'the last deepest level of her being was joy' (III, 321) – is now explored further with the introduction of two new aspects.

The first of these is the discovery of silent utterances, of 'things speaking silently' (III, 233), which represent a marvelling at the world, a close and unmediated encounter with things. Increasingly, she views silence as the locus of true language, declaring that 'things come up and life speaks directly, to the individual' (III, 366) and that 'being in the silence was being in something alive and positive; at the centre of existence' (III, 327). The second new element is that Miriam associates the notion of 'forgetfulness' more and more with the notion of reality, in the sense that she experiences 'moments of reality *in* forgetfulness' (III, 498). This state of forgetfulness involves liberating oneself from the material world, distancing oneself from unstable events and from talk and movement in the outside world. Furthermore, forgetfulness signifies a attitude of indifference which provides relief from the need to take sides and to defend an incomplete, exclusive point of view.

As a result, Miriam's own 'world' becomes more and more divided between a conscious subject and an inner world. The unchanging and enduring essence, experienced in silent, forgetful and tranquil solitude, which constitutes one aspect of the real, is frequently coupled with spatial attributes expressing profundity, interiority and depth: *'far away below* all interference' (III, 17), *'underneath* was something else, the same in everybody' (III, 429), 'reaching *down into* the life that rose faintly to meet her' (III, 17). She articulates her sense of her self in terms of a centre: 'this far cool place where she now was' (III, 307). Here, then, Miriam's identity is again depicted as a kind of doubling; a union between two selves: one which is always in motion, involved and living in time, and one which is unchanging and tranquil. Unlike before, however, the two aspects of the self are sharply differentiated from one another, the first conceived as being 'unreal' and the second as possessing an 'unchanging reality':

> Always in being thrown back from outside happiness, there seem to be two. A waiting self to welcome me . . . Being quite still . . . your mind, moving about in it without envy or desire, realizes the whole world. The future and the past are all one same stuff, changing and unreal. The sense of your own unchanging reality comes with an amazement and sweetness. (III, 283)

Significantly Miriam endows the imagination with the power to 'realize the whole world', so that solitude is not conceived as a place for recognition of the real and as a place which brings forth the reality of things; it is also a place which actually effects a re-creation of reality. If the most important insight gained in Volume Two was that there must be a dynamic interplay between subject and world, then, in the context of the emphasis on and the defence of the individual, the fundamental realisation in Volume Three is that solitude must necessarily occupy a central position in Miriam's psycho-topology, since it alone represents the locus of creative activity.

During her first experience of writing, a translation assignment, Miriam recognises that creative activity in solitude brings complete fulfilment as well as providing an extension of her material self and loosening her ties to materiality. She describes her experience:

> more oneself than anything that could be done socially, together with others and yet not oneself at all, but something mysterious . . . part of a separate impersonal life she had now unconsciously confessed herself sharing . . . herself, independently . . . her life coming back, as if narrated from the fascinating life of someone else. (III, 132)

Since it represents the point at which the self comes into contact with the immaterial inner world, this creative solitude is regarded as the 'centre of life' and as 'an everlasting various joyful coming back'. Furthermore, it enables her to contemplate her own life and the events and experiences in material exterior space with a gaze which is rooted in her own self but does not implicate it directly.

The emphasis upon immaterial contemplation and creation as features of this lonely private world is allied with the demand for multiple worlds and with a perception of reality as the replacement of sequential time with a kind of permanent present. The following description of the psychological state between waking (as material, conscious space) and sleeping (as immaterial, unconscious space), a position not dissimilar to that of writing, addresses the phenomenon of immaterial contemplation. Miriam anticipates her future as follows: 'Holding worlds and worlds, all the many lives ahead. And I lie wandering within them, a different person every moment . . . until some small thing brings back the present life' (III, 478). The process of recollection is described in similar terms:

> She found . . . she was once more in that zone of her being where all the past was with her unobstructed; not recalled, but present, so that she could move into any part and be there as before. (III, 322)

> Fragments of forgotten experience detached themselves, making a bright moving patchwork as she watched, waiting, while she passed from one to another and fresh patches were added, drawing her on. (III, 323)

It is telling that Miriam sets her vision of reality in creative solitude against the externally determined, outside world in both descriptions. This introduces a new mode of ordering past or anticipated events, whereby these events, freed from what Miriam views as a flat sequentiality, and placed in such a way that they are juxtaposed conterminously, thus acquire a simultaneous presence. Solitude gives these past or anticipated events a double immediacy by yoking together the *present* (i.e. presence in time) and *presence* (i.e. existence in space).

Finally, solitude is also viewed as the 'real' because it is there that Miriam creates her own reality in her immaterial imaginings. Not only does she deny the outside world that quantum of reality which she is equally capable of realising in tranquil, silent contemplation. She also sets the given material world, with its sequential succession of events, in opposition to her own creation in which she explores the depth of events, their continual essence and their simultaneous order and juxtaposition, a reality preferable to her: 'Life was being spent in watching the glint of sunlight upon waves, believing it her own sunlight and permanent, while all the time it was light created by others, by millions of lives in the past, by all the labour that now kept the world going' (III, 507).

Having decided to reject the other, unacceptable reality because, in passively accepting the system in the outside world, she has been spiritually dead and living in unreality, she decides to withdraw from the material world and to enter further into the immaterial world of solitude. Significantly, she also justifies this withdrawal as a step which is necessary in order to protect her own individuality: 'I must create my life. Life is creation. Self and circumstances the raw material . . . And in going off to create my own I must leave behind uncreated lives' (III, 508).

Volume Three thus brings with it an increasing emphasis upon the primacy of the individual, with solitude conceived as Miriam's means of protecting and preserving her self and her own distanced world as the centre and locus of the real.

Ultimately, then, Miriam does adopt a clear position, since she increasingly pronounces the outside world, with its manner of ordering events and worlds in temporal sequences and spatial distances and its demand for continual motion and superficial existence, as 'unreal'. Experiencing immateriality in solitude, which facilitates a temporally and spatially juxtaposition of worlds, is in turn endowed with the status of being 'real'. Furthermore, Miriam becomes more and more convinced that the developments in her own life are governed by an 'inner arrangement' (III, 237), fulfilling a pre-ordained pattern. Increasingly, Miriam believes that the so-called eternal, recurring 'same' controls all events. This conviction provides her with additional justification for her preference for a state of still, tranquil being rather than one of transformative becoming. Although she insists that the individual forms the centre of her own world, she includes only the individual's ideas and thoughts and not his or her actions, which necessarily require presence in the material world. The subject is thus viewed not as being a self-determining actor in the world but as fulfilling a pattern; rather than structuring events, events happen to the subject. Nevertheless, individuals are active in the privileged, immaterial world in the sense that they create their own reality.

This new emphasis upon the individual, accompanied as it is by the definite notion of a centre, as well as the topological arrangement of the inner region and the surface as an explanatory device, also inscribes her notion of gender difference, focused primarily on differences in perception and representation of reality. In an attempt to encompass the various positions which men and woman in England adopt in relation to reality, Miriam draws up the following topology:

> The English differences, the women moving, more and more ... towards the heart of life and men getting further and further away from the living centre? Ought men and women to modify each other, each standing, as it were, half-way between the centre and surface, each with a view across the other's territory? Or should they accentuate their natural differences? *Were* the differences natural? (III, 271)

Even if Miriam does not wholly accept specifically feminine attributes and continues to perceive her identity as a conflictual, intermediary position, she nevertheless postulates two opposing worlds. She continues to view the masculine world as eloquent but ultimately unknowing ('cleverness and ignorance' (III, 279)), since men's blinkered verbal formulae only grasp the surface of things, their abstract ideas and theories leave out the essential and, as her conflict with Hypo demonstrated, they seek to explain everything with reference to ideas rather than to life, that is, 'in terms of things': 'Skimmed off the surface, which was all they could see, and set up neatly in forcible quotable worlds. The rest could not be shown in these clever, neat phrases' (III, 62). She argues that the masculine mode of representation can have no exclusive claim to truth because it lacks contact with life: 'There was truth in it, but not anything of the whole truth ... all their thoughts false to life; everything neatly described in single phrases that are not true' (III, 14).

Masculinity comes to be located at the surface, 'away from the living centre', precisely because it so highly values the unceasing superficial movement and change but in so doing alienates itself from an immediate understanding of reality and from an orientation towards the self as a permanent centre. Miriam states: 'But men have no sense of atmosphere. They only see the appearances of things, understanding nothing of their relationships' (III, 100). Not only does she deny the masculine world an understanding of reality in its entirety, she also claims that its emphasis upon becoming as opposed to being is rooted in men's 'absence of personality' and their lack of a sense of self ('unselfconscious' (III, 278)). She declares that 'it causes them to be moulded by their occupations, taking shape, and status, from what they do' (III, 280).

Having in Hypo and Michael key representatives, the masculine world is associated as a whole with subordination to, and dependence upon, an abstract system of ideas and thus with the loss of individuality: 'men invent systems of ethics, but they cannot weigh personality; they have no individuality, only conformity or non-conformity to abstract systems' (III, 37). Miriam invests the world of women, which she localises at the centre, 'in the heart of life', with an immediate, non-linguistic, silent wisdom which is based upon lived experience. In contrast to men's changeability, she regards women as true to their own selves and as untouched by external changes: 'remain herself . . . at home in life, central' (III, 280). While this feminine world may lack verbal eloquence, women possess in its stead a comprehensive wisdom derived from life: they are 'illiterate, hampered . . . and yet with a perfect knowledge' (III, 280). Women, Miriam argues, assess life from within ('seeing from inside' (III, 37)); they do not allow themselves to be distracted or deceived by appearances; instead, they focus their attention on the permanent essence in things and always ensure that their knowledge and utterances spring from a still centre within the self. This renewed affirmation of the attributes of the feminine world enables Miriam to explain more precisely why feminine speech must be inconstant and unclear:

> Views and opinions are masculine things. Women are indifferent to them . . . a woman's opinions and interests change with her different husbands . . . It is that women can hold all opinions at once, or any, or none. It's because they see the relations of things which don't change, more than things which are always changing, . . . but behind it all their own lives are untouched. (III, 259)

Once again, Miriam emphasises that women have a double allegiance in the sense that they occupy, usually even simultaneously, the superficial position of masculine 'views and opinions' *and* the permanent centre. In this way, their knowledge involves a simultaneous awareness of multiplicities as well as a many-*layer*edness, both of these standing in direct contrast to the one-sidedness and confinement to *one* level in masculine speech.

Thus, Miriam finally assigns an artistic skill to the feminine world, one which she views as an expression of the permanent being and immediate contact with life peculiar to women. This skill is defined as an 'art of making atmospheres' (III, 257) which is associated with 'self-sacrifice' (III, 258) and in which women act as a medium for life to express itself; that is, life achieves its expressive power in and through women. Miriam opposes this gift to men's art, which she sees as consisting in 'self-realization' (III, 258) as well as in their orientation towards the future which reveals their failure to live in the permanent present: 'Men weave golden things; thought, science, art, religion, upon a black background. They never are. They only make or do; unconscious of the quality of life as it passes ... men have no present ... That would explain their *ambition* ... their doubting speculations about the future' (III, 280).

Although women alone share a non-linguistic marvelling at existence – 'the utter astonishment of life ... before speech' – this being an integral part of their sensitivity to atmospheres, Miriam is nevertheless forced to concede that it would be possible to share this insight clearly and intelligibly only in the masculine world: 'Yet it would be easier to make all this clear to a man than to a woman. The very words expressing it have been made by men' (III, 280).

Since Miriam herself seeks to promote self-realisation and the ability to communicate experience in language as aspects of her own world, she distances herself from this feminine art – 'I don't want to exercise the feminine art' (III, 258). She fears that embracing women's inner power would mean 'becoming a slave' (III, 37) for, like men, she is capable of conceiving abstract ideas and thus has 'a masculine mind' (III, 236). In Miriam's view, it is precisely this intermediary position which enables her to recognise the plurality of life: ' I'm as much a man as a woman. That's why I can't help seeing things' (III, 221). Moreover, in proclaiming poetic creativity to be androgynous, as when she speaks of Yeats and the 'half man's half woman's adoration he gave to the world' (III, 502), she gives a further justification for assuming this in-between position, viewing it as the prerequisite for her own creative activity.

In her attempt to fulfil both her paternal and her maternal inheritance, she recognises the pattern which dictates the direction in which her life is leading. From her mother she inherits the following supposedly feminine position: 'Resisting the drawing of lines and setting up of oppositions ... More and more consciously ranged on all sides simultaneously' (III, 245). She adopts her father's 'sceptical intuitive mind' (III, 246). In this way, she interprets her continual shifting and curiosity as well as her indecision, which leads her to withdraw into the uncommitted multiplicity of her own solitude, as direct manifestations of an androgynous position:

> Within me ... the third child, the longed-for son, the two natures, equally matched, mingle and fight? It is their struggle that keeps me adrift, so variously interested and strongly attracted, now here, now there? ... Feeling so identified with both, she could not imagine either of them set aside. Then her life would be the battlefield of her two natures. (III, 250)

In order to express the contradiction inherent to any representation of existential reality, Miriam draws up a topology which is structured along the same lines as the opposition between the masculine and feminine worlds. She divides reality into two layers, into a surface reality which is always mobile and can be rendered through facts and verbal eloquence, and a reality which exists beneath the surface and is located in an inner region. This second layer of reality may be recognised only in silence and embodies a form of invisible and unnameable, yet continuous and coherent centre: a permanent, continual essence:

> Underlying things... But the words belonging to the underlying things were far away only to be found in long silences, and sounding... irrelevant, often illogical and self-contradictory, impossible to prove,... There are two layers of truth. The truths laid bare by common sense... founded on apparent facts, are incomplete. They shape the surface,... recognizable, in a sort of general busy prosperous agreement; but... enormous things are left behind, unsuspected, forced underground, but never dying, ... The surface shape is powerful... but in everyone alone, often unconsciously, is something, a real inside personality that is turned away from the surface. In front of every one, away from the bridges and catchwords, is an invisible plank, that will bear. Always. Forgotten. (III, 181)

It is a question not of giving one layer exclusive precedence over the other but rather of rearranging and redefining the priorities. Miriam indicates that the one layer, conceived as the *surface*, cannot be viewed as having supreme validity since it never comes into contact with the other *underlying* layer, the latter left undescribed as a result of the limited expressive capacity of language. In this manner, she gives renewed emphasis to this unrecognised aspect, indeed giving it privileged status, yet not an exclusive validity. She thus draws attention to her vision of the individual as a permanent centre, as well as to that which is invisible on the surface in the material world, but is nevertheless present and exerts an unseen influence. Miriam's earlier conviction that language cannot express anything – 'the way words express almost nothing at all' (III, 369) – may now be seen to signify that a true expression of the real necessarily encompasses both the superficial, linguistic level and the layer of the un-speakable which expresses itself in silence.

Here, too, it is significant that the real is localised in transcendence of temporal succession and in the individual's creative rearrangement of experienced events. The individual, as the creative centre, constitutes the locus of the real: 'But this was life! These strange unconsciously noticed things, living on in one, coming together at the right moment, part of a *reality*' (III, 133).

Although the expressive power of language is still assigned to the 'superficial' layer of truth and thus cannot, in the context of these spatial metaphors, articulate the deeper layer of reality, there is now increased emphasis on Miriam's opportunity to transcend the boundaries of her own linguistic capacities in language. Miriam progresses beyond her realisation that language is not sufficiently able to capture reality and now considers that it might be possible to express the overlooked or un-speakable aspects by employing a mode of oblique representation. In this way, her awareness of the limited opportunities for representing reality in language itself leads to an awareness of the very things that it does not express. Miriam explains: 'Faintly everyone knows that nothing can be said. Then why listen any more? Because if you know, exactly, that nothing can be said and the expert reasons for it, you know for certain in times of weakness, how much there is that might be expressed if there were any way of expressing it' (III, 173). Miriam's consciousness of the limited expressive capacity of language thus creates a silence, an aporia, around something, and it is precisely in this imposed silence that the underlying layer is expressed; as a promise which lies beyond the boundary.[17]

Miriam sees a further means of articulating that inner region of reality in the infinite variety of linguistic expression. She considers whether it might be possible to repeat a description in such a way that the repetition does not necessarily deaden the object of speech but instead encircles it and creates it anew, in a process of constant transformation:

> Speech did something to things; set them in a mould that was apt to come up again; repeated, it would be dead ... Perhaps the same thing could be said over and over again, with other things with it, so that it had a different shape, sang a different song and laughed all round itself in amongst different things. (III, 129)

At stake is a negative mode of representation communicating something by highlighting what it is *not*.

A further attempt to preserve the power of language, without falsifying the represented object, consists in viewing language without regard for its use or application. This would require one not to give evidence, not to assume one point of view nor to attempt to take control of an object of speech. Miriam becomes increasingly fascinated by a linguistic experience which does not provide a clear transfer of meaning and does not labour under the false assumption that an object of speech has been captured by representing it in language. For a time, she ceases to demand that an object of speech which is situated in the inner region of truth ought to be captured using a language which is situated on the surface of truth. This facilitates a simple, aimless enjoyment of the play of words, a pleasure which neither generates a binding relationship between signifier and signified nor mediates any determinable meaning. It is precisely this *absence* of linguistic reference which gives voice to something 'impossible to explain' directly. As Miriam explains: 'Finding things without following the story was like being interested in a lesson without mastering what you were supposed to master and not knowing anything about it afterwards that you could pass on or explain ... Why did everything seem alive in a way it was impossible to explain?' (III, 69).

The final volume of *Pilgrimage* revolves around Miriam's embrace of creative solitude and the spiritual, inner world in an effort to attain a condition of abstinence, a spiritual 'annihilation of every known aspect of her external world' (IV, 296). In the first three volumes, Miriam either undertook to divide the 'outside world' into multiple worlds in order to discover correlations between these and her own world, or criticised the outside worlds and distanced herself from these as a means of ascertaining her own position. From the novel *Oberland* onwards, however, she privileges an uninvolved, spiritual detachment. Miriam declares of herself: 'in the recent past, she had rounded an unseen corner, grown observant and therefore detached' (II, 25). Since she has finally established the features of her own world, she loses all interest in entering even briefly into contact with the outside world. The description of Miriam during her stay in Oberland as 'an onlooker, appreciative, but resistant' (II, 39) is an accurate summary of her behaviour throughout Volume Four, for, in contrast to her previous behaviour, her contact with other worlds serves only to reinforce her sense of self. She can now fully embrace her fantasy of 'floating free of all attachments' (IV, 301) and relinquish all definite and judgmental positions in relation to others. As a result, she ceases to regard that which is foreign and unacceptable to her as a threat, since she no longer needs to assure herself that the positions which do not correspond to her own world are false. Instead, she is able to acknowledge that their unacceptable features are 'other' without having to incorporate them as negative qualities into her own world-making. Ultimately, what she achieves is a position of complete impartiality: 'I'm not taking *sides* any more. You can't have a middle without edges, right and left. Or edges without a middle' (IV, 164).

However, this new position also generates an increasingly rigid boundary between Miriam and the other worlds, in contrast to the previous volumes, where this boundary was more fluid, with Miriam at times situated between worlds, at other times belonging to one world or another. One might say that her final, absolute rejection of all one-sided positions enables her to perceive the boundaries dividing the various different worlds even more clearly. The dividing lines between the worlds and her separation from all of the worlds is thus postulated as relatively final; characters and certain experiences are assigned more decisively to one single world. And if the shifting boundaries of the previous volumes were accompanied by Miriam's unwillingness to commit herself entirely to one world, so the increasingly distinct boundaries between Miriam and the other worlds is contingent upon her willingness to commit herself to one world, not, however, limiting herself to a material world but rather to the immaterial world of writing. In the following passage, Miriam voices her new desire to belong to a world:

> The worlds from which one after another she had retreated, gathered round her redeemed from bondage to time and place, each, now, offering a brimming cup her unsteady hands had been unable to hold, each showing as a most desirable dwelling-place ... The desire to commit oneself came from the sense of having, at last, an available identity. (IV, 424)

This indifferent detachment, with its tendency towards abstinence, has two consequences for Miriam's assessment of the outside world. On the one hand, she recognises for the first time that each world has an independent and intrinsic value; she accepts that what the other constructs as 'real' does not consist in its correlation with herself, but in its fundamental difference. As she sees Harriett sitting on the Barnes' veranda, she becomes aware of her sister's own loneliness:

> There she was gazing, in solitude into her own being ... For the first time I realized the unique, solitary person behind the series of appearances that so far represented in my mind the sister called Harriett ... Returned to the heart of the darkness, I begged myself to remember, every day, this sudden glimpse of reality. (IV, 608)

In the course of her world-making, Miriam did not engage in social interaction for its own sake; she always had an ulterior motive, namely, to create her own world by discovering aspects of herself in the other. Other characters thus tended to be reduced to certain key attributes, regarded as representatives of certain particular worlds. It is not until she has fully established her own world and ceases to have a vested interest in contemplating the other, that she is in a position to look beyond herself and her own needs and genuinely able to recognise and understand the other's unique, separate reality.

This is admittedly an indirect awareness of the other, born of Miriam's consciousness of her own boundaries, and thus implicitly enabling her to recognise the presence of something beyond herself, even if she is unable to grasp it. Now that Miriam has completed the phase of her world-making, she is able to reassess the accuracy of her judgments. She concedes that the validity of her world-making with its extremely idiosyncratic judgments, may actually be confined to herself alone; that it neither necessarily speaks for others nor necessarily does justice to the other characters and their own unique realities. In qualifying the validity of her world-making, she acknowledges that others possess separate realities, realities which she may not necessarily be able to grasp: 'We all have different sets of realities' (IV, 309).

This realisation has considerable implications for a shift in Miriam's understanding of communication as an encounter in a third space. Whereas in the first three volumes she regarded successful communication between two separate subjects as consisting in a shared occupation of a third 'same', she now comes to value a shared awareness of mutual solitude (being 'together in solitude') and of the insurmountable division between two individuals as the most privileged mode of communication with another.

Furthermore, this disinterested detachment from the outside worlds (the psycho-topological analogue to contemplative space) leads to a continuation of Miriam's comparative shifting between different worlds which was discussed earlier. Thus, as before, her contact with Hancock's 'world of silent or speechful communion' (IV, 210) makes all other worlds appear relative: it 'set her other worlds at a distance' (IV, 210). Similarly, Selina's alien presence in the Wimpole Street, as Miriam says, 'in one of my worlds' (IV, 183), also makes her aware of its enduring appeal. Miriam briefly entertains the idea of married life with Guerini in Italy, yet a comparison with her London world swiftly dispels this fantasy: 'In London it at once fell into proportion and became absurd' (IV, 123).

However, the comparisons and correlations undertaken here possess a new quality: they no longer help Miriam to clarify the most suitable world but instead reinforce the decision which she has already taken, namely to abandon all of these different worlds. In the context of this new mode of comparing worlds, Miriam describes her withdrawal back into her own world as follows: '[She] slipped back into her own world, into the half-conscious conspiracy of avoidance. Orderly world. A pattern world, life flowing in bright set patterns under a slowly gathering cloud' (IV, 106). Now that she is no longer directly involved in them, these worlds acquire a new charm. She continues to view the most diverse characters as representatives for one particular kind of world, stating, for example, that the majority of the guests in Oberland are 'representative of England, the middle-class . . . their world of villa and garden, their gentle enclosed world' (IV, 90). Likewise, she still regards encounters between strongly opposed opinions as 'the spectacle of two worlds in collision' (IV, 236). Significantly, however, she now no longer feels compelled to defend her own position, since she is able to observe these unacceptable worlds dispassionately, as a kind of distant, independent panorama. Her earlier Lycurgan Socialist attempts to show Vereka and Eden (as representatives of the 'enclosed world' of the English bourgeoisie) that their world represents 'innocent mental oblivion' and that it is based on a disregard for other worlds, now appear irrelevant. Indeed, her detached attitude even leads her to mitigate her judgments. Now viewing it with an impersonal gaze, she discovers a charm in the English middle class, the world which she had previously judged as wholly unacceptable: 'a deep, common understanding exists at the heart of English hypocrisy . . . A deep quality that comforts' (IV, 252). Using this so-called 'quality' as a criterion, she sorts the different worlds into two groups and thus establishes a comprehensive explanatory pattern for her past experiences. The presence of this 'deep quality' unites the following, hitherto divided worlds: 'home, a tolerant, liberal atmosphere in a conservative home . . . In the English girls in Hanover, in the Pernes . . . In the Corries. In the Orlys and Mr. Hancock and the majority of their patients. In all kinds of Oberlanders . . . of all classes?' (IV, 252). The absence of this attribute in turn links all the other worlds: 'All the others, the German girls and the north-country Brooms, Irish Julia Doyle, the Tansley Street people and Michael and radical Mag and cynical Jan, had been adventures outside the world where that deep quality persisted' (IV, 252). This process of division is typical for the whole of Volume Four. Judgments and assessments of the worlds – embodiments of Miriam's strategy of forming her identity – are replaced by a comprehensive explanatory pattern and a final coherence; marked by the establishment of clear boundaries and by the precise assignment of meaning. Miriam also uses this process of division to justify her decision that she must renounce her ties to the material worlds because she refuses to declare exclusive allegiance to any single world:

> The old-world people . . . Sooner or later, they discover that you belong mentally elsewhere as well as to them, and you become an object of suspicion. And the anarchists and Lycurgans bring sooner or later the feeling of living in a void. Yet if the links with them were cut, there was no life ahead. Only the lonely joy that comes and goes. (IV, 252)

Miriam's mitigation of her previously critical attitude towards the familiar and commonplace, which resulted from her detached, impersonal mode of observation, is revealed also by a marked change in her treatment of the Russian girl, Olga. This is the last example concerning a representative of foreign countries in *Pilgrimage*. Miriam also perceives Olga as standing for Russia: 'Here, once more, is Russia. But not quite the Russia brought by the Lintoffs. The girl . . . is here as an interested investigator' (IV, 632). Like all of the foreigners before her, Olga has the disinterested outsider's capacity to observe and is thus able to clarify the meaning of the English world, to notice its characteristics, such as an avoidance of the subject of death as well as a certain complacency.

Now, however, Miriam also emphasises the limits of this way of seeing – 'But sees only in terms of her own values: mental, aesthetic' (IV, 633) – and highlights the advantages of her own unifying position as an 'onlooker as well as participant' (IV, 634). Since she has finally succeeded in clarifying her own identity and has established a state of detached, creative solitude as the primary feature of her own world, she is able to play a brief part in the YWCA world, without viewing this as bondage to a site of alterity. Miriam refers to her stay there as 'togetherness on neutral territory, keeping us independent in unity' (IV, 635). In taking up this double position, she also learns to appreciate certain features of this world, without needing to condemn the women's insecurity and lack of self-awareness or feeling that her own sense of self is under threat:

> Even the simplest of these young women live, even if unknown to themselves, in the Now, the eternal moment, fully; . . . their sense of Being, whatever their discontents and longings, outdoes for most of them, the desire to Become. Will triumph, throughout their lives . . . an awareness . . . of the strangeness of the adventure of *being*, of the fact of existence, anywhere, of anything at all. (IV, 635)

Unlike the YWCA women, Olga stands aside, a judgmental observer, and, as a result, she remains oblivious to their albeit unwitting awareness of being.

With regard to Miriam's relationship to the alterity of the various different worlds, this condition of 'unity-in-difference' (IV, 638) assumes the privileged position. Until now, the predominant attitude had been an intermediary position, implying a shifting alliance to different worlds. Now, Miriam's final assumption of her own world, accompanied as it is by a renunciation of such forms of belonging, renders this shifting between worlds unnecessary and is replaced by a desire for synthesis and unity. The privileged position constitutes no longer a state of 'hovering' but a dynamic peace: 'a movement that is perfect rest'. In this, Miriam's ideal of attaining a simultaneous multiplicity of worlds and opposites finally becomes psychic reality.

In the final volume of *Pilgrimage* three worlds prove to be seminal in Miriam's final encounter with the material world, not least of all because they reinforce her decision to renounce all in favour of the scene of writing: Hypo Wilson's 'world of science', with its focus upon evolution and progress; the 'womanly women', represented by Amabel, and the Quaker world of the Roscorla family in Dimple Hill.

In *Dawn's Left Hand* and *Clear Horizon*, Miriam's conflict with Hypo's world centres on their conflicting perception of 'being' and 'becoming' and on their respective recognition or omission of that layer of the real which cannot be directly captured in language because it is located in an inner centre, invisible on the material surface. Since Hypo's world is driven by a scientific notion of material, human evolution and by belief in progress as the central moment in human development, Hypo emphasises the progressive sequentiality of events in human life and believes that human existence is fulfilled in a worldly plan. The main features of his world are, Miriam argues, a constant movement which is orientated towards the future and a one-sided concern with his own becoming: 'Achieving, becoming, driving forward to unpredictable becomings, delighting in the process, devoting himself . . . to a ceaseless becoming, ceaseless assimilating of anything that promised to serve the interests of a ceaseless becoming for life as he saw it' (IV, 220). In her view, it is this world's focus upon 'ceaseless becoming' which blinds it to the reality of each individual's permanent essence: 'He saw only what they were becoming or might become, and of the essential individual knew, and wanted to know, nothing at all' (IV, 220). Miriam realises that her emphasis upon constant being is destined to be meaningless in this world: 'There was no way of proving the importance of the individual deep sense of being that for them meant little or nothing' (IV, 167). She views her own world, 'wherein should be included also the fact of "being"' (IV, 220) as an ideal adaptation of Hypo's 'world of ceaseless becoming' and is even prepared to sacrifice their friendship in order to protect this conviction. In contrast to the Wilson world, one of the most important features of her own world is a permanent, personal centre which lies outside temporal sequentiality, a 'timeless experience independent of evolutionary development' (IV, 325). She sets her vision of 'present eternity' against Hypo's 'doomed and passing "future"' (IV, 280).

Nevertheless, it is significant that Miriam does not entirely reject the notion of 'becoming', wishing instead to change its emphasis and thus to affirm that 'being' is the centre of human life and, furthermore, that all human developments issue from this centre. Accordingly, Miriam offers a new description of her belief that a group movement is dependent upon change occurring in each individual:

> Being versus becoming. Becoming versus being. Look after being and the becoming will look after itself. Look after the becoming and the being will look after itself? Not so certain. Therefore it is certain that becoming depends upon being. Man carries his bourne within himself and is there already, or he would not even know that he exists. (IV, 362)[18]

Miriam's criticism of Hypo's world is that it places *exclusive* emphasis upon the notion of 'becoming' and, moreover, that Hypo's perception of the world reduces 'becoming' to a one-dimensional, flat surface which is restricted to a material, sequential ordering of events, making him incapable of perceiving, or unwilling to perceive, any other layers of reality. Since his vision of the world remains confined to one layer, it represents a metonymic mode of thought. Miriam counters this with her own desire to think metaphorically and, by so doing, to achieve a simultaneous awareness of different layers of reality. In looking beyond the temporal and spatial ordering on the material surfaces, she seeks to generate a simultaneous juxtaposition of events which, when viewed from the vantage point of this surface layer, might appear to be separate or mutually exclusive.

The return to her own centre ('the heart of her being' (IV, 219)) is posited more and more insistently as an alternative to her inhabiting Hypo's world, which would necessarily be unsatisfactory. The return to her centre also involves a preference for a metaphorics of space and for a mode of expression which lies along the vertical and associative linguistic axis: 'Down and down . . . that self within herself, who was more than her momentary self, . . . down in the innermost sphere of happy solitude' (IV, 222). Permanent being is viewed as being more than a momentary self, for the reason that it is not bound to one single, superficial and sequential layer, but instead contains and unites within itself multiple manifestations of the momentary self.

Miriam becomes more and more convinced that Hypo's world, a 'world of hard fact' (IV, 282) confined to a linguistic registration of the world's surface and to scientific explanations, propositions and formulae, 'wide shallow definitions and interpretations all neatly in place' (IV, 222), can never articulate her vision of reality. The 'inside things' (IV, 417) which are privileged in her vision of the world – metaphysical wonder at the fact of human existence, the non-linguistic inner world, 'an unseen world and an unseen power in communication with every single soul' (IV, 228), 'reality that thought could neither touch nor express' (IV, 281), 'the being far away within' (IV, 225) – none of these central features of her world can be expressed in Hypo's scientific mode of expression, even though Miriam insists upon their status as truths which can balance out his theoretical, evolutionary plans for human development without fitting into his explanatory patterns. These truths represent 'alternative interpretations of his overpowering collection of facts' (IV, 142).

Again and again, Hypo tries to understand Miriam's experiences of transcendence using his scientific terminology – 'his mind extended a verbal tentacle to grasp the miracle and set it within the pattern of doomed and disappearing things of which his world was made' (IV, 280).

Yet these attempts lead to misunderstandings and, finally, to their break-up because Miriam recognizes the inadequacy of Hypo's intellectual brilliance and of the dazzling displays of eloquence which characterise his world. Gaps and inconsistencies begin to emerge in his comprehensive plan: '[she felt] the insufficiency of these to encompass reality . . . growing . . . increasingly impatient of the scientific metaphors tyrannizing unquestioned within so much of his statements . . . the gaps in this scheme of salvation' (IV, 361).[19] For women to be a part of Hypo's world, they must either sacrifice their own world unconditionally by becoming a 'disciple' or play a role which enables them to follow his discourse, while at the same time returning to their 'own deep world' when they are alone again:

> Being obliged to shut off, in order to meet him in his world, his shaped world, rationalized according to whatever scheme of thought was appealing to him at the moment, three-fourths of their being . . . There was no place in his universe for women who did not either sincerely, blindly, follow or play up and make him believe they were following. (IV, 223)

Miriam sees 'the vast strange promise within' (IV, 141) as an alternative to the self-deception and failed communication associated with belonging to his world, concluding from this that she cannot have a relationship in which the other individual, does not share in her own vision of essential permanence and of the continually present personal centre:

> She demanded of herself whether she cared for him ... so much as the certainty of being in communion with something always there, something in which and through which people could meet and whose absence, felt with people who did not acknowledge it, made life at once impossible, made it a death worse than any dying. (IV, 229)

Miriam's final decision to withdraw from Hypo's world is also reinforced by a comparison with Amabel and her feminine world. Amabel, in offering an alternative attitude towards reality, characterised by respect for the individual – 'a real rare love for the essential human being' (IV, 245) – enables Miriam to apprehend further points of conflict between her and Hypo's world. Miriam regards the meeting which she stages between her two friends as 'a meeting between the representatives of two countries, incomparable and incompatible' (IV, 315). In Miriam's eyes, Amabel stands for the 'world of womanly woman', a woman who uses her feminine charm and weakness strategically to gain influence: 'managing men by means of masked flattery' (IV, 343). At the same time, however, Amabel also embodies the other attributes of this world: immediate contact with one's own being and unity with the reality at the centre, features which Miriam sets against men's inner conflict and their position on the surface of reality. She refers to Amabel as 'certain in the way a man so rarely is certain, whole where he is weak. Deeply ensconced within her being, and therefore radiant' (IV, 345). Amabel embodies the 'specifically feminine' art, in the sense that, conscious of her effect upon others, she turns herself and her personal experiences into a work of art in everyday life. In contrast to 'masculine' art, which looks to self-fulfilment, Amabel's so-called 'specifically feminine' creativity is represented as a form of self-sacrifice. Woman, become selfless, acts an instrument in and through which life and atmospheres may be rendered tangible. Miriam interprets Amabel's performance of her own self in the following way: 'What she so rejoicingly exploits is not only herself, but what she impersonally represents; moving in all her exploitations, from self to selflessness. Willingly dedicated? She is what a man can never fully be: the meeting place of heaven and earth' (IV, 345).

If one recalls the earlier discussion of the semantic encoding of actual material spaces, it becomes clear that, in her function as a mediator at the threshold between two worlds, Amabel herself represents, figuratively speaking, a *significant space* on two levels.

Firstly, she is able, *through* and *with* her corporeal self, to generate a meaningful, artistic gathering of different levels of being. It is this significant gathering which Miriam seeks to realise in immaterial artistic production, by withdrawing from the material world and creating her own text. In this way, Amabel acts as a complete fulfilment of Miriam's demand that one should create in and with life or, as she says, 'in terms of life'. This is revealed particularly clearly in the passage in which Miriam describes Amabel's manner of writing a letter, which stands in sharp contrast to Hypo's 'cool critical facts':

Between each letter of each word was as much space as between the words they were supposed to compose. Yet each was expressive, before its meaning appeared. Each letter, carelessly dashed down, under pressure of feeling, was a picture, framed in the surrounding space. It was this strange, direct, as if spoken communication, that was making the reading of this letter so new an experience . . . These written words were alive in a way no others she had met had been alive . . . it called her directly to the girl herself, making her, and not the letter, the medium of expression. Each word, each letter, was Amabel . . . was one of the many poses of her body. (IV, 215)

Furthermore, by dispensing with conventional means of signification, Amabel's letter also circumvents the dilemma that language can never fully permit intersubjective communication. Amabel's writing resembles a speech which draws attention to the speaker and not to the words. It is a direct form of self-expression, in the sense that it leads straight to Amabel herself rather than to the content of her writing, which does not attempt to render tangible a immaterial idea; the written communication instead renders language itself physical, since it is placed at the service of Amabel's own self-performance. This is an example of an non-reflective, purely atmospheric mode of expression; the complete artistic application of one's own self. Unlike Miriam, who sees herself and her experiences in the material world as the starting point for a textual re-creation of the world, Amabel's creativity is firmly rooted in the material world.

Miriam also regards Amabel in terms of a 'significant space' owing to the particular nature of their relationship, to its 'inexpressible quality' (IV, 658). Miriam finds in Amabel a response to her own reality, a reality which she had previously encountered only in solitude. For the first time, Miriam is able to share her reality with someone else: 'The girl's reality appealing to her own . . . acknowledged . . . in herself and the girl, . . . somehow between them in the mysterious interplay of their two beings, the reality she had known for so long alone, brought out into life' (IV, 217). This deep, mutual encounter allows Miriam to glimpse new opportunities for 'wordless communion' (IV, 245), sharing the space that unites them with an hitherto unknown intensity: 'Alternating between intense awareness of the beloved person and delight in every aspect, every word and movement, and a solitude distinguishable from the deepest, coolest, most renewing moments of lonely solitude only in the enhancement it reaped by being shared' (IV, 242). In creating a state of mutual, shared solitude, the friendship with Amabel fulfils the demands which Miriam makes of interpersonal communication. Miriam repeatedly measures Hypo's world against the standard of this shared 'rich deep world' (IV, 317) and this contrast intensifies her vision of Hypo as being 'enclosed and enmeshed' (IV, 316) in an unfulfilling world. Interestingly, however, Miriam would have been unable to express this relationship in language without having at least briefly occupied Hypo's world. In other words, even though essentially non-linguistic experiences, as, for example, her mental flight, are entirely alien to Hypo's 'masculine' world with its unambiguous language, it is only by availing herself of this 'masculine' mode of expression that Miriam can communicate these other states. It is not until Miriam attempts to tell Hypo about Amabel that she finds words with which she can express the quality of their friendship.

And yet, precisely those features which make Amabel so vital to Miriam prove to be why she finds she must ultimately distance herself again.

For one, she rejects the feminine route Amabel opts for – marriage to Michael Shatov and maternity – in favour of creativity, which according to the rules of her world-making belongs into the masculine realm. Indeed Miriam equates Amabel's marriage with a complete sacrifice of her own world: 'Amabel watches the disappearance of her world . . . In a few hours, Amabel will be isolated, for life, with an alien consciousness . . . a death' (IV, 545). At the same time Amabel's rejection of the silence practised by the Quakers provides Miriam with final confirmation that Amabel cannot share in the central feature of her creative production, namely tranquil detachment. Ultimately, Miriam comes to regard Amabel's marriage as a satisfactory way of extricating herself from two further worlds, such that at the end of her London years she is able to conclude that all worldly hindrances have been removed from her path: 'And now she was for ever excluded from this world [Hancock], and the world she had entered [Hypo] was closing against her and the one she had inhabited with Amabel was breaking up. Ahead, nothing was visible' (IV, 365).

Although Miriam continues to reject allegiance to one single world, since it would require her to take sides – 'except in spirit one cannot join all the societies' (IV, 331) – she also recognises that her own inconstancy is a sign that no single world was ever able to hold her undivided attention. At the same time, however, she entertains the thought of committing herself exclusively to the Roscorla family's Quaker world in Dimple Hill, for initially Miriam thinks that she has found in Dimple Hill a completely satisfactory correlate of her own world since, like herself, the Roscorla family cherish solitary individuality ('the depth of her being' (IV, 594)) as well as the indestructibility of this individuality and the constant inner world beneath the surface. The Quakers' attitude towards reality demands a tranquil, silent and contemplative state of mind as well as a concentration upon one's own centre and upon permanent being: 'Be still and *know*. Still in mind as well as in body. Not meditation, for meditation implies thought. Tranquil, intense concentration . . . leads presently to contemplation, recognition' (IV, 498).[20] Precisely such non-thought-oriented concentration upon 'silent contemplation' (IV, 506) allows her to be continually conscious of the permanent essence – 'the everlasting source within and without' (IV, 588). In the Quakers' world she discovers an alternative to the usual concern with becoming and the hurried, shallow speech which revolves around defending one of a wide range of often contradictory standpoints: a distanced impartiality towards things which lie on the surface of reality, such as opinions, as well as a continual return to one's own centre. She focuses her attention not upon becoming in the future but rather upon astonishment at the depth of the present: 'Current existence, the ultimate astonisher' (IV, 611).

All actions and utterances are used only in order to communicate the essential; their mode of communication is conceived as carefully 'weighting' and patiently 'waiting'. The Quakers do not seek to use rhetorical brilliance to the test their visitor but instead they steadfastly endure the meaningful silence: 'unembarrassingly hanging fire in a stillness... deep shared stillness' (IV, 441). In using language only with the greatest reserve and care, the Quakers highlight the border between language and silence, making their speech appear to Miriam like a 'knife-edge balance between two worlds' (IV, 470). Having experienced this continual silent contemplation, Miriam feels justified in her judgment that the spoken word either wholly inhibits the emergence of the real or at the very least blunts it, 'dimming its lustre' (IV, 488). By emulating the Quakers' silence, she comes to realise that one becomes conscious of one's own being at those times when speech is held back: 'a sudden touch upon one's inmost being... bringing the sense of being, for the fraction of a second, oneself the dynamic centre of advancing life' (IV, 540). Furthermore, it is the sparing use of speech, resulting from a sense of one's separation from others and expressing a solitary centredness upon one's own being, which renders the spoken word so significant: 'Enabling the speakers to address each other indirectly, impersonally, from a distance, so that even the simplest words became jewels set in a spacious light' (IV, 589).

Accordingly, it is shared silence, not the spoken word, which unifies the inhabitants of the Quaker world. Miriam terms this silence 'a sense of recovery, of a return to a common possession, the richer for having been temporarily forgotten' (IV, 473). In contrast to conventional silence, this unifying 'space', however, enables people to experience permanent essence and liberates them from the temporally sequential surface layer of reality: 'The moment we found ourselves together, time stood still... our intermittent silences... rather than tension-creating searches for fresh material, were fragments of a shared eternity' (IV, 567). In this way, the Quaker meeting, characterised as it is by silence, distance and concentration in one's own being, represents a privileged position for Miriam, since it cancels the opposition between solitude and contact and thus generates distanced interest and dispassionate fascination in the other: 'The richest depth of social experience is to be had only in relation to those who, while exercising a poignant appeal, make no demands' (IV, 510). In this silent encounter, one's own world is preserved and, at the same time, this togetherness is experienced as a complement to solitude: 'a serenity... far richer than the same kind of serenity achieved in solitude' (IV, 470), 'silence that would deepen, by enabling it to be shared' (IV, 437).

In addition to this, the Quakers' impartial, distanced attitude – their attempt to live out a perfect, constant balance between their own centre and connection to the material world – confirms Miriam's growing conviction that distance is a precondition for true vision: 'Distance does not *lend* enchantment. It shows where it is. In the thing seen, as well as in the eye of the beholder. And I realized one of the Quaker secrets. Living always remote, drawn away into the depths of the spirit, they see, all the time, freshly. A perpetual Sunday' (IV, 491).

Despite her attempts to enter into the Quaker world (IV, 463), Miriam recognises that the strong attraction which she feels towards this world is nevertheless flawed, since it necessarily excludes other worlds which also correspond to features in herself. The Dimple Hill world, for example, derives its significance from its opposition to the different London worlds and from being linked solely to one site, namely the countryside. Miriam asks herself upon arriving there for the first time: 'If she had heard of the Roscorlas as living in London, would she have sought them out?' (IV, 433). The implicit negative reply to this hypothetical question is reinforced when, during her stay in London, Miriam talks to Amabel about Richard Roscorla with Amabel, for in this world his presence is 'inconceivable . . . Reduced to nothing. Indifferent. Apart from his surroundings, Richard is nothing to me' (IV, 546). At the same time all her other worlds cannot be sustained in Dimple Hill. There is no place here for Hypo's science and reason, issues of feminism or ethnic alterity, nor for her perfect friendship with Jean: in the Quaker world everything that does not belong to it is 'without significance' (IV, 464).

Thus Miriam recognises that the attraction Dimple Hill has for her is that she inhabits this world as a welcome guest, without being permitted to become a member. She differentiates sharply between her own world and that of the Roscorlas, not least of all because the pleasure she derives from reading and writing secular fiction is foreign and disagreeable to them: 'Yet the delight of this reading is profane, dependent upon a kind of culture alien to these people. Read downstairs in their company the text would lose much of its savour' (IV, 454).

Miriam learns that she cannot belong exclusively to this Quaker world either, because it demands that she should turn her back not only on her other worlds but especially on the scene of her own aesthetic creation: 'The business of minute to minute living in the spirit which gives them their perspective and their poise and serenity, is the best I've met. But the thought of the missing letters makes the idea of Quakerized world intolerable' (IV, 603). Discovering that she may not remain a permanent guest, but must ultimately choose to belong exclusively to their community, Miriam leaves the Quakers, in favour of her solitary room, where she is able to belong 'in spirit' to many worlds.

In the course of the last volume of *Pilgrimage*, Miriam continues to maintain that a tranquil, silent state of mind is necessary in order to recognise the continual essence. As before, she encodes solitude semantically as containing a refreshing, unknown quality: 'Loneliness . . . shelter[s] strangeness that can be known only in solitude' (IV, 24). Solitude is also a privileged place because it is there that the real may be experienced and preserved: 'in solitude amongst things whose being was complete, towards that reality of life that withdrew at the sound of a human voice' (IV, 126). The real vanishes when it is confronted with material ties to a world or with memory and anticipation. Above all, any attempt to bind oneself wholly to another individual leads to alienation from this reality. The world of marriage is unacceptable for this very reason: it is synonymous with 'the loss of unthreatened solitude' (IV, 605). Most importantly, solitude is finally acknowledged to be the only possible locus of creative production so that, at the close of *March Moonlight*, Miriam decides to abstain from all material worlds and thus clears the way for her re-creation in art: 'Solitude . . . Every distance a clear perspective . . . Each vista demands for portrayal, absence from current life, contemplation, a long journey' (IV, 655).

As became apparent in the previous discussion, Miriam increasingly comes to regard herself as possessing a 'persistent, unchanging, personal identity' (IV, 304) which is untouched by change. She distances herself from a sequential ordering of events which is located on the surface of reality and centred upon becoming, instead emphasising as the most important features of her own world the unchanging, permanent essence of being ('changeless central zone of her being' (IV, 299), the depth of her own being ('deep quiet sense of *being* . . . Perfect in itself' (IV, 172)) as well as the uniqueness (IV, 134) and eternity of every event – 'immortal moment' (IV, 561), 'continuous moment that was always and everywhere the same' (IV, 176). The layer of reality central to her world is the invisible one which is situated behind or beneath each single thing: 'the reality underlying the thin criss-cross pattern of events' (IV, 384) and is untouched by the temporal dimension: a 'timeless reality' (IV, 298). In this way, the crucial decision for the development of her own identity is to occupy this immitable centre, rather than anticipating changes in the future: 'To know beforehand where you are going is to be going nowhere. Because it means you are nowhere to begin with. If you know where you are you can go anywhere, and it will be the same place and good' (IV, 172). Miriam still conceives of her own world as a point at which different irreconcilable aspects converge, each aspect corresponding to something in the outside worlds: 'Being a collection of persons . . . Yet the lives she lived with each one were sharply separated lives, separable parts of herself, incompatible' (IV, 122). Her vision of her own identity as a worldly, intermediary position thus stems from her desire to share simultaneously, in multiple worlds, a position which is available only to the dispassionate, reserved observer: 'certain outsiders . . . see *all* the game . . . People who have never plunged into life' (IV, 238). At the same time, however, she views her identity as a place in which she gathers together and preserves her own correlates for several worlds which are irreconcilable in the outside world.

As a result, even greater emphasis is placed upon her sense of her own existence as being split between two levels. At one level, there is the material outside world, which she views as a 'superficially dynamic world of external change and new ideas' (IV, 406) in which she sees her existence as a 'ceaseless stream of events set in a ceaseless stream of inadequate commentary' (IV, 305). The second level contains her own immobile, unchanging centre (IV, 305), a place which embodies 'continuous reality' (IV, 406) and preserves her eternally youthful essence. The division between the inner and outer worlds is strengthened, with the inner world representing a preferable substitute (IV, 224) for an outside world which threatens to lose all traces of charm and which Miriam even at times refers to as unreal and illusory.

Miriam expresses her relentless gaze upon reality, characterised as it is by a desire to reject her familiar world in favour of a distanced inhabitation of her inner world, as follows:

> Supposing this cold contemplation of reality stripped of its glamour were all that remained, there was still space in consciousness, far away behind this benumbed surface, where dwelt whatever it was that now came forward, not so much to give

battle as to invite her to gather herself away . . . and watch, from a distance, unattained. (IV, 296)

In one respect, her preference for her inner world thus stems from her realisation that only detachment from the world leads to real vision and that only mediated experiences are productive: 'Vicarious suffering is the only kind that instructs' (IV, 183). Furthermore, the emphasis upon this spiritual world confirms her in her conviction that her own self-created ordering of the world is her only reality. Only by observing from within her inner world is she able to experience this personal reality, which she describes as an 'independent light on the scraps of reality she was being offered' (IV, 47). She withdraws from Hypo's world of action, explaining 'there's more space within than without' (IV, 168) and uses this discovery of an 'inner vastness of space' (IV, 307) in order to complete her independent ordering of events. The following passage, which introduces an increased concern with exploring the inner world, addresses this form of ordering past reality anew and also points implicitly to the world of the text which Miriam is to write. The primary features of this world appear to be its infinity as well as its capacity to render her own reality tangible: 'I pursue the pathway so suddenly opened last night. Towards the past. Inexhaustible wealth . . . Distance in time and space does not *lend* [enchantment]. It reveals. Takes one into heaven, or into hell' (IV, 607). In the ensuing discussion about the conditions necessary for this kind of spiritual journey, Miriam stresses the importance of restricting herself to one part of the outside world, which ought to be as small as possible: 'Perhaps the sudden return of lost reality is the result of temporarily losing freedom to move, of being compelled to concentrate, for a whole evening, upon affairs other than my own' (IV, 607).

Miriam's increased inhabitation of her own 'world of solitude', her concentration upon her own centre, as well as her recognition of the immeasurability and vastness of the 'space within', are reinforced textually in *Dimple Hill* and particularly in *March Moonlight* by an increasing use of the first person pronoun. This 'I' signals Miriam's contemplative position, her ability to look beyond herself as a subject which is bound to one or many worlds and to rearrange successive events in the outside world in a manner which corresponds to her own reality. Thus the 'I' may also be regarded both as a locus of inner-worldly events and as a site of an artistic re-creation of the world. *Pilgrimage* thus ends with Miriam's final decision to abstain from the outside world and devote herself to her own permanent centre, her 'I', marking her final acknowledgment that her own creation of the world, as opposed to the material outside world, is her chosen reality: 'Contemplation is adventure into discovery; reality. What is called "creation", imaginative transformation, fantasy, invention, is based upon reality. Poetic description a half-truth?' (IV, 657). The issue of gender difference continues to engage Miriam, especially the conditions under which women are able to inhabit the masculine world. And if in the course of her psychic pilgrimage Miriam repeatedly came to emphasise women's need to take up a double position, one possibility which now presents itself to her is that of emancipation, characterised by a complete adoption of the masculine world and an uncritical appropriation of masculine thought systems such as 'abstract reasoning' (IV, 378). However, Miriam tends to view emancipation as 'deranging and dehumanizing' (IV, 378) and as a self-imposed imprisonment, since it is tantamount to women denying and giving up their own world: 'Modern women, assimilating, against time, masculine culture, and busying themselves therein and losing, in this alien land, so much more than they gain' (IV, 381). Alternatively women can play a double role, which Miriam continues to judge as being behaviour typical of the so-called 'womanly woman', with the woman acting as 'both her husband's guardian and a masked being' (IV, 202). Such women leave their own world behind – 'turning their backs upon their own territory' (IV, 441) – in order to support and entertain their husbands and briefly inhabit an alien world, 'alert at the front gates of consciousness' (IV, 158). Nevertheless, they remain indifferent towards this foreign world, are conscious of betraying themselves and thus preserve their own individual feminine world. Of this type of woman, Miriam comments: 'She was really indifferent to the system within which she spent her outward life, aware of a world where it had no importance, perhaps taking refuge in it when she was alone' (IV, 202).

In Miriam's world, there is no overlap between the masculine and the feminine world, since the masculine world is, for women, always associated with self-deception, just as men are able to recognise the 'world of woman' only as a 'flattering echo of his own imaginings' (IV, 441). As a result, direct contact between the representatives of each world is inconceivable since they lack a common language: 'by every word they use men and women mean different things' (IV, 93). However, Miriam allows that the two worlds might be able to draw closer to one other by achieving what she terms 'shared solitude', which is to say in the encounter in a third, separate space – a kind of intermediary territory, which would enable both men and women to preserve their own worlds. Accordingly, Miriam suggests, 'People can meet only in God? The shape . . . a triangle. Woman and man at either end of the base, the apex: God' (IV, 224).

As in the previous volume, Miriam still emphasises 'becoming' and hence the 'creation of things' as attributes of the world of men, and 'being' and 'creation using one's own life' as attributes of the world of women. Within this opposition, acknowledgment in the masculine world is always related to work and achievement; in the feminine world, however, it involves a 'recognition of themselves, of what they are and represent' (IV, 230). Miriam takes the sexes' differing usage of their creative faculties as an opportunity to put into question the traditional valorisation of works of art, and the comparative disdain for creations which are firmly rooted in life and being: ' "Art", "literature", systems of thought, religions, all the fine products of masculine leisure that are so lightly called "immortal" . . . Who has decreed that "works of art" are humanity's highest achievement?' (IV, 93). In Miriam's opinion, this judgment is at fault, since it is based on a typically masculine preference for 'making things' as opposed to an ability 'to love what is made' (IV, 464) and always regards feminine creativity as inferior. In counter-distinction, for Miriam it is women whom she perceives as 'eternal being . . . eternity personified' (IV, 139).

At the same time, she avails herself of the opposition between these two models of creativity, using it as a means of situating her own identity and her own mode of recollecting and representing the past in a hybrid, intermediary position, so that she comes to recognise aspects of the feminine world within herself: 'There was a woman, not this thinking self who talked with men in their own language, but one whose words could be spoken only from the heart's knowledge, waiting to be born in her' (IV, 230). Likewise, Miriam continues to feel drawn towards 'womanly women' who radiate an intimacy with eternity, while at the same time feeling that this very admiration makes her complicit with 'the world's manhood' (IV, 162). Most importantly, she rejects a view of female creativity as being merely reproductive, declaring her frustration with conventional notions of maternity: 'No man or woman, can ever engage the whole of my interest who believes . . . that my one driving-force, the sole and shapely end of my existence is the formation within myself of another human being' (IV, 331).

Ultimately, she seeks to synthesise allegedly masculine and feminine attributes, in the sense that her creativity combines aspects from both worlds. Though using the representational strategies of the masculine world, Miriam hopes to communicate her knowledge of a non-linguistic permanent 'deep being': an awareness she tends to assign to the feminine world.

Gender difference continues to inform her search for the adequate mode of representing reality. In a passage where she considers the possible ways of describing her meeting with Selina, Miriam explains that the utterance, 'I was pleased to see Selina', would exemplify a masculine use of language, since it is concerned with the surface of the occurrence and represents the event as a fact within a sequence of events: 'stated simply, in a brief poetic lie . . . A man's statement, carrying one sanguinely along the surface of life that is so plain and simple' (IV, 184). Miriam's own poetic rendering of the meeting, in which she uses a spatial metaphor and attempts to capture the multifaceted, elusive and yet nevertheless enduring quality of this event reads, on the other hand, as follows: 'there we were meeting, each with a *solid piece of* eternity in hand. Now isn't that sort of thing wonderful, untouchable, whatever may happen afterwards' (IV, 184).

These comments expose Miriam's profound ambivalence towards the ability of language to grasp and articulate reality. Her recognition that there are limits to the possibilities of linguistic expression is linked to her awareness that she needs language if she is to communicate her psychic reality. Thus she refers to her speech as 'a barrier and yet the vehicle of her everlasting communion . . . by virtue of the echo within it of the way of being from which it had come forth' (IV, 138).

In this final phase of world-making, then, Miriam is not only concerned with establishing the precise components of her own world and defining her position in relation to the outside worlds as one of distanced, solitary and creative abstinence. More importantly, she also attempts to present her own poetics, which transcends and supplements the conventional system of ordering the world – a poetics in which, given that language proves to be a barrier between two subjects, silence emerges as the true locus of reality and the place in which individuals may communicate with one another. As a result, Miriam's realisation of how limited language is actually leads her to find ways of putting these limitations to positive use.

Miriam begins by emphasising language's dividing function: 'Words are separators, acknowledgment of separateness . . . Spirits meet and converse and understand each other only in silence' (IV, 620). True communication, she argues, occurs in silence, it runs beneath the words which are uttered (IV, 322). In her view, spoken communication is inadequate, because individuals use language to transmit thoughts rather than as a means of directly communicating their true being. Thus, she does not condemn the spoken word itself as the cause for the communicative rift, but rather its claim to unequivocal referentiality: 'One must use words embodying special references, prejudices, ways of thought, a hundred and one hidden powers amongst which communications must be steered across to someone who remains, however, well known, several times removed' (IV, 381). Miriam situates her own world *behind* the surface reality of sequential succession, with her own utterances emerging from this deep and permanent centre. In this way, she perceives her own speech as having a claim to multiplicity: 'She proposed to communicate, with all these voices that were speaking at once within her, each presenting a different aspect of what she wanted to say and leaving her to choose' (IV, 226). This ideal of multiplicity is, however, in conflict with a concise, clear and unambiguous manner of speaking: 'In speech the straight and narrow way is always either a *lie* or an *exhibition*. That is the curse of speech: its inability to express several things simultaneously. All the unexpressed things come round and grin at everything that is said' (IV, 164). Miriam's alternative to modes of utterance that claim universal validity, and privilege the transmission of ideas over the communication of permanent being is a manner of reading that does not view language as being related directly to one specific meaning. She describes her joy upon discovering a mode of reading which does not render the text clearly comprehensible:

> The miracle of intelligibility, the taken-for-granted, unconsidered revelation lying behind the mere possibility of so arranging words that meaning emerges from their relationship. And presently I ceased to look for meanings, took a phrase or a single word from its context and let it carry me into fresh contemplation of familiar realities . . . that made even advertisements read like lyrics. (IV, 454)

Miriam is not, however, prepared to banish intelligibility wholly from her own communications, so she settles in the end for a use of language in which there is a certain referentiality towards ideas, but in which this referentiality is nevertheless sufficiently flexible to permit an encounter between the speaker and the addressee. Thus, for example, she decides to impart her experience of mental flight, with its 'incommunicable essence', by using ambiguous language and silence, writing to Hypo, 'I've been up amongst the rejoicing cloud-tops' (IV, 280), convinced that this oblique representation is the only way to capture the essence of the experience: 'Just these revealing, misleading words. And then silence, indefinitely. An indefinite space for realization, free of the time-moving distractions of plans' (IV, 283). This formulation seems so appropriate to her, since it expresses the multifaceted quality inherent in every event, though necessarily absent from any univocal rendition. The silence following upon an oblique utterance is, however, so significant for Miriam, because it marks an infinite and dynamic space which is freed from the sequentiality of events in which her addressee can reconstruct Miriam's experience for himself. The fact that Hypo fails to understand this communication and interprets her words as metaphors for an expression of joy, of being *in seventh heaven*, is less crucial than the fact that this passage provides an outlet for Miriam's own poetic ideas.

One of the key's to Miriam's poetics is the question as to what the wrong, and thus implicitly also what the right, metaphors might be, for Miriam criticises conventional poetics for controlling thoughts and words by virtue of a kind of *metaphorisation*, which, rather than bringing the speaker closer to the essence of the object of speech, actually separates the speaker from it. This separation arises when metaphors are viewed as communicating one coherent notion: 'About thought. About the way its nature depends upon the source of one's metaphors. We all live under a Metaphorocrasy . . . thought is cessation, cutting one off from the central essence, bearing an element of calculation' (IV, 607). At the same time, because they require the speaker to combine two distinct paradigms, metaphors give an indication of the speaker's personality. It is not so much the superficial meaning of the words chosen but the way in which they are joined together which is today the speaker's preference for certain juxtapositions, which make it possible to infer aspects of his or her personality from the metaphor chosen. Miriam affirms that 'the metaphor you choose will represent you more accurately than any photograph' (IV, 331). This recalls her belief that it is possible to understand an individual only by learning about the quality of his or her experiences as 'images in the mind', as opposed to outlining facts of his or her life. A considerable portion of these 'linguistic images' which are formed in the identity-forming process of world-making are, in fact, metaphors. Miriam's comment about the accuracy of metaphors may be read as an indication that worlds are characterised above all by their unique configuration of metaphors and that the metaphors which are selected determine a world's entire structure.[21]

Miriam's obvious interest in metaphors would suggest that it is not metaphors as stylistic devices per se which are inadequate but the level of reality which they are conventionally used to express, namely the surface of reality, seeking to compress phenomenological and psychic existence into a coherent narrative sequence. In response to Michael's explanatory metaphor that 'the whole is greater than the parts', Miriam wonders: 'The catch in the metaphor . . . Are all the blind alleys and insufficiencies of masculine thought created by their way of thinking in propositions, using inapplicable metaphors? "See these silent wonderful". Are all coherent words, in varying measure, evidence of failure?' (IV, 427). Similarly, she sees the unacceptable feature of Hypo's world, his emphasis upon evolution, as summed up by his inapplicable metaphor for the spirit as an 'endless spiral' (IV, 607). She feels this definition to be a 'nightmare. Wrong metaphor. Spirit is central' (IV, 607).

Within her poetic world, then, metaphors lead to false modes of registering and describing reality whenever they betray one-sidedness, lack of ambivalence and sequentiality. In her poetics, the right metaphors[22] are those which reveal the central essence, as well as the 'eternally same' permanence of reality, without being reduced to a one-sided and superficial linguistic meaning, which is tantamount to being deadened.

If one recalls once more the definition of significant space as a simultaneous gathering of opposites or as a clarifying threshold between several modes of being, then the 'right metaphor' emerges as a textual representation of significant space, both as a stylistic device and in terms of what it communicates. Deleuze writes of metaphor in relation to Proust: 'The metaphor is essentially metamorphic and indicates how the two objects change their meanings, and even exchange the name by which they are identified, in the new environment which confers upon them a shared quality.'[23] In terms of its fundamental formal structure, the metaphor establishes a connection between two semantically separate objects (or paradigms) in a shared third space and thus, as a rhetorical device, achieves the simultaneous multilayeredness which characterises significant space.[24] It is not only at a stylistic level that metaphors enact a textual performance of 'significant space'. They also generate a simultaneous intersection between opposites at a *thematic* level: a point at which silence, which contains permanent essence and the real, yet cannot articulate it, converges with language, which is capable of naming but also falsifies reality in its sequential one-sidedness and omissions. Genette writes of Proust's use of metaphors: 'the metaphor is the privileged expression of a profound vision: that which transcends appearances in order to gain access to the essence of things'.[25]

The attraction of the metaphor thus lies in its creation, both thematically and as a rhetorical device, of the spatial and temporal simultaneity which constitutes the 'real' in Miriam's world-making. Achieving a successful balance between associative language and silence, the spatial metaphor represents a rhetorical device which is ideally suited both to the world of Miriam's poetics and to the entire textual world of the novel *Pilgrimage*. For this narrative as a whole contains a veritable network of spatial metaphors, spatial circumscriptions, spatial adverbs and deictic words, even while most of the relationships between characters and objects are represented in terms of space. That Dorothy Richardson did not confine her treatment of the dangers and joys of metaphors to *Pilgrimage* can be seen in a letter she wrote to Henry Savage: 'Language is a very partial medium of expression . . . Oh the helplessness surrounding the helpfulness and manifold uses of speech, the dangers within the delights of metaphor. By their metaphors ye shall know them. Metaphorocracy, that is what really all thought lives under, all the philosophies.'[26]

NOTES

1 N. Goodman, *Ways of Worldmaking* (Hassocks, 1978), 22. See Lawrence Leshan and Henry Margenau, *Einstein's Space and Van Gogh's Sky: Physical Reality and Beyond* (Brighton, 1983) for a study which applies theories from the natural sciences (especially from physics and psychology) so as to describe how reality is constructed by the observer at the moment of experience or narration.

2 In contrast to the textual formation of Miriam's lived space, her world-making does not function as a point of identification for the reader. Rather it expresses Miriam's character. However, if one considers the frequently malicious remarks which various critics have made about *Pilgrimage*, it nevertheless seems to be the case that the reader needs to feel a certain degree of sympathy for Miriam's frequently polemical claims and judgments in order to find *Pilgrimage* pleasurable. Since the novel's credibility and comprehensibility are based upon an identification with the depiction of lived space, the reader also needs to identify with the protagonist and her behaviour in this lived space, although not necessarily with the way in which she organises these experiences by creating, evaluating and differentiating her own meta-world. The weakness of both the extremely laudatory and extremely disapproving critical comments lies in their inability to overlook their subjective sympathy for, or rejection of, Miriam's judgments and, as a result, their failure to recognise that these judgments are a poetic expression of a process leading to the formation of identity. More fruitful, I would argue, are questions which, rather than addressing Miriam's polemic, consider what this constant renegotiation of her personal world-making achieves, where and how she carries this out, and where and how it is represented in the text.

3 Goodman, *Ways of Worldmaking*, 6.

4 *Ibid.*, 15.

5 *Ibid.*, 97.

6 *Ibid.*, 2.

7 The similarity ought to be noted here between this concept of the multiplicity of worlds and Bakhtin's concept of polyphony which is also adopted by Lotman. See Mikhail Bakhtin, *The Dialogic Imagination: Four Essays*, ed. Michael Holquist (Austin, 1981) and J. Lotman, *The Structure of the Artistic Text* trans. R. Vroon (Michigan, 1977). Although I am not concerned with Richardson's socio-historical context, it is interesting to note that the emphasis which she places upon the individual as opposed to the group, as well as her interest in multiplicity, simultaneity and in a constant present, reflects the dominant interests of a particular circle of modern artists and scientists. See Stephen Kern, *The Culture of Time and Space 1880–1920* (Cambridge, MA, 1983).

8 Goodman, *Ways of Worldmaking*, 21.

9 D. Richardson, 'Data for a Spanish Publisher', *London Magazine*, 6 (June 1959), 18. See Richard Macksey, 'The Architecture of Time: Dialectic and Structure', in *Proust: A Collection of Critical Essays*, ed. René Girard (Westport, 1962), 106. In his essay, Macksey traces a developmental curve in the psychotopology for Proust's novel cycle which could be applied in its entirety to *Pilgrimage*. He describes the dialectic between interior and exterior as 'expansion and concentration . . . The first movement in each case is outward toward the flux, the second a turning back on the center'. He terms the centre aptly the place for 'the remembering and reconstructing of these experiences'.

10 The following may be seen as the five basic categories: firstly, the professional English middle class with offices like the Wimpole Street practice and homes in suburbia such as the Henderson family home but also the Corries' luxury house; secondly, the women like Mag and Jan and the girls in the YWCA who earn an independent living; thirdly, the foreigners; fourthly, the representatives of various groups of intellectuals, scientists and artists, particularly the world of the Wilsons and of Tansley Street; fifthly, the religious, primarily Quaker world.

11 At this point, it is important to remember that the notion of 'world' is also crucial to the recognition of one's own spatial existence, for Richardson conceives of metaphys-

12 In *The Structure of the Artistic Text*, Lotman refers to the division of the single world of the text into different worlds which are under the influence of different characters, as a 'polyphony' of spaces and notes that 'the clash of various characters' may also represent 'a clash between their respective ideas regarding the structure of the world' (231). As I hope to show in the following individual analyses of each of the four volumes, Miriam's encounter with different characters involves such a confrontation or clash between her perception of her own world and those worlds which the characters individually represent. This is most pronounced in Miriam's encounters with Michael Shatov, Hypo Wilson and the Roscorla family.

13 The spatio-metaphorical description of the Corrie children is typical: 'They would grow up and be exactly like their parents . . . a kind of prison' (I, 363).

14 Only in solitude is Miriam able to experience her inner world. This, too, is circumscribed in spatial terms: 'her short sleep . . . had carried her down and down into the heart of tranquillity where she still lay awake and drinking as if at a source' (I, 149). Reading alone, which is characterised as 'erecting a little wall of unapproachability between herself and her family', is encoded semantically as one of the first places in which she became conscious of her inner self: 'it was the most intimate self she had known' (I, 282).

15 For a general exploration of the conventional perception of femininity, with particular emphasis upon the historical era described in *Pilgrimage*, see Viola Klein, *The Feminine Character: History of an Ideology* (London, 1946). Though their writings are separated by half a century, Richardson's notion of the double position of feminine speech is reconfirmed by Luce Irigaray's critical analysis of the image of femininity in Western philosophy, *Speculum de l'autre femme* (Paris, 1980).

16 See also R. Arnheim, *The Dynamics of Architectural Form* (Berkely, 1977), 21. He addresses the analogy between a spatial and a social experience of emptiness: 'Extreme emptiness is experienced where there are no objects at all . . . the absence of all points of reference and orientation . . . can cause ultimate terror. It social equivalent is the experience of a person who feels totally abandoned: the environment is complete without him, nothing refers to him, needs him, calls him, or responds to him. This lack of external definition destroys the internal sense of identity, because a person defines the nature of his own being largely by his place in a network of personal relations.' In a manner similar to its presentation in *Pilgrimage*, he views the occupation of a centre as analogous to positive solitude: 'a strong personality may cope with aloneness by establishing himself or herself as the center and irradiating the surrounding from the center with a sunburst of forces that animate emptiness' (22).

17 In her understanding of silence as a marker of the outermost limits of language and, equally, as an independent means of expression, Richardson addresses concerns shared by her contemporaries. Samuel Beckett is similarly interested in silence: 'the extraordinary evocation of the unsaid by the said'. See Marianne Kesting, 'Verlust des Kosmos: Kopernikanische Wende des Bewusstseins. Zur Geschichte einer Desillusion und ihrer ästhetischen Konsequenzen', *Kosmische Bilder in der Kunst des 20. Jh.s*, Staatliche Kunsthalle Baden-Baden, 1983/84, 20. In his *Tractatus logico-philosophicus* (Frankfurt, 1976), Ludwig Wittgenstein also localises the outermost border of language in silence: 'That the world is *my* world is shown by the way in which the boundary *of* language (the language which I alone understand) constitutes the boundaries of my world . . .

I am my world' (90). At a later stage, he continues: 'There are, however, things which cannot be expressed. This becomes apparent, it is the mystical . . . If one cannot speak of it, then one must be silent' (115).

18 Miriam's demand that one should embrace simultaneously both becoming and being may be compared with the following words by Max Bense in *Raum und Ich* (Munich and Berlin, 1943), 84: 'he whose being expresses only becoming or transformation cannot understand tranquillity in the abstract . . . The question of development is at once a question of the unceasing new creation of form and of nature's tendency to preserve form.' In *The Dynamics of Architectural Form* Arnheim expresses a similar view of the importance of a dynamic tension between being and becoming in human existence: 'This productive opposition of Being versus Becoming . . . the counterpoint of mobility versus dwelling place is one of those indispensable antinomies' (146).

19 Miriam's doubts about Hypo's scientific explanations and his belief in pure reason are also, of course, expressions of various philosophical disputes waged by her contemporaries, especially the conflict between theories which were orientated towards science, as well as towards material and social reform, on the one hand, and theories which focused upon phenomenological, mystical and existential issues. Richardson's treatment of these themes may be compared with the thought of Lev Shestov. *Clear Horizon* is dedicated to Shestov's translator, S. S. Koteliansky. Like Miriam, Shestov bases his rejection of evolutionary theories upon their failure to acknowledge the unique, individual essence, in short, anything which cannot be expressed or understood. In *Job's Balance*, he writes: 'However much we may have attained in science we must remember that science cannot give us truth . . . For truth lies in the singular, uncontrollable, incomprehensible, . . . and fortuitous . . . The fundamental property of life is daring; all life is creative daring and thus an eternal mystery, irreducible to anything finished or intelligible'. Cited by George L. Kline, in his piece on L. Shestov in the *Encyclopedia of Philosophy*, 7/8 (New York, 1967), 432.

20 J. Linshoten, in his essay 'Anthropologische Fragen zur Raumproblematik', describes the sense of stillness and detachment which is also explored in *Pilgrimage* as a place 'where I am simultaneously in two places and have drawn two different points in time virtually into one and where, in the simultanous double aspect of things, I have one single impression which is deepened by an extra dimension (of space and time)' (*Studium Generale*, 11 (1958), 96). Likewise, he emphasises cognitive detachment as the site which facilitates simultaneity: 'in cognition [we look upon] the multiplicity of directions as a simultaneous whole'.

21 Although the following analogy, made by E. E. Frank in her book *Literary Architecture* (Berkeley, 1979), is actually between the human mind and material, architectural buildings, her description is none-the-less relevant to the structure of the meta-world which I am discussing here. She states: 'not only may buildings express the mind of their builders, but buildings may also impress that expression on an observer's mind' (239).

22 For a treatment of the issue of the 'right' metaphors, see the following passage in which Miriam reflects upon a letter which she is intending to write to Hypo: 'Meanwhile she was launched in a tide flowing brightly to music. Launched with her own hands still steering the fragile barque . . . how to continue the metaphor? . . . the bright firelight was intruding another. The launched barque was best, suggesting cool freedom and movement. If it stayed in mind, it would serve to shape the letter to be written to-day or to-morrow' (III, 466). In this respect, one can also understand why Richardson rejected the term *stream of consciousness* which, in her opinion, misleadingly stressed the

sequentiality of individual consciousness and not its eternal essence. In an interview with V. Brome, 'A Last Meeting with Dorothy Richardson' (*London Magazine*, 6 (June 1959), 26–32), she explains: 'it is a muddle-headed phrase. It's not a stream, it's a pool, a sea, an ocean. It has depth and greater depth and when you think you have reached its bottom there is nothing there, and when you give yourself up to one current you are suddenly possessed by another' (29).

23 G. Deleuze, *Marcel Proust et les signes* (Paris, 1964), 42.
24 See Nelson Goodman, *Languages of Art* (Indianapolis, 1976), 72. He defines the metaphor as a connection beteeen two fields of meaning: 'Now metaphor typically involves a change not merely of range but also of realm. A label along with others constituting a schema is in effect detached from the home realm of that schema and applied for the sorting and organizing of an alien realm'. See, too, Stephen Ullman's similar definition in *Style in the French Novel* (Cambridge, 1957), 214: 'It is an essential feature of a metaphor that there must be a certain distance between tenor and vehicle. Their similarity must be accompanied by a feeling of disparity; they must belong to different spheres of thought.'
25 G. Genette, *Figures I* (Paris, 1966), 39.
26 Undated letter, headed Good Friday. Bernecke Rare Book Library, Yale University.

CHAPTER SIX

THE SPATIALITY OF PSYCHIC STATES

The previous chapter dealt with the way that identity-formation in *Pilgrimage* comes to be expressed as a process of world-making. I shall now explore how the key concepts of Miriam's philosophy – 'communication', 'ecstasy' and 'creative contemplation' – are assigned spatial traits.[1] While communication tends to be conceived by Miriam as a third space, as a meeting-point at which the various characters' separate worlds converge, failed communication emerges as the absence of such a shared space. Ecstasy and creative contemplation, in turn, are conceived as movement through space or movement between several levels of being.

The treatment of each subject as a world in *Pilgrimage* has important implications for the concept of communication, in the sense that all relationships *between* subjects thus imply a spatial nature. Miriam compares her successful relationship with Jean to an accession to foreign territory: 'one of the prices of this perfection she taught me: to accept incursions without evasion or resentment' (IV, 575). Another form of successful communication, in this case with Richard, is evoked as a brief, communal experience of ecstatic absorption into infinite space: 'It was only for an instant that his eyes rested, showing . . . a calm grave scrutiny . . . For an eternity during which everything vanished, leaving us alone in space. In eternal life' (IV, 515).

Spatial characteristics are likewise used to describe a breakdown in communication. Miriam depicts her argument with Guerinin over the woman question in terms of a concrete barrier: 'And suddenly there was a wall dividing. No more communication possible' (IV, 92). Hypo says of his estrangement from Miriam: 'Lucky Miriam. Sailing Free . . . Isolation; in space' (IV 225). Spatial metaphors are used also to communicate characters' realisation of their estrangement from one another. When Miriam sees her first lover Ted again, she recognises that they inhabit separate worlds: 'The face grew dim and far off and at last receded altogether into darkness. That darkness was dreadful. It was his own life. She would never know it. However well they got to know each other they would always be strangers' (IV, 206). Communication becomes possible between two subjects if one steps into the other's territory or if both enter a third space. The breakdown of communication either reveals the barrier between two subjects or makes each subject recognise that they are unable to experience the other's separate world.

As I have already argued, when occupying lived, contemplative space, the subject is able to overlook his or her own restriction to one point in space. This capacity to think in terms other than one's own centre may also be applied to the subject's restriction to his or her mental world. Gölz states: 'This eccentricity offers the possibility for identification between the space which we experience and space as others experience it . . . Thus, it is precisely the fact that our conception of space *is* eccentric and off-centre which enables us to live in an intersubjective shared space at all.'[2] It is in encountering another subject and recognising the irreconcilable differences between one's own world and that of the other that the subject is ultimately able to glimpse the limits of the personal world, just as the knowledge of those differences inspires the subject to seek contact with the other's world, that world which will always remain in some way unknowable. As seen with actual material spaces, such contact between the various individuals' unique psychological worlds is made possible when the individual partially transcends his or her own world and overcomes the knowledge that his or her world is limited. It is this step which allows a mutuality to develop in or through a third space, in the sense of an intersubjective, universally valid space.[3]

In my discussion of actual material spaces, I argued that what unites two characters may be a shared experience of a landscape. Concomitantly, Miriam succeeds in communicating with another person if she is able to get this other person to perceive a given place in precisely the same manner as she does. In relation to the metaphorical psycho-topology of *Pilgrimage*, the concept of communication proves to be somewhat different. Although communication is, in certain exceptional cases, equated with entry into the world of the other, it is primarily engendered by virtue of a third space valid to both. The notion of a third shared space is based on the assumption that two subjects are completely isolated from one another, that their sense of self is irreducibly attached to their corporeal emplacement and psychological world. The third space transcends this fundamental separation because it contains something which is shared by both and, at the same time, enables the subjects to preserve their own 'territories'.

The desire 'to be perfectly in two places at once' would thus also appear applicable to this issue of human communication, in the sense that Miriam images successful communication as occurring when one subject simultaneously occupies his or her territory as well as that of the other. This shared third space is thus conceived figuratively as a neutral territory and is analogous to material neutral space, since neither one subject nor one world dominates in this intermediary meeting point. Ultimately, Miriam envisages successful communication as follows: 'With others, providing they have no claim. Provided one is neither guest nor host. With others on neutral territory, where one can forget one is there and be everywhere' (IV, 657).

However, only certain events may engender a successful communicating, given that it depends upon whether the third element in the other subject corresponds to that within herself. Apodictically put, two subjects may encounter one another only if they already have something in common: 'It's finding the *same* world in another person that moves you to your roots . . . Your sense of the world and of the astonishingness of there being anything anywhere . . . is confirmed when you find the same world and the same accepted astonishment in someone else' (IV, 333). Recognising the other is seen to be tantamount to recognising oneself in the other, with recognition being viewed as a form of anticipation. Miriam asserts that we can understand only those aspects in someone else which we already have in ourselves, that another subject must to a degree act as an external mirror of that which is present within ourselves: 'We can take only what we have. Even from genius. The accepting party must have within himself the same genius. Otherwise, no taking what is given' (III, 464). As a result, successful communication offers Miriam an opportunity to preserve her own world, to perceive the other both as a completely separate subject even while this other also functions as a reflection of her own self.

When Miriam is reading one of Hypo's texts and sharing her comments with him, one of the few successful encounters between the two takes place:

> Sharing... a discovered extension of herself, available for companionship she had had with herself... feeling alone and independent of him and yet supported by his unusual silence... a lonely, impersonal joy... the inmost essence of her being and yet not herself; but something that through her... was addressing the self she knew, making her both speaker and listener, making her, to herself... strange... and mysterious. (IV, 208)

In this encounter with Hypo, mediated through his work and his ideas, Miriam discovers the same ideas within herself and perceives Hypo as part of her own world. At the same time, she is able to look beyond the parameters of her world; she experiences an 'impersonal joy... not herself', an expansion of her own world which is accompanied by an insight into an essential part of Hypo's own being. A particular quality within Miriam is coaxed into existence only by contact with another. Only in communication – by finding itself resonating in the other – does this quality come to be articulated.

Communication emerges as an encounter between two worlds, where each world is expanded and heightened through its encounter with the other; the world is enriched and becomes greater than when it stands in isolation. In the following description of a group bible-reading at the Roscorlas', this experience of a similarity with the other and of seeing a characteristic of the other mirrored in oneself is demonstrated particularly clearly:

> The deep vibrant monotone, simple, childlike, free from unfelt, tiresomely elucidatory expressiveness, leaving the words to speak for themselves, was the very sound of the Old Testament... It gave the reading a power independent of the meaning of the read words which presently sank away, leaving only the breathing spirit of their inspiration, sending the hearers down and down into depths within themselves, kindred to the depths whence it came, till the emotion creating this scripture became current and the forms seated in the golden lamplight fellows of those who had brought it forth, sharers of its majesty; a heritage bringing both humility and pride. (IV, 474)

The bible-reading is represented as a shared space in which the readers' individual essences ('depths within themselves') experience a communion with the essence which generated the Holy Scripture ('the emotion creating this scripture'). The nature of this encounter is such that the surface plays a subordinate role. The similarity, the permanent essence which resonates silently beneath the words, 'the breathing spirit of their inspiration', acquires chief significance and the readers see this essence mirrored in their own selves.

In this third space of reading, the sequential ordering of events fades from view; the original, religious feeling from the past is actualised in space and time and enables the readers to be simultaneously present with the 'fellows ... who had brought it forth'. In this, the passage also emphasises that this religious fervour is alive within the readers and, at the same time, that the readers, as 'sharers of its majesty', become part of this spirituality and thus become greater than they were.

In other words, then, the readers' encounter with the original religious feeling, vividly rendered in the text through the reading of the shared space of the biblical text, focuses on that which they both have in common. It is this shared essence which allows the readers to comprehend the biblical text, whereby their awareness of this essence is itself called into existence by this encounter in the act of reading. Although the similarity is evoked obliquely, it nevertheless forms the actual subject of this particular encounter.

In *Theory of Literature*, Warren and Wellek define the difference between metonymy and metaphor as follows: 'poetry of association by contiguity, of movement within a single world of discourse, and poetry of association by comparison, joining a plurality of worlds'.[4] In an examination of Diese and Jakobson's[5] definition of metaphor, Lodge[6] also points out that metaphor, in belonging to a selective rather than a combinative form of language, is based upon a principle of recognised similarity: 'Selection involves the perception of similarity ... metaphor is substitution based on a kind of similarity ... the coexistence of similarity and dissimilarity.' The two key features which characterise metaphor are thus, firstly, that it binds together two separate semantic paradigms into one sign, whereby each becomes greater than itself and, secondly, that it combines these two paradigms on the axis of a perceived similarity, a similarity which is not named directly but is implicitly present in the rhetorical figure of speech. One may, therefore, postulate an analogy between the characteristics of metaphor and the way in which communication is discussed in *Pilgrimage*, namely as an encounter between two separate subjects in a third shared space which is, if only implicitly, characterised above all by the recognition of similarity.

In the sense that 'communication' represents the point of contact which unites two subjects, it is clearly treated as a *spatial* phenomenon. Moreover, the concept of communication also expresses a *metaphorical* process, in that the unification takes place within the framework of a process of selection which requires there to be a similarity between the two territories and is concerned primarily with capturing the precise quality of this similarity: in short, it renders this similarity palpable without naming it. This analogy between communication and metaphor may be extended with regard to their spatial formation since, by uniting two separate semantic worlds, both communication and metaphor lift these worlds out of flat sequentiality (located linguistically on the syntagmatic plane) and create a simultaneous relationship of parallelism on the associative, paradigmatic plane, a multi-layered space. In this way, the concept of communication is assigned spatial characteristics and, like metaphor as a whole, also represents space in the text.

Turning to the different instances of successful and failed communication in *Pilgrimage*, Miriam's statement comes to mind: 'Art, sex and religion; one and the same' (IV, 228), for this may be taken to mean that all three concepts may potentially make up a third shared space of encounter between two separate subjects. For example, Miriam notes of the volume by Emerson which she gives Michael to read that 'if he found anything in it, if he understood it at all, they could meet on that one little plot of equal ground' (III, 26). However, it is not only texts themselves which may foster successful communication: the shared, silent reading of a book may also effect a similar encounter, as is shown in the following description of a scene in which Miriam and Michael read Spinoza together:

> It did not occur to him that his serenity, in which were accumulated all the hours they had passed together, *was* realization, the life of the world in miniature, making a space where everything in human experience could emerge like a reflection in deep water, with its proportions held true and right by the tranquil opposition of their separate minds . . . It [serenity] was the place where everything was atoned. (III, 189)

Shared reading creates a tranquil space, a terrain on which the 'opposition of their separate minds' may come together and in which they can recognise what they have in common, the 'hours they had passed together'. The comparison between human experience and a 'reflection in deep water' indicates that the silence and clarity of this space of shared reading also engender a materialisation of the permanent essence in their two separate lives.

The description of the scene in which Miriam and Eleonor Dear read the novel *Villette* aloud to one another gives a particularly clear indication that shared absorption or reflection not only leads to a recognition of the third element but also facilitates an intimate communion between two separate subjects. One might also say that the encounter between the characters is realised *in* and *through* the text.

> They were looking and hearing together . . . The book was cold and unreal compared with what it was when she read it alone. But something was happening. Something was passing to and fro between them, behind the text; a conversation between them that the text, the calm quiet grey that was the outer layer of the tumult, brought into being. If they should read on, the conversation would deepen . . . the reading did not separate them like a man's reading did . . . A man's reading was not reading; not a looking and a listening so that things came into the room . . . They had been both absent from the room nearly all the time. (II, 260)

Miriam's encounter with Eleonor Dear is possible because they have shared a contemplative space while reading; they have managed to overlook their phenomenal and psychological belonging to their own world: 'they had been both absent from the room'. In this scene, too, the true nature of their communication — a silent communion running beneath their spoken words, beneath the text which is being read – is only implied. Richardson's choice of a poetic text as a means of illustrating a shared third space, as a point of contact between separate characters, of course self-reflexively addresses the function of Richardson's narrative, which by implication is itself meant to facilitate an encounter between the author and the reader.

'Sharing a common vision' (IV, 621) is conceived by Miriam much along the lines of the other third spaces she invokes. For she explains, 'People can meet only in God? The shape . . . a triangle. Woman and man at either end of the base, the apex: God' (IV, 224). A shared religious emotion projected as a point of unity between two separate subjects is significant on two scores. Firstly, communication is possible for Miriam only if it enables her to continue to occupy her own centre, which is possible if the two subjects share a particular belief, which emphasises silent contemplation: 'Only in silence, in complete self-possession, possession of the inwardness of being, can lovers fully meet. An enthusiastic vocal engagement is a farewell. Marriage usually a separation, life-long. Life-long unless resting upon the foundation of shared belief' (IV, 645). Secondly, religious experience is also a shared space in the sense that one's own centre is preserved and, while concentrating upon another person, one also recognises one's own permanence, as Miriam notes in relation to her involvement with the Roscorlas: 'When we are together, we are conscious mainly of each other, of something unchanging and trustworthy far away within the personal depths. Such a moment, with man or woman, is a spiritual experience, moving body and soul' (IV, 515). Here, sharing in a common faith reinforces Miriam's permanent centre and deepens the correspondence between her own essence and that of the other.

Finally, the erotic is also encoded semantically as a shared space. Miriam describes the world of love, which she first encounters through Michael, as follows: 'The world it shows is the biggest world there is. It is *outer* space where God is and Christ waits' (III, 202). Miriam's rendering of her communication with Michael as a world is emphasised even more clearly in the representation of Michael's kiss:

> His solid motionless form, near and equal in the twilight, grew faint, towered above her, immense and invisible in a swift gathering swirling darkness bringing him nearer than sight or touch. The edges of things along the margin of her sight stood for an instant sharply clear and disappeared leaving her faced only with the swirling darkness shot now with darting flame . . . she was at last, in person, on a known highway, as others, knowing truth alive . . . as on a journey . . . A voyage swift and transforming, a sense of passing in the midst of this marvel of flame-lit darkness, out of the world in glad solitary confidence with wildly, calmly beating morning heart. (III, 192)

The shared space which the kiss embodies and renders tangible is characterised as a 'swift gathering swirling darkness . . . shot now with darting flame'. More so than in the passages cited previously, transcendence of one's ties to space is represented as a necessary prelude to communication. In the shared space of the kiss – 'in the midst of this marvel' – Miriam moves beyond her own world, 'transforming . . . passing . . . out of the world'. If this kiss is understood as a shared space briefly uniting the divided characters Miriam and Michael, then it becomes clear that the solitary ecstasy which ensues, her 'glad solitary confidence', has been made possible only by their togetherness: 'Yet it was ... through some essential quality in him, that she had reached this haven and starting place' (III, 202).

Finally, this passage also indicates that, by rendering the kiss as a journey through space, Miriam is able to offer an oblique representation of this ecstatic, erotic experience. It is not until after the description that we are told: 'He had kissed a foreign woman' (III, 193). This scene is structured according to Richardson's conviction that the essential quality of an event may be better demonstrated using a spatial comparison than by directly naming the event in any factual manner.

If one contrasts this representation of this kiss with that description of the sexual encounter between Miriam and Hypo, one finds that an erotic encounter does not necessarily lead to entry into a shared, third space. On the contrary, it may also be used to reveal precisely the lack of communication between two characters, emphasising their isolation from one another:

> It was uncanny, but more absorbing than the unwelcome adventure of her body, to be thus hovering outside and above it in a darkness that obliterated the room and was too vast to be contained by it. An immense, fathomless black darkness through which, after an instant's sudden descent into her clenched and rigid form, she was now travelling alone on and on, without thought or memory or any emotion save the strangeness of this journeying. Whose end came in a light that seemed the pale light of dawn. She was up at the high, glimmering window, saw clearly its painted woodwork and small blemishes upon the pane against which she was pressed; through which, had it been open, she felt she could have escaped into the light that had called her thither. (IV, 257)

In this passage, too, the erotic is represented as a darkness through which one journeys. Unlike the kiss scene, however, the space of inadequate communication is characterised by an immeasurable darkness which is not illuminated by a flame, such that Miriam realises after the event that 'extended darkness ... had been the central reality of her ... experience' (IV, 306). Likewise, the journey which follows is not an ecstatic transcendental movement into endless space but rather a confirmation of Miriam's belonging to her phenomenological emplacement. Without having communicated with another individual, Miriam appears unable to move beyond her own world. Rather than revealing the possible similarities between herself and Hypo, this encounter simply reaffirms 'their essential unrelatedness' (IV, 257). Miriam emphasises the divisions between them by describing their sexual encounter as an 'unshared journey' (IV, 258), a 'lonely journey through uninhabited darkness' (IV, 259) and states that 'within her was something that stood apart unpossessed' (IV, 258). The separation between the two characters is further highlighted by the way in which this journey's foremost feature, far from being a breakthrough into infinite space, is the experience of being pushed up against a windowpane ('the pane against which she was pressed') and thus of encountering a barrier which actually prevents movement towards the light. This experience begins with Miriam feeling uncomfortably trapped in her own body. The descriptions emphasise that what this experience lacks is a transcendence of their individual bondage to space. Miriam's mental journey towards the window is prefigured by a 'descent into her clenched and rigid form' and by 'the void to which it [her self] had withdrawn' (IV, 258).[7]

In addition to art, faith and the erotic, silence is also frequently conceived by Miriam as a potential point of contact between two separate subjects, given that it is one of the seminal qualities of all those places she considers to be significant. Silence emerges as the 'perfection of social intercourse' (IV, 456) while encounters are felt to be successful if occurring in silence as a 'wordless meeting'. In one of the rare occasions of successful communion between Selina and Miriam, Richardson illustrates how it is in silence that 'being' comes to the fore and the permanent essence which is omitted from discourse is able to emerge. Miriam notes:

> And now the strange something was growing clearer. Their prolonged silence was speaking ... 'C'est dans le silence que les âmes se révèlent.' ... Clearly, almost audibly, the silence was knitting up the broken fabric of their intercourse ... At the centre of her consciousness there was an image of her new friend, not as she appeared to be, but as she really was; just as within her own consciousness there was an image of the real Miss Holland. (III, 430)

In shared silence, the unspoken aspects of their relationship surface and an immediate, mutual encounter can take place between Miriam's reality and the reality of the other woman.

Thus, while communication may occur in the most disparate shared spaces, whether in the shared reading of a text, the shared experience of an event or in shared silent contemplation, the one condition it must fulfil is that this space enables those involved to be both with themselves and with the other. Accordingly, Miriam's walk with Mendizabel is described as 'a companionship ... they threaded their way together, meeting and separating and rejoining, unanimous and apart' (II, 392). In the course of the novel, however, the most fulfilling form of communication takes place only if it is permanent essence which constitutes the terrain upon which the two divided subjects meet, so that Miriam comes to express this ideal communication as 'the certainty of being in communion with something always there, something in which and through which people could meet and whose absence, felt with people who did not acknowledge it, made life at once impossible, made it a death worse than any dying' (IV, 229). For Miriam, then, permanence is not simply one space among many; it is *the* single true shared space and a fundamental element of all other shared spaces. However, whether permanence is the decisive unifying similarity depends upon whether the communication between two subjects truly captures their individual reality and essence, which is situated beyond ties to time and beneath the surface of reality, or whether it merely represents a peripheral and superficial encounter. Miriam explains: 'It was only ... with the unlocated being of these people that she desired communication and not at all with the sight and sound of their busy momentary selves' (IV, 141).

THE SPATIALITY OF PSYCHIC STATES

Since the only windows and doors which we have are spiritual ones, as Deleuze writes of Proust,[8] and since we may experience communication with another only in contemplative space, that is, in an imaginative disregard for our bondage to the phenomenological world, Richardson ultimately conceives the site of intersubjectivity as immaterial and mediating. The meeting-point between two subjects is represented as a space which both share, in and by virtue of their imagination, a space which tends to express itself in art, faith and the erotic as well as in silence. Since subjects may communicate successfully only if they discover a correlation between their worlds and achieve a state which is described as being 'alone together . . . a balance of side-by-side, not opposition . . . rising from the same depth' (IV, 43), it is furthermore clear that the seminal precondition for the successful encounter between subjects involves a spiritual reality, namely an awareness of the all-embracing permanent being.

Along with communication, Richardson also casts imaginative and philosophical thought processes in spatial terms.[9] However, 'ecstacy' and 'creative contemplation' – marking a solitary communion with things spiritual – are far more consistently aligned with the notion of travel, and are represented either as movement through space or as movement into another immaterial space.[10]

In the following, I am no longer concerned with exploring the actual circumstances which lead to an experience of ecstasy, given that this has been analysed in earlier chapters. Rather what is at stake is to illustrate how the concept of 'ecstasy' – refering to a psychological process – is treated as a spatial category. My point is that Richardson uses spatial metaphors in addition to and independently of her representations of material lived spaces, even while she implies analogues to the ecstatic experiences which relate to the protagonist's phenomenological perception of lived space.

Music is one of the most frequent catalysts for Miriam's experiences of ecstasy, represented as a movement into infinite space. Dancing, Miriam proclaims, 'brings an endlessness . . . in a room, till the walls disappear – in the open, till the sky, moving as you dance, seems to cleave and let you through' (IV, 496). This form of ecstasy tends to facilitate a sense of liberation from temporal existence: 'Everything was dissolved, past and future and present and she was nothing but an ear' (I, 205). In addition Miriam also describes ecstasy as the act of liberating her from the spatial ordering of surface reality, that is, as allowing her to encounter an immaterial world. Not only does the experience of music itself inspire 'the sense of going forward and forward through space', but recollecting this experience also produces a similar sense of enspacement, as when Miriam 'fell asleep somewhere outside the world' (I, 50).[11]

Entering boundless space is also used to express the spiritual independence and freedom of movement, so fundamentally inscribed in Miriam's notion of ecstasy, given that she equates spiritual freedom with the potential for free, endless movement. Thus, when imagining her future as devoid of any opportunities for personal fulfilment, Miriam speaks in terms of an 'absence of any opening prospect', while expressing her sense of hopelessness in similar spatial terms: 'dreams for the future faded. They would never be realized . . . All the space was behind. Things would grow less and less' (I, 289). Miriam's hope that she may still achieve independence is, in turn, conceived as follows: 'she would go away, to some huge open space' (I, 288). After Miriam leaves London, this form of freedom seems to be within her reach and is consequently described in more emphatically spatial terms. During her stay in Grace Broom's home, Miriam thinks of her future independence as 'the ocean beatitude wherein, at the end of this short week, she would be ready to plunge; alone' (IV, 408). Likewise, Miriam directly associates the smiles worn by independent women whom she repeatedly seeks to emulate, with this kind of free space. She refers to their smile as the 'smile of these wide vistas . . . it was *alone* in its vision of the spaces opening beyond the world of daily life' (III, 198). The metaphors of an infinite space which is nowhere is used also to describe negative experiences of ecstasy as well as unpleasant forms of independence, albeit less frequently, as in Miriam's description of her sense of responsibility for her mother's suicide: 'I am in eternity . . . where their worm dieth not and their fire is not quenched' (I, 490). Similarly, she equates the stasis of her own loneliness with 'being nowhere . . . In the bottom of the lake . . . hidden, and forgotten' (III, 148).

The ecstatic joy associated with metaphysical wonder and astonishment is almost always recast in spatial terms, for example as 'the feeling that in a moment one will disappear into space' (IV, 182), or as 'standing and singing till everything split with your joy and let you through into the white white brightness' (II, 98). And if ecstasy is seen to bring liberation from bondage to the material world, such transcendence helps Miriam become conscious of her own reality: 'To *see* the earth whirling slowly round, coloured, its waters catching the light . . . I've no right to be in it; but I'm in' (II, 98).

Concerning the semantic encoding of imagined spaces, I have already argued that reading and creative activity are usually conceived as an inner journey into imaginative space, journeys which enable Miriam either to appropriate a foreign space or to render tangible and grasp something immaterial by localising it in a space. At the same time, imagination involves simultaneously occupying the present lived space and one or more imagined spaces. Butor asserts that the parallel between reading and travel may be applied to all experiences of reading literature: 'All fiction inscribes itself in our space as a journey.' This leads him to conclude that 'any novel which narrates a journey is thus more clear and more explicit than one which is not capable of metaphorically explaining this distance between the site of reading and the place to which the tale transports us'.[12] In the previous discussion of imagined spaces, what was at stake was how Richardson explicitly thematises the distance between the reader's space and the space of the text by directly comparing the act of reading with a journey. I will now discuss how the process of cognition and imagination is cast in the spatial metaphor of a 'journey' independent of any reference to actual places of passage. These metaphorical depictions of the cognitive process as a journey in *Pilgrimage* are founded in a particular vision of the way in which immaterial or imaginative objects are perceived, which has much in common with Lyons's interpretation of the visual perception of material things. He describes perception as 'making a kind of visual journey from a point-of-reference, as source, to the object of perception, as goal'.[13] So as to illustrate the extent to which such a spatial conception of mental processes is much more concerned with the process – the journey or movement itself – than with the attainment of a goal, I would like to return to Miriam's definition of imaginative thought.

Miriam expresses her sense of the endless opportunities for realising images and fantasies as follows: 'you can go on and on, filling space' (II, 93). She then continues by offering her definition of a way of thinking which would match these endless possibilities, a definition which embraces the imaginative movement contained in this thinking and does not try to name and thus limit the object of speech. She explains: 'You can think in your brain, by imagining yourself going on and on *through* it, endless *space* . . . You don't GRASP it. You go through it' (II, 93). While Miriam conceives all mental processes as movement through endless space, the direction of this voyage often differs. An ecstatic journey usually leads to a brief contact with endless, permanent nothingness, much as the act of reading calls forth a similar outward movement, which is linked to a sense of liberation from all phenomenological emplacement. Contemplation, on the other hand, emerges as movement through immeasurable inner space and as the individual's concentration on his or her own unchanging essence. Creative activity, in turn, unites both of these tendencies – the imaginative journey into other outer spaces, an exercise in rereading events that occurred in the past, and the focus upon one's own permanence learned in contemplative concentration. Indeed, it links the imaginative thought process with the concept of understanding and recognition, as a recreation of meta-worlds. For Miriam, invention encompasses an act of construction in the middle of a process which is perceived as an enlightening, imaginative journey.

If, for Miriam, meditative contemplation always leaves her 'poised between the inner and outer worlds' (IV, 497), it is also experienced as a journey towards her own permanent centre:

> Journeying, down through the layers of her surface being . . . Down and down through a series of circles each wider than the last, each opening with the indrawing of a breath whose outward flow pressed her downwards towards the next, nearer to the living centre. Again thought touched her, comparing this research to a kind of mining operation. For indeed it was not flight. There was resistance from within. (IV, 498)

In contrast to her ecstatic experience, permitting a brief liberation from phenomenological enspacement, this mental journey consists of a dynamic tension between the centre and the material world: 'the small cross-section of the visible world by which she was surrounded' (IV, 499). It is only by sheer will-power and by suppressing all thought that Miriam is able to continue the journey. The contemplative journey thus needs to be grasped as being primarily an imaginative transcendence of the material world, which is closely bound up with inner reflection, and less as a rupturing of ties to the material world.

The experience of reading, on the other hand, is compared with an outward movement into a permanent, endless space. Miriam's state while reading Hypo's letter is expressed as follows:

> That indeed she had been transported beyond time and space, that her being, at the moment of reading, had become an unknown timeless being, released from all boundaries, wider as the world and wider, yet still herself. And when her breathing was even again and her surroundings motionless, she turned to him in boundless gratitude. (IV, 364)

In this state, having been 'released from all boundaries', Miriam becomes unconscious of her physical existence; she passes beyond the boundaries of the material world, which stretches 'wide as the world and wider'. In transcending her own ties to space and moving into immaterial space, Miriam's existence becomes impersonal ('an unknown timeless being'), in the sense that her experience extends beyond her own specific, limited personality. At the same time, she retains a powerful awareness of her own self: 'Yet still herself.' Reading, like contemplation, does not describe an unconscious dissolution of the material world and movement into nothingness, but rather a deliberate transcendence of conscious knowledge of material ties within the framework of a movement into immaterial space.

In creative activity, then, links are forged between elements found in contemplation and in the reading situation. Writing is likewise compared with a journey leading to a brief triumph over spatial and temporal ties to the material world. Miriam explains: 'Each vista demands, for portrayal, absence from current life, contemplation, a long journey . . . While I write, everything vanishes but what I contemplate' (IV, 656). This movement shares features with contemplative journeys, to the extent that it also involves a focus on her own permanent being ('centre of being' (IV, 609)). As with contemplation, Miriam also attempts to free herself in writing from physical ties to surface reality and, more importantly, from its medium of expression, namely thought. Miriam declares her goal to be to 'evade thought. Travel, while I write, down to that centre where everything is seen in perspective; serenely' (IV, 619).

In this permanent centre, the various contradictory aspects of her personality and the different temporally and spatially separate events in her life meet to form a simultaneous unity. They provide Miriam with an experience of her own self which is at once indeterminate and clearly defined, not part of any one actual event, yet, nevertheless, self-reflexively aware of her own essence. However, writing also signifies an 'engrossed forgetfulness of time and place' (II, 144) in which Miriam, however, also draws upon foreign outside worlds.

Thus, for example, Miriam's translation involves an imaginative process of creating a new textual world; she reshapes the unfamiliar world of the text to produce a second, transposed version, which she endows with an independent existence, it reaches 'a life of its own' (III, 142). Miriam refers to the three separate stages of this process as three different journeys, the first being depicted as 'plunging thus roughshod from language to language . . . to see, through the shapeless mass the approaching miracle of shape and meaning . . . this first headlong ramble down the page'

(III, 142). The second phase consists in 'the dark length of the second journey . . . the plunge down into oblivion of everything but the object of contemplation . . . but leading always . . . to the return, with the shining fragment' (III, 142). This journey finally culminates in

> [the] serene third passage, the original banished in comforting certainty that the whole of it was represented, the freedom to handle until the jagged parts were wrought into a pliable whole . . . She read from an immense distance. The story was turned away from her towards people who were waiting to read and share what she felt as she read.
> (III, 143)

Translation for her is, thus, closely bound up with a desire to create something tangible from something intangible, even while Miriam undertakes this journey with the intent to return to the material world bearing a textual world, which is itself directed outwards, since it is aimed at the attention of a readership. Writing unifies an inward and an outward imaginative movement, for, as Miriam insists: 'Imagination means holding an image in your mind. When it comes up of itself, or is summoned by something. Then it is not outside, but within you' (IV, 613).

As Vladimir Nabokov notes, 'The sharpest feeling of nowness, in visual terms, is the deliberate possession of a segment of Space collected by the eye. This is Time's only contact with Space . . . To be eternal the Present must depend on the conscious spanning of an infinite expansure. Then, and only then, is the Present equatable with Timeless Space.' In so doing he addresses Richardson's tendency to encode the concept of time as a space, so as to explore its continuity and permanence.[14] Lyons differentiates between two traditional means of speaking about time: one mode of expression which is dynamic or 'tensed' and one which is static or 'tenseless'. The dynamic form situates events in the past, present and future and depicts them as being always changeable, whereas the static form treats events as part of an unchanging order, even though these events are continually subject to change with regard to their past, present and future.[15] Although both the past and the present tenses are used in *Pilgrimage*, Richardson's treatment of the concept of time falls primarily into Lyons's second category, namely the emphasis on a permanent temporal whole which unites disparate events. Ultimately, events are conceived not as sequential or successive but as occurring simultaneously side by side, such that time takes on the form of space.[16]

According to Miriam, there are two reasons for such a spatialisation of time. Firstly, the emphasis placed on reality's permanent essence is accompanied by a focus on the limitations of the temporal dimension: 'time that was unendurably narrow and confined' (III, 255). As a result, time, expressed as a continual dynamic sequence of events, is denied any claim to an accurate expression of reality: 'The future and the past are all one same stuff, changing and unreal' (III, 283). Secondly, in terms of its occurrence in time, an event may be depicted only as past and never as present. As Miriam notes, 'if you can speak of a thing, it is past . . . Speaking makes it glow with a life that is not its own' (II, 317). Since Richardson, however, has a special interest in expressing the 'continual presence' of an event, she circumvents the problem of belatedness by avoiding any representation whatsoever of an event's temporal dimension, and instead directing our attention towards its spatial dimension. The issues of mutability, and, by extension, of the loss of presence in representation, lose their relevance. For, by shifting her gaze on to the spatial dimension, Richardson, and by implication her heroine focus on depth as opposed to sequentiality, so as to represent an event's continual presence as the expression of a spatial, rather than temporal, category.[17]

The metaphorical spatialisation of the concept of time is furthermore in keeping with a more widespread tendency in *Pilgrimage*, namely that events are experienced, imagined and described in the text at a remove from Miriam's time, yet never beyond the parameters of her space. Not only is it always possible to locate Miriam's actions and thoughts in a particular space, though not necessarily at a particular time. What emerged in my discussion of experiences of transcendence and ecstasy was that, although they are accompanied by a temporary rupture of Miriam's temporal bonds to the material world, Richardson still employs spatial images to describe her heroine's sense of being nowhere. Even where the concept of simultaneity is concerned, the temporal dimension is suspended as an ordering structure, but not the spatial dimension.

Part of Richardson's tendency to spatialise time is that the concept of eternity conventionally thought of as temporal endlessness is replaced with the notion of infinite depth. The eternal permanence of an event may thus be captured in terms of spatial expansion, as in the following description of a spring day: 'Midspring . . . now that it was here it opened before her so spaciously, and with such serene assurance of its eternity, that she paused on her way to its centre' (IV, 278). Here, Miriam moves as if she were traversing a space in a phenomenon which is in actuality temporal.

Richardson also makes use of metaphorical spatialisation in order to trace the progress of time. The changing seasons are thus transposed into a spatial image: 'Time pressed. The year was widening and lifting too rapidly towards the heights of June . . . sweeping . . . towards September' (III, 144). Again and again, the future is compared to a river – 'the tide of her own life flowed fresh all about her' (IV, 406) – so as to draw attention to the phenomenon of continual essence. Miriam refers to this as 'the sense . . . of time pouring from an inexhaustible source: gentle, marvellous . . . It came in through the window' (IV, 56). Such temporal spatialisation also magnifies the similarity between Miriam's feelings and the textual representation of her lived space, with time conforming to her mood. Miriam feels that she is capable of either expanding her lived time or contracting it, according to her needs. When Rachel-Mary Roscorla informs her that she is welcome to return to Dimple Hill after a summer interlude, a description follows of 'the summer whose months, only just now, she had transformed into a brief enchanted bridge towards the strange promise of September' (IV, 627). This conjunction between her psychic state and her perception of time as space is articulated most pertinently when an event's passing in time is compared with the disappearance or extinction of space. At the close of a working day, Miriam notes that 'her day scrolled up behind her' (II, 74).

[186]

Time is also described statically when events in time are assigned spatial characteristics. In the following examples, anticipated events are characterised, using deictic words and spatial concepts, in terms of spatial distances or boundaries, or as something situated in the foreground: '*far distances* of the afternoon' (IV, 185), 'tomorrow will pour *in over* the *surface* of the hours' (IV, 185), '*Ahead*, nothing was visible' (IV, 365). As one might expect, the past is likewise conceived as a background or, as a space which is shut off from the present: 'His coming brought the earlier time to an *end*; made it a past, *expanding* in the *distance*' (IV, 96).

This technique of attributing spatial features to temporal phenomena is also applied in descriptions of the present; whenever the use of a spatial metaphor is able to add emphasis to the depth or expansiveness of one moment or period of time: 'boundless immensity of Sunday' (III, 313), 'large quiet moments' (III, 467), 'expansive moments' (III, 282) and 'To-day was an unfathomable loop within the time that remained' (IV, 96). All of these descriptions are founded in an understanding of time as the cessation of movement. By treating events in time as part of an overall static and continual unity, that is, by presenting time as a metaphorical form of space, Richardson avoids confronting the problem of expressing time in language. In this way, the quality of time as a continually changing phenomenon, which it would be impossible to describe directly, is rendered tangible and intelligible though spatialisation.

These general observations concerning the possibilities of writing about time are true also of depictions of Miriam's own personal time. Not only is it impossible to capture the temporal presence of an event in words, in the sense that events, as temporal phenomena, are continually engaged in a process of becoming and cannot be held in suspension. For her own experience of an event, Miriam also realises that she is unable to experience the temporal present consciously since, as soon as she begins to reflect upon an event, it has already passed. Conscious experience is facilitated only in anticipation or memory: 'Future flows into the present . . . on entering an experience one is already beyond it, so that most occasions are imperfect because no one is really quite within them, save before and afterwards' (IV, 347).

Since Miriam regards the 'becoming' of an event as its primary quality, she frequently experiences an event in the present retrospectively, as already past (IV, 198). Instead of concentrating upon the temporal present, she resolves to distance herself from it, since it will inevitably elude her, and instead directs her attentions to the future: 'the in-flowing future that already was driving this short evening into the past' (IV, 168). She avoids confronting the dilemma that it is impossible to perceive the present consciously and only ever possible to comprehend it as a becoming, by completely dismissing any descriptions which would take into account the succession and changes in time. Instead, she separates events from their temporal bond and confines herself to those features of an event which remain constant.

This solution to the problem of capturing or avoiding the temporal phenomenon of becoming, by positioning it in space and not in time, is of course a further expression of the realisation that reality ought not be viewed as a succession of events but as a permanent state. As Max Bense writes, 'in reality things never [stand] in succession but only in parallel'.[18] Temporal causality and causes as a whole seem as though banished from Richardson's vision of the world, since all events, all of Miriam's experiences and insights, are interpreted as part of a continual whole, of an eternally same essence. Experiences are often felt to take place in confirmation and repetition of a prior event, or in anticipation of the future; they are united by their immutable attributes, while the perceived congruence between different events in turn renders their essence even more resistant to change. In opposition to a vision of reality as diachrony, as a continuous and always changeable succession, Miriam favours one which emphasises synchrony and which enables the multi-faceted depth and simultaneous unity of different events to be expressed. In the course of recollecting the past she seeks to rearrange events in such a way that all the disparate instances which could be conceived in temporal and linear fashion come to be spread out in a relation of *spatial depth*. In other words, she substitutes simultaneous parallelism for sequential linearity.

According to Bense, simultaneity creates space:

> Space presupposes the presence of multiplicity ... We do indeed relate our perceptions to consciousness and thus to time. However, a perceived multiplicity itself compels us to relinquish perception in temporal sequence. The perception of multiplicity reforms perception as temporality into perception which is spacing ... Perception becomes spacing [*Raumung*]. Here, spacing is intended to signify awareness or experience of space.[19]

Space in this context is intended to denote not a physical bond to the surface of the material world but a liberation from all surface-located sequentiality. The term 'space' here describes an immaterial depth and a manifestation of permanence, in which separate events are lived simultaneously and in which the many different aspects of one event are experienced, recognised and articulated in spatial metaphors. For Bense, such an awareness of multi-layered reality is the hallmark of creativity:

> The imagination [*Geist*] has no terminology – that belongs to the intellect –, however the imagination has the images, the impetus toward unity within multiplicity. In this, it reveals its spatial nature ... Every tendency to embrace multiplicity stems from the imagination. It is in the imagination alone that we recognise perception as spacing [*Raumung*].[20]

Precisely along the lines suggested by Bense, Miriam experiences a concert as utterly unsatisfactory because the absence of a sense of space proves to be coterminous with the absence of any experience of reality:

> But the movement of time, because she was consciously passing along the surface of its moments as one by one they were measured off in sound that no longer held for her any time-expanding depth, was intolerably slow. And so shallow, that presently it was tormenting her with the certainty that elsewhere, far away in some remote region of consciousness, her authentic being was plunged in a timeless reality within

which . . . she might yet rejoin it and feel the barrier between herself and the music drop away. (IV, 298)

The unsatisfactory state of being bound to the temporal sequence of one experience ('intolerably slow', 'tormenting') is conveyed in spatial metaphors: 'along the surface of its moments' and 'shallow'. In opposition to this state, Miriam sets up permanence as an alternative experience of reality. This permanence is expressed by depicting time as a space: 'time-expanding depth', a 'timeless reality', located 'in some remote region'.

The following description offers a sharply contrasting example, in which the rendering of time as a metaphorical space serves to depict an experience of ecstasy:

> She stood still, moving rapidly into the neutral zone between the two days, further and further into the spaces of the darkness, until everything disappeared, and all days were far-off strident irrelevances, for ever unable to come between her and the sound of the stillness and its touch, a cool breath, passing through her unimpeded. (III, 165)

Expressions, such as the 'neutral zone between the two days', and the comment that 'all days were far-off strident irrelevances', not only highlight Miriam's sense of timelessness, they also emphasise the fact that abandoning temporality immediately leads to an experience of space, which indicates an actual space, as well as an imaginative intimation of the *depth* of reality; 'further and further into the spaces of the darkness'.

In her desire to capture the essence of the 'real' – the timeless depth of its multiple layers which is compressed into one moment – Miriam assigns to a particular period of time the quality of spatial elasticity, when, for example, she claims 'the actual life of the passing moment . . . the deep loop it made' (III, 314). Above all, this manner of divesting an event of its temporal dimension emphasises its continual essence, so that when the event is reconstructed in memory the restrictions of temporal sequentiality – the material perception of the brevity or length of a period of time – can be relinquished. As she remembers a particular Sunday she not only recalls the eternal permanence of this moment; she also articulates what is special about this moment in time by virtue of having recourse to a spacial metaphor: 'And now, the longest part of that day that seems so vast a stretch is the moment of being out again on those steps, with all the oncoming hours in my heart . . . for ever' (IV, 209). This moment does not only live on 'for ever' in Miriam's memory; its continual essence also comes to the fore by virtue of its having been perceived as part of a temporal whole, since it already contains an anticipation of the 'oncoming hours' within itself.

The treatment of memory in *Pilgrimage* thus involves presenting time as space in the sense that Miriam attempts to understand original experiences and impressions retrospectively by organising different episodes into a uniform pattern of simultaneous parallelism. In its overall structure, Miriam's creation of a coherent autobiographical narrative involves substituting a method of ordering events temporally for one which is determined spatially. As J. Hillis Miller notes, such detached reflection and recollection involve spatial patterning:

> To say 'pattern' is to use a spatial term ... The change from infatuated movement forward to a detached seeing of the past is also a change from time to space. Detachment spatializes time, freezes in into a fixed space ... [one sees] all moments in time as simultaneously present, juxtaposed side by side in a spatial design. The movement in orientation from future to past is a transformation of time as it is lived from moment to moment into the spatialized time of a permanent destiny ... [a] change in relation to life from existential temporality to spatialized time.[21]

By virtue of recollection the past is transformed into a unity of juxtaposed events so as to be treated like a space in which one can mentally move from one event to the next. As Miriam insists,

> The past was with her unobstructed; not recalled, but present, so that she could move into any part and be there as before ... Fragments of forgotten experience detached themselves, making a bright patchwork as she watched, waiting, while she passed from one to another and fresh patches were added, drawing her on ... this ramble into the past. (III, 322)

Concomitantly, Miriam's understanding of her own past is quite explicitly conceived as a spatialising time. Describing her personal development, she refers to her life's path as a spatial progression through the years, 'passage through years' (III, 134). At the same time, she removes past events from their original sequentiality, interpreting them increasingly as a continuous whole. As her memory engenders spatialisation of diverse temporalities, past and present events appear simultaneously juxtaposed:

> she found her years of London work set in the air, framed and contemplable like the pictures on the wall, and beside them the early golden years in snatches, chosen pictures from here and there, communicated, and stored in the loyal memory of the Brooms. Leaping in among these live days came to-day. (II, 312)

Indeed, Miriam has the tendency to reduce her past to the sum of certain especially significant events, conceived as an expanding space. When she wishes to emphasise that certain events belong to the past, she reviews those moments as 'a beautiful distance outspread behind her' (III, 237) or as 'a manageable space and at last only an indifferent distance' (III, 135). If, on the other hand, she seeks to invest the past events with a profound meaning, then they are represented as a distant image, as a panorama of lived experience.

The following example of one such panorama of life illustrates with particular poignancy how memory reinforces past experiences by the use of spatial metaphors. Miriam's change of mood is evoked as follows:

> She seemed to have reached the summit of a hill up which she had been climbing ever since she came to Newlands. The weeks had been green lanes of experience, fresh and scented and balmy and free from lurking fears. Now the landscape lay open before her eyes, clear from horizon to horizon, sunlit and flawless, past and future ... The old troubles ... her own personal thoughts ... had moved and changed, melted and flowed away. (I, 424)

The spatial metaphor, 'reached the summit of a hill', signifies not only her sense of exuberance but also the fact that she has achieved a detached and indifferent position in relation to painful aspects of her past. Not only does Miriam observe her life, the most recent past and the anticipated future, as a collated image of disparate events – 'the landscape lay open before her . . . past and future' – she also renders events which occurred in time as spaces. Weeks are referred to as 'green lanes of experience' and the disappearance of her past unhappiness leaves the vista 'clear from horizon to horizon'. By facilitating a simultaneous presence of various past events, such work of memory belatedly confers upon these moments the attribute of continual presence.

In *Pilgrimage*, descriptions of spatialised time are, then, used above all in order to represent an all-encompassing unity between the past, the present and future so as to endow Miriam with a panoramic view of life, which visualises the similarities between different events, the coherent structure subtending all modalities of experience. By representing time as a spatial unity, Richardson gives voice to her conviction that reality knows no progression in time and no change, but only a 'continual presence'. The essence of an individual and of an event remains constant despite the continual shifts in the superficial world. The following description of an encounter with music poignantly articulates Miriam's sense that different temporal periods are all mutually related to each other:

> She rushed up . . . following the claim of the music . . . flowing swiftly on across a tide of remembered and forgotten incidents in and out amongst the seasons of the years. It sent her forward to to-morrow . . . It came from far back amongst the generations where everything was different; telling you that they were the same. (II, 301)

The present, which, as a temporal category, cannot be represented without factoring in the deferral inherent to representation, can be depicted once it is transposed into spatial terms. For, to argue that the act of recollection allows the essence of an individual or an event to become endlessly reiterable and thus made present again is tantamount to claiming that an event can never truly be past. Miriam expresses her sense of the endless presence of an event in a statement about the time which she spent with Richard. She declares: 'vivid in your memory, as in mine, is the eternal vast interior of last summer's revealing moment. A destination never to be lost . . . even now . . . the whole of our past electric about us' (IV, 622). To characterise something as 'eternal' is not merely to describe the permanence of the past moments. The word 'eternal' refers also to the way in which the event is denied its temporality so as to conceive it as eternally present. A seminal aspect of Miriam's projected poetics of memory thus consists in performing her discovery that 'The whole of what is called "the past" is with me, seen anew, vividly . . . the past does not stand "being still". It moves, growing with one's growth' (IV, 657).

Genette refers to the double effect of spatial metaphors as follows: 'One does not speak of space: one speaks of something else in terms of – space – and one might almost say that it is space which speaks: its presence is implicit and implied at the source or foundation of the message rather than in its contents.'[22] Richardson's philosophical and poetological preference for space is reinforced by the powerfully metaphorical prose and by the frequent usage of spatial metaphors to describe reality and states of being, yet it is also mirrored in the poetic debate concerning metaphor in the text. For both space and metaphors alike involve grasping disparate events (or signifiers) simultaneously in order to represent reality. The subject of metaphors is brought into play, firstly, at the thematic level of Miriam's explicit statements on metaphors. Secondly, it also emerges in the text where different imaginative techniques which aim to create a simultaneity of events (such as the memory or fantasy of an imaginary space, an encounter in a third space or creative activity as a simultaneous gathering of disparate events) clearly employ a method analogous to that used in metaphors and thus also describe a metaphorical process. For both these psychological experiences and metaphors enact an attempt 'to be in two places at once'.

One may in consequence recognise a close relation between space and metaphors based on the similar manner in which they are used to represent reality. Just as space gathers multiple levels of reality in its depths, so metaphors simultaneously juxtapose two disparate signifiers and, furthermore, gather these along the vertical, paradigmatic axis and not along the horizontal, syntagmatic, one. At the same time, the coupling of two signs in metaphor is founded on the existence of a similarity (albeit unspoken) which is rhetorically circumscribed yet rendered tangible by virtue of an oblique utterance. Genette, in his remarks on the contemporary elevation of space over time which he regards as a response to Bergson, notes that the term 'spatial metaphor' is in some respects redundant – not only because metaphors tend to make use of the lexical field of expansion but also because space is in fact their unspoken subject and they may thus be said to be formative of space in their expression. In spatial metaphors, the signified is not spatial, whereas the signifier is. As a result, space comes to function as an attribute of the object of speech. If a spatialisation of time is used to express those realities which recede from any direct representation, it also turns space itself into an object of speech. As Genette explains:

> The term 'spatial metaphor' itself is almost a pleonasm, since metaphors are generally drawn from the lexis of expansion . . . our language is woven out of space . . . Today literature – thought – speaks of itself only in terms of distance, horizons, the universe, the countryside, locations, sites, paths and dwelling places: naive figures of speech which are nevertheless characteristic, figures of speech *par excellence* in which language transforms itself into space in order that space in itself, having become language, should speak itself and write itself.[23]

Genette's description of modern literature's self-conscious performance of the mutual implication of space and language quite accurately addresses the poetic unity which informs Richardson's decision to focus on her protagonist's surroundings rather than upon biographical data; her understanding of reality as the juxtaposition of spaces and as continual essence, and her stylistic preference for spatial metaphors. Performing space in and through language is the shared issue, the common concern subtending and gathering together the various textual layers of *Pilgrimage*.

NOTES

1 See J. Lotman, *The Structure of the Artistic Text* (Michigan, 1977), 217. In his view, this derives from the particular mode of visual perception peculiar to human beings.
2 W. Gölz, *Dasein und Raum* (Tübingen, 1970), 70.
3 See *Ibid.*, 26.
4 Rene Wellek and Austin Warren, *Theory of Literature* (New York, 3rd edition, 1977), 195.
5 See R. Jakobson, 'Two Aspects of Language: Metaphor and Metonymy', in *European Literary Theory and Practice*, ed. Vernon W. Gras (New York, 1973), 119–129.
6 D. Lodge, *The Modes of Modern Writing* (London, 1977), 75.
7 A further indication of Miriam's and Hypo's failure to communicate is possibly that Miriam's 'unshared journey' is immediately succeeded in the text by a starkly contrasting experience of transcendence, a mental flight, which acts as an example of successful communication. The next morning, Miriam watches in the mirror as three birds fly in the form of an 'elongated triangle' and asserts that 'the sight of them as they passed had smitten through her as though she were transparent and left her thrilled from head to foot with the sense of having shared their swift and silent flight' (IV, 259).
8 G. Deleuze, *Marcel Proust et les signes* (Paris, 1964), 88.
9 This provides further indication of Richardson's conviction that spatial metaphors are the 'right' metaphors with which to represent thought processes as well as of her deliberate use of spatial metaphors in *Pilgrimage*. In her letters, Richardson also describes imaginative insights as spatial insights and as a journey through space, as the following letter to Peggy Kirkaldy (October 1946) shows especially clearly: 'If you drop all "tensions" ... and move forth, "imaginatively" ... among the "myriad of spheres" in the "vastness of space" is it not odd ... that "the cosmos" no matter how extensive, is too small to imprison your consciousness, and that however far things go, you can outstrip them and reach a region, maybe a centre (all metaphors, as ever, like all language and all art and all science, are inadequate to convey reality, but if Einstein is on the right track, a centre, unfathomable, would seem to come nearest ... whence comes, or flows, or streams, or radiates, whatever you-like-to-call-it, that keeps things going).' Beinecke Rare Book Library, Yale University.
10 I. Rice Pereira likewise equates spatial perception with imaginative insight into the immaterial world in her book *The Nature of Space* (New York, 1956), 46: 'But unlike the object, man's perceptions are spatial and extend beyond the boundaries of his physical limitations. This is the reality which links him with the universe. He senses immeasurable depths; he soars to spiritual heights.'
11 Similarly, the ecstasy which Miriam experiences when playing the piano is also described in spatial and metaphorical terms, since Miriam is able to transfer the emotion into imaginative space. This process emphasises the enduring and timeless quality of this experience. Miriam's piano-playing is described as follows: 'All round her was height and depth, a sense of vastness and grandeur beyond anything to be seen or heard, yet stretching back like a sheltering wing over the past to her earliest memories and forward ahead out of sight' (II, 335).
12 M. Butor, 'L'espace du roman', *Répertoire II*, (Paris, 1964), 44.
13 J. Lyons, *Semantics* (Cambridge, 1977), vol. 2, 700.
14 See E. E. Frank's discussion of Proust's understanding of metaphor in *Literary Architecture* (Berkeley, 1979), 150. She writes: 'the metaphor connects, but in so doing it preserves

the distinctness of each term ... because it comprises the "essence" of "the two separate terms of the experience", essences which are similar and extractable without threat to the terms themselves'. It is this feature of metaphors which she views as antithetical to time, since it presents essences outside the context of their dependence on time. See also M. Butor's essay 'Recherches sur la technique du roman', especially the sixth part entitled 'Les propriétés de l'espace', in *Répertoire II*.

15 Lyons, *Semantics*, vol. 2, 682.
16 See Georges Poulet, *L'Espace proustien* (Paris, 1963).
17 Here reference should be made to Heisenberg's uncertainty principle, which prescribes that it is only ever possible to measure either spatiality or temporality, i.e. the progress of an event, at any one point. The necessity of localising an event in one dimension in the course of describing it makes it impossible to describe the other dimension, so that one may conclude that when one dimension is described (the temporal dimension, in the case of the spatialisation of time), the other is necessarily negated.
18 M. Bense, *Raum und Ich* (Munich and Berlin, 1943), 25.
19 *Ibid.*, 29.
20 *Ibid.*, 30.
21 J. Hillis Miller, *Thomas Hardy: Distance and Desire* (Cambridge, MA, 1970), 197. See also Frank, *Literary Architecture*, especially the fifth part entitled 'The Analogical Tradition of Literary Architecture'.
22 G. Genette, *Figures I* (Paris, 1966), 102.
23 *Ibid.*, 106.

PART III

TEXTUAL SPACE – SPATIAL TEXTUALITY

CHAPTER SEVEN

THE SPACE OF LITERATURE

By privileging simultaneity, silence and the desire to present an individual's life as the sum of the images in his or her imagination, rather than as a chronological sequence of events, Richardson argues in favour of a spatial mode of description. This emerges as a rejection of a chronological narrative style in favour of drawing together separate events simultaneously into one spatial whole. Miriam's notion of narrative typifies this view: 'Of course you can go back, and round and up and everywhere. Things as a whole' (I, 443). And yet this fascination for simultaneity characterises not only Miriam's quest for self-identity but also the narrative Richardson undertakes to represent this pilgrimage. So as to explore at more length the way questions of space not only involve the actual places her heroine passes through and the worlds she constructs so as to make sense of her experience but rather also Richardson's own poetic project, it is useful to turn to more general discussion of literary space.

Speaking of space in relation to literary texts, which are conventionally viewed as temporal phenomena, may, Genette states, seem paradox: 'Apparently, a work of literature's mode of existence is in fact essentially temporal, since the act of reading in which we realize the virtual existence of a written text . . . is made up of a succession of instants which reaches completion over a period of time, in our time.'[1] I nevertheless propose exploring the analogy between narrative textuality and space, because within the framework of, and in addition to, the temporal, sequential dimension of the novel (its chronology), each literary text also possesses a spatial dimension, although this is indeed more pronounced in some novels than others. In the novels, for example, which J. Frank gives as instances of a 'spatial form', it is used with particular intensity and appears to have become the dominant formal dimension.[2] This spatial dimension of the text is by no means exhausted in observations such as that literature describes actual material places, that reading may be viewed as a journey or stay in unfamiliar imagined spaces, nor by noting that the fascination of what Richardson calls 'surroundings' is one of the crucial features of poetic description. For, as Genette notes, like other art forms which are conventionally perceived as spatial, what is at stake in narrative representation is not that it depicts expansion but that this representation itself is accomplished in expansion.[3] Genette gives Saussure's spatial description of language as one justification for speaking of a characteristic, as opposed to a merely characterised, spatiality in the text; 'a representative rather than represented spatiality'.[4] He draws upon Saussure's model according to which every word occupies a particular site within a vertical and horizontal network of relations. Leading on from this, Genette suggests that spatial textuality should be located in the fact that a book is to be perceived not as narrative sequences but as a unified object, so that in the act of reading our attention is drawn to 'the atemporal and reversible disposition of signs, words, phrases and discourse in the simultaneity of that which one calls a text'.[5] In so doing he implicitly refers back to Lessing's distinction in *Laokoon* (1766) between temporal art, which he defines as successive and thus irreversible in its essence, and spatial art, which he defines as simultaneous and thus essentially reversible. Indeed, Genette does not only suggest that narrative texts contain both a temporal and a spatial dimension. By speaking about literary spatiality his interest is above all in the way the act of reading involves overcoming the text's temporality entirely, giving precedence to a conception of the text's simultaneity and reversibility.

For Genette and J. Frank argue that the reading process[6] involves two distinct frames of perception. The first is concerned with a successive sequence of time, namely when a text is first read chronologically. The second one, however, involves a spatial dimension, namely when the reading has been completed and the reader gathers together into one entity all of the chronological episodes which make up the text. At this point in the reading process, reading for plot development is exchanged for an attempt to grasp the multiplicity of the text simultaneously. Whereas the text is felt to be a temporal work of art during the initial act of reading, while meaning gradually emerges, it comes to represent a spatial work of art as soon as the pattern of the text's internal relations and references is seen to form a meaningful whole.

Likewise, when one is reading, the meaning does not emerge solely along a horizontal axis of language – in the textual chronology of the successive words, descriptions and episodes – but also along the vertical axis, which establishes relations between chronologically separate passages in the text. In this way, the reader must, on the one hand, comprehend the chronological development of the narrative sequence and, on the other, recognise and combine the parallels set up in the text, the significant symmetry between the various narrative threads, the cross-references and allusions, in order to grasp the full implications of the text. Descriptions of memories inserted into the body of the text, references and links to past episodes, hints of future events and so forth, all interrupt the chronology and briefly cause the reader to stop reading sequentially and to read instead in a mode of 'reflexive reference' (Frank). They require the reader to take up the challenge of grasping different episodes simultaneously, in the sense of constantly referring back to past episodes, and of recognising the implicit connections between two non-sequential descriptions.[7] It goes without saying that some texts permit or demand this form of reading to a greater extent than others; however, Genette regards any mode of reading which attempts to grasp the meaning of a text over and above its narrative chronology as a spatial, atemporal activity:

> It is always already rereading, incessantly running one's eye across a book in all its meanings, all its directions, all its dimensions. One may therefore say that the space of the book, like that of the page, is not subordinated passively to the duration of successive reading, but that even if it reveals and fulfils itself in that reading, it never ceases to inflect it and to turn it around and thus, in a sense, to undo it.[8]

The aspect of spatial textuality which creates the text's atemporal dimension, its simultaneity and reversibility, thus consists in the following: meaning is generated in the text, in the framework of the cross-references which appear independently of the narrative chronology, whereby the overall pattern of internal relations, in which the episodes are brought together in simultaneous unity, is not completed until the end of the text. Thus, a text's 'simultaneity' does not relate solely to a description of the end of the novel, nor to the observation of the novel as an entirety (and therefore as a simultaneous gathering of all the episodes). On the contrary, this principle of simultaneity may be applied also to each individual episode. As part of the internal network of interrelations, each episode may act as a point at which several episodes converge, may associatively gather various other textual events and thus become a unifying focus for the artistic illusion of simultaneous multi-facetedness.[9]

The reversibility of a text has two primary characteristics, the first being that it permits cross-references and thus enables the reader to travel forwards and backwards in the text and the second being that each episode may be viewed also as an independent unit. The significance of a single episode is thus not exclusively determined by its position within a sequence of events and may also be read and interpreted in isolation from the narrative chronology. Both the simultaneity and reversibility evident in a text are opposed to the chronology and undermine its dominant position in the creation of meaning. Of course, it is also a question of the extent to which spatial textuality stands in opposition to the textual chronology. Just as it would be wrong to deny a literary text its temporal dimension, so it would be impossible to deny outright that chronology contributes to textual meaning, since both are an inherent part of linguistic expression. Nevertheless, there are texts – and *Pilgrimage* certainly belongs in this category – in which the formal structure places extra emphasis on the text's simultaneity and reversibility, while the chronology of plot events is relegated to second place.

The meaning generated by spatial textuality has two main features. By virtue of the non-chronological referential relations and allusions contained in the text, the reader can grasp separate events simultaneously within the narrative's sequentiality. The final, complete meaning of the different cross-references in the novel comes to the fore when all of the episodes are drawn together as one coherent unity. At the same time, the reversibility of spatial textuality confers significance on every single episode, regardless of its referentiality to preceding or succeeding passages.

Without referring explicitly to spatial textuality, Edel highlights these two characteristics in his description of *Pilgrimage*. He writes:

the works of [Richardson] . . . belong to that category of fiction of which T. S. Eliot spoke when he said that 'only sensibilities trained on poetry can wholly appreciate' them. By this he meant . . . that the novel is read not as a time sequence but as a heterogeneous series of perceptions each catching its moment of intensity without reference to what lies on the succeeding pages, but the entire reading of which conveys a poetic synthesis.[10]

My exploration of spaces in *Pilgrimage* was based on the assumption that, at one level, the text represents a *Bildungsroman* which, in outlining Miriam's pilgrimage through different material spaces together with her psychological development, confers significance through narrative chronology. Both in the descriptions of her movement through actual spaces and in the psycho-topology of her world-making, a certain progression played a crucial role, the significance of which arose by way of the sequential succession of episodes. At this level, the reader perceives the progression of the narrative in *Pilgrimage* as an occurrence in time: firstly, since reading represents a temporal process and, secondly, because the story of *Pilgrimage* traces the development in time of Miriam's life unfolding a narrative chronology which can be retold.

However, owing to *Pilgrimage*'s pronounced spatial textuality, such chronological retelling captures merely the novel's narrative scaffold. As my previous discussion suggested, the text allows one to read episodes divorced from their chronological sequence, without undermining the novel's overall meaning. Indeed, it was precisely by contrasting separate narrative episodes as a simultaneous whole that a reading became possible. In other words, the separate novels and many, if not all, of the diverse episodes contained in them may be read independently of the chronological sequence of *Pilgrimage* as a whole without appearing incomprehensible to a reader unfamiliar with the preceding parts of the novel. That it should be possible at all to read the text in such a way exemplifies the formal aspect of simultaneity which *Pilgrimage* performs. At the same time, however, *Pilgrimage* contains internal cross-references, some of which are separated only by a few pages, some of which are scattered across hundreds of pages. Not only are certain localities always endowed with the same meaning; rather, as my discussion of the three renditions of Teetgen's tea-shop illustrated, *Pilgrimage* works by establishing connections between experiences of space, with alterations in their depiction signalling that a change has occurred in the protagonist as well. Thus, Miriam returns in memory to characters and events from past episodes in order to compare the worlds, the moods and the values which they represent with her present experiences, or as a means of revealing continuity by alluding to and thus creating links with past events.

Thus, although most of the episodes may be read separately from each other, other passages become meaningful only when the implicit cross-references are taken into account. As a result, the meaning of one description may depend on its relation to another; likewise, certain different descriptions make sense only when viewed as forming a unit with internally related parts. A typical instance of the use of textual interrelations is an allusion to Oscar Wilde's homosexuality, of which Mrs

Corrie declares: 'It's the most awful thing there is. It's in the Bible' (I, 428). The person spoken of here and the precise nature of the scandal becomes clear only if the added description – 'the name of the man who wrote the plays . . . Miriam could only recall that it was a woodland springtime name' – is seen in relation to an earlier passage in which Mrs Corrie speaks of Wilde's genius and Miriam associates his name with 'wild spring' (I, 413). Similarly, it becomes clear that Miriam's realisation at the end of *Dawn's Left Hand* – 'Disadvantage had fallen from her and a burden leaving a calm delightful sense of power' (IV, 267) – is an allusion to her loss of virginity only when it is seen in the context of the preceding description of her sexual encounter with Hypo.

Examples of the second way in which textual interrelations are used would be the various hints at Miriam's pregnancy and her miscarriage. Miriam's interpretation of her meeting with Hypo – 'the occasion had originated in his careless misreading of her second note' (IV, 320) – as well as Hypo's remark – 'Miriam . . . is allusive . . . when you said you had come down from the clouds, I thought you meant you were experiencing the normal human reaction after a great moment, not that you had been mistaken' (IV, 325) – are textual descriptions which do not make much sense when seen in isolation. They need to be understood in connection with Miriam's evocation of her mental flight (IV, 280) and the subsequent discussion in which both Hypo and Amabel interpret her 'flight' as a metaphor for pregnancy, and also in the context of Miriam's conversation with Michael during a concert which is not recorded in the text but which leads Michael to propose to Miriam a second time. Only when viewed as a whole do these various descriptions yield their meaning.

The different cross-references and repetitions of descriptions which create such textual reversibility and simultaneity may be said to help reveal a completed pattern at the end of the novel. What is, however, also of particular significance for the use of spatial textuality in *Pilgrimage* is that the text contains a narrative development of the psycho-topological aspects of Miriam's world-making, as well as the production of a final overall pattern of all events. Nevertheless, this development tends to assume a secondary role in the production of meaning. The end of the text may not be read as the desired closure of narrative suspense, nor does the final unity of all episodes constitute the text's ultimate meaning. The spatial textuality emerges as a tension between a horizontal, chronological development, which is focused on one final image as the ultimate completion and resolution of textual signification, and an opposing, vertical level of meaning which enables the simultaneity and reversibility of textual episodes to be created. In the context of such an anti-chronological gesture, the narrative resolution has already been anticipated and the conclusion serves only to complete both a pattern which has long since been recognised and a message which has long since been heard.

Although Miriam experiences changes in the course of her pilgrimage so that the novel's central subject appears to be Miriam's assumption of creative activity in a movement towards an empty room and towards a phenomenological and psychological position between the material and the immaterial world, she does in fact acquire the insights which make up the novel's subject long before the end. The final episode may therefore be regarded more as a final affirmation of an already familiar message concerning Miriam's formation of her own identity, reality and its poetic representation than as a final narrative explanation. *Pilgrimage's* spatial textuality does not only reinforce the thematic description of reality as simultaneity, continual essence and thus also as spatialised time at a formal level. Ideas which are explored in the text (such as the notion that insight is a form of cognition and that development acts as a confirmation of anticipation) may be said to be explored at a formal level, too, in the sense that simultaneity and reversibility themselves undermine the primary semantic status of chronology in the text.

Up to now, I have defined spatial textuality as a synchrony of events which is opposed to narrative chronology. Genette, however, addresses another aspect of spatial textuality which is applicable to *Pilgrimage*, namely the power of language to express not only literal but also figurative meaning and thereby to achieve a highly evocative circumscription of an object of speech. This linguistic doubling, as well as the tension which is generated between literal and figurative meaning, may be recognised as a further characteristic of space in the text. Genette states:

> That a word ... may transport two meanings at once, one which would be said in rhetoric to be literal and the other figurative, the semantic space which is driven between the obvious signified and the real signified at the same time abolishing the linearity of discourse ... the figure is at once the form which space takes and the shape which it gives itself in language, and it is itself a symbol for the spatiality of literary language in its relation to meaning.[11]

This doubling effect, contained in every single linguistic expression, also engenders semantic heterogeneity. The density of textual meaning which may be achieved along the vertical, paradigmatic axis of linguistic expression forms a complementary opposite to the horizontal, syntagmatic axis of language, without the figural putting the literal in question or cancelling it. Whereas the literal level of the text is what allows different readers to agree upon the events of the narrative, the protagonist's activity, her philosophical and poetic ideas – the figural level of meaning is what makes it possible for each reader to modify the text for his or her own needs. Thus, the concept of spatial textuality is also related to the tension between the literal or referential function of language, and the figural, affectively coloured function which leaves room for association and thus calls forth a reaction in the recipient which transcends the mere recognition of the object of speech. For Genette, the way in which a text contains many different levels of meaning at once is a further expression of its atemporality: 'It is ... this simultaneity ... which constitutes the style as the semantic spatiality of literary discourse ... like a depth of meaning which may never ever be truly plumbed nor, still less, exhausted.'[12] Of course, the relevance of this aspect of spatial textuality is determined by the extent to which the text in question may or may not make use of the technique of suggestive circumscription.'[13]

As early in this study as my discussion of the extent to which reality may be represented in language, as well as of the appeal and the dangers of metaphor, it became evident that Miriam is interested in applying poetic language in such a way that it does not communicate an idea directly but rather gives voice to it obliquely. At the same time, however, she concedes that a text ought to be comprehensible. The kind of language which would meet Miriam's requirements may thus be defined as a language which refers to an idea, yet is sufficiently flexible in order to enable a connection or *partial* correspondence to take place between the speaker and the addressee; a language which allows the addressee to understand, while at the same time offering the opportunity to modify that meaning.[14] The deliberate use of vague, suggestive language and textual omission, that is, significant silence, forms in Miriam's words, 'an indefinite space for realization' (IV, 283). This mode of linguistic description creates an infinite dynamic space which removes an event from its sequentiality. Furthermore, in abandoning any claim to a direct, definite referentiality between word and object, it allows the reader to reconstruct the essential meaning of that event.[15] As Simon notes, it is the figural dimension of language which enables an unoccupied space to be created within the certainty of meaning, this 'certainty' being understood as a fundamental precondition of *intersubjective* linguistic communication. He states:

> 'Space' is the (abstract) moment which leaves room for meaning which is directly opposed to the abstract clarity of meaning contained in every linguistic concept in the speech situation. Without 'space', it is impossible to understand how I can achieve such agreement with others and that *others* are truly involved *in* this agreement.[16]

The enspacement performed in *Pilgrimage* can, then, be related to the manner in which figural language undermines the literal utterance, even while it enables the reader to produce meaning actively, and allows him or her to share in the creation of the text and to encounter the self and also the other (to discover 'the same world in another'). As a result, the text becomes a site of intersubjectivity. Consequently, every single linguistic expression needs to provide a space which can turn the communicative act into a shared experience. Nevertheless, the degree to which this scope for meaning is used in a text varies, and this determines the extent to which the reader is able to bring his or her own meanings and ideas to bear upon the text, or to use them in order to create his or her own form and meaning for the text actively.

In my earlier discussion of the tension between narrative chronology and synchrony, I defined spatial textuality as being present when the reader is called upon to recognise the cross-references so as to reconstruct the implied meaning. The second crucial aspect of spatial textuality, emerging as the tension between the literal and the figural mode of representation, calls upon the reader to supplement textual allusions with his or her own ideas and to incorporate these into the unspoken: the blank spaces in the text. In other words, on the one hand, meaning is produced when the connections between different descriptions are perceived as a result of the text's reversibility: that is, when the reader juxtaposes two textual descriptions. On the other hand, meaning results from the deliberate textual omissions in the following manner: the reader embellishes a textual description with his or her own ideas, that is, an intersubjective encounter takes place between the text and the reader. To a much greater degree than in the first example of spatial textuality, the emphasis on the production of meaning lies firmly with the reader: the reader must be prepared to engage in creative activity.

With regard to this second aspect of spatial textuality in *Pilgrimage*, it is nevertheless important to stress that, although the narrative unfolds in an extremely suggestive descriptive mode and there is, as a result, considerable scope for the reader to bring meanings to bear upon the text, the text never completely abandons the referential level of meaning. As was seen in my discussion of Miriam's poetic ideas, *Pilgrimage* incessantly oscillates between, on the one hand, its referential function (its intention to communicate a particular idea as unequivocally as possible) and, on the other hand, an embrace of a heterogeneity in reading liberated from all constraints of intention. While there is no space for an equivocal interpretation of the overall development of Miriam's life, the events she experiences, the people she meets and of her actions and thoughts, the potential density and heterogeneity of meaning emerges as a supplement to this clearly defined narrative chronology. The deployment of evocative circumscriptions and allusions which avoid directly naming the object of speech, as well as the absence of actual description, invites the reader to add the unspoken information, to embellish the textual descriptions, that is, to take an active part in the construction of the text. Frequently the reader is required to imagine for himself or herself a speaker's name, the subject of a speech, sometimes even the object to which the entire description is referring, as well as the characters' circumstances and activities. Such textual omissions encourage the reader to appropriate the spatial experiences, the depictions of characters, and particularly the descriptions of emotions, by enhancing these details with meanings derived from his or her own experience.

The following passage, which evokes an important emotional experience without directly naming it, exemplifies the way in which spatial textuality exploits a tension between the literal and figural mode of representation:

> She remembered with triumph a group of days of pain two years ago. She had forgotten . . . Bewilderment and pain . . . her mother's constant presence . . . everything, the light everywhere, the leaves standing out along the tops of hedgerows as she drove with her mother, telling her of pain and she alone in the midst of it . . . for always . . . pride, long moments of deep pride . . . Eve and Sarah congratulating her, Eve stupid and laughing . . . the new bearing of the servants . . . Lilly Belton's horrible talks fading away to nothing. (I, 137)

On the one hand, the reader recognises that Richardson is referring to Miriam's first experience of menstruation. On the other hand, however, this kind of description deliberately calls upon the reader to draw her own personal palette of associations into the text, using her own imaginative faculties to reconstruct the significance of the event described in the passage. In this sense, the reader arranges the text so as to make it meaningful to herself, indeed, one might also say that she transforms it into a significant space.

The omission of clearly designated references to the events to which Miriam's perceptions respond, the general absence of a narrator who might explain or interpret Miriam's actions and intentions calls upon the reader to participate in producing the meaning of the text for herself. Since the narrator does not offer any such orientation, the reader is required to participate as a partner in the gradual development of Miriam's experiences, thoughts and her growing cognitive awareness, in order to recognise, and later to judge, her character and her world as a result of this 'shared' process. As demonstrated earlier, the reader tends to experience the material places Miriam passes through or inhabits from her point of view, passing through them with her or observing them as she does as a distant image. In the similar absence of narratorial mediation, the reader also shares in Miriam's thoughts as a gradually emerging, explanatory pattern and is asked to endow them with a personally meaningful structure. *Pilgrimage*, one could say, represents a dynamic space in the sense that the reader has to establish relations between different, chronologically disordered episodes and is asked to embellish the different levels of textual meaning with his or her own associations. In this, the text clearly makes room for plural meanings which, in one respect, allow the text to become a site of intersubjective communication between the reader and the author. In another respect the text encourages the reader to become involved in the creative process by partaking in the production of the text and thus generating a unique and personal version of the read events. Barthes comes to understand the reader's own active recreation of the text as a revision, produced in accordance with each individual reader's narrative desire. Seen in this light, the novel is conceived not only as a dynamic space but also as a *generative* one.

Distinguishing between a readerly and a writerly text, Roland Barthes points to the degree of semantic plurality which emerges at the figural, expressive level of the text.[17] According to him, a text is readerly if it demands to be read sequentially and thus assigns the reader a passive, consumerist role; it is writerly, if it helps the reader to establish correlations with meanings beyond the text. Liberated from the role of consumer, the reader is permitted to produce the text himself or herself to be inscribed in it:[18]

> Reading is not, however, a parasitic gesture, the active complement to a writing which we crown with all the prestige of creation and anteriority. It is work (... in that I write what I read) and this work has a topological method: I am not concealed in the text, I am simply irreparably there: my task is to move and to translate systems, the future destiny of which does not stop at the text, nor at myself.[19]

Since, in purest form, a readerly text would be absolutely definite and a writerly text plural in its meaning, David Lodge is right to note that one should view this differentiation as 'one of degree rather than essence'.[20] Just as it is impossible to imagine a completely readerly text, since linguistic expression is always also figurative, so, too, a complete writerly text is conceivable only as an ideal, as, for example, in the form of a blank page. *Pilgrimage* can be said to be a writerly text in the sense that it employs an internal chronology and articulates clearly postulated aesthetic doctrines concerning the representation of reality and the creative as well as cognitive process. Furthermore, its marked spatial textuality permits, indeed calls for, the type of productive reading Barthes designates for a writerly text, not least of all because *Pilgrimage* reflects upon its own structuration and aesthetic effect.

Although I have previously isolated passages that illustrate the self-reflexive gesture of *Pilgrimage*, one may now apply this to the use of spatial textuality, which undermines the textual chronology and the clear referentiality of the text and compels the reader to supplement and recreate the text actively, precisely because this exposes the similarity between Miriam's world-making and the reading process. Just as Miriam takes her bearings in her lived world by creating a meaningful explanatory pattern in the form of a meta-world, so too the reader, guided by ideas and expectations derived from his or her personal world, orients himself or herself within the world represented in the text by creating a meaningful meta-world as a supplement to the text. The reader's reconstruction of the text broadly resembles Miriam's recreation of her lived world, although the former also reflects the reader's personal disposition, values and judgments and will thus differ from Miriam's reconstruction.

Similarly, the final situation depicted in *Pilgrimage* corresponds to the reader's own situation upon finishing reading. At the close of the novel, Miriam is in a bare room, objectifying in phenomenological terms the psychic reality of writing in a scene of detached solitude; here she faces an immaterial world, a blank sheet of paper, caught in the act of creation, in a second process of world-making which is neither a direct reaction to the material world nor meant to help her orient herself in it. More than anything, this second, invented world of her text has a reality of its own which is independent of the material world, even if it aims to recollect and represent Miriam's first world-making process. Thus, her concluding activity may truly be said to enact the scene of writerly textuality. The reader, having finished reading, is faced with a similar challenge, namely to reshape read text and by virtue of such recreation make it meaningful to himself or herself. In analogy to Miriam, the reader is actively able to create an independent world as the result of the world-making process of reading, while still drawing on the world described in the original text. For, recalling Goodman's statement that 'comprehension and creation go on together',[21] the reader may be said to retell or rewrite the text, beginning with the original work, yet supplementing it according to his or her own cognitive interests. In bringing together the separate worlds of the reader and the text, such an act of reading contains both worlds and, at the same time, elevates them. Thus, analogously to the metaphor, active, productive reading at once remains the same and creates something new and unique.

Barthes is particularly eager to apply his reading of textual space to his own sense of identity as a literary critic, since it allows him to be a producer of texts. Genette, in turn, interprets literature as a unified realm, so that textual spatiality ultimately allows him to explore the way in which a text always stands in relation to other texts. According to Genette, the reader not only ought to recognise cross-references within one particular text but must also establish relations between this text and diverse other, external texts in order to produce a further level of the text's meaning.[22] He thus compares literature – seen as a simultaneous whole – with space: 'literature [is] like a vast simultaneous domain which one must know how to cross in every possible direction'.[23]

Rather than discussing how Richardson inscribes intertextual references into *Pilgrimage*, I will turn one more time to the way Richardson and her heroine perceive chronologically separate events as a simultaneous whole, so as to call forth a multiplicity and heterogeneity of textual meaning. Basing my discussion on the description of Miriam's stay in Vaud and of her relationship with Jean in the last novel of *Pilgrimage*, I do not wish to give a comprehensive interpretation but merely, by way of a conclusion, to discuss the formal treatment of spatial textuality and its implications for the reader.

NOTES

1 G. Genette, *Figures II* (Paris, 1969), 43.
2 See Joseph Frank, 'Spatial Form in Modern Literature', *The Widening Gyre* (New Brunswick, 1963), 3–62, and 'Spatial Form: An Answer to Critics', *Critical Inquiry*, 4 (1977), 231–252. Although I have adopted some of Frank's concepts for my discussion of spatial textuality, I would nevertheless like to disagree with his conclusions. I do not share his claim that space takes priority over time at the *formal* level of modern texts. Since I regard the issue of spatial textuality not as an affirmation of the priority of space over time but as an explanation of the way in which a text not only represents space but also *produces* space Genette's essay seems more fruitful. Even if certain modern texts seem to be predominantly concerned with spatial form in the sense of the abandonment of narrative chronology, I view spatial textuality above all as a tension between chronology and simultaneity, as a free space between the syntagmatic and the paradigmatic axis of verbal utterance. In this respect, then, spatial textuality seems to me to be valid for all texts, even if it assumes a greater significance in some. Naturally, in simultaneously placing episodes side by side and in reversing them, the form of *Pilgrimage* does mirror the thematic philosophical and poetic discussion in which the eternally present, 'being' and essence are celebrated and in which 'becoming', progression and change are rejected as modes of interpreting reality. However, one cannot deny that the text also possesses a chronological sequence, progression and development, even if these play a lesser role than in the realistic novels which Richardson criticises.
3 Genette, *Figures II*, 44.
4 *Ibid*.
5 *Ibid*., 45. See too Michel Butor, 'Le livre comme objet', *Répertoire II* (Paris, 1964).
6 See also the essay collection by J. R. Smitten and A. Daghistany, *Spatial Form in Narrative* (Ithaca, 1981), the essay by William Holtz, 'A Reconsideration of Spatial Form', *Critical Inquiry*, 4 (1977), 271–283, and J. Kestner, *The Spatiality of the Novel* (Detroit, 1978). All of the above take Frank's essay on spatial form as their starting point; they may further his conclusions but do not make any significantly new contributions to the subject. Alexander Gelley, in his essay 'Metonymy, Schematism and the Space of Literature', *New Literary History*, 11 (1980), 469–487, and J. J. van Baak, in his study *The Place of*

Space in Narration: A Semiotic Approach to the Problem of Literary Space (Amsterdam, 1983) are among those who criticise and reject Frank's position.

7 For Frank and supporters of his concept of spatial form, texts of this kind replace at a fundamental level the temporal dimension inherent in language with the spatial principle of reflexive reference. The synchronic relations in the text are seen to take precedence over diachronous referentiality. In their view, the reader needs to relate the chronologically separate episodes reflexively to one other in order to be able to recognise, when he or she has finished reading, the meaning of the text in its entirety. Frank declares: 'readers are required to suspend the process of reference temporarily until the entire pattern of internal references can be apprehended as a unity . . . the synchronic relations *within* the text [take] precedence over diachronic referentiality, and [it is] only after the pattern of synchronic relations [has] been grasped as a unity that the "meaning" . . . [can] be understood'; 'Spatial Form: An Answer to Critics', 235. The fact that it is impossible for the reader to establish any of the references or interrelations until he or she has finished the book, and is in a position to grasp it as a whole, shows that it is essential to know the whole in order to understand the parts. Problematic aspects of this explanation seem to me, firstly, the low opinion of the role of the temporal dimension of narrative chronology in generating meaning in a text and, secondly and more importantly, that the autonomous meaning which each episode acquires in a reversible text is consequently overlooked. The claim that a text's meaning may be understood only in the final observation of its overall unity, however, also exposes a perception of reading as an activity in time, as a process of creating a chronology (albeit of cross-references rather than of textually successive episodes) which culminates in one overall picture which is the ultimate and single site of textual meaning, and which must be reached before it is possible to recognise the meaning of the individual textual episodes and of the entire text. In this, the text is seen to be simultaneous but not, however, reversible since, for a text to be reversible, each episode must have an autonomous meaning and exist independently of the narrative chronology and, furthermore, be independent of any gradually acquired overall unity. Frank's model might offer an adequate description for certain texts of the modern period, but it seems to me to fall short as a model for spatial textuality.

8 Genette, *Figures II*, 46.
9 See M. Butor, 'Recherches sur la technique du roman', *Répertoire II*, 68.
10 L. Edel, *The Modern Psychological Novel* (New York, 1972), 137.
11 Genette, *Figures II*, 47.
12 *Ibid*.
13 This question will be dealt with in more detail when I examine R. Barthes's differentiation between a *texte scriptible* and a *texte lisible*. Barthes sees the suggestion used in a text as an expression of its openness and, comparably with the above discussion, he recognises this openness as a basic condition of all aesthetic pleasure and all aesthetically organised works of art. At the same time, he stresses that different poetic texts seek to achieve this openness to a varying extent.
14 See J. Simon, *Sprache und Raum* (Berlin, 1969), 116.
15 See Ronald Foust, 'The Aporia of Recent Criticism and the Contemporary Significance of Spatial Form', in *Spatial Form in Narrative*, ed. J. Smitten and A. Daghistany (Ithaca, 1981). In his discussion of spatial form, Foust foregrounds the reader's participation and states: 'Meaning, as Frank implies, resides somewhere between the past activity of the author and the present activity of the engaged reader' (199).

16 Simon, *Sprache und Raum*, 118. The addition in parentheses is Simon's own.
17 R. Barthes, *S/Z* (Paris, 1970), 17.
18 *Ibid.*, 10.
19 *Ibid.*, 17.
20 D. Lodge, *The Modes of Modern Writing* (London, 1977), 68.
21 N. Goodman, *Ways of Worldmaking* (Hassocks, 1978).
22 For Barthes, a cultural context may also constitute an external text, as his discussion of codes in *S/Z* shows.
23 Genette, *Figures II*, 48.

CHAPTER EIGHT

WHEN THE TAPESTRY HANGS COMPLETE: *MARCH MOONLIGHT*

The description of Miriam's stay in Vaud, which takes up the majority of Chapter 1 in *March Moonlight*, begins with the arrival of a letter without a named sender that leads Miriam to wonder: 'To whom, so much letter-writing?' (IV, 555). Following a description of her present stay in her sister Sally's guest room, Miriam imagines attaining a state of juxtaposed spatiality in which the chestnut tree which she is watching is perceived simultaneously with the larches which she had experienced in the past in Vaud as 'a participant of mystery' (IV, 556). Furthermore, Miriam poses the key question of the chapter, namely 'What can Jean mean?' (IV, 556). In these passages, Richardson determines right from the beginning both the fundamental formal structure of the description – consisting in the reversibility and simultaneity, as well as the associative power of events – as well as the theme of the representations which are suggested by the textual form. Again and again, three phenomenological situations, which are at a spatial and temporal remove are juxtaposed into meaningful unity: Miriam's present stay with her sister, Jean's present stay in Vaud (and thus her experiences after parting from Miriam) and, lastly, various events which occurred during their stay there together. At one level, Miriam's reconstruction of these disparate sites into a significant unity is an attempt to solve the question as to what Jean's utterance meant. Her simultaneous perception of these different situations allows her to represent obliquely the essential quality of her friendship with Jean, without naming it directly. The subtle overtones of this relationship unfold gradually in the course of the chapter, even though the meaning that ultimately emerges always refers back to these initial descriptions.

Concerning the text's reversibility, the sequentiality of the events is interrupted not only by the overall narrative's continual shifting between the three different situations in time but equally by the non-chronological narration of each individual situation. Likewise, the single episodes interspersed within the description of the events in Vaud are either depicted disconnectedly (not in order of occurrence) or strung together loosely by associations and parallels. A second aspect of the textual reversibility is that the reader is required to place the individual episodes in a certain relation to one another and to decipher the cross-references before being able to understand the meaning of the different utterances and allusions.

The following is a list of the references made to events in Chapter 1, excluding

Miriam's comments which also refer to further events. The initial depiction of Miriam's stay in Vaud (IV, 555) is followed by a memory of the tea party in Vaud (IV, 556). This is succeeded by an extract from an earlier letter from Jean in which she tells Miriam about the bishop (IV, 559), which is an associative trigger for the next memory. This memory concerns Miriam's conversation with the bishop and his peculiar question on her first day in Vaud (IV, 560). This exchange with the bishop itself in turn contains two further episodes: Miriam's arrival in Vaud and an experience in Dimple Hill (IV, 561). Two further memories of her stay in Vaud follow on from this: a Sunday with Jean (IV, 563), trips they took together (IV, 567) and, above all, Miriam's recollection of two episodes which, viewed in hindsight, seem to offer an answer to her question, namely a breakfast with Jean and the bishop (IV, 570) and a trip to Gruyère (IV, 571). This memory seemingly having resolved Miriam's question, the final memories are centred wholly on her relationship to Jean. Firstly, Miriam recalls their first meeting (IV, 573) and then, having associated Jean with Jim Davenport, she is reminded of a road accident which Jim Davenport skilfully managed to avert (IV, 574), although this description is interrupted by Sally's reaction to Miriam's narrative. This is immediately followed by a description of the arrival of Jean's first letter (IV, 575) and Sally's reaction to the handwriting. Then come various memories, of a walk at night with Jean which she had to share with Miss Lonsdale (IV, 575), and of their successful escape from the other guests (IV, 576). Then the narrative returns to the motif with which it began, namely the contents of Jean's letter (IV, 576), followed by a description of Miriam reading it (IV, 577) and, subsequently, a return to the letter's closing lines. Miriam's perusal of the letter, and the memories and thoughts of Jean which it calls forth, are interrupted by Sally entering the room and inviting Miriam to come downstairs and sit at the fireplace. The chapter comes to a close with Miriam's rhapsodic declaration of her feelings for Jean. In the following chapters, Vaud (and with it always Jean) is mentioned five more times, at irregular intervals: in relation to Mrs Harcourt's loan (IV, 586); in a memory of Jean skating (IV, 595), regarding Miriam's first attempt, in Jean's absence, to write an article (IV, 609); as a realisation that Jean's departure is not a real separation since Jean is always present (IV, 613) and, lastly, in a comparison between Amabel's baby and the child which Jean might have with Jim Davenport (IV, 658).

This list illustrates the extent to which the three temporally and spatially separate situations are interwoven even while, rather than producing a chronological narrative, they form an associative combination of disparate events, which illustrate what they have in common. She thus recreates the most important events during her stay in Vaud as one significant unity in order to find an explanation therein for Jean's utterance and thus for the nature of Jean's relationship with the bishop.

More crucially, however, it is Sally's reaction to Miriam's manner of relating her experiences in Vaud which acts as a pertinent commentary on the overall mode of textual representation: 'Patiently at first, buoyed up by the expectation of hearing at any moment something that would serve as a basis for hope. But always in the end revealing her disappointment in the smile that plainly said ... this is all very well, but leads nowhere' (IV, 575). The reader's expectations, too, are disappointed, in two respects. There is no development of narrative suspense which might lead to a climax and resolution and, more significantly, the narrative fails to provide any definite explanation of the events, offering no interpretative closure to the event. When all episodes are juxtaposed, we end up with no clear pattern of meaning, but rather with a highly suggestive, metaphoric representation of Miriam's declaration: 'Jean, my clue to the nature of . . . reality. With Jean, for me, friendship reaches its centre' (IV, 623).

The fact, though never expressed overtly, that the nature of Jean's relationship with the bishop is revealed only by comparing different events retrospectively, does of course bring about a certain narrative suspense. Miriam's memories are repeatedly interrupted by questions, or supplemented by her thoughts and comments, in such a way that the significance of the individual descriptions begins to become clear. These numerous cross-references use the narrative device I have been calling spatial textuality. In a form of enforced collaboration, confined to Miriam's perspective, the reader traces with Miriam her developing awareness of Jean's relationship with the bishop and, like Miriam, discovers the answer to her question as a result of a detached, comparative observation of past events. Importantly, the reader's conclusions also lead to a second insight, namely into Miriam's relationship with Jean – one which is not posed as a question in the text.

If one strings together the cross-references which are used in the text, then the following emerges. Miriam's first question in the chapter, 'To whom, so much letter-writing?' (IV, 555), suggests that Miriam is indeed aware from Jean's description of her morning's writing that there is a second addressee. However, it does not become clear that this addressee is the bishop, nor how Jean's relationship with him is to be regarded, until one sees the separate statement and inferences as being related. It is not until she recalls the tea party and Jean's letter about the new boarding house that Miriam recognises that the bishop is the other addressee and, furthermore, that the reader realises the significance of the initials 'B.V.' (IV, 555) in Jean's letter. In order for it to make sense, the question 'What, as seen by Jean, is wrong with his religious beliefs' (IV, 559) must be read as a reference to the bishop's conversion to Catholicism which precedes it ('going over to Rome' (IV, 559)) but it also explains the subject of Miriam's earlier question: 'What can Jean mean?' (IV, 556, 558). For this new question clearly refers back to the letter cited at the beginning of the chapter, in which Jean expresses her sadness that B.V.'s religious convictions prevent him from enjoying life as other men do, although his health would indeed permit him to do so.

While Miriam, and equally the reader, are indeed able to conclude from these disparate textual signifiers that Jean and the bishop are friends, they may do no more than infer that they might be romantically involved and only then if Jean's complaint is interpreted as a reference to the Catholic rule of celibacy. Miriam returns to this surmise after thinking back over some of the times she shared with Jean, and asks herself: 'It is the puritanism of his Anglo-Catholicism that troubles her . . .?' Moreover, it is Miriam's desire to discover the truth of this inference which leads her to make associations between the different events, whereby the reader must in each case establish the relations between the comments, questions and explanatory descriptions for herself. Thus, Miriam sees a link between Jean's comment in her earlier letter upon the bishop's parting words – 'he said we shall never meet again on this side of the grave – but beyond' (IV, 560) – and her own conversation with him in which he posed an 'astonishing question' (IV, 560), the subject of which did not become apparent until two days later, namely whether it is possible to meet a loved one again after one's death beyond the material world (IV, 562). In retrospective, Miriam believes that the bishop was in fact referring to Jean, and not, as she thought at first, to an earlier friend. This memory both begins (IV, 560) and ends (IV, 563) with this realisation ('It *was* Jean').

Although Miriam does then speak her mind about the feelings which she now imagines the bishop to have – 'found himself... in the midst of revelation, in love, for the first' (IV, 563) – the reason for the impossibility of their ever living this love in the material world is only implied. For the bishop's part, this is characterised only as 'torment. Keen enough to drive him to open his heart to a stranger' (IV, 563), although the reader needs to see this in the context of the bishop's earlier exchange with Miriam. Miriam's conclusion concerning Jean reads as follows: 'in emotional response. And when the barrier made itself felt ... able only to deplore the belief that inexorably built it up' (IV, 563). This comment may indeed be viewed as related to the other passages concerning the bishop's religious convictions (IV, 555; IV, 556; IV, 558; IV, 559), yet the precise nature of the 'barrier' is never declared.

Led by her new belief, Miriam recognises her own blindness (IV, 558) as well as the hidden significance of events which had until then seemed wholly unambiguous and concludes: 'And I saw nothing' (IV, 570), 'Blind, I was, to the drama playing itself out under my nose ... I believed that she and I together ... irradiating our surroundings, she for me, I for her' (IV, 573). She now sees a second meaning in two events: firstly, Jean's claim not to know Miriam in the bishop's presence during a breakfast, which she mistakenly believed to be politeness (IV, 571), and, secondly, Jean's choice of the bishop as her companion on a trip to Gruyère, which she had previously and equally mistakenly interpreted as a 'fatherly pride in being singled out'. Placing these events in the context of other events and comments made by both Jean and the bishop, Miriam now believes them to be signs of an intensely romantic attachment, proof of her supposition that Jean is 'more deeply involved than her letter admits' (IV, 571). Miriam's commentary, which seems at first unclear and unfounded, acquires significance if one relates these insights to an earlier passage in which Jean declares joyfully to Miriam following the tea party, 'I have seen you radiant'. The reader is, then, able to realise in retrospect that Miriam's reaction, 'as if, for her his new vision of her friend had been the afternoon's chief gift' (IV, 558), is an expression of her suspicion that she is not, at least not alone, the reason for Jean's enthusiasm.

What these examples illustrate is the way in which a pattern of meaning is created: Miriam perceives separate events simultaneously, the reader recognises the links between them and must at the same time establish the relations between

Miriam's questions, comments and memories in order to grasp both the meaning of individual descriptions and the overall explanation which emerges in the simultaneous collation of events. At the same time, the explanation which Miriam discovers, while confirming a romantic involvement between Jean and the bishop, significantly omits any details of their relationship.

Such a preservation of ambiguity goes in tandem with a further aspect of the spatial textuality in *March Moonlight*, namely the plurality of meanings and the figural mode of description, which Miriam privileges in her rendition of the relation between Jean and the bishop. Furthermore, Miriam's own realisation that certain events have a hidden significance in turn sharpens the reader's awareness that the text may contain multiple meanings. The reader's ability to discern, analogously to Miriam, two possible explanations for these events is, of course, one instance of textual plurality. Furthermore, however, the plurality emerges by virtue of the way in which the reader is also in a position to judge the nature of Miriam's own relationship to Jean, independently of Miriam's point of view, by considering her reaction to Jean's utterance and her retrospective new interpretation of Jean's relationship with the bishop. The nature of Miriam's relation to Jean may be divined in part by relating different events to one another and in part by examining subtle descriptions and comments on shared experiences with Jean.

If one juxtaposes Miriam's descriptions of, and comments on, the episodes which drew her attention to the romantic aspect of Jean's feelings for the bishop with the passages in which she complains of having to share Jean with the other guests, then the possessive intensity of her feelings becomes very clear. Although she claims that Miss Lonsdale is jealous of the close contact between herself and Jean since 'she had had, before I came, the largest share of Jean' (IV, 570), the very terms in which this statement is couched reveal her own jealousy as well as being an implicit declaration that she herself now has a right to 'the largest share' of Jean's attention. Miriam's enraged reactions to the least interruption of her companionship with Jean – such as her reaction to Miss Lonsdale's request to accompany the two on their walk at night – 'I could have slain her' (IV, 575), or her response to the appearance of acquaintances or other English people during their trips together, 'either of whom I would desire to strangle' – also reveal that Miriam believes herself to occupy a unique and privileged position in her friendship with Jean. In this context, her insights into the intensity of Jean's feelings for the bishop do not represent simply the clarification of a question but, above all, her own disappointment. Although one might accordingly view all of the passages concerning the bishop as signs of her own jealousy Miriam's feelings are expressed particularly clearly in her final realisation: 'Then all our deep happiness, never confessed, never even alluded to, was nothing more than a background. Lit by glowing rays from an unsuspected source. Yet it had seemed so real, so independent' (IV, 575).

The primary theme of this chapter thus proves to be a description of the unique quality of Miriam's friendship with Jean. The description of her stay in Vaud and the clarification of Jean's utterance, which at first appear to constitute the main subject, prove to be pretexts which conceal Miriam's true concerns. Viewed as a whole, this chapter traces the way in which Miriam refuses to accept that her friendship might be less important to Jean than her relationship with the bishop and, furthermore, it outlines how this causes Miriam to rifle, so to speak, through the different past events in search of evidence for the uniqueness of her relationship with Jean. Formally, this is shown to be the primary textual communication, in the sense that the bishop's importance recedes while Miriam's realisation that 'it had seemed so real, so independent' is instead privileged.

In one respect, the comparison between her own departure from Jean and that of the bishop gives Miriam reason to view her relationship with Jean as the more significant one, although the reader has to establish a link between separate textual events in order to recognise this. Jean depicts the bishop's departure in her letter thus: 'On his last day here he said we shall never meet again on this side of the grave – but beyond. And then followed a dissertation on his ideas of a meeting there. Of its happiness and naturalness. He may be right; but I wonder' (IV, 560). Since Jean depicts their separation here as absolute and since the prospect of a resumption of their friendship is projected into an unknown future beyond life, Miriam in turn emphasises precisely the immediacy of her relationship with Jean. Repeatedly she declares that separation from Jean reinforces their friendship (IV, 565) and that the thought of separation is associated with 'promised reunion' (IV, 567). Not only does she stress, when describing her departure from Jean, that their separation is only temporary; she actually claims that it is not really a separation at all, since her friend will remain ever present in her imagination. Departure is coupled with a knowledge 'that in separation we should not be parted . . . with Jean, for me, friendship reaches its centre. All future friendships will group themselves round that occupied place, drawing thence their sustenance' (IV, 613).

Jean assumes the status of an ever-present standard against which Miriam judges her relations with others, with Miriam holding imaginary conversations with Jean, even speaking through Jean ('Jean speaking, herself speaking to Jean, to Sally' (IV, 578)). Miriam regards these facts as evidence that her friendship with Jean is of greater value than Jean's relationship with the bishop, since they emphasise precisely an intimate presence between the two women, the possibility of which the bishop himself denied on his departure. Miriam's repeated characterisation of Jean as 'eternal' is also a sign of the emphasis which she places on Jean's presence. For she treasures certain shared experiences as 'eternal moments' (IV, 565) safely stored in her memory, such as their first encounter in which she said of Jean: 'There, for ever, she sits' (IV, 574). Above all, it is the moments of intimate communion which express her sense of permanence and eternal presence: 'The moment we found ourselves together, time stood still' (IV, 567). By implication, this feeling returns each time she recalls these moments. Miriam's desire to affirm the unique quality of her friendship with Jean, by reviving it completely in memory, is also fulfilled in the sense that their friendship is ultimately endowed with an eternal, because textual, presence.

This leads me to the second way in which the unique quality of their friendship is communicated in the text, namely through associated descriptions which are resonantly figural. The significance of this friendship is never named directly, either in the individual episodes or in the overall collection of descriptions. This encourages the reader to supplement the description of the friendship with her own associations. In fact, by omitting a direct naming of significant aspects of this relationship, she reinforces its uniqueness. Jean expresses the link between uniqueness and the rule of silence in her letter as follows: 'I don't say much about our friendship. It is a very precious thing. I am silent before the wonder of it . . . For me you are like the most refreshing of sea breezes. No, that won't do. There is nothing to compare with the effect you have on me' (IV, 577). In her many descriptions of, and comments upon, Jean, Miriam tends to employ allusions, metaphorical comparisons and oblique designations in such a way that the evocation of the events which they experienced together indirectly articulates their mutual joy, shared understanding and deep, mutual communion. In accordance with this method, the textual apotheosis of their friendship is not a direct declaration of love between the two nor a commentary conveying it, but in fact a description of their laughter:

> Whenever we were together laughter enfolded us coming from her to me, from somewhere to both of us. Sometimes I deliberately drove it away, desiring, for one of my elucidations, a surrounding gravity. And gravely she would listen. But in her response there was always laughter, in her quietest responsive smile a dancing laughter. (IV, 579).

The special quality of their friendship is thus apoetic, since laughter is in itself a form of communication which does not support a referential linguistic function.

In an autobiographical essay, Richardson justifies her dissatisfaction with the traditional forms of the novel, so as to justify her own narrative innovations:

> I believed myself to be, even when most enchanted, intolerant of the romantic and the realist novel alike. Each so it seemed to me, left out certain essentials and dramatised life misleadingly. *Horizontally*. Assembling their characters, the novelists developed situations, devised events, climax and conclusion. I could not accept their finalities. Always . . . one was aware of the author and applauding, or deploring, his manipulations. This, when the drama was a conducted tour with the author deliberately present telling his tale . . . what one was assured were the essentials seemed to me secondary to something I could not then define, and the curtain-dropping finalities entirely false to experience.[1]

In so doing Richardson directly addresses the question of how reality can adequately be represented. For, as I have sought to illustrate, she favours a technique of suggestive and metaphorical circumscription and a deliberate use of ellipses over the overt definition and naming of a subject. The themes which Miriam prefers to see treated in fiction are descriptions of the phenomenal world; the 'surroundings' rather than human relationships; 'human drama' and, above all, explorations of the way in which the surroundings affect and influence fictional characters (III, 243). Her chosen method of describing a character is not by relating the facts of his or her life, but instead by presenting 'her own images. What she sees and thinks' (III, 285) as well as the metaphors which a character applies to the world, that is, the way in which a character reacts to and perceives his or her phenomenal world, gives it a meaningful order and articulates this in words.

Richardson's notions of an adequate novelistic form, which are a polemic against, and a response to, more conventional forms of the novel, may be summed up as follows. In accordance to the conviction voiced in *Pilgrimage* that reality consists of lived events in a continual essence and that it ought thus to be grasped in spatialised time, with events set side by side, Richardson regards it as the task of fiction to record such a juxtaposition of events. It is not the illusory, sequential succession of events – 'appearing piecemeal, chronologically and, so to say, horizontally' – which ought properly to determine fictional forms, but rather a transformation and reordering which would express the true relations between events, 'revealing their essential depth of relationship'.[2] Her objection to the romantic and the realistic novel is founded in a belief that, in depicting the chronological sequence of events as the true one and representing this in the text in a dramatised narration, 'a story complete with beginning, middle, climax and curtain', these narrative modes drive a wedge between dramatic representation and the actual experience of reality even while they also leave out essential aspects of reality.

Richardson's second primary objection to the traditional novel relates to their use of the referential function of language. By placing novels in the service of the unequivocal communication of an idea, all events are presented as part of an 'orderly scheme', thus reducing reality (understood by Richardson as being present when 'things state themselves from several points of view simultaneously') to a one-sided and predetermined explanatory model, 'large superficial statements' (III, 275). In addition to their one-sided schematisation, Richardson accuses these novels of failing to focus primarily upon the creation of an imaginary world and upon their own fictionality and of instead subordinating this self-referentiality to the communication of an idea. As a result, these novels are 'about something else ... a masterly study of some single thing' (III, 61), 'all teaching something' (III, 46), 'witty exploitations of ideas' (IV, 239). Since their primary significance is to be found in the reference to an idea, they reduce, as far as is possible, the plurality which makes up the space of the text, thus turning it into a 'dreadful enclosure' (IV, 239). Miriam declares: 'The torment of *all* novels is what is left out' (IV, 239). This insufficiency is especially pronounced in the novels in which plurality, which is potentially able to bring forth the unnamed aspects which have been 'left out' and which enables the reader to supplement these omissions with his or her own images, assumes a subordinate position.[3]

Above all, Richardson criticises the authorial narrators of these novels, both because their support of one-sided descriptions, in which the essential is left out, represents a claim to omnipotence and, furthermore, because these unambiguous explanations of the events impede the reader's freedom. Authorial narrative shifts its focus from the text's self-reflexivity, to reassessments of ideas that are external to it. The text's dominant meaning thus ceases simply to be its communication of an idea and instead draws attention to the foreign presence of the author: to the author's intentions and interpretation of the narrrated events. Miriam thus objects to Hypo, a key representative of the novelistic form which Richardson attacks: 'You weaken the whole argument by coming forward . . . to tell your readers what they ought to feel . . . attention is turned from the spectacle to yourself' (III, 251). Significantly, Richardson here constructs a polemic against explicit authorial intervention, since this forces the reader to look to the writer and not to the text (I, 385), while she at the same time regards the author as the primary subject of all fiction: 'the novel will remain a tour of the mind of the author'.[4] Accordingly, the primary meaning of a text is located neither in the chronologically developed story nor in the referentially mediated authorial message, but rather in the author's self-presentation. Miriam declares that chronological narration merely serves a peripheral function: 'I don't read books for the story, but as a psychological study of the author' (I, 384). Likewise, her relationship to the author's message is described as follows:

> reading *everything* so that she grasped only the sound and the character of the words and the arrangement of the sentences, and only sometimes a long time afterwards . . . anything . . . of the author's meaning. . . but always the author; in the first few lines; and after that . . . going about for days thinking everything in his shape. (III, 131)

Richardson regards the text as the scene of an intersubjective encounter, yet augments her general definition of the novel as a representation of the author's imagination with the comment that 'the decisive factor is his attitude towards phenomenon'.[5] When she states that the author is engaged in self-presentation, Richardson means that each part of the novel bears the indelible stamp of his or her consciousness, his 'attitude towards reality, inevitably revealed; subtly by his accent, obviously by his use of adjective, epithet and metaphor'.[6] Recognising the author is thus far less a question of understanding his or her message than of gaining insight into his or her mode of perceiving the experiential world by restructuring and recreating it. For Richardson, then, the text's primary communication consists in its attitude towards the phenomenal world, an attitude which expresses the author's world-making and not the message which it serves. Although she regards this definition as a comprehensive description of literature, it is especially pertinent to her preferred novelistic form, in which the narrator withholds his or her judgments and explanations and the reader is encouraged to participate in and to supplement the text.

From Richardson's criticism of the traditional novel one may infer her own poetology: Richardson seeks to bring forth the 'essentials' which are conventionally left out of the novel, namely an unchanging, continual essence and a centre beneath the surface which is oblivious to the passage of time. She does this by deliberately drawing attention to omissions and ambiguity and, furthermore, by abandoning any attempt to provide a comprehensive explanatory scheme. For her, fiction's primary concern is with surroundings, with the phenomenal world, and not with 'human drama'; with the character's or author's standpoint in relation to these surroundings and not with explanatory facts. Fiction ought not to refer to a world beyond the text, to a message or idea to which the fictional description is subordinated, but should rather refer to itself and express an awareness of its own fictionality. Fiction should draw attention to its position as a newly created world, in the sense that the particular mode of fictional description and the composition of the words and metaphors are an accurate mirror of the author's perception of the phenomenal world.

In the new novelistic form which originated at the turn of the century and which she regards as a fusion between romance and realism, with Joyce, Proust and implicitly herself [7] as its representatives, Richardson sees an alternative to the aspects of the traditional novel she finds so unsatisfactory. This type of novel does not leave the reader 'searching for superficial sequences in stretches of statement regarded horizontally'[8] but instead foregrounds the text's spatial dimension. Correspondingly, Richardson also draws an analogy between space and the text in the article, arguing that this kind of novel is a challenge to the reader 'to plunge provisionally, here and there; *enter* the text and look innocently about'.[9] The spatial dimension of this form of text is also evinced by its profound reversibility; the individual sections may be understood without reading the text sequentially: 'Such novels may be entered at any point, read backwards, or from the centre to either extremity.'[10] As in the theoretical texts which I discussed earlier, Richardson's description of this textual reversibility is closely bound up with a simultaneity of textual events, a simultaneity which enables the reader to discern a significant pattern at the end of the novel and which communicates a particular message and weaves an explanatory pattern. At the same time, however, this marked reversibility renders each individual part of the text significant. Richardson says of this novelistic form:

> the reader . . . finds himself within a medium whose close texture, like that of poetry, is everywhere significant and although, when the tapestry hangs complete before his eyes, each portion is seen to enhance the rest and the shape and the intention of the whole grows clear, any single strip may be divorced from its fellows without losing everything of its power and of its meaning.[11]

As well as rendering each part of a text autonomous, then, reversibility also helps to articulate a text's self-referentiality: it encourages sheer pleasure in the narrative mode of a single episode, so that the reader may enjoy its poetic expressive power independent of the overall narrative and fundamental textual communications.

Richardson regards the novel as a dynamic site for an encounter between reader and author, in the sense that a novel either directly or implicitly betrays an author's tastes, prejudices and philosophical position and thus provides the reader with a 'conducted tour . . . into the personality of the author . . . the writer's self-portrait'.[12] In addition, the new type of novel she envisages is especially well equipped with a further dynamic quality. It is not merely the site of an encounter with the other, but also gives the reader insight into his or her own self by challenging him or her to share in the production of meaning and thus to engage in creative activity. As Richardson explains, 'It weaves for the reader the eternal romance of *his* own existence and demonstrates that aesthetic recreation is to be had not only by going far enough out, but also by coming near enough home.'[13]

For Richardson, human consciousness – a contemplative and creative attitude towards reality – is the bearer of literature. This consciousness leaves its indelible mark on every single page of the novel; this assures that all of the episodes are interdependent as well as making each episode in itself a representation of the author's mind. Furthermore, contemplative consciousness is precisely what the author and the reader have in common – 'the sole link between reader and writer'[14] – and it is their consciousness which transforms the text into the scene of a dynamic encounter between two subjects, an encounter which also leads to the creation of a new text, the reader's thoughtful recreation of the text in the image of his or her own ideas. The act of reading also sharpens the reader's contemplative awareness and makes him or her willing to co-operate in exploring and recognising his or her own way of seeing reality, the 'stable contemplative human consciousness',[15] as well as that of the author. The force and appeal of literature are found not in the communication of an idea, the depiction of events nor in the creation of a meaningful explanatory pattern, Richardson claims, but rather in the text's ability to conduct a tour through the author's contemplative consciousness and, as a result, its power to create a dynamic space in which the reader's creative contemplation can be brought to fruition. She declares of the relevance of literature as a whole:

> [it] resides in its power to create, or arouse, and call into operation . . . the human faculty of contemplation. In other words: while subject to the influence of a work of art, we are ourselves artists, supplying creative collaboration in the form of a reaction of the totality of our creative and constructive and disinterested being.[16]

NOTES

1 D. Richardson, 'Data for a Spanish Publisher', *London Magazine*, 6 (June 1959), 19: the italics are my own.
2 Letters to H. Savage; February 1947 and 18 March 1950 respectively. Beinecke Rare Book Library, Yale University.
3 The extent to which this is an adequate judgment of the romantic and the realistic novel may be questioned, since these may be seen to possess a much greater degree of plurality than Richardson admits. However, the accuracy of her judgments of other novels is not in question here, but rather the fact that she regards novels which highlight the spatial qualities of the text as those which achieve the most accurate representation of reality.
4 D. Richardson, 'Novels', *Life and Letters To-day*, 56 (March 1948), 191.
5 Ibid.
6 Cited by S. Kunitz in his contribution on Richardson to *Authors Today and Yesterday* (New York, 1942), 562.
7 D. Richardson, 'Future of the Novel', in *The Future of the Novel*, ed. Meredith Starr

(Boston, 1921), 90. Richardson calls this 'the third form of the novel . . . a reaction from realism, though within it realism finds its fullest aesthetic development, or . . . a new birth of romance'.
8 D. Richardson, 'Adventures for Readers', *Life and Letters To-day*, 22 (July 1939), 51.
9 *Ibid.*, 51.
10 Richardson, 'Novels', 192.
11 Richardson, 'Adventures for Readers', 47.
12 Richardson, 'Novels', 190. See also the following letters to H. Savage: 19 November 1947, 1 February 1951, 11 March 1950. Beinecke Rare Book Library, Yale University.
13 Richardson, 'Future of the Novel', 91.
14 Cited by S. Kunitz in his piece on Richardson in *Authors Today and Yesterday*.
15 *Ibid.*, 562. See the unpublished manuscript, 'Authors and Readers', in which Richardson emphasises the reader's participation and proposes a new term for the reader's relation to the author: 'expressing both partnership and collaboration. Readers are . . . the authors' counterpart.' Beinecke Rare Book Library, Yale University.
16 Richardson, 'The Artist and the World To-day', *Bookman*, 86, ed. Geoffrey West (May 1934), 94.

APPENDIX

CRITICAL LITERATURE ON DOROTHY RICHARDSON

The first decades of research on Richardson, in so far as it is not limited to simplistic labelling of Richardson as the 'inventor of the stream of consciousness novel', can be divided into three main categories. The majority of critical commentaries take the form of reviews dealing with the single volumes as they came into print successively up until 1938; after 1938 with the first collection of the novels in four volumes, and from 1967 onwards with the second and final edition of *Pilgrimage* (which included the unpublished novel *March Moonlight*). Certain critics also use these publications as an opportunity to comment upon Richardson's biography.[1]

Richardson is not only, as Ford Madox Ford once wrote, 'abominably unknown' as a modern English writer. Her work has often provoked arbitrary judgments and sharply contradictory responses, as Jane Carol Bangs demonstrates in her dissertation.[2] These numerous reviews on Richardson tend to be influenced considerably by personal taste and prejudice. As John Cowper Powys rightly assesses: 'It is a queer and significant thing that you either love [Richardson's] writings deeply, quietly, intimately – like a large and yet minutely detailed landscape by Hobbema – or you just find them "dull".'[3] Readings which are either personally or ideologically inflected may be said to form the first and by far the broadest category of criticism. Certain value judgments are applied to the text, so that one is more likely to gain insight into the critic's expectations than into the text itself. The second group concerns itself with the relationship between the author's life and her work and accordingly interprets *Pilgrimage* as autobiographical fiction. The most interesting research falls, in my view, into the third category which deals with the text itself, whether it is read as an example of the stream of consciousness technique in literature, as a psychological novel or as an example of *écriture féminine*.

In the first group of commentaries, the critics evaluate the text according to their own ontological, poetic and psychological expectations. The critical reception, be it praise or censure, is then made dependent upon whether these expectations are fulfilled. The assessment that the narrative structuring of the novel is 'inconsistent' and 'incoherent', in that it represents a departure from the conventions of literary realism and fails to deliver a plot which is rich in suspense and can be retold, is in turn viewed as the text's strength or weakness. Other authors take this assessment as the starting point for studies which seek to prove that the novel does in fact possess a meaningful coherence. May Sinclair, who coined the term 'stream of consciousness' in her discussion of the first three volumes of *Pilgrimage*, praises Richardson's experiment because she views this new narrative technique as corresponding most adequately to contemporary requirements as to the proper representation of reality. In her call for the abandonment of the omniscient narrator and of dramatic narrative construction, which she justifies with the argument that a fragmentary, one-sided and limited representation of subjective perception, postulated as 'real' perception, is more true to life, May Sinclair's contentions typify the understanding of the relationship between reality and its representability which was emerging around 1919. She writes: 'people are presented to us in the same vivid but fragmentary way in which people appear to most of us. Miss Richardson has only imposed on herself the conditions that life imposes on all of us'.[4] She resists the accusation that the novels lack both method and form, explaining:

> In this series there is no drama, no situation, no set scene. Nothing happens. It is just life going on and on. It is Miriam Henderson's stream of consciousness going on and on. And neither is there any grossly discernible beginning or middle or end ... Miss Richardson produces her effect of being the first, of getting closer to reality than any of our novelists who are trying so desperately to get close ... What we call the 'objective' method is a method of after-thought or spectacular reflection ... Miss Richardson seizes reality alive ... nothing happens, and yet everything that really matters is happening ... we close with life.[5]

Here, Sinclair is referring not only to Richardson's literary output, but also to that of other significant representatives of modern literature such as Woolf, Joyce and Proust.

The points which are given priority in the controversial debate over the stream of consciousness technique's adequate or insufficient representation of reality, and over Richardson's specific use of the technique, are whether her experimental prose is successful, whether she achieves a certain artistic coherence and whether this form of prose is desirable.[6] One would be justified in asking whether a novel with such a 'faithfulness to reality' (consisting in the portrayal of the world as unconnected and fragmented, as the perceiving subject experiences it) is actually comprehensible and worthwhile for the reader, or whether it simply degenerates into boredom. Some of Richardson's contemporaries position the novel's appeal directly in its apparent formlessness. R. A. Scott-James offers his opinion of *Dimple Hill*: 'it is beautifully proportioned and none the less complete because it leads us nowhere'[7] and Ethel Hawkins states: 'Any volume read singly has much the same inconclusiveness that would be felt if a chance segment of one's life were considered separately; the composite effect is of significance and unity, and leaves us that rare impression of a soul entirely known.'[8] For others, it is exactly this so-called subjective formlessness which inhibits identification with the novel. Robert Humphrey argues: 'It is a psychic autobiography, which means that it is almost impossible for a reader to be empathetic toward it or to understand the importance of its implication. It is difficult to see either a microcosm or an exemplum here.'[9] Derek Stanford writes: 'All we can say is that the unrelieved impact of the ego, in life as in art produces monotony. We tire ourselves, and tire others also; and Miriam is, in her effect, truly life-like.'[10] Joseph Beach merely remarks on the absence of an overall formal structure and regards this as reason enough to deny that the novel might possess any thematic structure whatsoever:

> They [the first three books] are books that can hardly be said to have a social or philosophical theme. They are altogether lacking in formal characterization. There is no dramatic issue. And there is the almost irreducible minimum of story. There is certainly no story in the sense of some relationship developing, some plot engineered, some opposition overcome.[11]

Robert Kelly, on the other hand, attempts to explain his sense of the novel's aesthetic failure as resulting from its lack of structure:

> she gives her novel no structure whatsoever. She follows the stream of consciousness technique stolidly to its uttermost implications, and arrives at simple chronological sequences . . . every fragment floats in a void. We are rarely sure where we are, or who is present, or what has happened . . . there is not only no organisation, there is ostensibly no selection. And this is to be expected, for there is no longer any basis for selection . . . There are no categories in Miriam's world; one thing cannot represent another; everything is unique.[12]

In a dismissal of this accusation of formlessness, Jane Miller questions the relevance of these categories:

> It is ironic that [Richardson] should so often have been taxed with inconsistency and her novel with being endless 'inchoate experience and style' when her heroine would accept both inconsistency and formlessness as necessary attributes of her own mind. The novel is about . . . its heroine's search for some ways of immersing herself in 'current existence' . . . which would not be in conflict with the effort to communicate such experience . . . it involved a grasping at the central predicament of novel-writing.[13]

Other authors seek, in contrast, to analyse the novel precisely in terms of its structure. C. R. Blake thus explains his intentions as follows:

> The meaning of *Pilgrimage* will be apparent . . . in its 'reading of life' through Miriam's impressions of, and reactions to, life. The analysis of meaning will imply a definite structural pattern in the novel . . . We may then be able to conclude that *Pilgrimage*, recently discussed again as an enigma of form and meaning, has both coherence and integrity as a novel.[14]

Similarly, Lesley Fiedler's judgment that 'it is with the dullness of [Richardson] that we must begin'[15] cannot be verified by virtue of its obvious bias. Joseph Prescott says of Richardson: 'The author too often lavishes her surpassingly delicate perceptiveness upon dull material',[16] and C. P. Snow goes so far as to condemn the style as a whole: 'Reflection had to be sacrificed; so did moral awareness; so did the investigatory intelligence . . . hence the experimental novel . . . died from starvation, because its intake of human stuff was so low.'[17] Olive Heseltine, on the other hand, writes: 'The sense of wonder and suspense is on every page of the book as it is in every moment of the living day.'[18] Babette Deutsch also locates the human relevance of her novels squarely in Richardson's style: 'The significance is that of life itself, in the mere living . . . [the books] leave the reader with a heightened awareness of the most unconsidered elements in his own daily experience. They perform the supreme service of literature, that of increasing consciousness even when they seem to deal with trivia.'[19] The question as to how far Richardson succeeds in conveying Miriam as a multi-dimensional personality in the novel provokes similarly contradictory responses. In stark contrast to Hugh Walpole's comment that '[Richardson's] characters are like people seen for a moment in a tube and no more, and their philosophy is merely transient emotion',[20] Harvey Eagelson argues: 'But it is Miriam herself who mainly interests us. Before we have finished the series she has become for us a more distinct and vivid personality, a creature of greater reality than many of our actual associates. We know all about her.'[21]

When considering this juxtaposition of contradictory statements about the novel's aesthetic value and the extent to which it achieves its aims, it is important to keep in mind that issues of a text's appeal (or lack of it) will always result in subjective utterances. As Roland Barthes states: 'If I accept to judge a text in terms of pleasure, I cannot permit myself to say: this is good, this is bad . . . the text . . . may provoke nothing but the following judgment, stripped of all adjectives: that's it! And yet more: that's it for me!'[22] For this reason, the comments cited above, more than anything else, give the writers the chance to present their own views on modern literature and to express either their fascination with, or their own subjective unease in the face of, this particular avant-garde style. Commentaries which address the novel's textuality at an analytical level are, however, notably absent.

Arbitrary or self-reflexive critical texts, in which obvious prejudices are brought to bear on the text, reveal the critics' own attitudes even more plainly. By this I mean critical texts which concentrate upon the protagonist Miriam. Here it is critics' own ontology of the feminine which comes to the fore, their own ideas of female psychology and a specifically female aesthetic, and of the strengths and weaknesses of a novel written solely from a feminine perspective, as well as their own opinions on the representation of women in literature.

In Leon Edel's opinion, it is the fact that the novel is developed almost exclusively from a woman's perspective which poses one of the main problems in the critical reception of *Pilgrimage*: 'Few men – few critics of their sex – have been willing to climb into Miss Richardson's boat; the journey is long; the "stream of consciousness" difficult – and then the need, Orlando like, to become the girl or woman, to become Miriam if we are to be her consciousness.'[23] Other critics admire the novel precisely because it offers such an opportunity to identify with Miriam Henderson. They view the novel as an accurate depiction of the political and social position of women in the England of the early twentieth century. Margaret Lawrence, for example, writes:

> To understand the years just before the culmination of the feminist movement in England, women must study [Richardson's] series of novels under the general title of *Pilgrimage*. More than this, to arrive at an even tentative understanding of women this magnificent portrait of a woman must be read.[24]

Others praise *Pilgrimage* not only because Richardson achieves an accurate representation of female psychology – 'she has actually produced . . . the history of a woman's mind . . . so intimate and penetrating'[25] – but above all because she pioneered a literary style which enables the female consciousness to be revealed. Virginia Woolf describes her achievement as follows:

> She has invented, or, if she has not invented, developed and applied to her own uses, a sentence which we might call the psychological sentence of the feminine gender . . . It is a woman's sentence, but only in the sense that it is used to describe a woman's mind by a writer who is neither proud nor afraid of anything that she may discover in the psychology of her sex.[26]

Powys founds his great admiration for Richardson in her 'peculiarly feminine reaction to life . . . her genius is that of the nature of all women. Women represent the eternal growth to life itself'.[27] Scott-James argues, with a little less extravagance, that her femininity is the source of her 'unique claim to distinction':

> She is perhaps the most perfect incarnation . . . of one of the warring elements in the eternal sex war. Hers is . . . the authentic voice of essential woman using the distinctively feminine faculties to express the world . . . Miriam's part was to act, think, feel and experience life with the sentience that belongs to the feminine side of human nature and to do so in full consciousness of what she was doing.[28]

Although one cannot avoid questioning the various ideas of 'femininity' which are tacitly implied in these remarks, an even more obvious construction of femininity lurks beneath the objections voiced by those opposing *Pilgrimage*. Since neither the fictional character nor the author exhibit these traits consistently, the critics believe that the novel may be faulted not only at a moral but also at an aesthetic level. J. Prescott describes the heroine as follows:

> an attractive, spinsterish and mystical New Woman. Unfortunately more new than woman, since, for a character committed to the stream of consciousness technique of self-revelation, her reactions to her various experiences are selected and edited with peculiarly improper reticence; while hers is entirely a woman's consciousness, it is not nearly a woman's entire consciousness.[29]

The sheer arbitrariness governing subjective expectations as to the proper fictional handling of sexuality is exposed in Horace Gregory's contrasting commentary: 'This is not to say that her remarkable love scenes lack intensity. I have yet to read anything finer or more delicately poised than the love scenes between Miriam and

Michael, Miriam and Mr. Hancock, Miriam and Hypo; they are among the superlative examples of realistic art in English fiction.'[30]

The absence of any explicit reference to, or depiction of, the sexual act, as well as the fact that Miriam fails to correspond to conventional images of femininity – she neither exhibits a constant concern with her own sexual needs nor appears to place the desire for a man and the longing for motherhood above her work and her artistic activity – do not (as Edel suggests) alone provoke reproach from the male critics who speak of Richardson's 'daphnean furtiveness',[31] her 'fatal coldness'[32] and her 'spinsterishness'.[33] Sydney Janet Kaplan does concede that the absence of explicit descriptions of Miriam's sexual desire is a sign of the times in which Richardson was writing. Nevertheless, she still judges Miriam's attitude towards nature, her spontaneous sympathy for women, her decision to become an artist rather than a wife and mother and, above all, her reserve towards men, as resulting from her 'basic insecurity as a woman'. In this way, she too brings her own criteria of femininity to bear upon the text:

> it is precisely in the areas of sex that she has so much trouble . . . the demands for submission, loss of identity, loss of self, called for in sexual relationships are unbearable for her . . . the 'feminine consciousness' remains strangely abstract and separated from its normal connection with the body – which is the basic source of femininity – and its fullest revelation is to be a state of mystical awareness and communion with God. This is a lonely and asexual achievement with being.[34]

Whereas Kaplan limits her criticism of the novel to its representation of female psychology and sexuality, Elaine Showalter compounds this with the political dimension of feminism. She applies her own understanding of 'femininity' and her view of the proper aims of 'feminine writing' to the novelistic form itself. As a result, she judges Richardson's vision of the 'female aesthetic' to be insufficient:

> *Pilgrimage* can be read as the artistic equivalent of a screen . . . an aesthetic strategy that protected her [Richardson] enough from the confrontation with her own violence, rage, grief, and sexuality that she could work. The female aesthetic was meant for survival . . . But how much better it would have been if [Richardson could] have translated the consciousness of [her] own darkness into confrontation instead of struggling to transcend it.[35]

The varied and contradictory interpretations to which the terms 'feminism' and 'feminist writing' themselves are subject become apparent in Gillian Hanscombe's reading of the novel, which also derives from a feminist position. In her view, Richardson's genius may be summed up in the following claim: 'she is one of the very few to attempt the very complex task of explicating a feminist world-view at the same time as developing a feminist aesthetic in a work of imaginative literature.'[36] In a second group belong those critics who address the problematic relationship between life and art, asking to what extent the novel give us insight into the writer's life and whether such knowledge assists one in interpreting the text. Here, too, one encounters mutually exclusive arguments. Powys, a close friend of

Richardson, is most quick to attack the argument that the novel should be read as autobiography:

> Even if Miriam Henderson is more closely akin to [Richardson] than the Idiot is to Dostoievsky . . . she is not a whit more akin to her than the young Marcel and Swann are to Proust . . . Miss Richardson's friends could point, one may be sure, to countless important differences between the novelist herself and her heroine.[37]

All the same, most critics do take the statement made by H. G. Wells that 'her *Pilgrimage* books are a very curious essay in autobiography'[38] as the starting point for their research.[39] In his book on Richardson, Horace Gregory undertakes to expose a correlation between the events in Richardson's life and in the life of her fictional character Miriam: 'To reread *Pilgrimage* today is to recognize that this particular work of art is closer to the art of autobiography than to fiction. *Pilgrimage* took the course of an extended memoir.'[40] Gregory even goes so far as to refer to the subject of his study as Dorothy–Miriam, yet his analysis does no more than simply relate particular episodes in Richardson's life which are also described in the novel. John Rosenberg likewise views the novel as autobiography and uses the sequence of the events in the novel as an opportunity for comment upon Richardson's life:

> Since *Pilgrimage* is closely autobiographical as Dorothy Richardson herself confirmed from time to time, and since it was her life's work as well, I devote several chapters to setting out briefly the main characters, incidents and issues of *Pilgrimage*, so that these may be related to the actual events and people of her life.[41]

He does, however, distinguish the author from her heroine and concentrates his discussion of the novel on the insights which it offers into Richardson's own life. Blake, on the other hand, who is concerned above all with a detailed analysis of the novel, uses Richardson's life as a basis for discussing the novel:

> the analysis will trace the stages of development of Miss Richardson's life view as those stages are implied in the development of Miriam's consciousness. The effect of her experiences is to achieve self-discovery, or the reality of identity in Miss Richardson's terms.[42]

Rather than seeking possible parallels between the author's life and its representation in the novel, Rosenberg emphasises the way in which the author's poetic and philosophical convictions relate to those of her fictional character.

Gloria Fromm, who for the most part deals with Richardson's biography, nevertheless draws conclusions about the nature of Richardson's work and declares that it is

> indeed an autobiographical novel . . . and any portrait of [Richardson] must takes its fundamental lines from her own novel, because it was here that she felt she had fully revealed herself. She once said that the usual facts about a writer are 'secondary to his work', that 'we should meet him first in his achievements'.[43]

She exploits the potential for comparison between a writer's life and its presentation in fiction in order to prove her central thesis: namely, that the novel did not simply offer Richardson the opportunity to solve conflicts in her own life through fiction but that it also came to shed light upon her fundamental dilemma. Fromm characterises this dilemma as Richardson's refusal to separate life clearly from art and her resulting inability to favour one over the other: 'if her novel was not absolutely first-rate, it was because she could not ignore "the human demand" that life ... made upon her'.[44]

In her work on Richardson, which can in part be read as a direct response to Fromm, Hanscombe reveals the extent to which Fromm makes implicit assumptions about artistic production and consciousness in her analysis, assumptions which cannot be taken as universally applicable nor as corresponding absolutely to Richardson's work and her sense of herself as an author. Hanscombe writes:

> Fromm suggests that Richardson did not achieve greatness because she could not choose between art and life ... a possible, but ultimately unhelpful, interpretation – unhelpful in that it pays insufficient tribute to the unique way in which Richardson struggled to unify the divisions in her personal universe and to make coherent the experiential reality she perceived.[45]

In her study, Hanscombe attempts to assess the interrelation between life and art; she interprets Richardson's work almost wholly as a response to insoluble conflicts in her life, some of which were of a personal nature and some of which were related to the wider sphere of her socially determined position as a woman:

> [Richardson's only] solution to her personal alienation ... was to become a writer, but a writer who could manipulate relationships so that they would affirm her worldview in life, as well as in art. In this way, life and art would not be merely contiguous. That is why it is of special interest to the reader of *Pilgrimage* to know how exactly the important characters ... in the fiction accord with their real-life models ... and ... how in life Richardson manipulated her relationships with those people and then showed, in *Pilgrimage*, the meaning of those manipulations for her own liberation as a writer.[46]

With the exception of Blake, who does not address the issue of autobiography, Hanscombe is the only writer on the subject of autobiographical fiction among those mentioned above who carries out any close textual analysis. She attempts to elucidate Richardson's feminist consciousness both by means of a linguistic analysis of the text, for which she adopts Woolf's term, the 'feminine sentence', and by carrying out an analytical commentary of the constellation of characters in the novel. Although she does outline Richardson's feminist viewpoint convincingly, the terms 'feminine sentence' and 'feminist consciousness' are not defined sufficiently clearly. Her conclusion that Richardson succeeded in creating a feminist aesthetic thus appears, in the light of this analysis, speculative and incomplete.

The work which I place in the third group of criticism is primarily concerned with textual analysis and seeks to fit Richardson into a literary tradition. This results in a proposed outline of a canon of the 'great' writers into which, dependent on subjective preference, Richardson may be admitted, or from which she is rejected. One is justified in asking what useful purpose such a canon might actually serve. The value judgments and comparisons which are made in biographical texts on Richardson, such as that of Fromm, are simply transferred to the question of aesthetic merit. Gloria Fromm compares Richardson with Woolf and Joyce:

> It may well be that [Richardson] did not achieve greatness because she was never able to choose between art and life, to give herself up with her whole heart to the creative imagination that shapes and fashions art out of life – and leaves life behind ... In contrast the Joyce and Woolf novels have an almost classical calm, despite their intimate connections with the physical world of London, Cornwall and Dublin, because they have an independent existence of finished works of art.[47]

Setting out with similar expectations, Shiv Kumar examines the relationship between Richardson and Bergson and suggests that certain aspects of his philosophy are manifested in her novel. Particular emphasis is placed upon the conflict between being and becoming and the notion of reality as a continuous process.[48] Furthermore, he is concerned with the way in which Richardson employs the stream of consciousness technique, assessing this exclusively by comparison with her contemporaries:

> although [Richardson's] *Pilgrimage* has a certain historical importance ... it pales into insignificance when compared with the novels of Virginia Woolf and James Joyce. Devoid of any dramatic interest, symbolic meaning or skilful patterning, *Pilgrimage* remains at best only a literal and rather uninteresting record of Miriam's stream of consciousness ... [Richardson] appears to be unaware of the imperative need to superimpose some kind of aesthetic design on the indeterminate flow of Miriam's stream of sensory impressions ... [she] remains the least successful of all the stream of consciousness novelists.[49]

Leon Edel also compares Richardson with Proust and Joyce and classifies her as belonging to a group of 'hardy and plodding experimenters'.[50] Since he examines the text in terms of the psychological novel, it is precisely its subjective truthfulness which he views as achieving a successful self-portrait and a valid representation of a specific historical, social and, above all, feminine consciousness. He notes that *Pilgrimage*, written mainly in the form of an interior monologue, functions only

> when the reader achieves a certain state of identification or relationship with the sole mind that is offered to him in the pages of the book ... Miriam ultimately emerges as rounded, one might say a three-dimensional figure – just so long as we can stay with her ... and *feel* with her as we follow the play of her mind.[51]

Both Thomas Staley[52] and C. Blake[53] seek to demonstrate in their studies that the novel possesses a coherent structure, yet their arguments do not for the most part move beyond a summary of the plot and central themes. Staley's book offers an extremely shallow approach to Richardson's life and thought, and any discussion of her work tends to stop at mere retelling. Blake analyses the novel with reference to its style, to the constellation of its characters and to the passage of events. Since he was not familiar with the final volume, he interprets and at times misinterprets the novel as a psychological development towards a mystical consciousness.

Shirley Rose[54] is one of the first critics to move beyond a retelling of the novel's story and beyond the boundaries of subjective value judgments. She begins with a remarkable examination of Richardson's understanding of the concepts 'consciousness' and 'time' and in particular of Richardson's theory of literature, in order to clarify how these themes emerge and are developed in the text. Suzette Henke[55] explores Richardson's categories of 'male versus female consciousness' from a feminist perspective, and Arline Thorn[56] carries out a feminist analysis of Richardson's understanding of a 'feminine experience of time'. Thorn is particularly quick to acknowledge the dangers of creating such a gendered essentialism, in which 'masculine' and 'feminine' are viewed as completely separate categories. Both critics point towards to the way in which the word 'feminine' is given a broader significance in Richardson's novel, one which seeks to evoke a synthesis of intuition and reason: 'The expression "feminine realism" should be interpreted not as a label (signifying the gender of the mind) but as a convention, the antecedents of which are familiar to us as an aspect of romanticism.'[57] In his *Reader's Guide to Dorothy Richardson's Pilgrimage*, George H. Thomson notes that, because this text is both a subjective autobiographical and a realist narrative, it is particularly difficult to classify.[58] Indeed, the more recent Richardson scholarship continues to reflect the nosological challenge *Pilgrimage* poses to the critics. In the last decade, some critics have chosen to focus on the autobiographical aspect of the text, such as Avrom Fleishman, discussing the plot development of *Pilgrimage* in relation to Richardson's biographical development in general or, as is the case in Gillian Hanscome and Virginia L. Smyer's study of the modernist woman, emphasising Richardson's refiguration of her romantic relations with both men and women.[59] Gloria G. Fromm has not only supplemented her biography by discussing the manner in which Dorothy Richardson wrote about ageing in a text entitled 'Old Age' but has also put together the first collection of Richardson's letters, allowing the readers of *Pilgrimage* to trace the manner in which its author wrote her philosophical, political and aesthetic opinions into her narrative.[60]

However, the shift in Richardson scholarship has been particularly influenced by Rachel Blau DuPlessis's discussion of the way that 'the quest plots of twentieth-century women writers incorporate a critical response both to the ending in death and to the ending in marriage' of conventional narrative fiction. In *Pilgrimage*, she argues, Richardson 'shrugs off the well-charted narrative areas of sexuality and death', and instead explores the erotic and emotional intensity of women's friendships as well as providing a decisively feminine response to the way lives can be shaped, emphasising a holistic, synthetic, totalising vision of reality, so as to resist and rewrite the traditionally masculine approach to experience, conceived as instrumental, calculating, rational. This writing of a new plot, according to Blau DuPlessis, consists above all in rejecting both punitive, transcendent individual love and punitive, transcendent individual death and instead accepting a spirit of community and righteous convergence, which has 'both a spiritual and a political meaning'.[61] Along the lines suggested by Blau DuPlessis, Sabine Vanacker reads Richardson's autobiographic mode as a way of rejecting the traditional female plot; Kate Fullbrook discusses Richardson's novel as one of the most resonant narratives of the life of an independent woman; Anita Levy explores *Pilgrimage* in relation to the question of how modern fiction uses the figure of the middle-class working woman so as to critique the narrative of female domesticity such as *Wuthering Heights* and *Jane Eyre*, even though she judges Richardson's preference of the art world over that of female professionalism to be a limited subversion of the traditional domestic plot. Similarly Esther Kleinbord Labovitz reads *Pilgrimage* in the context of the female *Bildungsroman*, discussing Miriam's quest for self-realisation as a destruction of the various roles offered to women at the beginning of the twentieth century, notable those of domesticity and marriage on the one hand and white-collar labour on the other, while the choice of authorship emerges as a successful mode of self-development. Grace Steward, in turn, suggests that *Pilgrimage* rewrites a different cultural myth, namely the masculine *Künstlerroman*, negotiating the way feminine authorship can be gained only at the expense of conventional notions of womanliness, while Diane Filby Gillespie locates Richardson's political aestheticism in the fact that the end product of her pilgrimage 'is not adjustment to society and its values; rather, it is a demand that society adjust to her view of reality'. Though not concerned with issues of autobiography, Natascha Würzbach also comes to the conclusion that the highly subjective presentation of characters in *Pilgrimage* supports Richardson's constructionist project, at the end of which her heroine Miriam has poetically recreated herself.[62]

A second of feminist criticism addresses the question of gender and genre in relation to issues of poetic style. Elizabeth Podnieks suggests that the reason why Richardson, in comparison to a woman writer like Woolf, is still not canonised may reside in the fact that she depicts the woman's outlook with fanatical devotion. She uses her defence of *Pilgrimage* to critique the perseverance of a canon which will include only moderate women authors.[63] Stephen Heath suggests that, by writing the life of a woman artist at the beginning of the twentieth century, Dorothy Richardson was inevitably concerned in the debates around femininity, with her stream of consciousness technique a mode of self-creation that was explicitly developed in opposition to the novels of H. G. Wells: 'a critique of the idea of the novel, a perception of reality, and a psychology of women'. Following this suggestion, both Doris Wallace and Ellen Friedman see her narrative experimentation as a deliberate effort at pitting her feminine realism against the conventional masculine one. While Wallace offers autobiographical reasons for this stylistic preference, Friedman, however, sees this as an explicitly feminist departure from patriarchal discourse, meant to eliminate authorial dogmatism. Gillian Hanscome, in turn, emphasises that, like other women modernists, Richardson chose an experimental mode, so as to explore her individual voice against the expectations of style she found herself confronted with.[64] Seeing the prose of *Pilgrimage* primarily in terms of a spiritual exercise, Susan Gevirtz also argues that Richardson offers a deconstruction of the genre of male realism. However, she locates this stylistic subversion in the way Richardson uses spirituality to explore a prose more adequate for a representation of feminine subjectivity. At stake, she claims, is a narrative negotiation of the silence beyond words, in part related to the way Miriam's writing occurs in the wake of the traumatic impact of her mother's death, in part, however, also related to the way Richardson's interest in a continuous presence (which she came to explore also in her writings on film), reflects the feminine subject's relation to and conceptualisation of the maternal body.[65] In a similar vein Jane Miller's spirited appraisal of Dorothy Richardson's experimental prose links her concern with presenting feminine subjectivity in a less linear and less one-dimensional manner than was expected of the traditional feminine novel to the Bahktinian notion of novelistic polyphony, while Lynette Felber maps Richardson's exploration of feminine inner space on to the debate around *écriture féminine*, which was to emerge within a decade of the first publication of the completed four volumes of *Pilgrimage*. She sees in Richardson's privileging of silence over speech, as well as in her privileging of simultaneity as textual fluidity, not only an articulation of her distrust of male logocentricity but in fact an undercutting of gender binaries, an avoidance of paternal origins as well as marital closures, and thus an alternative to phallocentric discourse.[66] In contrast to most of the other critics addressing the construction of gender in *Pilgrimage*, Rebecca Egger, addressing primarily Richardson's discussion of cinematography, claims that her epistemological position in fact rests upon 'the denial or repression of difference', privileging cultural homogeneity. For, as Egger notes, in her rigidly gendered schema of the world she 'ends up encrypting – not elucidating – sexual difference'. Similarly critical, Jacqueline Rose astutely notes that, as Richardson rewrites 'woman's sexual and aesthetic participation in modern culture' in terms of 'her relation to nationhood', antisemitic representations of her time come to inscribe themselves in her notion of neutrality, as this is formulated in the dialogues between Miriam and Michael Shatov. Unwittingly, her relinquishing the domain of public existence in favour of writing proves, according to Rose, an 'inadvertent form of collusion', even if this occurs in the name of feminist self-determination and freedom.[67]

In her contribution to a discussion of *Pilgrimage* in the context of the debate around gender, genre and modernism, Sandra Kemp is one of the first to address the manner in which Richardson's suspension of linear sequences should be read in connection with her construction of new topography, where 'space turns the tables on time'. At the same time, such an all-encompassing notion of temporality, she adds, is a praticularly significant feminist modernist device when it is read in terms of the trope of death, for death 'is the moment of supreme identity with our bodies' and thus the 'complete objectivity/phenomenology – the literally unspeakable mystery of matter over mind; object over object'. In that she takes 'silence and stillness to their furthest extreme', refigures feminine perception in terms of an 'ultimate meditation on solitude' and sees as the logical consequence of her heroine's pilgrimage a move outside conventional time and space, Richardson's rearticulation of masculine modernism is not only always implicitly conceived under the sign of death. Its radicality, according to Kemp, also consists in the 'dismal image of how difficult it is for women (or "feminists") to possess their own consciousness in peace'. Continuing in the vein suggested by Kemp, Kristin Bluemel explores another issue that has been displaced to the margins of Richardson scholarship, namely the issue of corporeality. Pitting her argument against those critics who have faulted Richardson for avoiding issues of sexuality, Bluemel explores the manner in which lesbian desire is written into Miriam's narrative, though realised through a writing unfettered by narrative conventions. At the same time, she contrasts this experimental mode of representing an unspoken sexuality to the way the text also addresses discussions of the female body in relation to work, illness and ultimately, in the figure of Miriam's mother, violent death.[68]

The other three most recent full-length monographs on Richardson all highlight how her work fits into the concerns of modernism. Eveline Killian focuses on the manner in which *Pilgrimage* presents significant moments of transcendence as an immunity against contingency and future uncertainty. By virtue of memory and aesthetic recollection, time can be surpassed, yet the result is a supreme moment of ambivalence. For the distance from the self which impersonality affords also proves to be a moment of extreme subjectivity. Carol Watts, in turn, explores how, for Richardson, a move into modernism comes to be coterminous with a negotiation of the maternal figure, whose loss she must first screen and then recuperate in the form of writing. At the same time, becoming a woman writer also means addressing the shocks and euphorias which came with an experience of urban centres after the First World War. According to Watts, then, Miriam's pilgrimage consists in understanding the past she comes from and recognising that it has irrevocably been shattered; expressing prejudices and becoming self-aware of these; cultivating a distance to her experiences and admitting that all vision is clouded by subjectivity and finally fashioning an image of herself which continually breaks open past experiences by projecting these on to the future. It is in terms of such a constant renegotiation of the self that Watts asks us to understand Richardson's writing beyond the end.

Finally, in what is both a clear and at the same time a highly sophisticated discussion of Dorothy Richardson's work, Jean Radford presents *Pilgrimage* as a modern and feminine reiteration of Bunyan's *Pilgrim's Progress*.[69] Reading the novel in reference to Roland Barthes's discussion of the reader's collaboration in texts he calls writerly, she highlights the manner in which Miriam's narrative not only traces a quest for a mystical scene of rebirth but also performs a 'counter-discourse expressive of the kind of spiritual holism her heroine seeks', which draws the reader into a textual pilgrimage of their own. Exploring the manner in which Richardson plays through the various modern debates on masculinity and femininity, Radford argues that she repeatedly relinquishes an either/or position in favour of assuming both. Her heroine, she explains, 'crosses class as well as gender boundaries', as she comes to find that an authentic self-representation involves identifying with the masculine as well as the maternal position. In the most subtle psychological reading of

APPENDIX

Pilgrimage to date, Radford reads Miriam's psychic development as a refiguration of her family romance; the writer emerges only after she has used her various love objects to work through the maternal suicide and the paternal bankruptcy and thus put her psychic mourning to aesthetic use. Mapping Richardson's rejection of linear story-based narratives and her deferral of the ending on to the critical language developed by French feminists – notably Kristeva's notion of a semiotic *chora* based on bodily pulsations and affects that precede symbolic language, Cixous's notion of the woman's affirmative laughter as one breaking open masculine speech and Irigaray's discussion of what she call *le parler femme* as a fluid language, using ellipses, inversions and displacements – Radford brilliantly illustrates how Richardson writes feminine subjectivity as corporeal textuality, arguing that the body can be 'heard' in *Pilgrimage*, if one reads for it, if one listens 'differently'. At the same time, the intricacies of language and subjectivity are here played through 'without a master theory of either woman or writing'.

One can perhaps explain why the majority of critical writing on *Pilgrimage* ultimately reflects the reader's philosophical, aesthetic and psychological expectations – with critical evaluation being dependent upon the extent to which the text satisfies or disappoints these expectations – by turning to Richardson's own thoughts on the pleasures of reading. For she suggests that the power which a novel has to attract or repel can ultimately be linked to the author's personality, as it is revealed either directly or indirectly, and as it confirms the reader's own expectations,

> If we *like*, if we feel our consciousness, in any and every direction, enlarged, or our feelings and convictions, we 'like' that author. And it is by no means always a case of like to like, though perhaps more than usually so. It *may* be attraction of opposites.[70]

NOTES

1 See *Adam International Review*, 31 (August 1966); 310–12, Vincent Brome, 'A Last Meeting with Dorothy Richardson', *London Magazine*, 6 (June 1959), 26–32, and Rachel Trickett, 'The Living Dead – V: Dorothy Richardson', *London Magazine*, 6 (June 1959), 20–25, written in commemoration of her death. See especially Gloria G. Fromm, 'Checklist of Writings by Dorothy M. Richardson: An Annotated Bibliography of Writings about her'. Fromm gives a commentary of all reviews and critical publications on Richardson.

2 See Ford Madox Ford, *The March of Literature* (London, 1939). In her thesis, 'The Open Circle: A Critical Study of Dorothy Richardson's *Pilgrimage*' (University of Oregon, 1977), Jane Carol Bangs lists six key reasons for the prejudices held against *Pilgrimage* in order to expose 'the arbitrariness of [Richardson] criticism': firstly, a suspicion of the experimental novel; secondly, a specific concept of the plot which every novel ought to provide, that is, a demand for a harmonious and coherently presented story; thirdly, a lack of interest in, or dissatisfaction with, the heroine Miriam and, above all, with Richardson's image of femininity; fourthly, a perception of the novel's autobiographical character as presenting a barrier; fifthly, an attempt to compare Richardson with

other modern writers in order to conclude that she lacked genius; sixthly, misinterpretations of the text as a result of careless reading. Bangs ascribes all these points to obvious prejudices. Although I would adopt some of her classifications, I would like to add that the supporters of *Pilgrimage* also misinterpret the text in permitting an obvious predilection to govern their commentaries.

3 John Cowper Powys, *Dorothy M. Richardson* (London, 1931), 43.
4 May Sinclair, 'The Novels of Dorothy Richarson', *Little Review*, 4 (April 1918), 5.
5 Sinclair, 'The Novels of Dorothy Richarson', 6.
6 By no means all of May Sinclair contemporaries share her opinion that the stream of consciousness corresponds to reality. Lawrence Hyde, for example, voices a typical reservation in his review, 'The Work of Dorothy Richardson': 'the resulting work is a medley of heterogeneous impressions, connected together by practically nothing more than the fact that they have all been received by one mind . . . [a] failure to which her method of approach to life is doomed at the very outset. For Life, to be conveyed by a writer, has to be viewed from some mysteriously situated point of vantage which must ever be impossible of exact location . . . there is a certain serenity which pervades anything written from this particular angle. In *Pilgrimage*, written by a person who is so palpably wandering uneasily among the trees, this serenity is wanting. No, the stream of consciousness is not reality' (*Adelphi*, 11 (November 1924), 515).
7 R. A. Scott-James, 'New Literature: Journey Without End', *London Mercury*, 39 (December 1938), 214.
8 Ethel Wallace Hawkins, 'The Stream of Consciousness Novel', *The Atlantic Monthly*, 138 (September 1926), 356–360.
9 Robert Humphrey, *The Stream of Consciousness in the Modern Novel* (Berkeley, 1954), 12.
10 Derek Stanford, 'Dorothy Richardson's Novels', *Contemporary Review*, 1100 (August 1957), 86–89.
11 Joseph W. Beach, *English Literature of the Nineteenth and Twentieth Centuries* (New York, 1950); the addition in parentheses is my own. Compare also Paul Rosenfeld, 'The Inner Life', *Saturday Review of Literature*, 19 (10 December, 1938), 6 : 'It is a loosely strung sequence of sensation and experiences, a continuous stream of entertainment innocent of inner form, without particular conformation to a vital process of growing shape.'
12 Robert G. Kelly, 'The Strange Philosophy of Dorothy M. Richardson', *Pacific Spectator*, 8 (Winter 1954), 78.
13 Jane Miller, 'In the Element of Language', *Times Literary Supplement* (14 July 1978).
14 Caesar R. Blake, *Dorothy M. Richardson* (Ann Arbor, 1960), 196.
15 Introduction to C. R. Blake, *Dorothy M. Richardson*, vii. Walter Allen also argues in *The English Novel* (London, 1954), 332: 'one is bored by Miriam and by the method of rendering her'.
16 Joseph Prescott, 'Dorothy Miller Richardson', *Encyclopaedia Britannica*, 19 (London, 1958).
17 C. P. Snow, 'Storytellers for the Atomic Age', *New York Times Book Review* (30 January 1955), 11, 28.
18 Olive Heseltine, 'Life, The Tunnel', *Everyman* (22 March 1919), 582.
19 Babette Deutsch, 'Adventure in Awareness', *Nation*, 148 (18 February 1939), 216.
20 H. Walpole is cited by Frank Swinnerton in *Figures in the Foreground* (London, 1963), 46.
21 Harvey Eagelson, 'Pedestal for Statue: The Novel of Dorothy M. Richardson', *Sewanee Review*, 42 (January–March 1934), 42–53.

22 Roland Barthes, *Le Plaisir du texte* (Paris, 1973), 24.
23 Leon Edel, 'Dorothy M. Richardson, 1882–1957', *Modern Fiction Studies*, 4 (Winter 1958), 165–168.
24 Margaret Lawrence, *We Write as Women* (London, 1937).
25 Babette Deutsch, 'Adventure in Awareness'.
26 Virgina Woolf, 'Romance and the Heart', reprinted in *Women and Writing*, ed. Michele Barret (London, 1979), 191.
27 Powys, *Dorothy M. Richardson*, 17.
28 R. A. Scott-James, 'New Literature: Quintessential Feminism', *London Mercury*, 33 (December 1935), 201–203.
29 Prescott is essentially well disposed towards Richardson; he wrote the first entry on Richardson for the *Encyclopedia Britannica* and drew up the first bibliography of her work. See also Kelly, 'The Strange Philosophy of Dorothy M. Richardson', in which he objects that '[she] is a prude. Though we plumb the depths of Miriam's mind . . . we never meet any of her sexual observations, nor even her most commonplace physical observations. The slightest physical detail is concealed in an awkward gap in the narrative . . . Eventually she creates in the reader an impression not only of a chaste mind, but even of an intangible body' (79f.) Here, too, we learn more about Kelly's own notions as to how sensuality ought to be depicted in literature than about its actual representation in *Pilgrimage*.
30 Horace Gregory, 'Dorothy Richardson Reviewed', *Life and Letters To-day*, 21 (March 1939), 36–45.
31 Beach, *English Literature of the Nineteenth and Twentieth Centuries*, 387.
32 Hyde, 'The Work of Dorothy Richardson', 517.
33 Rosenfeld, 'The Inner Life'.
34 Sydney Janet Kaplan, *Feminine Consciousness in the Modern British Novel* (Urbana, 1975), 45.
35 Elaine Showalter, *A Literature of Their Own: British Novelists from Brontë to Lessing* (Princeton, 1977), 262.
36 Gillian E. Hanscombe, *The Art of Life: Dorothy Richardson and the Development of Feminist Consciousness* (London, 1982), 166.
37 Powys, *Dorothy M. Richardson*, 15.
38 H. G. Wells, *Experiment in Autobiography* (London, 1934).
39 Virginia Leigh Smyers begins her study 'Dorothy M. Richardson' *Book Collector*, 27 (1978), 60, with the assumption that '*Pilgrimage* is, in effect, the story of [Richardson's] life between the ages of seventeen and forty-four'. In 'A Last Meeting with Dorothy Richardson', Brome cites the author's declaration that 'My novel was distinctly autobiographical. Hypo was Wells, Miriam in part myself and Alma, Mrs. Wells' (28).
40 Horace Gregory, *Dorothy Richardson: An Adventure in Self-Discovery* (New York, 1967), x.
41 John Rosenberg, *Dorothy Richardson: The Genius They Forgot* (London, 1973), xf.
42 Blake, *Dorothy M. Richardson*, 29.
43 Gloria G. Fromm, *Dorothy M. Richardson: A Biography* (Urbana, 1977), xiii.
44 *Ibid.*, 169.
45 Hanscombe, *The Art of Life*, 165.
46 *Ibid.*, 32. In her article, 'The Living Dead – V: Dorothy Richardson', 25, Trickett explains: '[Richardson's] deliberate limitations, her fanatical devotion to the woman's outlook, is her unique claim on our attention, and, by its very completeness secures her a place among the writers whose work survives'.

47 Fromm, *Dorothy Richardson: A Biography*, 395.
48 Shirley Rose, 'The Unmoving Center: Consciousness in Dorothy Richardson's Pilgrimage', *Contemporary Literature*, 10 (Summer 1969), 370. Rose accuses Kumar of ignoring Richardson's actual philosophical position: 'Kumar's attempt to fit Miss Richardson into the Bergsonian System results from his misunderstanding her position.'
49 Shiv K. Kumar, *Bergson and the Stream of Consciousness Novel* (New York, 1963), 62.
50 Leon Edel, *The Modern Psychological Novel 1900–1950* (New York, 4th edition, 1972), 156.
51 Ibid., 74.
52 Thomas F. Staley, *Dorothy Richardson* (Boston, 1976).
53 Blake, *Dorothy M. Richardson*.
54 See the following articles by Shirley Rose: 'The Unmoving Center'; 'Dorothy Richardson's Theory of Literature: The Writer as Pilgrim', *Criticism*, 12 (Winter 1970); 'Dorothy Richardson's Focus on Time', *English Literature in Transition*, 17 (1964), 163–172.
55 Suzette A. Henke, 'Male and Female Consciousness in Dorothy Richardson's Pilgrimage', *Journal of Women's Studies in Literature*, 1 (Winter 1979), 51–60.
56 Arline R. Thorn, '"Feminine" Time in Dorothy Richardson's *Pilgrimage*', *International Journal of Women's Studies*, 1 (1978), 211–219.
57 Ibid., 212.
58 George H. Thomson, *A Reader's Guide to Dorothy Richardson's Pilgrimage* (Greensboro, 1996).
59 Avrom Fleishman, *Figures of Autobiography. The Language of Self-Writing* (Berkeley: 1983); Gillian E. Hanscome and Virginia L. Smyers, *Writing for Their Lives, The Modernist Women 1910–1940* (London, 1987).
60 Gloria G. Fromm, 'Being Old: The Example of Dorothy Richardson', in *Aging and Gender in Literature: Studies in Creativity*, ed. Anne M. Wyatt-Brown and Janice Rossen (Charlottesville, 1993) and *Windows on Modernism: Selected Letters of Dorothy Richardson* (Athens and London, 1995).
61 Rachel Blau DuPlessis, *Writing Beyond the Ending: Narrative Strategies of 20th-Century Women Writers* (Bloomington, 1985), 142 and 161.
62 Sabine Vanacker, 'Stein, Richardson and H. D.: Women Modernists and Autobiography, *Bête Noire*', 6 (1988), 111–123; Kate Fullbrook, *Free Women: Ethics and Aesthetics in Twentieth-century Women's Fiction* (New York and London, 1990); Anita Levy, 'Gendered Labor, the Woman Writer and Dorothy Richardson', *Novel: A Forum on Fiction*, 50–25:1 (1991); Esther Kleinbord Labovitz, *The Myth of the Heroine: The Female Bildungsroman in the Twentieth Century* (New York, 1986); Diane Filby Gillespie, 'Political Aesthetics: Virginia Woolf and Dorothy Richardson,' in *Virginia Woolf: A Feminist Slant*, ed. Jane Marcus (Lincoln, 1983), 132–151; and Natascha Würzbach, 'Subjective Presentation of Characters from the Persepctive of Miriam's Experience in Dorothy Richardson's Novel Pilgrimage: A Contribution to the Analysis of Constructivist Narrative', *Modes of Narrative: Approaches to American, Canadian and British Fiction* (Würzburg, 1990).
63 Elizabeth Podnieks, 'The Ultimate Astonisher: Dorothy Richardson's Pilgrimage,' *Frontiers: A Journal of Woman Studies*, 14:3 (1994), 67–94.
64 Stephen Heath, 'Writing for Silence: Dorothy Richardson and the Novel,' in *Teaching the Text*, ed. Susanne Kappeler and Norman Bryson (London, 1983), 139. See both articles by Doris B. Wallace; 'Secret Gardens and Other Symbols of Gender in Literature',

Metaphor and Symbolic Activity, 3:3 (1988), 135–145, and 'Stream of Consciousness and Reconstruction of Self in Dorothy Richardson's Pilgrimage', in *Creative People at Work: Twelve Cognitive Case Studies*, ed. Doris B. Wallace and Howard E. Gruber (New York and Oxford, 1989), 147–169; Ellen G. Friedman, '"Utterly Other Discourse": The Anticanon of Experimental Women Writers from Dorothy Richardson to Christine Brooke-Rose', *Modern Fiction Studies*, 34:3 (1988), 353–370; and Gillian Hanscome, 'Dorothy Richardson Versus the Novvle,' in *Breaking the Sequence: Women's Experimental Fiction*, ed. Ellen G. Friedman and Miriam Fuchs (Princeton, 1989), 85–98.

65 See Susan Gevritz, 'Recreative Delights and Spiritual Exercise: Pantheism as Aesthetic Practice in Dorothy Richardson's Pilgrimage', *West-Coast Line*, 26:3 (1992–93), 84–94; and *Narrative's Journey. The Fiction and Film Writing of Dorothy Richardson* (New York, 1996).

66 Jane Miller, *Women Writing About Men* (London, 1986); see Lynette Felber's article, 'A Manifesto for Feminine Modernism: Dorothy Richardson's Pilgrimage,' in *Rereading Modernism: New Directions in Feminist Criticism*, ed. Lisa Rado (New York, 1994) as well as her chapter on Dorothy Richardson in *Gender and Genre in Novels Without End. The British Roman-Fleuve* (Gainesville, 1995).

67 Rebecca Egger, 'Deaf Ears and Dark Continents: Dorothy Richardson's Cinematic Epistemology', *Camera Obscura: A Journal of Feminism, Culture, and Media Studies*, 52 (1992), 13; and Jacqueline Rose's chapter 'Dorothy Richardson and the Jew,' in *States of Fantasy* (New York and Oxford, 1996).

68 Sandra Kemp, '"But How to Describe a World Seen Without a Self?" Feminism, Fiction and Modernism', *Critical Quarterly*, 32:1 (1991), 109 and 113; Kristin Bluemel, *Experimenting on the Borders of Modernism* (Athens, 1997).

69 Eviline Kilian, *Momente innerweltlicher Transzendenz* (Tübingen, 1997); see both Carol Watts's article 'Releasing Possibility Into Form: Cultural Choice and the Woman Writer', in *New Feminist Discourses: Critical Essays on Theories and Texts*, ed. Isobel Armstrong (London and New York, 1992) and her book for the series 'Writers and their Work,' *Dorothy Richardson* (Plymouth, 1995); also see both Jean Radford's article 'Coming to Terms: Dorothy Richardson, Modernism, and Women', *News from Nowhere*, 10 (July 1989), 25–36, and her book *Dorothy Richardson* (Bloomington, 1991), 41, 125 and 138.

70 Unpublished letter to Henry Savage, 1 February 1951. Beinecke Rare Book Library, Yale University.

BIBLIOGRAPHY

THE WORKS OF DOROTHY M. RICHARDSON

Novels: first editions

Pointed Roofs, introduction by J. D. Beresford (London, 1915).
Backwater (London, 1916).
Honeycomb (London, 1917).
The Tunnel (London, February 1919).
Interim (London, December 1919).
Deadlock (London, 1921).
Revolving Lights (London, 1923).
The Trap (London, 1925).
Oberland (London, 1927).
Dawn's Left Hand (London, 1931).
Clear Horizon (London, 1935).

Collected works

Journey to Paradise: Short Stories and Autobiographical Sketches, selected and introduced by Trudi Tate (London, 1989).
Pilgrimage, including *Dimple Hill*, 4 vols (London and New York, 1938).
Pilgrimage, including *March Moonlight*, introduction by Walter Allen, 4 vols (London and New York, 1967), 2nd edition (New York, 1976), 3rd edition, with a new introduction by Gillian E. Hanscombe (London, 1970).
Windows on Modernism: Selected Letters of Dorothy Richardson, edited by Gloria G. Fromm (Athens and London, 1995).

Autobiographical texts

'The Future of the Novel', in *The Future of the Novel: Famous Authors on their Methods: A Series of Interviews with Renowned Authors*, ed. Meridith Starr (Boston, 1921), 90–91.
'Confessions', *Little Review*, 12 (May 1929), 70–71.
'Beginnings: A Brief Sketch', in *Ten Contemporaries: Notes Toward their Definitive Biography*, ed. John Gawsworth (London, 1933), 195–198.

'The Artist and the World To-day', *Bookman*, 86, ed. Geoffrey West (May 1934), 94.
'Data for a Spanish Publisher', *London Magazine*, 6 (June 1959), 14–19.

Reviews and essays

'The Reality of Feminism', *The Ploughshare*, 2 (September 1917), 241–246.
'The Perforated Tank', *Fanfare*, 1 (15 October 1921), 29.
'Talent and Genius: Is Not Genius Actually Far More Common than Talent?', *Vanity Fair*, 21 (October 1923), 118, 120.
'About Punctuation', *Adelphi*, 1 (April 1924), 990–996.
'Women and the Future: A Trembling of the Veil before the Eternal Mystery of "La Gioconda"', *Vanity Fair*, 22 (April 1924), 39–40.
'The Queen of Spring', *Focus*, 5 (May 1928), 259–262.
'Anticipation', *Focus*, 5 (June 1928), 322–325.
'Compensations?', *Focus*, 6 (August 1928), 67–71.
'Decadence', *Focus*, 6 (September 1928), 131–134.
'Puritanism', *Focus*, 6 (October 1928), 195–198.
'Where is Miss Jameson's Suburbia?', *Evening News* (London, 2 October 1928), 8.
'Peace', *Focus*, 6 (November 1928), 259–262.
'Adventures for Readers', *Life and Letters To-day*, 22 (July 1939), 45–52.
'Novels', *Life and Letters To-day*, 56 (March 1948), 188–192.

CRITICISM ON DOROTHY RICHARDSON

Adam International Review, 31, 310–12 (August 1966).
Allen, Walter, *The English Novel* (London, 1954).
Bangs, Jane Carol, 'The Open Circle: A Critical Study of Dorothy Richardson's *Pilgrimage*' (thesis, University of Oregon, 1977).
Beach, Joseph Warren, 'Imagism: Dorothy Richardson', *The Twentieth Century Novel* (New York, 1932), 386–395.
——, *English Literature of the Nineteenth and Twentieth Centuries* (New York, 1950).
Beresford, J. D. 'Experiment in the Novel', *Tradition and Experiment in Present-day Literature* (London, 1929), 23–53.
Blake, Caesar R., *Dorothy M. Richardson* (Ann Arbor, 1960).
Blau DuPlessis, Rachel, *Writing Beyond the Ending: Narrative Strategies of 20th-Century Women Writers* (Bloomington, 1985).
Bluemel, Kristin, *Experimenting on the Border of Modernism* (Athens, 1997).
Brome, Vincent, 'A Last Meeting with Dorothy Richardson', *London Magazine*, 6 (June 1959), 26–32.
Bryher, *The Heart to Artemis: A Writer's Memoirs* (New York, 1962).
Buck, Eva, *Die Fabel in Pointed Roofs von Dorothy Richardson* (Istanbul, 1937).
Chevalley, Abel, 'Les Lettres anglaises', *Vient de Paraître* (Paris, 1928), 55–56.
Church, Richard, 'An Essay in Estimation of Dorothy Richardson's "Pilgrimage"', *Pilgrimage: The Life of Dorothy Richardson* (London, 1938). [Publisher's brochure]
Deutsch, Babette, 'Adventure in Awareness', *Nation*, 148 (18 February 1939), 216.
Eagleson, Harvey, 'Pedestal for Statue: The Novels of Dorothy M. Richardson', *Sewanee Review*, 42 (January–March 1934), 42–53.

Edel, Leon, 'Dorothy M. Richardson, 1882–1957', *Modern Fiction Studies*, 4 (Winter 1958), 165–168.
——, *The Modern Psychological Novel 1900–1950* (New York, 4th edition, 1972).
Egger, Rebecca, 'Deaf Ears and Dark Continents: Dorothy Richardson's Cinematic Epistemology', *Camera Obscura: A Journal of Feminism, Culture, and Media Studies*, 52 (1992), 5–33.
Ellmann, Mary, *Thinking About Women* (London, 1979).
Felber, Lynette, 'A Manifesto for Feminine Modernism: Dorothy Richardson's Pilgrimage', in *Rereading Modernism: New Directions in Feminist Criticism*, ed. Lisa Rado (New York, 1994), 23–39.
——, *Gender and Genre in Novels Without End: The British Roman-Fleuve* (Gainesville, 1995).
Fleishman, Avrom, *Figures of Autobiography: The Language of Self-Writing* (Berkeley, 1983).
Ford, Ford Madox, *The March of Literature* (London, 1939).
Friedman, Ellen G., '"Utterly Other Discourse": The Anticanon of Experimental Women Writers from Dorothy Richardson to Christine Brooke-Rose', *Modern Fiction Studies*, 34:3 (1988), 353–370.
Friedman, Melvin, 'Dorothy Richardson and Virginia Woolf: Stream of Consciousness', *Stream of Consciousness* (New Haven, 1955), 178–187.
Fromm, Gloria Glikin, 'Dorothy M. Richardson: The Personal Pilgrimage', *PMLA*, 78 (December 1963), 586–600.
——, 'Checklist of Writings by Dorothy M. Richardson', *English Literature in Transition*, 8 (1965), 1–11.
——, 'Dorothy M. Richardson: An Annotated Bibliography of Writings About Her', *English Literature in Transition*, 8 (1965), 12–35.
——, 'Through a Novelist's Looking-Glass', *Kenyon Review*, 31 (Summer 1969), 297–319.
——, 'Dorothy M. Richardson', *English Literature in Transition*, 14 (1971), 84–88.
——, *Dorothy Richardson: A Biography* (Urbana, 1977).
——, 'Being Old: The Example of Dorothy Richardson', in *Aging and Gender in Literature: Studies in Creativity*, ed. Anne M. Wyatt-Brown and Janice Rossen (Charlottesville, 1993), 258–270.
Fullbrook, Kate, *Free Women. Ethics and Aesthetics in Twentieth-century Women's Fiction* (New York and London, 1990).
Gevritz, Susan, 'Recreative Delights and Spiritual Exercise: Pantheism as Aesthetic Practice in Dorothy Richardson's Pilgrimage', *West-Coast Line*, 26:3 (1992–93), 84–94.
——, *Narrative's Journey: The Fiction and Film Writing of Dorothy Richardson* (New York, 1996).
Gillespie, Diane Filby, 'Political Aesthetics: Virginia Woolf and Dorothy Richardson', in *Virginia Woolf: A Feminist Slant*, ed. Jane Marcus (Lincoln, 1983), 132–151.
Gregory, Horace, 'Dorothy Richardson Reviewed', *Life and Letters To-day*, 21 (March 1939), 36–45.
——, *Dorothy Richardson: An Adventure in Self-discovery* (New York, 1967).
Hanscombe, Gillian E., *The Art of Life: Dorothy Richardson and the Development of Feminist Consciousness* (London, 1982).
——, 'Dorothy Richardson Versus the Novle', in *Breaking the Sequence: Women's Experimental Fiction*, ed. Ellen G. Friedman and Miriam Fuchs (Princeton, 1989), 85–98.
Hanscombe, Gillian E. and Virginia L. Smyers, *Writing for Their Lives: The Modernist Women 1910–1940* (London, 1987).
Hawkins, Ethel Wallace, 'The Stream of Consciousness Novel', *The Atlantic Monthly*, 138 (September 1926), 356–360.

Heath, Stephen, 'Writing for Silence: Dorothy Richardson and the Novel', in *Teaching the Text*, ed. Susanne Kappeler and Norman Bryson (London, 1983), 126–147.
Henke, Suzette A., 'Male and Female Consciousness in Dorothy Richardson's *Pilgrimage*', *Journal of Women's Studies in Literature*, 1 (Winter 1979), 51–60.
Heseltine, Olive, 'Life: The Tunnel', *Everyman* (22 March 1919), 562.
Humphrey, Robert, *The Stream of Consciousness in the Modern Novel* (Berkeley, 1954).
Hyde, Lawrence, 'The Work of Dorothy Richardson', *Adelphi*, 11 (November 1924), 508–517.
Kaplan, Sydney Janet, *Feminine Consciousness in the Modern British Novel* (Urbana, 1975).
Kelly, Robert G., 'The Strange Philosophy of Dorothy M. Richardson', *Pacific Spectator*, 8 (Winter 1954), 76–82.
Kemp, Sandra, '"But How to Describe a World Seen Without a Self?" Feminism, Fiction and Modernism', *Critical Quarterly*, 32:1 (1991), 99–118.
Kilian, Eveline, *Momente innerweltlicher Transzendenz* (Tübingen, 1997).
Kumar, Shiv K. 'Dorothy Richardson and Bergson "Memoire par excellence', *Notes and Queries*, 6 (January 1959), 14–19.
——, 'Dorothy Richardson and the Dilemma of "Being versus Becoming"', *Modern Language Notes*, 74 (June 1959), 494–501.
——, *Bergson and the Stream of Consciousness Novel* (New York, 1963).
Kunitz, Stanley J., ed., *Authors Today and Yesterday* (New York, 1933).
——, and Howard Haycraft, eds, *Twentieth Century Authors* (New York, 1942).
Labovitz, Esther Kleinbord, *The Myth of the Heroine: The Female Bildungsroman in the Twentieth Century* (New York, 1986).
Lawrence, Margaret, *We Write as Women* (London, 1937).
Levy, Anita, 'Gendered Labor, the Woman Writer and Dorothy Richardson', *Novel: A Forum on Fiction*, 25:1 (1991), 50–60.
Miller, Jane, 'In the Element of Language', *Times Literary Supplement* (14 July 1978), 788.
——, *Women Writing About Men* (London, 1986).
Morgan, Louise, 'How Writers Work: Dorothy Richardson', *Everyman* (22 October 1931), 400.
Podnieks, Elizabeth, 'The Ultimate Astonisher: Dorothy Richardson's Pilgrimage', *Frontiers: A Journal of Women Studies*, 14:3 (1994), 67–94.
Powys, John Cowper, *Dorothy M. Richardson* (London, 1931).
Prescott, Joseph, 'Dorothy Miller Richardson', *Encyclopedia Britannica*, 19 (London, 1958).
——, 'A Preliminary Checklist of Periodical Publications of Dorothy M. Richardson', *Studies in Honor of John Wilcox* (Detroit, 1958), 219–225.
Radford, Jean, 'Coming to Terms: Dorothy Richardson, Modernism, and Women', *News from Nowhere*, 10 (July 1989), 25–36.
——, *Dorothy Richardson* (Bloomington, 1991).
Rose, Jacqueline, *States of Fantasy* (New York and Oxford, 1996).
Rose, Shirley, 'The Unmoving Center: Consciousness in Dorothy Richardson's *Pilgrimage*', *Contemporary Literature*, 10 (Summer 1969), 366–382.
——, 'Dorothy Richardson's Theory of Literature: The Writer as Pilgrim', *Criticism*, 12 (Winter 1970), 20–37.
——, 'Dorothy Richardson: The First Hundred Years. A Retrospective View', *Dalhousie Review*, 53 (1973/74), 92–96.
——, 'Dorothy Richardson's Focus on Time', *English Literature in Transition*, 17 (1974), 163–172.

Rosenberg, John, *Dorothy Richardson: The Genius They Forgot* (London, 1973).
Rosenfeld, Paul, 'The Inner Life', *Saturday Review of Literature*, 19 (10 December 1938), 6.
Scott-James, R. A., 'New Literature: Quintessential Feminism', *London Mercury*, 33 (December 1935), 201–203.
——, 'New Literature: Journey Without End', *London Mercury*, 39 (December 1938), 214–215.
——, *Fifty Years of English Literature 1900–1950: With a Postscript 1951–1955* (London, 1956).
Showalter, Elaine, *A Literature of their Own: British Women Novelists from Brontë to Lessing* (Princeton, 1977).
Sinclair, May, 'The Novels of Dorothy Richardson', *Little Review*, 4 (April 1918), 3–11.
Smyers, Virginia Leigh, 'Dorothy M. Richardson', *Book Collector*, 28 (1978), 60–63.
Snow, C. P., 'Storytellers for the Atomic Age', *New York Times Book Review* (30 January 1955), 11, 28.
Staley, Thomas F., *Dorothy Richardson* (Boston, 1976).
Stanford, Derek 'Dorothy Richardson's Novels', *Contemporary Review*, 1100 (August 1957), 86–89.
Steward, Grace, *A New Mythos: The Novel of the Artist as Heroine 1877–1977* (St Albans, 1979).
Swinnerton, Frank, *Figures in the Foreground* (London, 1963).
Thomson, George H., *A Reader's Guide to Dorothy Richardson's Pilgrimage* (Greensboro, 1996).
Thorn, Arline R., '"Feminine" Time in Dorothy Richardson's "*Pilgrimage*"', *International Journal of Women's Studies*, 1 (1978), 211–219.
Trickett, Rachel, 'The Living Dead – V: Dorothy Richardson', *London Magazine*, 6 (June 1959), 20–25.
Vanacker, Sabine, 'Stein, Richardson and H.D.: Women Modernists and Autobiography', *Bête Noire*, 6 (1988), 111–123.
Wallace, Doris B., 'Secret Gardens and Other Symbols of Gender in Literature', *Metaphor and Symbolic Activity*, 3:3 (1988), 135–145.
——, 'Stream of Consciousness and Reconstruction of Self in Dorothy Richardson's Pilgrimage', in *Creative People at Work: Twelve Cognitive Case Studies*, ed. Doris B. Wallace and Howard E. Gruber (New York and Oxford, 1989), 147–169.
Watts, Carol, *Dorothy Richardson* (Plymouth, 1995).
——, 'Releasing Possibility into Form: Cultural Choice and the Woman Writer', in *New Feminist Discourses: Critical Essays on Theories and Texts*, ed. Isobel Armstrong (London and New York, 1992), 83–102.
Wells, H. G., *Experiment in Autobiography* (London, 1934).
West, Paul, *The Modern Novel* (London, 1963).
Woolf, Virginia, 'Romance and the Heart', *Times Literary Supplement* (19 May 1923), reprinted in *Women and Writing*, ed. Michelle Barret (London, 1979).
——, *Women and Writing*, ed. Michele Barret (London, 1979).
Würzbach, Natascha, 'Subjective Presentation of Characters from the Perspective of Miriam's Experience in Dorothy Richardson's Novel Pilgrimage: A Contribution to the Analysis of Constructivist Narrative', *Modes of Narrative: Approaches to American, Canadian and British Fiction* (Würzburg, 1990), 278–302.

BIBLIOGRAPHY

GENERAL CRITICISM

Arnheim, Rudolf, *Art and Visual Perception: A Psychology of the Creative Eye. The New Version* (Berkeley, 1974).
——, *The Dynamics of Architectural Form* (Berkeley, 1977).
Assert, Bodo, *Der Raum in der Erzählkunst: Wandlungen der Raumdarstellungen in der Dichtung des 20 Jh.s.* (thesis) (Tübingen, 1973).
Baak, J. J. van, *The Place of Space in Narration: A Semiotic Approach to the Problem of Literary Space* (Amsterdam, 1983).
Bachelard, Gaston, *La Poétique de l'espace* (Paris, 1957).
Badt, Kurt, *Raumphantasien und Raumillusionen* (Cologne, 1963).
Bakhtin, Mikhail, *The Dialogic Imagination: Four Essays*, ed. Michael Holquist (Austin, 1981).
Barthes, Roland, *Elements de sémiologie* (Paris, 1965).
——, *S/Z* (Paris, 1970).
——, *Le Plaisir du texte* (Paris, 1973).
Beckett, Samuel, *Proust* (New York, 1931).
Bell, Michael, ed., *The Context of English Literature 1900–1930* (London, 1980).
Bense, Max, *Raum und Ich: Eine Philosophie über den Raum* (Munich and Berlin, 1943).
Bilz, Rudolf, 'Pole der Geborgenheit: Eine Anthropologische Untersuchung über raumbezogene Erlebnis- und Verhaltensbereitschaft', *Studium Generale*, 10 (1957), 552–563.
Binswanger, Ludwig, 'Das Raumproblem in der Psychopathologie', *Ausgewählte Vorträge und Aufsätze II* (Bern, 1955), 174–225.
Blanchot, Maurice, *L'Espace littéraire* (Paris, 1955).
Bloomer, Kurt C. and Charles W. Moore, *Body, Memory and Architecture* (New Haven, 1977).
Bollnow, Otto Friedrich, *Mensch und Raum* (Stuttgart, 1963).
Bourneuf, Roland and Réal Ouellet, *L'Univers du roman* (Paris, 1972).
Braegger, Carlpeter, ed., *Architektur und Sprache* (Munich, 1982).
Butor, Michel, *Répertoire II: Etudes et Conferences 1959–1963* (Paris, 1964).
Casey, Edward S., *The Fate of Place: A Philosophical History* (Berkeley, 1997).
Cassirer, Ernst, 'Mythischer, ästhetischer und theoretischer Raum', *Beilageheft zur Zeitschrift für Ästhetik und allgemeine Kunstwissenschaft*, 25 (1931).
Conrad-Martius, Hedwig, *Der Raum* (Munich, 1958).
Culler, Jonathan, *The Pursuit of Signs: Semiotics, Literature and Deconstruction* (London, 1981).
Daidalos: Berlin Architectural Journal, 'Ummauerte Wildnis', 3 (March 1982).
——, 'Treppen', 9 (September 1983).
Deleuze, Gilles, *Marcel Proust et les signes* (Paris, 1964).
Derrida, Jacques, *La Voix et le phénomène* (Paris, 1967).
Doczi, György, *The Power of Limits: Proportional Harmonies in Nature, Art and Architecture* (London, 1981).
Dürckheim, Graf Karlfried von, 'Untersuchungen zum gelebten Raum: Erlebniswirklichkeit und ihr Verständnis. Systematische Untersuchungen II', *Neue Psychologische Studien*, 6, ed. Felix Krueger (Munich, 1932).
Eco, Umberto, *The Open Work* (Cambridge, MA, 1989).
Edwards, Paul, ed., *The Encyclopedia of Philosophy* (New York, 1967).
Eliade, Mircea, *Le Mythe de l'éternel retour* (Paris, 1949).
——, *The Sacred and the Profane* (New York, 1959).
Erikson, Erik H., *Identity, Youth and Crisis* (New York, 1968).
Fisher, Seymour, *Body Experience in Fantasy and Behavior* (New York, 1970).

Fisher, Seymour and Sydney E. Cleveland, *Body Image and Personality* (New York, 1958).
Fonst, Ronald, 'The Aporia of Recent Criticism and the Contemporary Significance of the Spatial Form', in J. Smith and A. Daghistany, ed., *Spatial Form in Narrative* (Ithaca, 1981), 179–201.
Frank, Ellen Eve, *Literary Architecture: Essays Toward a Tradition* (Berkeley, 1979).
Frank, Joseph, 'Spatial Form in Modern Literature', *The Widening Gyre* (New Brunswick, 1963), 3–62.
——, 'Spatial Form: An Answer to Critics', *Critical Inquiry*, 4 (1977), 231–252.
Freedman, Ralph, 'The Possibility of a Theory of the Novel', *The Disciplines of Criticism*, ed. Peter Demetz et al. (New Haven, 1968), 57–77.
Freud, Sigmund, *Die Traumdeutung* (Frankfurt, 4th edition, 1972).
Garcia, Irma, *Promenade femmilière: Recherches sur l'écriture féminine* (Paris, 1981).
Gelley, Alexander, 'Metonymy, Schematism and the Space of Literature', *New Literary History*, 11 (1980), 469–487.
Genette, Gérard, *Figures I* (Paris, 1966).
——, *Figures II* (Paris, 1969).
Gibson, James, *The Ecological Approach to Visual Perception* (Boston, 1979).
Gölz, Walter, *Dasein und Raum: Philosophische Untersuchungen zum Verhältnis von Raumerlebnis, Raumtheorie und gelebtem Dasein* (Tübingen, 1970).
Goodman, Nelson, *Languages of Art* (Indianapolis, 1976).
——, *Ways of Worldmaking* (Hassocks, 1978).
Gosztonyi, A., 'Das Raumproblem', *Studium Generale*, 10 (1957), 532–541.
Hager, Werner, 'Über Raumbildung in der Architektur und in den darstellenden Künsten', *Studium Generale*, 10 (1957), 630–645.
Hall, Edward T., *The Hidden Dimension* (New York, 1966).
Hauser, Arnold, *Sozialgeschichte der Kunst und Literatur* (Munich, 1967).
Heidegger, Martin, *Sein und Zeit*, (Tübingen, 7th edition, 1953). Translated as *Being and Time* (New York, 1962).
——, 'Bauen Wohnen Denken', *Vorträge und Aufsätze* (Pfullingen, 1954), 145–162.
——, 'Die Kunst und der Raum' (St Gallen, 1969).
Hillebrand, Bruno, 'Poetischer, philosophischer, mathematischer Raum', *Landschaft und Raum in der Erzählkunst*, ed. A. Ritter (Darmstadt, 1975), 417–463.
Hoffmann, Gerhard, *Raum, Situation, erzählte Wirklichkeit: Poetologische und historische Studien zum englischen und amerikanischen Roman* (Stuttgart, 1978).
Holtz, William, 'A Reconsideration of Spatial Form', *Critical Inquiry*, 4 (1997), 271–283.
Illich, Ivan, *Gender* (New York, 1982).
Ingarden, Roman, *Das literarische Kunstwerk* (Tübingen, 2nd edition, 1960).
Irigaray, Luce, *Speculum de l'autre femme* (Paris, 1980).
Iser, Wolfgang, *Der Akt des Lesens* (Munich, 1976).
Jakobson, Roman, 'Two Aspects of Language and Two Types of Aphasic Disturbances', *Fundamentals of Language*, eds R. Jakobson and Morris Halle (The Hague, 1956), 57–82.
——, 'Linguistics and Poetics', in *Style in Language*, ed. T. A. Sebeok (New York, 1960), 350–377.
——, 'Two Aspects of Language: Metaphor and Metonymy', in *European Literary Theory and Practice*, ed. Vernon W. Gras (New York, 1973), 119–129.
Jammer, Max, *Das Problem des Raumes: Die Entwicklung der Raumtheorien* (Darmstadt, 2nd edition, 1980).

Jantzen, Hans, *Über den kunstgeschichtlichen Raumbegriff* (Munich, 1938).
Jochims, Reimer, *Visuelle Identität: Konzeptionelle Malerei von Piero della Francesca bis zur Gegenwart* (Frankfurt, 1975).
Kern, Hermann, *Labyrinthe* (Munich, 1982).
Kern, Stephen, *The Culture of Time and Space 1880–1918* (Cambridge, MA, 1983).
Kesting, Marianne, 'Verlust des Kosmos: Kopernikanische Wende des Bewusstseins. Zur Geschichte einer Desillusion und ihrer ästhetischen Konsequenzen', *Kosmische Bilder in der Kunst des 20. Jh.s.*, Staatliche Kunsthalle Baden-Baden (1983/84).
Kestner, Joseph, *The Spatiality of the Novel* (Detroit, 1978).
Klein, Viola, *The Feminine Character: History of an Ideology* (London, 1946).
Klotz, Volker, *Die Erzählte Stadt: Ein Sujet als Herausforderung des Romans von Lessing bis Döblin* (Munich, 1969).
——, 'Architektur als Zeichensystem', *Konzept*, vol. 1 (Tübingen, 1975).
——, 'Stadtbild?', *Konzept*, vol. 2 (Tübingen, 1976).
——, 'Die Stadt als Text', *Konzept*, vol. 3 (Tübingen, 1976).
Kruse, Lenelis, *Räumliche Umwelt* (Berlin, 1974).
Lenk, Elisabeth, *Die unbewusste Gesellschaft: Über die mimetische Grundstruktur in der Literatur und im Traum* (Munich, 1983).
Leshan, Lawrence and Henry Margenau, *Einstein's Space and Van Gogh's Sky: Physical Reality and Beyond* (Brighton, 1983).
Lewin, Kurt, *Grundzüge der topologischen Psychologie* (Stuttgart, 1969).
Linshoten, J., 'Anthropologische Fragen zur Raumproblematik', *Studium Generale*, 11 (1958), 86–99.
Lodge, David, *The Modes of Modern Writing: Metaphor, Metonymy and the Typology of Modern Literature* (London, 1977).
Lotman, Jurij, *The Structure of the Artistic Text*, trans. R. Vroon (Michigan, 1977).
Lyons, John, *Semantics*, vols 1 and 2 (Cambridge, 1977).
Maatje, Frank C., 'Versuch einer Poetik des Raumes', *Landschaft und Raum in der Erzählkunst*, ed. A. Ritter (Darmstadt, 1975), 392–416.
Macksey, Richard, 'The Architecture of Time: Dialectics and Structure', in *Proust: A Collection of Critical Essays*, ed. René Girard (Westport, CN, 1962), 104–121.
Marquand, Odo, 'Plädoyer für die Fähigkeit, einsam zu sein: Gegen die Schwächung der Kraft zum Alleinleben und -denken', *Frankfurter Allgemeine Zeitung* (6 April 1983).
Marquand, Odo and Karlheinz Stierle, ed., *Identität, Poetik und Hermeneutik*, vol. 8 (Munich, 1979).
Merleau-Ponty, Maurice, *Phénoménologie de la perception* (Paris, 1945).
Metzger, Wolfgang, 'Das Raumproblem in der Psychologie', *Studium Generale*, 10 (1957), 620–630.
Miller, J. Hillis, *Thomas Hardy: Distance and Desire* (Cambridge, MA, 1970).
Moles, Abraham A. and Elisabeth Rohmer, *Psychologie de l'espace* (Paris, 1972).
Nelson, Cary, *The Incarnate Word: Literature as Verbal Space* (Urbana, 1973).
Niederer, Arnold, 'Zur Ethnographie und Soziographie nicht-verbaler Dimensionen der Kommunikation', *Zeitschrift für Volkskunde*, 71 (1975), 1–20.
Norberg-Schulz, Christian, *Genius Loci: Toward a Phenomenology of Architecture* (New York, 1980).
Pereira, I. Rice, *The Nature of Space* (New York, 1956).
Petsch, Robert, 'Raum in der Erzählung', in *Landschaft und Raum in der Erzählkunst*, ed. A. Ritter (Darmstadt, 1975), 36–44.

Piaget, Jean and Bärbel Inhelder, *La Répresentation de l'espace chez l'enfant* (Paris, 1948).
Pignatelli, Paola Coppola, *Spazio e Immaginario: Maschile e femminile in architectura* (Rome, 1982).
Paul-Lévy, Françoise and Marion Segaud, *Anthropologie de l'espace* (Paris, 1983).
Pöppel, Ernst, *Lust und Schmerz: Grundlagen menschlichen Erlebens und Verhaltens* (Berlin, 1982).
Poulet, Georges, 'Proust and Human Time', in *Proust: A Collection of Critical Essays*, ed. René Girard (Westport, 1962), 150–177.
——, *L'Espace proustien* (Paris, 1963).
Rasmussen, Steen Eiler, *Experiencing Architecture* (Cambridge, MA, 1959).
Ricoeur, Paul, *La Metaphore vive* (Paris, 1975).
Ritter, Alexander, ed., *Landschaft und Raum in der Erzählkunst* (Darmstadt, 1975).
Said, Edward W., 'The Problem of Textuality', *Critical Enquiry*, 4 (1978), 673–714.
Sappok, Christian, *Die Bedeutung des Raumes für die Struktur des Erzählwerkes* (Munich, 1970).
Saussure, Ferdinande de, *Course de linguistique générale* (Paris, 3rd edition, 1955).
Scheller, H. 'Das Problem des Raumes in der Psychopathologie', *Studium Generale*, 10 (1957), 563–574.
Scherer, Anton, 'Die Erfassung des Raumes in der Sprache', *Studium Generale*, 10 (1957), 574–582.
Scruton, Roger, *The Aesthetics of Architecture* (London, 1979).
Simon, Josef, *Sprache und Raum. Philosphische Untersuchungen zum Verhältnis zwischen Wahrheit und Bestimmtheit von Sätzen* (Berlin, 1969).
Smart, J. J. C., ed., *Problems of Space and Time* (New York, 1964).
——, 'Spatializing Time', *Mind* (1965), 239–241.
Smitten, Jeffrey R. and Ann Daghistany, ed., *Spatial Form in Narrative* (Ithaca, 1981).
Sommer, Robert, *Personal Space: The Behavioral Basis of Design* (Englewood Cliffs, 1969).
Spencer, Sharon, *Space, Time and Structure in the Modern Novel* (New York, 1971).
Steinberg, Erwin Ray, ed., *The Stream of Consciousness Technique in the Modern Novel* (New York, 1979).
Ströker, Elisabeth, *Philosophische Untersuchungen zum Raum* (Frankfurt, 1965).
Teymur, Necdet, *Environmental Discourse* (London, 1982).
Todorov, Tzvetoan, *Qu'est-ce que le structuralisme? 2: Poétique* (Paris, 1968).
Toporov, V. N., 'Prostranstvo i tekst', in *Tekst: Semantika i Struktura*, ed. T. V. Tzivian, (Moscow, 1983), 227–285.
Ullman, *Style in the French Novel* (Cambridge, 1957).
Venturi, Robert, *Complexity and Contradiction in Architecture* (New York, 1966).
Wellek, Rene and Austin Warren, *Theory of Literature* (New York, 1977).
Wittgenstein, Ludwig, *Tractatus logico-philosphicus* (Frankfurt, 1976).
Woolf, Virginia, *A Room of One's Own* (London, 1928).
Zevi, Bruno, *Architecture as Space: How to Look at Architecture* (New York, 1954).

INDEX

Names of characters are indexed under the form in which they are predominantly referred to in the text. Entries such as 'friendships', 'own world' etc refer to Miriam unless otherwise specified.

above/below spaces 12, 14, 16, 17, 21, 22, 25, 28
action space 49–51, 56–58, 61, 62–65
 psycho-metaphorical 115, 143
Alma (Wilson) 128–129
Amabel 24, 26, 79, 101, 106, 157–159
anchorage in space 27, 39, 64, 73
anti-spaces 15, 21, 22, 27
architecture 74–75, 106–107, 171n
Arnheim, R. 170n, 171n
art 128–130, 164
atmosphere 32, 33, 34, 42–43, 44–45
atmospheric space 48–49, 50, 54–55, 59, 61, 65–67
authorial narration 105, 216–217
autobiography 5, 227–228, 231

Babington garden 15–16, 66, 75–78
Bachelard, G. 82
back/front spaces 50, 51
Backwater 13–16
Bailey, Mrs see Tansley Street
Barnes 14, 15, 16
Barthes, R. 204, 205, 224
Beach, J. 223
becoming 155, 162, 171n
being 3, 146, 155, 162, 164, 171n
 time and 4
Bense, Max 3–4, 171n, 187–188
bible-reading, as shared space 175–176
Binswanger, L. 31–32
bishop, Jean's relationship with 211–213, 214
Blake, C. R. 223, 227, 229, 230
Blanchot, M. 67–68, 82

Blau DuPlessis, R. 230–231
Bloomer, K. C. 74–75
Bluemel, K. 233
Bollnow, O. F. 81, 83
Bonnycliff 21, 24, 25
boundary/boundaries 27–28, 51
 crossings 62
 between interior and exterior spaces 34, 36
 with other worlds 151, 153
 between subject and experienced surroundings 57–58
Brand (Ibsen) 102
Brighton 15
brilliance 105
Brooms 153, 182
Butor, M. 182

centre, self as 146, 147, 155–156, 170n
centred orientation 49, 51, 57, 58, 61, 69
characterization 215–216
Charles 25, 26
childhood spaces 65, 66–67, 75–77
Chopin, Frederic 67, 104
Clear Horizon 154
club, as neutral site 94–95
cognition, in world-making 112–172
communication 152, 157–158, 166
 as encounter between two worlds 174–175
 spatiality of 173–181
 successful 78–79
 see also language
comparison between spaces 99–101

[249]

INDEX

composition/decomposition in world-making 113–114
consciousness 219
contemplation 144–145, 159–160, 163, 183
  creative 16–17, 25, 81, 173
  distanced 67–68
  and temperament 113
contemplative space 51–53, 58–60, 61, 62, 65, 67–69
  Miriam's room and 83
  psycho-metaphorical 115, 143
Corries 16, 40, 43, 91, 117, 121, 153, 200
creative activity 183, 184–185
  solitude and 123, 144
creative contemplation 173
  space for 16–17, 25, 81
creativity 164–165, 188
cross-references 199–200, 205–206, 211

Dawn's Left Hand 154, 200
Deadlock 136
'deep quality' 153
deletion in world-making 114
Deleuze, G. 61, 168
Descartes, R. 44
detachment 152–153, 171n
Deutsch, B. 224
different worlds 152–154
Dimple Hill 25, 26, 64, 100–101, 158–160, 163
distance 49, 160, 163
Dürckheim, K. von 31, 32–33, 39, 45, 46n
dwelling 2, 73

Eagelson, H. 224
eccentricity 69, 174
ecstasy 67, 78, 131, 173
  spatiality of 95, 181–182
  see also joy; transcendence
Edel, L. 198, 224, 229
Egger, R. 232
Eleonor (Dear) 20, 40, 112, 124, 177
Eliade, M. 72, 73
emancipation 163–164
Emerson, R. W. 103, 177
emotive value of spaces 34–45
empty space 11, 170n
Englishness 118–119, 137–138

erotic, as shared space 178–179
eternity 186
evolution 154–155
existential space 31, 36, 39–40, 42
expectations 114
exterior spaces 12, 13, 18, 20
  and inner spaces 28, 34, 36

Felber, L. 232
feminine novel 231–233
feminine speech *see* speech, masculine and feminine
feminine worlds *see* masculine and feminine worlds
femininity 119, 120, 147, 148, 157, 225–226
feminism 226, 228, 231–232
Fiedler, L. 223
figural descriptions 213, 214–215
first person, use of 68–69, 163
Flaxman's Court 21–22, 36–39, 94
Fleishman, A. 230
foreign spaces 12–13, 20, 27, 118–119
  confrontation with 137–142
forgetfulness 143–144
formless, Richardson's work as 222–223
Frank, Ellen 81, 106
Frank, J. 196, 197
free spaces 88–90
freedom
  in London 84
  in own room 23–24, 39, 80
Friedman, Ellen 231
friendships 24, 94–95, 127–128
  with Jean 210, 213–215
Fromm, G. 227–228, 229, 230
Fullbrook, K. 231

gender difference 132–133, 146, 163–165
  see also masculine and feminine worlds
Genette, G. 101–102, 168, 191, 192, 196–197, 201, 205
Germany 12–13, 16, 98, 118
Gevirtz, S. 232
Gillespie, D. F. 231
God 44, 164, 178
Gölz, W. 33, 69, 174

[250]

INDEX

Goodman, N. 112, 113–115, 172n
Gregory, H. 225, 227

Hancock, Mr 41-2, 153
    Miriam's relationships with 125–126, 127
Hanscombe, G. 226, 228, 231
Harriet (Henderson) 41, 151
Hawkins, E. 222
Heath, S. 231
Heidegger, M. 31, 73, 82
Henke, S. 230
'here' and 'there' 50, 51, 52, 55, 57
Heseltine, O. 224
Hoffmann, G. 53
Honeycomb 16–17, 21
Hotel Alpenstock 22, 103
Humphrey, R. 222
Husserl, E. 31
Huxley, T. H. 129
Hypo (Wilson) 21, 40, 141, 179
    and neutral space 24
    sexual encounter with 179
    shared space with 86–88, 175
    world of 128–129, 140, 154–157

identity 44
    English 118–119
    and gender difference 132–134, 146–148
    and individualism 138–139, 140–141, 145–146
    between two worlds 127–128, 136–137
    world-making and 113, 115–116, 118–119, 121, 124–125, 153
imagination 24, 105, 182–185
imagined space 15–16, 53, 62, 67, 96–104
immobile spaces 90, 92–96
independence 123, 125, 127–128, 182
    versus marriage 14, 119–121, 126
individualism 138–139, 140–141, 142, 145–146, 159
inner space 12–13, 14–15, 17–18
    and exterior space 28, 34, 36
inner world 150, 162–163, 170n
Interim 125
inter-spatial experience 91
intersubjectivity 180–181, 202–203
island spaces 19–21, 27, 28

Jan 20, 124, 127–128, 134, 153
Jean 26, 173, 209–210, 211–215
Jim (Davenport) 210
journey in imagined space 102, 179–180, 182
joy 36, 37, 45, 63, 78, 104, 143
Joyce, James 218, 229
Julia 119, 153

Kaplan, S. J. 226
Kelly, R. 223
Kemp, S. 232–233
Killian, E. 233
Kronen, Mrs 121
Kumar, S. 229

Labovitz, E. K. 231
landscape 22–3, 44, 108n
language 2, 134–136, 148, 149–150, 157–158, 160, 165–166
    and spatial textuality 201–202
    see also speech, masculine and feminine
Lawrence, M. 225
Lenk, E. 86
Levy, A. 231
liminality 2, 83, 89
Linshofen, J. 171n
literature, spatial dimension of 196–208
lived space 32–33, 54–69
    in *Pilgrimage* 34–45
    semantic encoding of 72–88
Lodge, D. 176, 204
London 15, 17–19, 20, 124, 125
    dialogue with 84–86
    freedom in 84
    north London 14–15, 117, 119
    spaces in 18–21, 26–27
    streets of 40, 42, 63
    and world of science 129–130
loneliness 36, 42, 124, 130, 161
Lotman, J. 10–11, 29
Lycurgan Society 25, 140
Lyons, J. 55, 60, 69, 182–183, 185

Macksey, R. 169n
Mag 20, 124, 127–128, 134, 153
March Moonlight 11, 25–26, 161, 163, 209–215

[251]

INDEX

marriage 21, 98–99, 117, 159
   versus independence 14, 119–121, 126
   versus solitude 120, 123
masculine and feminine worlds 126, 132–133, 146–147, 157, 163–165
   oscillation between 121–122, 133–134, 148
material spaces 1, 2, 4, 10, 11, 29–30, 43
Max 119
meaning/s 11, 104–105
   and dwelling 73–74
   multiple 213
   significant space and 88
   spatial textuality and 197–199, 200, 202–203, 204
memory 58–59, 77, 189–191
   see also remembered spaces
Mendizabel 135, 180
Merchant of Venice, The (Shakespeare) 133
Merleau-Ponty, M. 66
metaphors 3 167–168, 172n, 176–177
   spatial 1, 2, 4, 11, 190–192, 193n
Michael (Shatov) 26, 42, 108n, 137–139, 153, 178–179
middle-class world 21, 117–118, 119, 123, 127–128, 153
Miller, J. H. 189–190
Miller, Jane 113, 223, 232
mobile spaces 88, 89, 90–92
Moles, A. 34, 109n
Moore, C. W. 74–75
movement in space 27, 59, 63, 64–65
   see also mobile spaces
multiple worlds 114–115, 130, 132, 142, 145
music 40, 67, 104, 181, 191
mutual worlds 117

Nabakov, V. 185
narrative chronology 196, 199, 200
neutral spaces 20, 22, 24–25, 75, 88–96, 174
new worlds 116
Newlands 16–17, 77, 117–118
Norberg-Schulz, C. 73–74
Norway 102
novel, Richardson and 1–2, 43, 216–219
nowhere 67, 69, 90, 92, 94

Oberland 22–23
Olga 153–154
open/closed spaces 12–13, 15, 17, 20–21, 26
orientation 49, 50, 74
   centred 49, 51, 57, 58, 61, 69
Orlys 153
other 138, 174–175
   awareness of 152
outside world 116, 146
   relationship to 124–131, 136–137, 150–152
   withdrawal from 20, 24, 131, 139–140, 141–142, 152–153
own world 116–117, 136, 139–140, 141–142, 162–163

past 16, 83, 185, 190–191
perceptions of space 23, 24–25, 28, 57, 114
   differing 86–88, 89, 109n, 174
permanent essence 139, 140, 144, 180, 189
Pernes 40
perspective 48, 52, 53, 57
Pfaff, Frl. 12
Piaget, J. 66
Pilgrimage 1, 169n
   critiques of 221–234
   volume I 11, 13–18, 117–123
   volume II 19, 20, 123–137
   volume III 20, 21–22, 137–150
   volume IV 22–27, 150–167
Podnieks, E. 231
poetics 165–168
Pointed Roofs 11, 14, 121
porosity of space 12, 14, 27, 79, 80–81, 82
power of surroundings 34, 43–44, 45, 65
Powys, John Cowper 221, 225, 226–227
pregnancy 200
pre-reflexive experience 47, 65–66
pre-logical space 65, 66–67, 75–77
Prescott, J. 223, 225
progress 154–155
protective space 80
   own room as 12, 14, 16, 23, 24, 25, 27, 39

[252]

INDEX

Proust, Marcel 218, 229
proximity 49
psychic reality 3, 54–61, 80–81
    spatial situation and 57–58, 80, 84

Quakers 24, 159–161

Radford, J. 233–234
readers 197–198, 204, 205–206
reading 102, 103, 110n, 166, 170n
    and imagined spaces 182, 183–184
reality 81, 117, 126, 139, 142–143, 162, 188–189, 215–216
    metaphors and 167–168
    solitude and 144–145
    two layers of 148–149
    see also psychic reality
religious experience 123, 176, 178
remembered spaces 53, 67, 75–78, 90–91, 97–98, 103
    juxtaposition with experienced spaces 26, 77–78
    see also memory
reversibility 198, 200–201, 209, 218
Revolving Lights 136
Richardson, Dorothy 115
    comparison with Miriam 5
    critical literature on 221–238
    on the novel 1–2, 216–219
Rohmer, E. 34, 109n
role play 121, 122, 124, 126, 142
room (Miriam's) 22, 24
    at Dimple Hill 25
    at Flaxman's Court 21–22, 36–39
    freedom in 23–24, 39, 80
    at Newlands 16–17
    as protective space 12, 14, 16, 23, 24, 25, 27, 39
    return to 80
    and solitude 19, 26–27
    as space for creative contemplation 16–17, 81–82
    at Tansley Street 19, 34–36, 79, 80–82
Roscorlas 25, 26, 158, 159, 161, 173
Rose, J. 232
Rose, S. 230
Rosenberg, J. 227
Russia 102–3, 153–154

Sally (Henderson) 25, 210
sameness 76–77, 89
Saussure, F. de 196–197
Savage, Henry, letter to 3, 168
school, in Germany 12–13, 118, 119
science, world of 128–130
Scott-James, R. A. 222, 225
'secret societies' 124
self 124, 132
    as meeting point of different worlds 116, 121
    sense of 89, 91, 144
    two forms of 134
self-enclosed spaces 12, 13, 22, 25
self-presentation 217
self-realisation 136, 138, 142, 148
Selina (Holland) 37, 38–39, 94, 152, 165, 180
shared reading 176, 177–178
shared silence 160, 180
shared space 36–39, 41–42, 174–181
Shestov, L. 171n
Showalter, E. 226
significant space 2, 26, 27, 72–75, 105, 168
    Amabel as 157–158
    in *Pilgrimage* 75–88
silence 179n, 232
    shared 160, 180
silent utterances 143
similarity with other 175–176
Simon, J. 202
simultaneity 2–3, 96, 188, 196, 198, 200–201
Sinclair, M. 222
sites of recreation 14, 15, 17
Snow, C. P. 224
socialism 140–141
society, versus solitude 122–123, 130–131, 140–144
solitude 19, 26–27, 81–82, 138, 144–145, 170n
    and creative activity 123, 144
    dialogue with 85–86
    and ecstasy 78
    London and 84–85
    versus marriage 120, 123
    and reality 80–81, 161–162
    versus society 122–123, 130–131, 140–144

space, subject and 47–69
spacelessness 21, 88, 90, 91, 93, 95
spatial localisation 60–61
spatial possession 64–65
spatial representations 11–30, 64–65
spatial structuration 10–11, 29, 47, 72
spatial textuality 197–198, 201–202, 211, 213, 218
  of *Pilgrimage* 199–201, 203–205
speech, masculine and feminine 122, 126–127, 133–134, 170n, 225–226
spiritual detachment 150, 151, 152
stairs, as neutral site 92–93
Staley, T. 229
Stanford, D. 223
Steward, G. 231
stream of consciousness 6, 171–172n, 222, 229
Ströker, E. 32, 47–50, 52
sub-spaces 18, 20
suburban sites 21–22
supplementation, in world-making 114
Switzerland 22–23, 26, 104, 105–106, 151

Tansley Street 34–36, 80, 82, 124, 130, 136
teaching 119–120, 121
Ted 173
Teetgen's Teas, representations of 54–61
temperament 113
textual omissions 202–204
third space 174–176
Thomson, G. H. 230
Thorn, A. 230
time, spatialisation of 3, 185–192
toboggan ride 91–92
tranquility 159, 161
transcendence 59, 83, 89, 95–96, 156, 184
transitional spaces 12
translation 184–185

Trap, The 22, 136
Tunnel, The 125

utopian space 12, 16, 25

Vanacker, S. 231
Vaud 26, 100–101, 209–210
Venturi, R. 74
Villette (Brontë) 40, 177

Waldstrasse 12, 16, 103–104
Wallace, D. 231
Walpole, Hugh 224
Warren, R. 176
Watts, C. 233
weighting, in world-making 114
Wellek, A. 176
Wells, H. G. 227
Wilde, Oscar 199–200
Wilson, Hypo *see* Hypo (Wilson)
withdrawal from outside world 20, 24, 131, 136, 139–140, 141–142, 152–153
Wittgenstein, L. 170–171n
women 119–121, 121–122, 126–127, 133, 147–148, 163–164
  see also femininity; masculine and feminine worlds
Woolf, V. 225, 229
Wordsworth House 14, 16
work, independent 123, 125
  versus marriage 14, 119–121, 126
worldliness 123
world-making 112–172
writing 27, 115, 144–145, 151, 184
Würzbach, N. 231

Yeats, W. B. 148
YWCA 20, 154, 169n

Zionism 138

EU authorised representative for GPSR:
Easy Access System Europe, Mustamäe tee 50,
10621 Tallinn, Estonia
gpsr.requests@easproject.com

www.ingramcontent.com/pod-product-compliance
Ingram Content Group UK Ltd.
Pitfield, Milton Keynes, MK11 3LW, UK
UKHW021836140426
5217IPUK00021B/1474